ON MORAL CHARACTER

A PRACTICAL GUIDE
TO ARISTOTLE'S VIRTUES AND VICES

Based on a psychoanalytic perspective
and the theory of the four causes

Cross-referenced to both

THE NICOMACHEAN ETHICS
and THE ART OF RHETORIC

by

Jody Palmour, Ph.D.

A companion volume to the author's

THE ANCIENT VIRTUES AND VICES
Philosophical Foundations for the Psychology, Ethics
and Politics of Human Development

DEDICATION

TO the young men and women in all the various disciplines and professions who will dedicate not just their lives but their careers to mastering this ancient wisdom, comprehending modern life and thought in terms of it, and reawakening mankind's love of nobility and virtue.

AND TO the established men and women who will encourage, discipline and inspire them to attain this mastery and even to travel farther and climb higher along this path than they might be able to go themselves. - JP

A Publication of

The ARCHON INSTITUTE for LEADERSHIP DEVELOPMENT
Suite 121
3700 Massachusetts Avenue NW
Washington, DC   20016

© 1986 by Dr. Jody Palmour

ISBN 0-9616203-0-7
ISBN 0-9616203-1-5 (CLOTH)

contents

contents

INTRODUCTION

OVERVIEW

WHAT THIS BOOK OFFERS

A Conceptual Framework for Teaching, Leadership Training and Research

A Spiritual Workout

OUR CULTURAL SITUATION

Growing Awareness of the Problem of Moral Character

The Two Extremes Tell the Truth about Each Other

A Third Alternative

Early Modern Philosophy Temporarily Blinded Western Culture to the Reality of Nature and Character

Family Roots

Philosophical Roots

AN INTRODUCTION TO MORAL CHARACTER AND AN EXPLANATION OF THE THEORY OF VIRTUE AND VICE

Vision and Character

Leadership and Vision

Leadership and Character

The TABLE OF VIRTUES AND VICES

A Walk through the Causal Pathway

Moral Virtue and Cognition

Methodology in Creating the TABLE

Erikson's Stages of Human Development in the Light of the TABLE

Gilligan's Refinement of the Stages and Distinction between Paternal and Maternal Attitudes toward Morality

Character Traits and The Theory of the Four Causes

Purpose and Teleology

Establishing the Nature of Virtue and Vice

Dialectical Refutations of Competing Life Goals

Aristotle's Functional Conception of the Goal of Human Life and of the Nature of Human Development and Happiness

Synergism and the Concept of Proper Wish

Cybernetics and the Concept of Deliberation

The Decision Principle and the Concept of Choice and Weakness of the Will

The Definition of Moral Virtue

The Particular Virtues and Vices Illuminate the Meaning of Proper Wish, Deliberation and Choice in the Face of their Respective Agents

PHILOSOPHICAL ATTITUDES BLINDING US TO THE REALITY
OF HUMAN NATURE AND CHARACTER

BACKGROUND

ACKNOWLEDGMENTS

HINTS TO THE READER

RECOMMENDED READING

introduction

INTRODUCTION

WHAT THIS BOOK OFFERS

This is a work of friendly realism made possible by new discoveries about the Aristotelian theory of moral character which has inspired Western civilization since its beginnings among the ancient Greeks.
These new discoveries reveal the practical importance of moral education
if we are to prepare a new generation of leaders who will bring out the
best in our people at home and at school, in the work place and politics,
in the arts and communications. The book explains why the knowledge of
moral character is crucial to anyone who seriously wishes to promote
human development and to live an integrated and balanced life guided by
his own deliberations and choices. The theory presented here provides an
unexpectedly powerful explanatory principle for reintegrating the social
sciences and humanities around the central axis of the interaction between
psychology, ethics and politics and for grasping the indispensable place
of philosophy, culture and history in shaping human development.

**A Conceptual Framework for Teaching, Leadership Training and
Research.** The book's conceptual framework focuses on our powers to
handle the things which are the most important for our happiness and
well-being as well as for acting responsibly toward our children, spouses,
students, employees, customers and fellow citizens. The book is about
handling the painful things we fear, and about eating, drinking, sex and
drugs, about money, self-respect and status, about anger, friendship and
love, shame and social justice. The book offers a new explanation of the
difference between handling these things well and handling them badly,
and shows why the term "excellence" could be substituted quite properly
for the older term "virtue." It is by virtue of developing a virtuous character that we are able to handle life's challenges excellently. Our virtues
make us excellent at what we do--able to function properly and on a high
level of mastery in each of these areas.

The book examines each of these classes of things and explores
the interrelation between the different powers we have for handling them.
We examine, for example, various ways we can develop the power to
handle **money** and how they affect the development of our power to **love**.
By exploring different ways we can develop our character in each area, we
are able to examine which ways give us the fullest range of motion as intellectually and emotionally alive human beings and which leave us
stunted in our growth and driven by infantile desires.

Knowledge of this framework should provide great practical assistance to anyone trying to work with people and bring out what is best in
them in education, training, management, counseling or writing. But it
should also prove helpful to anyone doing research on people's attitudes,
perceptions, emotions and behavior who wants to understand how social
conditions, organizational structures and leadership styles can either em-

12

power or spiritually and politically impoverish people.

A Spiritual Workout. This ancient wisdom makes great demands on the reader, but surprisingly, it is more morally and emotionally demanding than intellectually so. It is personally challenging to learn that one can grow stronger by exercising his moral and emotional powers in the same way he can his physical powers. We do not have to settle for the character we might have slipped into unknowingly. This knowledge challenges us to change ourselves so we can function at our best as a good person. Such knowledge and self-development can only be gained through work and effort and through cultivating the desire for a deeper than average experience of ourselves and those who approach life in ways that differ from our own. This is why truly cultured people deserve to be honored.

Many of us are not very proud of who we have become. Feeling we are doing the best we can already, we grow afraid of learning about our shortcomings and the areas where we might work for improvement. As prevalent as it is today, such reluctance to acquire self-knowledge is not new to the human condition. Freud thought there is an uneasiness and discontent inherent in all civilized life. The best expressions of humanistic culture, whether religious or secular, have always challenged people to turn from their self-serving illusions and to recognize and discipline anxieties and desires which are incompatible with higher standards of love, work and community responsibility. True education will always be something of a spiritual workout. Just as with getting into physical shape, so too here, one must learn to pace his efforts at self-knowledge and distinguish between that discomfort which is part of the training effect of getting into better shape and that which is destructive. But in both contexts, it's equally true--No Pain, No Gain.

(Unless otherwise signaled, masculine pronouns refer to man generically considered and not to the male sex.)

In modern culture, we seldom talk about such lofty goals but have entered a period of cynicism and skepticism reminiscent of the declining culture of the Romans. While refusing to face what is wrong, a great many people no longer believe in the possibility of goodness. This has become so much the case that many people in a position to stand up for fine things feel they are not worthy of doing so and fear being accused of hypocrisy--as though one must already be good in order to start doing good.

To take up the challenge to live up to higher standards, we must revive the classical vocabulary of terms and concepts for thinking about character, motivation and values. **ON MORAL CHARACTER** attempts to do this--although the specific terms employed here are much less important than the concepts and realities to which the terms refer. In practical life as in the writing of literature, one must always search for the optimal term for expressing the associations one desires to bring to mind in one's audience. It is thus very telling about modern life that the associations we bring to our normal vocabulary for behavior and emotion has been largely sanitized to exclude any reference to the moral factors which we most need if we are to explain why we are acting and feeling the way we do. We've become so touchy and jumpy about this repressed dimension that simply noting the moral significance of someone's attitude sounds like a total condemnation of him as a person.

We have lost sight of the way these moral concepts empower us to put our deepest experiences of ourselves and others into words so that we might understand what is happening to us and how we might grow stronger in pursuing what we most value. I hope to have shown that when properly understood, Aristotle's **ETHICS** gives us the roots of a living vocabulary for our own moral discourse rather than simply a museum artifact from a dead language. The ideas presented here arose initially among an exceptionally articulate group of people who were committed to promoting human development and the flourishing of the human spirit. These ideas will always be revived when cultured people take up once again the practice of consciously, publicly promoting virtuous character development and the nobility of the human spirit.

Aristotle's contribution to the theory of human development and to the psychological, ethical and political dimensions of character formation has not been broadly appreciated, however, even by people who teach his works. The view presented here is thus not the traditional one. Even with the texts explicated in this volume, the importance of character does not become apparent until one reads them with a pre-existing appreciation for the nature and importance of character in human development--or approaches the texts through the eyes of someone who has done so. This is in keeping with Wittgenstein's principle that understanding the meaning of any language requires participating to some extent in the form of life activity in which that language arose and had meaning for its users. Someone like myself who has been deeply involved in character analysis for many years is thus more likely to find deeper meaning in these texts than people untrained in the study of character and who are possibly even uncomfortable with the subject.

OUR CULTURAL SITUATION

Growing Awareness of the Problem of Moral Character. People become conscious of things when they no longer work right. This is as true for moral character as for the carburetors in our cars. We Americans have become more conscious of moral character in the last decade or so. The relatives, neighbors and public figures we remember from our youth as having had great strength of character are dying off now and we miss their challenging but reassuring presence. Many of us are hungry to regain a lapsed sense of excellence and quality in our products and services and are striving for a heightened sense of mental and physical fitness to face today's opportunities and challenges. Yet no one on the national scene is calling for us to re-attain the most exalted sense of excellence and fitness--known from the ancient Greeks through the American founding fathers as VIRTUE.

One thing is certain, though. We simply won't succeed very much longer in ignoring our adult responsibility to maintain the principles of moral character which accounted for the highest accomplishments of our civilization in the past and which the best of our ancestors always tried to emulate in their own lives and pass on to succeeding generations. Today's leaders, however, have neglected the whole issue of moral character in both theory and practice and no longer encourage informed public reflection on the kind of people we are becoming and on our responsibilities to one another now and into the future. It will be from practical necessity, however, rather than ungrounded idealism that our people will return to the teaching of moral character.

Whether we use the term or recognize the concept, we refer to the reality of moral character whenever we talk about the drug and alcoholism problem, about criminality, divorce and family disintegration, "disconnected" youth and adolescent pregnancy. The reality of moral character is unavoidable in the declining work ethic and the ethics issue on Wall St., with defense contractors and in management generally, or in the so-called "character" issue of the public's trust in politicians.

Such neglect reflects powerful political-economic factors which have turned our people away from considering who we are becoming as a people and what we most value. Our stress in this INTRODUCTION, however, must be on the ideas which will help us regain this legacy as well as on those that have blinded us to the most basic truths about human nature and happiness. If the terms virtue and nobility no longer stir us, it is in significant part because the curators of Western culture have by and large displayed our most ennobling and passionate ideals in the pinched and prudish terms of Victorianism. Our intellectual leaders have failed to grasp the living core of this tradition and to rethink its truths in the light of modern knowledge.

A sign of this neglect of our cultural heritage is found in the way people who should have known better have allowed fundamentalists who call so loudly for a return to "traditional" values to belittle all forms of humanism when what they are really attacking is a modern form of skepticism about knowledge and relativism about values which Aristotelian humanism opposed from the start. Intellectuals have too often failed to acknowledge how right fundamentalists are in their criticism of the lack of moral principles in modern culture according to which people might confidently guide their lives. Yet, having said that, it is also true that fundamentalists have been allowed to treat their highly restrictive outlook as if it were the only moral tradition in Western culture and the only alternative to a liberal outlook rightly felt to be lacking in both values and strength.

The Two Extremes Tell the Truth about Each Other. The pendulum of Western culture has repeatedly swung back and forth between extremes of license and self-denial, as first one camp and then the other gains political power and sets the cultural agenda of the times by overreacting to each other's excesses. In recent days, liberals and conservatives have dominated public discussion by doing little more than telling the truth about one another while the rest of us have struggled without leadership to establish a more balanced stance in our moral and political lives.

Anyone seriously committed to human development must agree with most of what these groups say about each other. By ignoring the existence of standards of personal accountability, contemporary liberals have rationalized self-indulgence, dependency and irresponsibility. On the other hand, by appealing to individualistic standards of human worth, contemporary conservatives have rationalized a driven and self-seeking will to succeed without regard to quality or service and have engendered a deep fear of one's own punishing conscience and worthlessness should he fail. While contrary, these extreme attitudes actually feed off one another as each appears attractive only in relation to the other.

A Third Alternative. ON MORAL CHARACTER (OMC) offers those drawn to a more robust and life-affirming belief in mankind's potential goodness, creativity and excellence a modern reassessment of the classical humanist tradition which traces its roots back to Aristotle. (372-312 B.C.) Beginning even before the Christian era, this tradition went on to provide the philosophical foundations for the flourishing of Jewish thought in the work of Moses Maimonides (1135-1204 A.C.), Islamic thought with Avicenna (980-1037 A.C.) and Averroes (1126-98 A.C.), and Christian thought in the work of St. Thomas Aquinas (1226-74 A.C.). While itself making no appeals to revelation, this philosophy has been found time and again to provide an indispensable foundation not only for expressing what is best and most humane in these religious traditions but for protecting their spiritual integrity against those who would exploit faith in the service of power and hate.

History shows that whenever the best and brightest minds of a generation have returned to the Aristotelian tradition as the source of principles around which to synthesize their own advances and discoveries, their peoples and cultures have flourished. It is time that the best and the brightest at the end of the twentieth-century return to these same roots to bring forth the fruits and flowers of our own time in an integrated humanist framework. We might think of Aristotle's philosophy as providing a kind of master operating system for anyone interested in moving across the whole range of the human sciences and humanities with the goal of understanding and promoting human development.

For a culture truly to flourish, its leaders must integrate the Paternal and scientific spirit of universal law and rule by the head with the Maternal and emotional spirit of caring for one's own and rule by the heart. In philosophy, Aristotle epitomizes this integration of science and the humanities, of a powerfully developed head serving a loving and community-spirited heart.

As interpreted here, Aristotle's moral philosophy provides a theoretical and practical guide to the cultivation of truly independent men and women who will devote their strengths not to a shoddy materialism and self-promotion but to human development and the creation of institutions committed to furthering such a creative and community-spirited individualism. **OMC** sees the process of committing ourselves to the development of real people and to acquiring a craftsmanlike sense of mastery and excellence in our work as opening us to the fullness of life and the reality of the world rather than as tying us down and closing us off. Unless we commit our heads and hearts to real people and projects, we remain forever weak and empty inside.

Early Modern Philosophy Temporarily Blinded Western Culture to the Reality of Nature and Character. We still live today under the sway of 17th and 18th century philosophers like Bacon, Descartes, Hobbes, Locke, Hume, Bentham and Kant whose ideas still dominate much of our intellectual and academic culture even though they are at odds with the non-mechanistic spirit, computer technology and biologically inspired science of our times. Under their sway, we have lost sight of the classical ideal of integrating a truly loving heart with a scientific grasp of natural principles, of a truly individuated sense of personality wed to the love of community. By teaching us to treat knowledge as simply an instrument of power, for example, Bacon and Descartes repudiated the Aristotelian ideal of basing all our applied sciences on a reverence for natural structures and norms, and laid the intellectual foundations for the ecological crisis of industrial society.

Our generation has thus had to reinvent for itself the ideal of a scrupulously scientific study of nature committed to discovering and respecting nature's own normative and ecological principles. Contrary to their philosophical admonitions against seeking normative principles in nature, we now seek the fruits of an ecologically sensitive science so that we might learn how best to develop ourselves while respecting and husbanding the other living things we live from and share the planet with.

By teaching us to treat political and ethical theory as simply a means to regulate society so that people will be free to do whatever they want with their property and private desires, Hobbes, Locke, Bentham, Kant and others repudiated the Aristotelian ideal of basing public policy on reverence for human excellence and the encouragement of human development. In doing so, they paved the way for traditionalist over-reactions when people can no longer stand the lack of values in their lives.

Their belief that adopting any view of the nature of human development must inevitably crush the human spirit under an authoritarian imposition of arbitrary ideals deprived us of public support for the values mankind needs if we are to acquire inner freedom. As Erich Fromm taught, these modern philosophers conceived the problem of freedom simply in negative terms as freedom from outside interference. They neglected the positive side of cultivating the internal conditions of character which alone allow us to use freedom from external constraint to make something fine of ourselves. **(ESCAPE FROM FREEDOM)**

With their practical commitment to economic growth, expansion and the destruction of the ancient regime, the leaders of the early modern world set out to prove that the limits they confronted in industry, economics and social relations were not inevitable but could be transcended through intelligence and effort. And in this they were right. But with their intellectual fascination with Newton's powerful new mechanical physics, they thought they could base a whole civilization on a mechanical world-view denying that natural systems have any intrinsic norms which must be discovered and respected.

Alasdair MacIntyre has recently argued that turning against Aristotle's ethics has created a theoretical vacuum in which Western culture no longer possesses a coherent ethical theory. We have not been taught to recognize, however, that by repudiating the Aristotelian theories of substance, nature and the moral virtues, the modern philosophers laid the intellectual foundations for the practical crises we now face in our understanding of ourselves as well as of our place in the larger system of nature. We Westerners thus lost sight of our true place in the world of natural beings and of the fact that our moral and emotional functioning is just as subject to natural principles and causes as the functioning of any other natural being. Having been led to believe that all that is sound started with these supposedly enlightened thinkers, we no longer recognize the conception of an intellectual and spiritual quest for natural principles and guidelines as a central part of our birthright as Westerners.

Instead, many of our most sensitive people turn to Eastern forms of spirituality--not as respectful equals wishing to deepen and enrich their own knowledge and practice, but as philosophical and spiritual orphans feeling they have nothing in their own tradition to stand on and be proud of. They act as though there were no tradition of disciplined striving for such a distinctively Western form of spiritual knowledge and excellence which if mastered would give us the wisdom and strength of character to fashion technologies for the good of both man and planet, and which would allow us once again to be proud of our accomplishments and heritage.

The people professing to teach us how to read our classical texts seldom reveal any deep feeling, experience or wisdom about this strain in Western history. They seldom show insight into what it can teach us about what Faulkner called "the heart in conflict with itself." They show even more rarely a true love for mankind and belief in the goodness and promise of our developing into what this tradition shows we could be. Lectures and papers in the humanities more often bore and confuse than enlighten and inspire along these lines.

In the contemporary period, science and technology are no longer seen as inspiring, humanistic accomplishments in their own right as well as empowering us to serve mankind's development and meet our responsibilities toward all life on earth. By the same token the humanities are no longer seen as embodying scientifically confirmable truths about human nature and as providing a solid basis for training our leaders and shaping our public policy toward the goal of promoting human development. Yet if I am right in reaffirming the Aristotelian quest for natural principles and causes, C. P. Snow's famous description of the contemporary divorce between the "Two Cultures" of science and the humanities must be seen as reflecting an ebb-tide in Western culture and not its disastrous culmination. It is a mark of this nadir that we have ignored the Aristotelian tradition which would allow us to transcend the modern limitations on our thinking and reconnect with this central root in western culture. (THE TWO CULTURES)

Family Roots. Thanks to Alex Haley, and the practical and spiritual uncertainties of modern life, many people are eagerly searching to reconnect with their roots in family history, circling up their wagons and pooling resources to accomplish what they could not do alone. People are deepening their faith in biological and marriage bonds that don't break so easily as casual friendships, and are swelling with pride in one another's accomplishments and family solidarity. Young people are drawing strength and inspiration from their family's expectation that they will attain and even surpass their ancestor's standards of goodness and achievement, just as older people are finding an unexpected serenity in recognizing themselves as the living adult presence in an unbroken chain of life.

Many have rediscovered the sense of family that reaches backwards to departed ones who we keep alive in our respectful appreciation for the skills they taught, the artifacts they left behind and the ongoing social relations they established for us. But this renewed sense of family also reaches forward to the hoped-for maturing of the new lives who today's adults have brought into being and are nurturing. And with every new generation comes the heightened sense of adult responsibility to maintain and enhance the productive and cultural resources needed to support the living and which should be passed on as the next generation's birthright and inheritance too.

I believe we must re-establish our roots in the Aristotelian tradition in a similar way if we are to surmount the anti-naturalism and fragmentation of modern culture and pass on our cultural values and accomplishments to succeeding generations.

Philosophical Roots. We are all as deeply rooted in philosophical assumptions, attitudes and practices of life as we are in the unstated histories and traditions of our families. This is not because we consciously base our moral practices on philosophical assumptions but because philosophers try to formulate the assumptions implicit in the practices of life they share with others. The situation for the non-philosopher is rather like being an amateur chess player who is unaware that the opening moves he likes to play are part of the Nimzo-Indian Defense. After years of analysis these moves have been found to have certain strengths, but also certain potentially fatal weaknesses. The amateur doesn't know what they are except intuitively, however, because he has not learned to read the chess books as they relate to his own style of play.

Re-Establishing our philosophical roots and learning to read philosophy in this way is important because doing so will help us clarify the operating assumptions we base our whole lives on and refine our ability to live up to our highest hopes for ourselves and for those we care about the most. But just as most of us don't know very much about the biological and social stock we come from, we know even less about our own philosophic outlook and who we stand with in the history of western culture as a result of sharing the same moral attitudes and practices of life with them.

As a result of such theoretical and practical neglect, it should be no surprise that even our best educated leaders lack a solid framework for speaking confidently and objectively on the basic principles of humanistic character development and consequently know so little about how to bring out what is best in our people. No surprise that we are managed so often by highly-credentialed men and women who have no feeling for people's moral sensibilities and the factors affecting their morale. No surprise that even after obscenely expensive university educations, we send young people into the world so largely ignorant of their own character and of the people they will live among, marry and work with. No surprise that higher education so often creates trendy, facile sophists rather than courageous lovers of truth.

If we are to regain mastery of the wisdom of moral character and re-acquire the good judgment to apply it appropriately, we need our best-hearted and most gifted leaders to reintroduce this teaching at the highest levels of public discourse and at every level of the school curriculum from kindergarden to professional education. And they will need not only a well-crafted theory of moral character to draw on, but the practical experience, support and training to apply it in a spirit of friendly realism. They will have to acquire not only knowledge but the confidence to wield such powerful knowledge with profound courtesy and circumspection. For us to succeed, the leaders of this movement will also have to learn to defend themselves and the movement from those in the other traditions who challenge not only the existence of human nature and character but the morality of talking about them and assuming that we can know anything and act with any real confidence. This means they must free themselves from the intellectual spells cast by both rationalist and positivist assumptions.

In the next few sections, we will discuss realist philosophical ideas which should help readers benefit the most from ON MORAL CHARAC-TER. Some readers might, however, prefer to jump right in to reading about **courage, self-control, generosity** and the other moral and emotional attitudes discussed in the body of the text. Most readers should find, however, that these ideas can be followed rather easily with a little effort at concentration and that they do indeed clarify the text and place the theory of moral character in its larger philosophical context. But the reverse is true as well. Familiarizing oneself with the text first will also clarify the INTRODUCTION.

After this discussion of the theory of moral character, we will discuss the three philosophical traditions of rationalism, realism and positivism and suggest why only the realist tradition promotes the study and cultivation of moral character. This section should prove helpful to those troubled by the arguments and resistance one encounters in trying to take character seriously in the contemporary world.

Aristotle and his heirs opened and settled in this philosophical territory and gave us title to live there if we kept up the property. By and large we haven't done a very good job of it. Today the keepers of the tradition of the virtues and vices seem to lack a living faith in the legacy and are broadly ignorant of its great power. They do not know the content of the theory as a basis for either practical training or for theoretical research. While different camps of interpreters wrangle over who has title to this great estate of wisdom, the property lies fallow and the present generation goes hungry for its knowledge and guidance.

Aristotelian philosophers have a special responsibility as the keepers of the first principles and causes of this tradition. We must reach out to practitioners both in other academic disciplines and in all forms of social leadership to help those who are committed to human development ground themselves in the firmest possible moral and intellectual foundations.

AN INTRODUCTION TO MORAL CHARACTER
AND AN EXPLANATION OF THE THEORY OF VIRTUE AND VICE

Vision and Character. If Shakespeare, Jane Austen and Balzac are taken as trustworthy witnesses of their times, they alert us to the fact that cultured people were once highly conversant with the facts of moral character and its importance for mankind's well-being and happiness. If the reader does not recognize what I mean, he will if he goes back to such classics after reading this book. Today, one can no longer presume that even highly educated people know what character is. While literature departments are expected to teach about the characters in fiction, they aren't really expected to have studied character as such. We seem to expect that psychology departments are doing that--but they aren't either. And certainly very few philosophy departments are teaching moral character. As a result, any public discussion of character these days must always start by answering the question, What exactly do you mean by character, anyway?

We can gain a sense of the reality of character if we begin by describing some of the practical techniques people use to affect their own attitudes and performance as well as those of others. These techniques illustrate the reality and power of character even though practitioners rarely realize that it is character that they are dealing with. Discussing these practices will set the stage for our later explanations of the precise ways in which moral character underlies 1) what we wish for and fear, 2) how we picture the world and deliberate about pursuing our wishes and 3) the choices we make, the actions we take and how we feel about what we're doing and what's going on around us.

Our whole approach starts from a fact that we must simply announce for now but which we will document throughout **OMC**. The fact is that our moral character disposes us to picture the world in characteristic ways which have characteristic affects on our choices, actions and emotions. This fact allows us to explain, for example, why the psychological techniques of **directed imagery** and **visualization** help us change our character when we find we have characteristically gone into situations with the wrong attitude. And since we looked at things from a bad perspective, we performed poorly. Through these visualization techniques we try to put ourselves in the emotional and even physical states of readiness and focused attention required for the kinds of action (or inaction) we wish to perform. Athletes, public speakers, cancer patients and many others prepare themselves by visualizing handling things in virtuous or excellent ways so that they will be less tempted when the time comes to handle them in either excessive or deficient ways.

Since we have much greater control (though by no means complete) over our thoughts than directly over our feelings and actions, we can practice picturing the world in the ways that invite and challenge us to act properly. By doing so, we are building up our ability to handle them better in reality. These techniques are easily accessible vehicles of character development for anyone who can envision himself living on a higher plane of excellence. By envisioning ourselves actually performing well, we are subtly building up the character orientation, in both our heads and our hearts, that is required for performing well in fact when it really counts.

We find the same assumptions about the relation between visualization, action and emotion at work in drama, for example. Actors often follow the same technique to get into character on stage or before the camera. Rather than trying to act a feeling, most actors try to call to mind images from their own lives which stimulate the natural expression of the required emotion. By identifying himself with a situation similar to his literary character's, the actor actually feels something approaching the character's same emotion--instead of simply acting as though he did. As a film-maker, Sergei Eisenstein recognized that his own art, and indeed all literature, depended on exactly the same principle of constructing a structured sequence of images which will have the desired emotional effects on an audience. Because there are natural causal relations at work in this process, trained students can recognize what authors and directors are trying to do. Eisenstein used the word "montage" for the series of images an artist creates to arouse given emotions and even actions from his viewers. (See Eisenstein, **FILM SENSE.**)

But actor's also use a different and more comprehensive technique to get into character when they can't draw up an image that works to arouse the desired emotion. This technique shows us how an actor can acquire a feeling state he has either never experienced himself or that is hard for him to acknowledge. The approach thus illuminates the larger processes of acquiring new character traits and learning to identify with the thoughts and feelings of people unlike ourselves.

In this theatrical technique, the actor begins not by visualizing a time when he **saw** the world and thus felt the same way his character does, but by **doing** the things the character does or wants to do when feeling the way he does, for example, stomping around and slamming doors when he's angry. It is only after he begins to act and move in an angry way that the actor can begin truly to think about the unjustified slights against himself in the past or against his literary character in the play which would naturally cause a person to get angry.

By working himself into the form of life and literal physical state in which the given emotion is felt, the actor becomes more able to experience the picture of the world which arouses that emotion as a real perception and not just an idea. We could even say that a person believes in the truth of a picture or proposition only when his choices, actions and emotions reflect that assumption. And by the same token, just as belief gives rise to action, action gives rise to belief.

This expanded approach to getting into character helps us see why Wittgenstein was right to say that the meaning of words can only be understood in the context of their use and why we must always try to enter into the practice of life described by a theory or philosophy before we can have any true experience of its reality and power. We might even say that, when in Rome, doing as the Romans, we tend rather naturally to see and feel the world as the Romans do. And by the same token, we cannot know the true meaning of a picture of the world or of a philosophy about it unless we grasp the choices, actions and emotions from which it arose and which it encourages in turn.

We can trace our way backwards from a person's feelings, choices and actions to the cognitive beliefs which make them seem rational and desirable in the light of the person's characteristic desires and aversions. People's choices and feelings thus give us a profound insight not only into their beliefs but into the moral attitudes and desires animating their whole behavior. This is why Aristotle explained in the **POETICS** that playwrights must show people making choices between alternative courses of action if the audience is to build up a picture of the characters being portrayed on stage. He explains in a similar way in the **ETHICS** that the pleasure and pain people show in responding to different things is likewise a mark of their character and by implication of what they actually believe to be real and good. One's ability to perceive character is thus increased as he becomes more aware of the alternative courses of action open to people.

Leadership and Vision. The arts are not alone in their concern with the link between vision and image, on the one hand, and people's choices, actions and emotions, on the other. All effective leadership would seem to draw on the same theatrical techniques for getting people into character that a drama director might employ to help his actors get into the roles he expects them to play. Politicians, managers, teachers and coaches intuitively realize that since people base their choices and actions on how they picture and think about things, a group or team will accomplish very little together if everybody sees what the group is trying to do differently and nobody pictures himself playing the role he or she is most needed to fill. This is why the forging of a shared vision of what people are facing and trying to accomplish together is the central leadership function and why leaders have such a profound effect on character development. It is why philosophy, education and culture in general are so important for human development. They all give us a narrative vision of what mankind is about, who we come from, where we are going, and what we must do to fulfill our rightful place in the larger scheme of things.

Leaders, however, must not only help us picture ourselves and our functions within the world, they must set us in motion in ways which allow us to experience the reality and power of what they are talking about. Visions and ideas stir our emotions and move us to make choices and take actions only when we have some access to the practices of life and experiences which support our believing in their reality and power. Leaders therefore help us remember other times when we acted and felt in the desired way or they teach us about others who we can identify with who have done so. When they can, leaders set us in motion experimenting for ourselves in their desired direction while they try to show us how what we are doing, seeing and feeling is part of their larger vision of who we are and what we might become. Being caught up in a way of acting like this, we quite naturally catch on to its corresponding way of seeing and feeling too--especially if we feel it is making us stronger and bringing out what is best in us.

This is the basic truth about learning and leadership that Thomas Kuhn grasps so well in **THE STRUCTURE OF SCIENTIFIC REVOLUTIONS.** While Kuhn shares many of the philosophical limitations I later ascribe to the rationalist tradition, he is nonetheless right to insist that a revolutionary new scientific theory always entails a paradigm of scientific practices through which the theory can be confirmed and extended into new domains. The dissemination of the theory through the scientific community is then dependent on other people taking up the practices and problems which legitimate the theory.

A theorist becomes a leader in a scientific or philosophic revolution only to the extent that others succeed in making contributions, careers and names for themselves through using his theory to solve the kinds of problems it encompasses. A realist would add to this account that the same theory might nonetheless be totally ignored during a less opportune time when social forces did not favor the practices and problems the theory grows out of and solves--while still being true. It is not enough that theorists try to reach people with the truths they have seen, people's practical lives must make them reach for the discoveries theorists can place within their grasp.

In a more general way, in shaping the quality of moral and cognitive character most appropriate to the tasks at hand, leaders thus always start from the attitudes and problems people bring with them. They then create an ethos of both determinate ways of handling things and determinate ways of picturing them, what we are doing together and what we should feel about ourselves and one another if we are to get the job done.

To promote the virtues, for example, a leader will set us in motion handling painful things or challenges to our self-respect in appropriate ways and then draw our attention to how strong and good handling these things well makes us feel. They help us learn to value the difference, for example, between **courage** and **high-mindedness,** on the one side, and **cowardice** and **small-mindedness,** on the other. This is why the teaching of literature and history is so important for moral education. Writers with a keen perception of moral character must be taught by teachers who know what they are talking about.

Leaders must also think about the image of their own character they are projecting to their followers. If a leader is corrupt, this image will be designed to weaken them and dull their perception of both their own interests and the threats and opportunities they are actually facing. Good leaders, on the other hand, project an image which helps others grow stronger and more realistic about themselves and the world. Concern for one's image can thus be either self-seeking and **vain** or responsible and **high-minded**.

Aristotle stresses the role of the leader's image in the **THE ART OF RHETORIC** when he describes someone's "ethos" as the picture of his own character, experience and attitude that a speaker, teacher or writer tries to project to set the tone required for his audience to take seriously his vision of what is going on and of what people need to do to take the best care of what they value. "Pathos," on the other hand, refers to the corresponding emotions and attitudes the speaker wants to arouse in them and "logos" refers to the arguments and evidence he uses in making his case for choosing a given line of action over the alternatives.

All acts of leadership cover these three bases of ethos, logos and pathos. Any given act of leadership is effective in a morally-neutral way whenever its argument appears to follow naturally from the character of a speaker who appears worthy of being followed, and when it arouses the feelings the audience must have if it is to choose the line of action he presents as most choice-worthy in the circumstances. So here again reason or deliberation (logos) is seen as both arising from character (here, the leader's ethos) and as stimulating people's character to make choices, take actions and feel emotions (here, the audience's pathos).

Leadership and Character. In the light of these various techniques for improving people's performance by helping them get into the character orientation required to handle things well, we can understand why Aristotle said that

> The true student of politics... is thought to have studied virtue [i.e. virtuous character] above all things; for he wishes to make his fellow citizens good and obedient to the laws... clearly the student of politics must know somehow the facts about [the human] soul, as the man who is to heal the eyes or the body as a whole must know about the eyes or about the body; and all the more since politics is more prized and better than medicine; but even among doctors the best educated spend much labor on acquiring knowledge of the body. The student of politics, then, must study the soul, and must study it with these objects in view... (**NE** 1102a 8-25)

For Aristotle politics is the study and practice of leadership at all levels of society from the family through education, the economy and the legislative, judicial and executive functions. His own view was that all institutions must be organized, led and evaluated with an eye to their effect on the development of people's character, well-being and happiness. Different communities and even different institutions in the same community can be constituted in different ways and for different purposes. But whatever their constitutions and the differences in the environmental problems they have to handle, all institutions should be evaluated in terms of the kind of people they develop.

The TABLE OF VIRTUES AND VICES. OMC is written in the faith that leaders who accept this responsibility will welcome a contemporary reassessment of Aristotle's theory of the moral factors involved in human development. The reassessment is based on a systematic account of the relation between people's 1) choices, actions and emotions, 2) their ways

of picturing the world and 3) the character traits which dispose us both to
see the world in these ways and to choose, act and feel accordingly. The
TABLE on the next two pages lists in its first column fifteen classes of
agents which we must picture in one way or another in order to arouse
the feelings and attitudes listed in the second column. This second
column represents the moral and emotional powers we have for dealing
with the agents in the first column. The third, fourth and fifth columns
list the virtues and vices we can develop in each of our moral and emotional powers and which tend either to perfect or to distort how we perceive and handle the corresponding agent. They are the vice of excess,
the virtue and the vice of deficiency for each power.

At first glance, the TABLE might appear intimidating. Most readers
will be familiar, however, with all the terms with the possible exception
of "obsequious" which means roughly the same as "servile" and "irascible"
which means being prone to excessive anger. The TABLE's contribution is
in the way it helps us picture the relation between its various items.
Such an organization of the data allows a trained person to see the possible interactions between the elementary units and why the different
traits fit together in determinant constellations rather than in arbitrary
structures. Such systematized knowledge allows us to explain, for example, the popular wisdom that there is good chemistry between some
people and bad chemistry between others. The TABLE can thus function
like Mendeleyev's periodic table of the elements to organize our knowledge of the moral character traits including not only their relation to the
ultimate agents shaping them but their effects on perception and thought
and on choice, action and emotion.

A Walk through the Causal Pathway. We can locate these various
factors of character, thought and action within a causal pathway of human
action by using the following diagram. The diagram will help us explain
more precisely the role of moral factors in how we see the world and
come to act on it and will prepare the reader to use the book more effectively to improve his or her understanding and performance. In walking
through the pathway, we start with an agent in the external world (A1)
that stimulates or arouses us (M) in some way. Let's say this agent is a
person we just met. One should note from the beginning how the diagram
is drawn to reflect the fact that agents always stimulate both our moral-
emotional and our cognitive powers, both our heads and our hearts. Moral
virtue strives to integrate and balance these two sides of ourselves. This
is signaled by the arrow's pointing to the intersection between the moral
and cognitive parts of ourselves.

In the diagram, we treat the combined system of our moral-
emotional and cognitive powers as a **material** cause (M) disposing us to
see agents in the world (A) in determinant or structured ways (F). How we
picture and deliberate (F1) about the world (A1) is thus our initial form of
response to it. **OMC** documents throughout the ways our perceptions and
thoughts are effected by our moral and emotional attitudes. As we proceed
further along the pathway, we see that while our **cognitive** responses (F1)
are rooted in our moral and emotional powers (M), they nonetheless function as the proximal agents (Tfa) which go on to trigger these same
powers (M) to choose and act (F2) according to what we picture as the
most desirable thing to do in the circumstances. The diagram thus reflects
the fact that it is our picture of the world and our deliberations about it,
rather than the world itself directly, which stimulates us to choose and

TABLE OF THE VIRTUES AND VICES

THINGS WE HAVE TO HANDLE	OUR MORAL & EMOTIONAL POWERS TO BE	THE VIRTUES & VICES IN EACH POWER DISPOSING US TO BE		
		EXCESSIVE	APPROPRIATE	DEFICIENT
Ch. I Painful & Destructive Things	AFRAID	cowardly	COURAGEOUS	reckless
	CONFIDENT	macho-boaster	COURAGEOUS	cowardly
II Eating, Drinking, Sex & Drugs	PHYSICALLY PLEASED	self-indulgent	SELF-CONTROLLED	depressed
III Money & The Things It Will Buy On A Personal Scale	GIVING	extravagant	GENEROUS	hoarding
	RECEIVING	receptive	GENEROUS	
	TAKING	exploitative	GENEROUS	
On A Civic Scale	A COMMUNITY BENEFACTOR	vulgar	MAGNIFICENT	niggardly
IV Self Respect	NOBLE & PROUD	vain	HIGH-MINDED	small-minded
Status	AMBITIOUS	excessively ambitious	AMBITIOUS	deficiently ambitious
V Unjustified Slights	ANGRY	irascible	GENTLE	apathetic

		obsequious or flattering	FRIENDLY & COMPASSIONATE	contentious or contrary
VI Pleasure & Pain Of Others	FRIENDLY & LOVING			
Self-Revelation	TRUTHFUL IN SELF APPRAISAL	boastful	TRUTHFUL	mock-modest
Humor	LAUGH & BE FUNNY	buffoonish or ridiculing	WITTY	boorish
VII Disgrace	ASHAMED	abashed	PRINCIPLED	shameless
VIII Unjustified Bad Fortune Of Others	PAINED	soft	PITEOUS	hard
	PLEASED	spiteful	(NO VIRTUE IN THIS)	
Unjustified Good Fortune Of Others	PAINED	envious	INDIGNANT	apathetic
	PLEASED	flattering	(NO VIRTUE IN THIS)	
Justified Bad Fortune Of Others	PAINED	soft	(NO VIRTUE IN THIS)	
	PLEASED	spiteful	INDIGNANT	apathetic
Justified Good Fortune Of Others	PAINED	envious	EMULOUS	apathetic
	PLEASED	flattering	EMULOUS	envious

ASPECTS UNDER WHICH WE EXAMINE
STEPS IN A CAUSAL PATHWAY OR EXPLANATION

A – as an Agent or stimulator.

A_1 – as the first Agent in a pathway.

A_2 – as the second Agent in a pathway, etc.

M – as the Material stimulated by an Agent.

M_1 – as the first Material in a pathway, etc.

F – as the Form of response the Material has to an Agent.

F_1 – as the first Form of response in a pathway, etc.

T – as the Telos, goal, or function something accomplishes or performs.

T_{FA} – as a Form of response functioning as an Agent.

T_{FM} – as a Form of response functioning as Material.

T_{AM} – as an Agent functioning as Material.

T_{AF} – as an Agent functioning as a Form of response.

T_{MA} – as Material functioning as an Agent.

T_{MF} – as Material functioning as a Form of response.

CAUSAL DIAGRAM OF MORAL MOTIVATION,
PERCEPTION AND THOUGHT, CHOICE, BEHAVIOR AND EMOTION

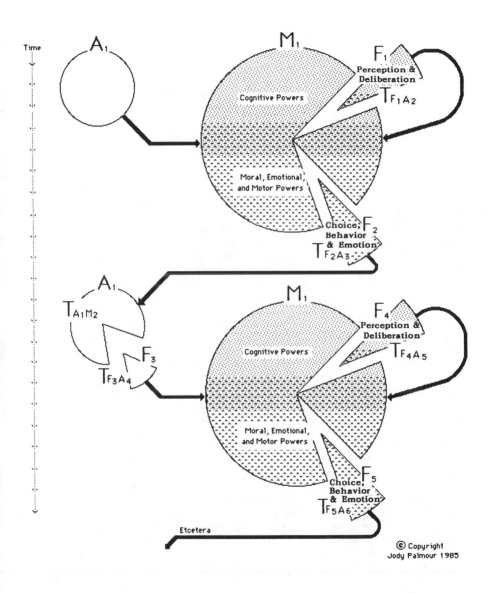

© Copyright
Jody Palmour 1985

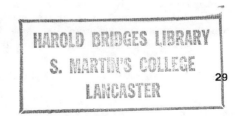
29

act the way we do.

Emotion comes into the diagram at that point in the pathway when we are desiring to choose and act on our picture and analysis of the situation. Emotion is the feeling associated with how we want to move, or are already moving, as a result of seeing things in the light of our moral desires and fears. It is literally an e-motion, a feeling associated with a desired or actual motion. Emotions and feelings are thus the physical expression of both a moral and a cognitive state. It is because we desire and see things in certain ways that we have certain feelings about them.

The next step in the pathway tracks the way in which our behavioral response at the level of action (F2) functions as an agent (Tfa) to stimulate the person or thing (Tam) which stimulated or aroused us in the first place. Let's say we pictured this new person as friendly and attractive (F1) and deliberated about what we could say or do to arouse their interest in wanting to know us too. When we thought of something to do that we actually felt like doing, however, our action (F2) expressed, let's say, a certain loud humor and **buffoonishness** that we often display when we want to draw attention to ourselves.

Unfortunately, though, as so often happens when we do this, our loud humor leads the person we wanted to be friends with to respond in a defensive way (F3), and that makes us feel bad (F5) and even **ashamed** for having done the same thing again. Feeling bad like this, we can either make the situation worse by talking still louder, or we can get more in touch with our wish to stimulate friendliness in others by acting with greater friendliness ourselves. Such negative feedback as the person's defensiveness (F3) can thus jar us into acquiring a clearer picture (F4) of other people's wishes, perceptions and feelings as well as of who we want to be and where we stand in the world today because of the limitations in how we have developed our character. Unless we practice visualizing the moral objective of being friendly that we so easily lose sight of, we will make no real progress in obtaining our objective even if we redouble our efforts again and again. By approaching the world with the wrong moral attitude, we do not picture what is really going on in the situation or what is truly at stake for our well-being and happiness. So how could we possibly handle the situation properly?

Moral Virtue and Cognition. The creation of the TABLE and the CAUSAL DIAGRAM required integrating Aristotle's assumptions and discoveries in **THE ART OF RHETORIC** with those in **THE NICOMACHEAN ETHICS** in a way which, while implicit in them, seems not to have been worked out before in this systematic fashion. Others have charted a partial listing of the virtues and vices but without reference to the moral andemotional powers analyzed in the **RHETORIC**, the agents each power responds to, or the impact of the virtues and vices on cognition. This neglect reflects a larger disassociation in the modern world between morality and epistemology. While David Ross notes that for Aristotle "the definition of moral virtue involves... an intellectual virtue," for example, he does not see the profound epistemological consequences of this fact. (ARISTOTLE, p. 194.)

Aristotle discovered in his study of rhetoric that he and his students could identify specific classes of people and behavior which arouse particular emotions, like those which make us angry or calm, or those which frighten us or give us confidence. They then listed these anger-arousing agents and those for the other moral and emotional powers in a handbook to help orators understand how to stimulate or resist the different ways an audience might feel and act. In addition to the lists of people and behavior arousing each emotion, they added lists of the states of mind disposing us to be more or less ready to see things in these ways and have the corresponding emotions.

To appreciate the practical and theoretical importance of their work, we must recognize that if we have to see the world in certain ways in order to be **afraid**, for example, it follows that if we are too often afraid, i.e. if we lack courage, we will too often picture the world in the threatening ways which cause us to be frightened. By the same token, if we have to see somebody as unjustifiably slighting us in order to be **angry**, and we have an excessively angry character, we will see people as unjustifiably slighting us even when they aren't. The excessive fearfulness or anger in our **moral** character will corrupt our **cognitive** character in a determinant way as well--and nobody should be expected to handle things very happily when both his desires and perceptions have been distorted. With such a vice in our moral character, no amount of education that ignores the moral dimension of our desires and fears will correct cognitive or behavioral problems for long. Our moral character will bring us right back to the same mistaken perceptions and inadequate behavior again and again.

By systematically correlating Aristotle's treatment of the moods in the **RHETORIC** and the virtues and vices in the **ETHICS**, we create a powerful new theory about the relation between moral character and cognition. The **RHETORIC** gives us careful descriptions of the various agents which arouse the different emotions and which shape the development of the different character traits. Aristotle's treatment of the virtues and vices in the **ETHICS** then allows us to explain the different forms of possible development in these moral and emotional powers and their differential effect on cognition, action or emotion. The **RHETORIC's** states of mind in which we are most likely to feel or resist a given perception, thought, choice, action and emotion are often the virtuous or vicious states of our other moral and emotional powers. The vice of **vanity**, for example, is a state of mind disposing us to excessive **anger**.

The identification of such cross-references to how one virtue or vice affects the others is enormously important both theoretically and practically. By learning to trace our responses back to the environmental agents stimulating them and to how the development of a virtue or vice in one power affects the development of the others, we come to picture our attitudes and actions as part of a natural system. We come to know our nature as human beings displaying the response of our nature to having developed ourselves within a given social environment. We can see more clearly the essential moral requirements for our well-being and development and how natural is our corruption and decay when we violate those requirements. When a person begins to see himself and others in this naturalistic way, he deliberates much more wisely before responding to things in one way rather than another. He can anticipate so much more realistically the impact of his actions not only on his own well-being but on the character and happiness of the people he cares about.

Methodology in Creating the TABLE. How did Aristotle come up with this particular list of moral and emotional powers? This is an important question because when one understands where a theory comes from, particularly the practices and methodology by which it was generated, he can better understand the theory and recognize that it is not an arbitrary construction. Of all the major philosophers, Aristotle most clearly saw man on a continuum of biological complexity with other living things and as literally a political animal endowed with the power or potency of reason. We should not be surprised then that Aristotle used the same methodology for studying man's moral and emotional powers as he did in explaining the general biological powers of nutrition, growth and reproduction, or in his pioneering explanations of man's five senses.

Aristotle explained this method in his book of principles for studying the animate as opposed to the inanimate world, **De ANIMA**. He taught that to identify any organic power for investigation one must first identify the class of agents to which it responds. To use hearing as an example, this means one must first examine audible things as agents (A) arousing our hearing response (F) before examining the power (M) within us that allows us to hear. Having recognized vibrations as the agents of sound, Aristotle thus proceeded to investigate the way our hearing apparatus was organized to collect, focus and amplify these vibrations. He did the same for all the five sensory powers or organs. This methodology follows the general assumption that we gain access to the underlying causal structures within things (M) by observing their forms of response (F) to given classes of agents (A) under given conditions.

The same methodology governed Aristotle's treatment of the moral and emotional powers in both the **RHETORIC** and the **ETHICS**. Aristotle always starts by identifying the kinds of agents we have to learn to handle in life before going on to analyze the forms of operation of the different powers we have for handling these agents under different conditions and in different states of virtuous or vicious functioning. He then organized the various attitudes people actually take in handling a given class of agents according to whether they were excessive, appropriate or deficient. This was in keeping with a deep cultural belief among the Greeks that in health as in all the arts either too much or too little of anything can destroy the desired effect. Aristotle raised this idea to the level of a central principle in his whole philosophy and not just the **ETHICS**.

In the **PHYSICS**, he explained how all change occurs between the contraries of deficiency and excess and that either extreme can destroy the integrity and identity of a substance. In modern physics, for example, we would say that if the atoms in a sample of a given element were to either gain or lose protons in their nuclei, they would no longer be the same element. The more pertinent application of the theory of the mean between extremes occurs in **De ANIMA**, however, where Aristotle speaks of the mean in a sensory power like sight or hearing. When in a virtuous state, these senses can perceive accurately through a broad spectrum of increased or diminished light and sound. If we are exposed to either excessive or deficient light or sound, our power of perception in these areas can be impaired. We might be able to see light of only a certain intensity or hear sounds only within a certain range of pitch. The damage might not be lasting, as when we are blinded when first entering a movie theater on a sunny day, or when we come back out into the light.

Aristotle's basic point about the mean, and the one that is most important in understanding his **ETHICS** is that a sensory or a moral and emotional power is in the mean, appropriate or virtuous state when it allows us to respond to the whole range of agents for which it is responsible. Our eyes are not in a mean state when they have grown accustomed to either the bright sun light or the darkened theater--as is born out by how hard it is to adjust to the contrary environment. In the sunlight our pupils are habituated to let in only small amounts of intense light. When we enter the theater, it is not the absence of light that blinds but our temporary inability to open ourselves to the light that is there. When we are finally able to see in the theater, it is because we have adapted ourselves once again to an extreme condition in a way which, while necessary at the time, nonetheless limits the range of operation of the power in question. What one has had to do to survive in an inhospitable environment tends to damage his power to handle other agents in a more appropriate way.

There is a group of contemporary pathobiologists who unknowingly use Aristotle's same theory of the mean to explain and classify disease states in the body. Following the work of Forbus in the 1940s, they argue that while disease is always a reaction to injury, it is not so much a matter of the insulting agents (A) attacking the body (M) as it is of the body's resulting excessive or deficient responses (F) in our regular processes for handling these agents. We are after all surrounded by pathogens all the time, so they cannot by themselves explain our being sick. The pathobiology conception of dispositions to either excessive, appropriate or deficient responses allows these theorists to pair up disease classifications in the same way Aristotle did with the virtues and vices, the powers or organs they are rooted in and the insulting or stimulating agents to which each responds. Perhaps the most commonly known such pairing is between hypoglycemia and diabetes. (LaVia and Hill, editors, **THE PRINCIPLES OF PATHOBIOLOGY**)

Aristotle's own focus in describing the vices was on that degree of excessive and deficient disposition which falls within the range of what psychologists today might call the psychopathology of normalcy. As the text of this work will amply document, the vices cripple our psychic functioning in more or less marked ways. These same moral and emotional attitudes can be taken to greater extremes of excessive or deficient responses, however, that fall into the neurotic or even psychotic range. It is a commonplace observation among psychologists that even the most extreme psychopathological states are distortions of the mental processes and emotional attitudes of everyday life. I have found in fact that clinical case histories by Freud, Jung, Adler, Horney, Sullivan and others are unknowingly written in terms of the more extreme forms of Aristotle's particular catalogue of moral and emotional attitudes and are fully in keeping with his functional explanations of their nature and operation.

Should this recognition be borne out by further research and established within psychological circles, Aristotle's theory of moral character could function as a kind of rosetta stone allowing us to translate the advances and accomplishments of each of their personality theories back into a common, more generic theory. We would see too that many of them give us a theory of human personality insofar as we are dominated by the struggle with particular vices, as with Freud's focus on the threatening consequences of excessive sexuality or Adler's focus on ambition and small-mindedness. From this perspective we would see that their seemingly contradictory theories of personality are actually complementary to one another and represent specific instances of a more generic theory of human development.

The pursuit of such research will appear desirable, however, only to those impressed with the power of Aristotle's theory within the less extreme range of excess and deficiency. The work of Erik Erikson and of Carol Gilligan provide significant inductive support for the power of Aristotle's conceptual framework to grasp essential dimensions of the process of human development. We will review their work briefly next to help the reader feel more at home and I hope feel more confident about the general schema of the virtues and vices. Yet, while we might intuitively recognize that people can be excessive or deficient in the various ways we will be describing, it is by no means obvious in Aristotle or even in Erikson or Gilligan what the standard is against which we judge an attitude to be excessive or deficient. But before we offer an answer to this decisive question, we must lay a still deeper foundation in Aristotle's theory of causality and scientific explanation. I wish to say something new in my answer to this question and it is important that the reader understand the practical perspective from which I believe we can establish what causes the virtues to be virtuous and the vices vicious.

Erikson's Stages of Human Development in the Light of the TABLE. Erik Erikson's "Eight Ages of Man" (in **CHILDHOOD AND SOCIETY**) and Carol Gilligan's **IN A DIFFERENT VOICE** allow us to illustrate the way in which contemporary researchers have unknowingly reaffirmed Aristotle's theory of the moral and emotional powers. They have empirically rediscovered the central place of Aristotle's virtues and vices in human development and have actually applied his conception of the natural history of a species much further than he did in the study of human beings. Erikson and Gilligan, however, offer no systematic account of the basic moral and emotional powers, the agents to which each of them responds, their various forms of development or the essential causal relations between them. They give us facts of human development (at least within the environmental conditions in which their studies were conducted), rather than the reasoned facts for why certain of these relations occur.

Still, as wonderfully perceptive observers and thinkers, they nonetheless describe human development in precisely the way Aristotle calls for and carry his tradition to a higher empirical stage. By translating Erikson's developmental stages into their corresponding Aristotelian terms, we can appreciate his contributions in identifying the periods in human life when we first begin working on developing the different virtues and are perhaps most vulnerable to acquiring the different vices.

Methodologically, Erikson assumes that the agents (A) which we are working on at a given stage reflect the material state (M) of our development at the time. Secondly, he recognizes that we can fail through developing either an excessive or deficient response (F) to these agents, and that we take the character (Tfm) we develop at one stage to all the tasks we must confront at other stages. No trait is ever won or lost for all time at a given stage but can be either undermined or acquired later through one's subsequent practice. He sees the successful resolution of each stage in terms of a person's growing together or integrating him or herself both physically and psychologically and that as a result one acquires a surplus of energy and a heightened sense of personal direction, autonomy and relatedness to others. Since he sees character as shaped through the quality of one's social practice, he situates the family's influence on character development within the larger political-economic context of other social institutions. Finally, he sees human development in explicitly ethical terms. Anyone properly trained in Aristotelian philosophy would have developed his cognitive character according to these same assumptions and could recognize Erikson as a contemporary contributor to this ancient tradition.

We offer here a telescoped re-description of Erikson's stages of human development in Aristotelian terms and of Gilligan's refinement of Erikson's schema with regard to the differences between the development of males and females. Those professionally involved with Erikson's or Gilligan's work will find that returning to it after having studied **ON MORAL CHARACTER** will give them a dramatically deeper grasp of the realities they describe as a result of understanding the nature of the moral and emotional powers involved at each stage. The Chapters in **OMC** where each of these powers is discussed are indicated in parenthesis.

1. **Basic Trust vs. Mistrust.** The mother and her role in the infant's feeding is the dominant agent at this stage. The child's power to be pleased in eating, drinking and sensuous experience generally (Ch 1) is the dominant need at this stage and is expressed through the **receptive** mode of acquiring the things he needs (Ch 3). This is Freud's Oral Stage. The trust or **confidence** (Ch 1) the child develops both in his mother and in his own ability to handle frustration affects whether he develops undue anxiety (the seeds of **cowardice** later, Ch. 1) or rage and **anger** (Ch 7). Consistency, continuity and sameness in the mother-child relation lays the foundation for the child's sense of ego identity, which we would speak of in terms of both **self-control** (Ch 2) and **high-mindedness** (Ch 4). Without this consistency, one loses confidence in both the world and himself, and becomes **small-minded** in what he expects both from and for himself (Ch 4). The establishment of an improper working relation between Mother and infant can lead to withdrawals into **indulgent** and **vain** (Ch 4) fantasies that cut one off from the world, promote **depression** (Ch 2) and inhibit the possibility of mutuality with others, i.e. the vices associated with **friendliness** and **love** (Ch 6). The great need at this stage is for parents to offset the inevitable frustrations of life with an experience of sameness and continuity that will help the child integrate himself within a larger sense of belonging to a benign and meaningful environment. Erikson believes that the needs of this stage seek institutional support in religions which encourage a sense of trust in life born through belief in a caring power which promotes inner unification.

2. **Autonomy vs. Shame and Doubt.** In this stage we first develop the power to hold on or let go, to **hoard** or to **give** (Ch 3). This is Freud's Anal stage. The development of this power awakens a "violent wish to have a choice, to appropriate demandingly, and to eliminate stubbornly" (Erikson, p. 252) Erikson notes that the desire for **self-control** (Ch 2) and choice develops prior to developing the power of discretion and deliberation which would allow one to control oneself well. The child needs adults who will both respect his developing power of choice and autonomy and yet protect him from experiences which might cause unnecessary **shame** (Ch 7) and **confidence**-destroying doubt (Ch 1). Hoarding control can become an obsessive preoccupation with detail with a corresponding inability to work out mutual self-regulation with others. Shame at failed self-control can become **anger** (Ch 5) turned inward and a **small-minded** sense of one's own worth (Ch 4). If people shame a child too much at this stage, he can become **shameless** (Ch 7) and develop a long-standing need to rebel against authority. Whether excessively or deficiently ashamed, the child who fails to develop a proper sense of self-

control will go into the next stages doubting himself and therefore **fearing** his ability to handle hard things and withstand attacks (Ch 1). When successfully mastered, this stage lays a foundation for the appropriate sense of **self-control**, self-esteem and good will toward others that we call **high-mindedness** (Ch 4). Erikson finds these virtues affirmed and protected by the principle of law and order.

3. **Initiative vs. Guilt.** Where the second stage centers on acquiring the power of choice, control, independence and even defiance, this stage adds the awakening sense of initiative and planning that we call "deliberation." Erikson speaks of this as the stage of "being on the make" of finding "pleasure in attack and conquest," in "aggressive manipulation and coercion." This suggests Freud's oral-aggressive stage and reflects what we describe as an **exploitative** orientation (Ch 3). When defeated and denied in their initiative, children can be **enraged** (Ch 5) and become **envious** (Ch 8), excessively **ashamed** (Ch 7), anxious and hopeless (Ch 1)-- unable to take initiative in their lives from the fear of retaliation. Such a child can develop a **small-minded** (Ch 4) and self-punishing view of himself that leads him to undercut his own promise if the adults he depends upon do not show him how to use his energy and gifts for good. This is the period when conscience and a sense of personal values first develop. It is the time of awakening of our power to **emulate** (Ch 8) others in responsibility and performance, to learn avidly and quickly, to plan and to build. The task is to developed a **high-minded** (Ch 4) sense of what one expects of himself so that his or her dreams and initiative can be later tied to realistic adult goals. The danger is that one's initiative will be forbidden as bad and aggressive. If defeated in his initiatives, the child can lose confidence in his powers and deny his own wishes. Alternatively, he can "stick his neck out" **recklessly** (Ch 1) to show he is not afraid. When his own initiatives are blocked and damned up, a person fixated at this stage becomes **envious** and **spiteful** (Ch 8) toward those who are not blocked. When more properly developed, he is capable of properly righteous **indignation** (Ch 8) against those violating the principles which he believes are necessary for the freeing of people's energies. The organization of work and the economic ethos is the crucial social institution for either supporting or thwarting the gains of this stage.

4. **Industry vs. Inferiority.** The third stage showed that the child must go beyond his family to fulfill himself if his sense of initiative is not to be thwarted. In the fourth stage he must learn to work industriously in the schooling that will prepare him later to go out in the world on his own. It is at this stage that one learns to "adjust himself to the inorganic laws of the tool world," to carry tasks through to completion and find joy in doing so. This stage lays the foundation for one's sense of competence and what we will call the power to generate the things one will need in life. This ability is the root of the virtue of **generosity** (Ch 3). The danger in failing to develop confidence in one's competence is that he will feel inadequate and inferior and thus become in our terms both **small-minded** and **unambitious** (Ch 4). He would lose the sense of how he might make his own way in the world, where he might fit in and the role of his own wishes and efforts in forging his own identity. Unless one develops a larger sense of generativity, he can become a conformist and slave to the technology of his work and those who can exploit it. The division of labor and of differential opportunities for mastering skills is the crucial social structure for this stage.

5. Identity vs. Role Confusion. Puberty and youth begin a whole new round of questioning the sameness and continuity established earlier. The troubling new task concerns how we appear to others, in our terms the **ambition** for honor and status in their eyes (Ch 4), and the problem of connecting up our own skills and wishes with the occupations available to us. The task is to integrate a sense of one's identity out of the mix of one's constitutional aptitudes, the character he has developed to this point, and the job market and income possibilities he must face. One strives to match one's internal **confidence** (Ch 1) and **self-esteem** (Ch 4) with one's public meaning for others. Socially, this is the quest for a career. Several dangers lurk here having to do with the danger of role confusion and the inability to get oneself together. As a reaction to this fear, youth tend to over identify through the **emulation** (Ch 8) they feel for the heroes of their cliques. They become **obsequious** and **flattering** (Ch 6) toward insiders and **contentious** and **contrary** (Ch 6) toward outsiders in their efforts to consolidate a sense of their own identity and protect themselves against confusion. In our terms, this is a matter of excessive **ambition** to find status in the eyes of others and often leads to a **reckless** desire to prove one's worth to them (Ch 1). With its preoccupation with the distinction between insiders and outsiders, this stage is marked by a deep attraction to ideology and to the criteria required for distinguishing aristocracy and excellence from sham and phoniness. They have a deep desire to believe that those who succeed in life thereby accept the responsibility to be the best at what they do. Without this belief, they are afraid they will become **apathetic** (Ch 5&8) and cynical--unworthy of the higher values they so want to believe in.

6. Intimacy vs. Isolation. As one becomes more confident of what he expects of himself and what others think of him, he becomes capable and even eager for intimacy with others. This means making concrete commitments and developing the ethical strength to stand by them even when sacrifice and compromise is required. Without a confident sense of **self-control** (Ch 2) and high **self-esteem** (Ch 4), one cannot risk the self-abandon and vulnerability involved in sexual intimacy with someone one **loves** (Ch 6), in being truly inspired by a teacher, **emulation** (Ch 8), or in opening oneself to his own deepest and most creative insights, see the contrast between **high-mindedness** and **ambition** (Ch 4). The fear of losing what is still only a fragile sense of oneself can lead one to avoid all such intimate involvements with others and to live in isolation. But it can also lead, on the other hand, to fearing he must control and dominate those he is close to so as to make them confirm the image he has of himself. (See the discussion of **insolent-sadism** in the GLOSSARY and text.) Erikson closes with the insistence that true genitality in sexual intimacy requires a blending of the virtues of **self-control, generosity, high-mindedness, friendship** and **love** in a process of mutual concern for one another.

7. Generativity vs. Stagnation. Erikson sees this as the central stage in which a person consciously becomes "the teaching and instituting as well as the learning animal... [who] needs guidance as well as encouragement from what has been produced and must be taken care of." This is the stage at which a person comes into full maturity and practices the kind of **generosity** and realistic responsibility toward later generations we describe in Chapter 3. By broadening our friendly interest in the world, we escape the bounds of our own finitude and selfishness and acquire an ongoing sense of life and of the persistence and development of natural structures. Without acquiring this generous broadening and deepening of interest and care, we become obsessed with a **self-indulgent** (Ch 2) sense of pseudo-intimacy that neither cultivates nor gives birth to further development and leaves one feeling stagnant and impoverished, see **depression** (Ch 2). **Vain** self-love (Ch 4), the lack of a **courageous** faith in mankind (Ch 1) and trust in the justice and goodness of community institutions all undermine the possibility of developing this sense of generativity. Erikson notes that "all institutions codify the ethics of generative succession," although we must qualify this to say that while all institutions affect our attitudes in this area their effect is not always a virtuous one.

8. **Ego Integrity vs. Despair.** Just as few people attain the generative stage, even fewer attain the degree of integrity described in this stage. It most closely resembles what we mean by **high-mindedness** (Ch 4) as the gradually ripening fruit of the prior stages. Erikson speaks of it as the "accrued assurance of [one's] proclivity for order and meaning" and the loving acceptance of both oneself and one's parents. This sense of integrity involves comradeship with the wisdom of other times and conditions of life, but also the readiness to defend one's own dignity and way of life against political-economic threats in one's own time. With such maturity, he sees standing up for the cultural principles which encourage personal integrity as the legacy or "patrimony of his soul" which he wishes to leave behind for others. Knowing that he will leave these principles and their fruits behind, he does not despair in the face of death. This **high-minded** sense of integrity can only be developed when one accepts that we must make the very best of the lives we have and not live in the **vain** illusion that we are living in a finer and more noble way than we really are. If we indulge in such illusions while. alive, we will be filled with **small-minded** (Ch 4) disgust, remorse and despair at having wasted everything when it is time for us to die. To attain such integrity one must first learn to follow "image bearers in religion and in politics, in the economic order and in technology, in aristocratic living and in the arts and sciences" before he can responsibly lead others to find such integrity in their own lives. Erikson closes his description of these stages by noting that children growing up among high-minded adults with enough integrity not to fear death are the most likely to develop the courage and trust not to fear life--thus completing the life cycle as those mastering the eighth stage are able to contribute most effectively to those at the first.

Gilligan's Refinement of the Stages and Contrast between Paternal and Maternal Attitudes toward Morality. Carol Gilligan has courageously reaffirmed the traditional wisdom that men and women tend rather naturally to develop in somewhat different ways and has insisted that unless these differences are acknowledged and respected women will continue to be treated as failed men. She argues that both Erikson's descriptions and Kohlberg's influential of developmental stages in moral reasoning are both based on the natural history of male rather than female development and that as such they stress autonomy and rules over intimacy and responsibility toward others. With regard to Erikson's fifth and sixth stages, she observes that research suggests that women tend to develop and consolidate their own **identities** through developing **intimate relations** with others rather than consolidating their identities as a preparation for intimacy. Female identity tends to be defined through the creation of responsible caring relations with others rather than through establishing one's autonomy and independence from them. This basic difference stems from the fact that while boys must separate themselves more dramatically from their mothers and prove their autonomous power if they are to establish their sex-role identity and ultimately found families of their own, girls are not threatened in their sexual identity by maintaining their initial focus on the quality of their relation with mother and family. Women thus maintain a deeper sense of empathy with those around them. As a result, males tend to have problems with close relationships and attachment while females tend to have problems with separation and individuation.

Gilligan argues that this difference in male and female development produces a characteristic difference in male and female views of morality. Where men tend to see morality in terms of rights and rules guaranteeing fair play and non-interference in the autonomy of others, women tend to see morality in terms of maintaining caring relations and not hurting the feelings of others. She is particularly critical of Kohlberg's ordering of developmental stages of moral reasoning which places the more feminine concern with caring for others on stage four while placing the male's more abstracted and unrelated concern with rules and principles at stage five or six. She seems to miss, however, the support she could find for her contention of the moral worth of caring in Erikson's sense of generativity and maturity and Kohlberg's conception of a "just community" at school.

Where from a female perspective, treating morality as simply a matter of rights, rules and autonomy seems coldly indifferent to others and negligent toward the community of relations within which we live; from a male point of view, a morality of responsibility and caring seems potentially arbitrary, unprincipled and intrusive. Gilligan recognizes the merits in each position and the need to integrate the strengths of both the male and the female perspective. But she does not recognize the Aristotelian pedigree of her own position which becomes most apparent in her description of the characteristic vices women are tempted to as a result of their strong focus on relationships.

With their preoccupation to please other's, women are prone to become **obsequious** (Ch 6) and unable to stand up for their own wishes in the face of the pain it might cause and the threat that doing so might destroy the relationship. Such excessive **fear** (Ch 1) promotes a deep sense of **apathy** and inability to be effectively **angry** (Ch 5) when one is slighted and put down. Since one feels she can't risk standing up for her own wishes, she tends rather naturally to lose respect for herself and so becomes **small-minded** (Ch 4) and **depressed** (Ch 2). As a result, her general ability to deliberate and plan based on her own wishes is undermined and it becomes harder and harder to make her own choices. A literal vicious circle is thus set in motion that can only be checked by her developing a sense of her own rights and autonomy through turning obsequiousness into a capacity for true **love**, fearfulness into **courage**, apathy into appropriate **anger**, small-mindedness into **high-minded** self-respect and depression into an appropriate sense of **self-control**.

Tracing the unrecognized place of Aristotle's schema of the virtues and vices through some of Erikson's and Gilligan's contemporary research as we have just done might build up a certain plausibility for the theory, but we would still be hard pressed to defend in any philosophical sense why we should say that any character trait was virtuous or vicious. Precisely in what way is a vice excessive or deficient? To answer that question we must first explain what character traits are and how we can know them. And to do that we need to know how to explain what causes anything to be what it is.

Character Traits and The Theory of the Four Causes. To help the reader grasp Aristotle's theory of moral character and its practical applications, I have employed a new system for the annotation of causal explanations--(A), (M), (F) and (T). Aristotle's view of causality allows for a more nuanced conception of what causes something to be what it is than that permitted by the positivist's bipolar conception of cause and effect, stimulus and response. An Aristotelian speaks of what positivists mean by "cause" as an **agent** cause and what they mean by "effect" as a form of response or **formal** cause, in our annotation as (A) and (F). This bipolar concept must be supplemented, however, with the two further factors of **material** and **functional** causality if we are to explain what causes virtues to be virtuous--or anything else to be what it is for that matter.

What Aristotelians call **material** causality comes from the Latin "mater" or "mother" and is used to designate the internal source of potency within a thing from which comes its power to give birth to a new form of response when properly stimulated. Recent neo-behaviorists in psychology recognized the importance of this neglected material factor when they abandoned the simplistic conception of Stimulus-Response in favor of a conception they refer to as Stimulus-Organism-Response. Where in their annotation this is a move from S-R to S-O-R, in our annotation it is a move from A => F to AxM => F.

The S-O-R formula expresses the recognition that an organism's response to any stimuli is determined not just by the stimuli (A) but by the organism's state (M) when stimulated. In fact, in most cases, the response (F) is determined far more by these internal factors (M) than by the external stimuli (A). This is especially true when it comes to people. Since we all have different constitutional gifts, experiences and social resources to draw on, we are in significantly different states when stimulated, and obviously do not respond to the same stimuli in the same ways. Even when people have the same character traits (M), they will not respond in the same ways (F) when their resources and/or the larger system of agents (A) they must face differ. For example, even though a noble Cheyenne Indian and a noble character in a Shakespearean play shared many of the same virtues (M), their forms of behavior (F) would be different because of the different environmental agents (A) they had to handle. Yet for years positivist and rationalist philosophers spoke as though any scientific or causal account of human nature and development must assume that everyone will respond in the same way to the same thing.

The AxM => F formula is particularly important for leaders, teachers and writers to understand and apply in their work. The formula explains why one cannot lead, teach, speak or write to different groups of people in the same way if he wants to bring out what is best in them. Students, sectors of the electorate, employees in different jobs and at different levels in an organization are at different stages of their development, have different backgrounds and interests, and different kinds of resources to draw on emotionally, intellectually, physically and socially. And they must be addressed accordingly if they are to have access to the meaning of one's message. One must not only speak their language but sing to them in their own tune. **OMC** is designed to help the reader learn to see and hear people in just this sense so that by cultivating a sounder sense of judgment we might have a more stimulating an furthering effect on one another.

Purpose and Teleology. If we are to know what causes a thing to be what it is, however, we must also explain what its function, telos or purpose is. There are two dimensions to teleology that are especially important when it comes to thinking about character. The first is how character traits function when once developed, the second is how traits come into being. In trying to explain teleology (T) to students, I discovered that in describing the function of anything (M) we are always talking about how its form of response (F) functions (T) after an agent (A) has stimulated it. This is as true for character traits as for anything else.

There are only three possible functions a form of response can perform according to the AxM => F schema. A form of response can be the end of a causal chain, at which point it functions as an (F). We can annotate this as Tff, a form of response functioning simply as a form of response. Much more interestingly, a form of response can function as an agent (Tfa) stimulating some other material (M) as when the output of one process becomes an input in another. We saw this in the causal diagram when describing our perceptions and deliberations as both the output of the cognitive process and the input into the process of making choices. "Input" is ambiguous, however, because not all inputs are agents. This is where the third form of teleology comes in. The output of one process can also become the seat of another process as when a thing's form of response functions as the material (Tfm) which further agents (A) stimulate.

We need the concept of a thing's form of response functioning as an agent (Tfa) in order to explain how to identify what someone's character (M) is. All character traits are defined with reference to how they function in our pursuing particular purposes. Both our actions and reactions reflect our purposes and what our character leads us to wish for. As in all real science, we infer the underlying causal structure within a thing (M) from our experience of its various forms of response (F) to the agents (A) which stimulate it. This pattern of analysis allows us to explain what character is and how it differs from habit. When we say that someone has a loving character, for example, we mean something far more dynamic than that he habitually pleases others and causes them no pain. We mean instead that he maintains a constant purpose to encourage the development and happiness of the people he loves (T) even though that purpose might require him to cause them pain by telling them things they don't want to hear or by denying them pleasures that aren't good for them.

Character traits (M) are thus defined by their ability to pursue and maintain a constant purpose (T) through adapting their form of response (Tfa) to the different agents (Tam) they must deal with. From this account, we can see why it is by observing a person over time and recognizing that his responses under markedly different conditions all promote the same purpose and intention that we are able to infer the nature of his character.

The student of character tries to put himself in other people's situation, but he does not do so by asking how he would act and feel pursuing his own purposes in their place. He tries instead to discover what his purposes would be if he were acting the way they actually are. A deep appreciation of history and memory is crucial if one is to place himself imaginatively at the center of other people's behavior and form of life in order to reconstruct whatever continuity of purpose and character one can find there. This epistemological process is beautifully described by R.G. Collingwood with regard to how an historian is able to build up his picture of the plans and motives of people in the past through an analysis of the artifacts they left behind. (AN AUTOBIOGRAPHY) By looking at how their forms of response function as agents in pursuit of common purposes (Tfa) one is able to infer their underlying motives and character (M). OMC should help historians and intelligence officers examine their data with much greater care and precision.

We must also use the (Tfa) annotation in explaining how developing a certain form of character (F) in one of our moral and emotional powers (M) can function as an agent (Tfa) affecting our other moral and emotional powers (M). We see this on the virtuous side, for example, when building up our power to be **friendly** (Tfa) helps us control our **anger** (M) as our more sympathetic understanding of others keeps us from feeling so easily slighted by them. On the vicious side, we see this effect when surrendering to **self-indulgence** (Tfa) undermines our power of **self-respect** (M).

On the other hand, if we are to explain the process by which people build up their character, we must refer to the (Tfm) case where the form of response of one process becomes the seat of the next one. The form of someone's character (F) is always rooted in the constitutional gifts and capacities (M) he brought with him into the world. We want the (Tfm) annotation to express how a socially cultivated character structure functions as the seat of the person's later responses to the world. While from one point of view the person's character is his form of response (F) to the earlier agents (A) he had to deal with, from another point of view his newly acquired character functions as the material cause (Tfm) determining his forms of response (F) to the next agents (A) he will have to handle. Character thus becomes a kind of second nature to us.

Since handling things in certain ways shapes and forms our character in those ways, we must always try to identify the environmental agents and opportunities (A) which shape and nurture constitutional capacities into the characteristic forms they assume in people's lives. The English term "character" originally signaled the importance of these environmental factors quite explicitly. The word originally referred to a mark or imprint like the characters of the alphabet that was purposefully left on something by its maker, as when a silversmith was said to put his character on a pitcher or candlestick. When applied to people, the term reflects the way we pick up from the ethos of our environment, from parents, teachers, neighbors, employers, etc. a sense of what purposes we should go after in life and the kind of people we should become. These social agents set us in motion and teach us to evaluate what we are doing. And each time we desire to pursue a given object, deliberate about how to attain it, and choose to act accordingly, we are building up a neurologically-based disposition to pursue the same kind of goal the next time we have to handle a similar situation.

Establishing the Nature of Virtue and Vice. By now the reader should have some idea of what character is, what kinds of things might affect its development in a general way and why it is important in so many ways. But we really haven't tackled the thorniest issue. What makes us say one kind of character is virtuous while another is vicious? Until now, the realist tradition has not had an adequate answer to this important question. At best, it was claimed that the virtues were just naturally better than the vices and that it is only rational to choose to live this way. But no one has really been able to explain what makes each of the virtues virtuous and the vices vicious. Without such an explanation, Aristotelian advocates have had no real theory of the essential properties of man's moral nature and thus could not defend Aristotle's account from charges that it reflects little more than Greek prejudices and connects with nothing truly essential about human nature. As a result, they normally ignore the specific teaching on the particular virtues and vices assuming that it lacks scientific content and philosophic significance.

This picture of the teaching changes, however, as soon as we recognize that Aristotle uses the same dialectical and inductive procedures for establishing the first principles and causes of the morally-developed and happy person in the **ETHICS** that he had justified in the **POSTERIOR ANALYTICS** and applied in establishing the first principles and causes of mobile being in book one of the **PHYSICS** and of animate being in book one of the **De ANIMA**. By following these methodological practices ourselves, we can develop a new picture of Aristotle's ethical teaching that one totally misses unless he approaches these texts from the practical perspective of trying to explain the nature of the morally developed and happy person. By taking up Aristotle's own methodological practices, we can enter ever so much deeper into the meaning and reality of Aristotle's picture of man's moral nature.

Many Aristotelians have been misled into thinking that because Aristotle says ethics is a practical, applied science that he could not have constructed a theoretical science of ethics to explain the difference between the proper and improper functioning of man and the necessity of the virtues which make proper functioning possible. Contrary to the common interpretation, I believe that just such a theoretical science lies unrecognized at the very core of the practical science expressed in the **NICOMACHEAN ETHICS**. Yet, just as with any other applied science like medicine or engineering, the application of its **scientific** proofs and certainties about man's moral nature to specific instances will always be a matter of **art** in which practitioners with a truer feel for the actual materials they are working with will always bring about finer results than people whose knowledge is only theoretical.

For us here, this means that while we can explain in theory what properties cause a character trait to be virtuous and can demonstrate why a morally developed person must be virtuous, we must nonetheless acknowledge that identifying specific instances of the different virtues and vices will always be a matter of art and practical judgment. Ethics, however, is no different from any of the other theoretical and applied sciences in this regard. The most gifted theoretical physicists and biologists are often dependent on the superior empirical judgment and experimental skills of others in their discipline. Knowledge of theory can contribute greatly to the refinement of perception and practical technique, but it can never replace them and in an important sense depends on their prior cultivation.

Our present concern is with re-establishing the methodological grounds for believing in the theory presented in the rest of the work. In striving to regain this ethical perspective, we can do no better than return to the very Aristotelian canons of scientific explanation which guided these giants of modern science not in their ecologically and philosophically disastrous "mechanization of the universe" but in their positive discoveries. Thanks to the pioneering research by William A. Wallace and other contemporary philosophers and historians of science, we now know that Gilbert, Harvey, Newton, Galileo and other giants of modern science all based their work on the Aristotelian methodological principles enunciated in the **POSTERIOR ANALYTICS** and **TOPICS**. Where Wallace, for example, has traced the history of the former's influence on the development of science in his two volume **CAUSALITY AND SCIENTIFIC EXPLANATION**, his student Andrea Croce has begun to do the same with the latter in her outstanding dissertation on **A LOGIC OF SCIENTIFIC DISCOVERY BASED ON ARISTOTELIAN DIALECTIC**. Many others have taken up this important research of providing a truer picture of Aristotle's seminal role in the rise of Western civilization.

Historians of early modern science have come to recognize that Aristotle's methodology of causal demonstration provided the "rules of the game" that Gilbert, Harvey, Galileo, Newton and others used to determine whether a scientist had demonstrated the truth of his discoveries about the essential nature and properties of a given subject. I have found that by playing by these same rules, we can construct a causal definition of what makes a character trait a virtue and can demonstrate why the morally-developed person must be virtuous. Following these rules uncovers the logical structure of the **NICOMACHEAN ETHICS** in a way that has not been recognized before and raises the tradition to a whole new level of penetration and clarity about the nature of human nature. William Harvey's famous demonstration of the circulation of the blood and the role of the heart in maintaining that function provides an apt analogy for our demonstration here and makes the whole procedure appear a most contemporary natural one.

Harvey (1578-1657) was dissatisfied with medical science's description of the flow of the blood through the body and of the nature and function of the heart. In designing his research and constructing his proof of an alternative theory, he explicitly acknowledges his adherence to the Aristotelian rules of the game for discovering and establishing scientific truths--even while breaking with Aristotle on the conclusions which should be drawn from applying this method in Harvey's area of special expertise.

The most important methodological assumption for our purposes here is that one must first establish the proper functioning (T) of an organism or system before he can establish the material (M), formal (F) and agent (A) factors required for that functioning to occur. Where Harvey's ultimate target for explanation was the heart as the agent of the blood's circulation (A), ours will be virtue as the material factor (M) underlying our purposes (T) and animating our forms of response (F) to all the agents (A) we have to handle in life.

Through painstaking observations over many years, Harvey gathered the data required to dialectically refute the accepted theory that the blood flowed continually outward to the appendages where it was totally absorbed--only to be continually replenished by the body's ingestion of new fluids. He showed that such a quantity of blood production was impossible and concluded that the blood had to flow in a circle. Having refuted the accepted view of outward flow, he then supported his own view of circulation through numerous inductive observations about the structure of the system of arteries and veins, etc. His conclusion that the blood circulates seems so obvious to us now, but it was not at all obvious at the time. The microscope was not yet in use and the capillaries joining the arteries to the veins had not yet been discovered. Harvey was thus demonstrating why the fact of circulation must be acknowledged even though there was no single experience that unambiguously testified to it.

Harvey used this demonstration of the fact of circulation as the first principle in his demonstration of why the heart must be made like a pump for the sake of stimulating this circulation, rather than like a bellows that would simply force blood outward to the body's extremities. Technically, his demonstration proceeded from a teleological or functional assumption that blood moves in a circular form to the conclusion that the heart, as the agent stimulating this circulation, must have a pump-like shape or structure if it is to do so. (See Herbert Ratner, "William Harvey, M.D.: Modern or Ancient Scientist?" in **THE DIGNITY OF SCIENCE** edited by Weisheiple, 1961.)

This general explanatory strategy of always starting with the functional outcome to be attained has passed anonymously into our intellectual culture like so much else we owe to the Aristotelian tradition. Systems analysts in the management field, for example, have intuitively recognized the same logic in their description of the four essential factors involved in the management function. The governing principle is always a firm's purpose, taken to be the function (T) it will perform in the market. They then argue that the firm's function necessitates that it be organized in a certain form (F) if it is to function (T) in that way. With a given organizational structure (F), certain kinds of people (M) must then be recruited who are capable of staffing such an organizational structure. Finally, management must stimulate (A) these people to carry out their responsibilities if they are to implement the firm's function. System analysts have not realized, of course, that these factors of planning, organizing, staffing and controlling illustrate Aristotle's concepts of functional, formal, material and agent causality or that they are part of an ancient tradition in showing how the last three factors all follow from the prior establishment of a thing's function or purpose. Their doing so is a tribute to their seriousness and creativity. (For passing references to Aristotle's influence on systems theory, see Schoderbek, Schoderbek, and Kefalas, **MANAGEMENT SYSTEMS.**)

Aristotle follows this same explanatory strategy in his study of ethics by first establishing a conception of proper human functioning (T) in order to define the difference between the virtuous and vicious character traits. Together, the definitions of proper human functioning and of virtue will allow us to demonstrate why the virtues are necessary if the morally-developed person is to function properly. Our argument will be that since the disposition to function according to proper wish, deliberation and choice is what characterizes the virtues, and a morally-developed and happy person is somebody who functions this way, a morally-developed and happy person must have the virtues. We can express this in classical syllogistic form this way. Where B = functioning according to proper Wish, Deliberation and Choice, and C = Moral Virtue, and A = the Morally-Developed, Happy Person, it follows that the Morally-Developed, Happy Person must have the Moral Virtues.

$$B \quad is \quad C$$

$$A \quad is \quad B$$

$$\overline{}$$

$$A \quad is \quad C$$

To my knowledge no one before has argued that Aristotle characterizes the most properly excellent human functioning in terms of **proper wish**, **deliberation** and **choice** or that it is the capacity to promote this kind of functioning that defines the moral virtues.

On my reading of Book I of the **ETHICS**, Aristotle first distinguishes between what we do for its own sake and what we do for the sake of other things and between what is sufficient by itself to make a good human life and what must be complemented with other things (Bk I, 1-3). With these criteria in mind, he then conducts a dialectical refutation of competing ideas about what people should aim at in their lives. His purpose here is to show that people often pursue means as though they were ends and as though they should be sufficient to make one happy and fulfilled in life even though they cannot (Bk I, 4-6). He then presents his own view of what people should aim at and strive for (Bk I, 7) which he goes on to support inductively by appealing to the common wisdom of the recognized authorities of the time (Bk I, 8-12). In the rest of the work he elaborates and refines the starting points introduced here, most importantly with regard to the individual virtues and vices and the concept of proper wish, deliberation and choice which characterizes their appropriate functioning. This series of moves in the **ETHICS** squares perfectly with the dialectical and inductive procedures for establishing the first principles of any theoretical science that are explained in the **POSTERIOR ANALYTICS**.

Dialectical Refutations of Competing Life Goals. A glance at my demonstrative syllogism reveals that my whole argument turns on establishing the meaning of functioning according to proper wish, deliberation and choice. This term (B) defines both what a virtue is and what the proper functioning of a person is insofar as he is developed and truly happy. As we saw above in talking about teleology, all character traits are identified by their purposes and how they function. So any talk about promoting character development should always require one to establish the kind of human functioning we wish to promote.

The concept of proper human functioning takes on much more significance when it is contrasted with basing one's life on improper wishes. Basically, the proper wish is to try to satisfy and fulfill oneself as a whole human being instead of gratifying a part of oneself at the expense of the whole--and to do so not only for oneself but for the sake of others and stimulating their development in turn. The virtues lead us to focus our desires in this way while the vices lead us to maximize or minimize our responses to things without regard to their effects on our well-being as a whole. Deliberating and choosing for ourselves about how best to act is an essential part of what we mean by proper human functioning.

Since Aristotle's goal in the **ETHICS** is to establish what we should aim at and go after in our lives, it was natural for him to conduct a dialectical analysis of what people do go after in fact whether rightly or wrongly. People tend, of course, to feel that whatever they are going after will make them happy--otherwise they would feel miserable about how they are living. But if we really look closely and with compassion, we see that some people have either never known what real happiness is or that they have lost touch with themselves and don't know what they feel anymore. Such people are poor judges of what is worth wishing and striving for. It's a hard thing to say, but some people have been so defeated by life that they simply don't wish to be happy anymore. Their not really caring anymore about their own well-being and development then becomes the practical starting point of all their perceptions and problems. If they don't wish to live better and see the world in a spirit of friendly realism, there's little anybody else can do to help them because their own wish is the starting point of everything they do.

Aristotle believed that in thinking seriously about what we should go after in our lives, we can move from a merely nominal definition of whatever people happen to think happiness is to a real definition of the way people are functioning when they are most truly themselves, happy and mature. In the intellectual equivalent of the game "King of the Mountain", he examines the claims that we should go after 1) pleasure, 2) honor and status, 3) virtue or 4) money as the ultimate good for man, and finds that none of them can withstand the challenge of close scrutiny. (He also examines the idea that a life devoted to theoretical science or to Plato's concept of the Good, but his arguments are too involved to be discussed here.) These four are all good things, but they are partial and not self-sufficient and should be treated more properly as means to the broader end of mankind's well-being and happiness as a whole. If one looks at real instances of people who treat these things as ultimate goals, he will see the meaning and reality of Aristotle's idea of proper wish, deliberation and choice.

First principles are ultimately justified by experience and the impossibility of accepting the alternatives to these principles. If they could be proved logically on the basis of a more fundamental principle, they would not be the first principles in the science in question. The very concept of a first principle entails that it cannot be theoretically derived from a still more fundamental idea. So whenever we are dealing with fundamentals, we must leave the closed system of ideas that we can manipulate without ever leaving our heads and examine whether our ideas are adequate to our experience of the subject we are examining. When we do this, we can disprove false principles by showing that they violate our broadest experience of the subject in question or that they are logically inconsistent like Bentham's treating utility as a first principle when utility implies usefulness in attaining a more fundamental end. This means learning to take one's own experience seriously and evaluating its possibly distorting limitations and not just look for rational arguments for why the fundamental principles are the way they are.

It would be foolish, for example, to mistrust the proposition that all mass has inertia until physicists can explain why this has to be the case. Inertia is a first principle which physicists have discovered about the essential nature of mass. While they can disprove propositions denying this claim and cite all sorts of empirical evidence supporting it, they have found nothing more basic about mass that would prove why mass has to have inertia. The serious student will start out wondering why a first principle should be so but will end up assured by the knowledge that everything he critically examines bears out the principle and that the alternatives can be disproven.

introduction

To evaluate what I am treating as Aristotle's first principle in ethics, the reader should repeat Aristotle's dialectical refutations of competing claims with a group of friends or students. First, ask them whether some people do in fact treat maximizing pleasure (and by implication, minimizing pain) as a first principle or starting point in their lives. And ask them the same about status and honor, about simply being a good person (rather than doing good), and about money. Most will agree that people often base their lives on one or other of these principles. And if the group is made up of Americans, they will probably start out by assuming that we shouldn't presume to tell other people what will make them happy. But the real task for the group will be to determine from their own direct experience of themselves and people they have known whether treating these things as ultimate goals to organize our lives around will open us to the fullest happiness and experience of ourselves and the world we know man to be capable of, or whether it's possible to succeed at attaining these things and still be a miserable human being. The issue is what they think themselves and not whether they think they can sell their views to others or whether they ought to force their priorities on them.

Aristotle's own strategy for refuting these competing conceptions of what people should go after in their lives becomes clear when we realize that each of them is rooted in a different part of ourselves or is simply a means to functioning properly. A life governed by the pursuit of **pleasure** is centered in the second power on the TABLE we described earlier, the desire for **status** and **honor** is centered in the fifth and **money** is in the third. The problem with each of these popular conceptions of the proper goal and function of man is that it confuses what is only a means with the end of human life and gives us a target to aim at that is by no means a self-sufficient conception of how we are functioning when we are most truly happy and mature. One can gain confidence in Aristotle's fuller conception of what is truly important in human life by recognizing the inadequacy of these competing views.

Aristotle explains in the **ETHICS**, Bk. I, Ch. 5, that a life devoted primarily to attaining

- **pleasure** leaves one slavish and underdeveloped. Aristotle speaks of such people as preferring "a life suitable to cattle." He explains much more about this attitude in his discussion of **self-indulgence** (NE III, 10-12) and of the nature and place of pleasure in human life (**NE** VII, 10-14 & X, 1-5). When people treat pleasure as ultimate, they lose control of their lives in the face of any pleasing distraction. Not only do they become unreliable to others, they can't rely on their own intelligence either. They tend to betray their own best thinking when it conflicts with their chaotic desires and thus betray the other parts of themselves that are most dear to them, like loving and being true to their families and friends, their work or the other caring activities which support their **self-respect**. Pleasure is an essential component of happiness, of course, but does not make one a happy person by itself. One can indulge in abundant pleasures and still be miserable. The pursuit of pleasure as an ultimate goal should thus not be treated as the proper function of man--even though celebrated people in high places have since ancient times encouraged the view that it should be. (For more on this attitude, see Chapter 2-B.)

- **status and honor** makes one dependent on what the people who confer it feel is worthy rather than on one's own sense of what is proper and good. Aristotle observed that people who live primarily for honor and status tend to be seeking reassurance for their **small-minded** lack of self-respect (**NE** IV, 3). Since trying to please others or gain status in their eyes as one's ultimate goal will lead to **excessive ambition** (NE IV, 4), **obsequiousness** (NE IV, 6) and all sorts of duty-centered forms of self-denial and **depression** (NE III, 11), it should not be treated as the proper function of man. (For more on these attitudes, see Chapters 4-B, 6-C & 2-B.)

  – **virtue** makes one confuse the internal means to living happily with the end of actively functioning in the proper way. The mere possession of virtue cannot make one ultimately happy because one can have a virtuous character while asleep or otherwise inhibited by bad fortune from acting happily on the basis of one's virtue. The equivalent would be for an athlete to say that being in shape was a higher happiness than playing the games or pursuing the other activities his superb conditioning would make possible if he were only more active and interested in doing things. To think more about one's virtue than about the contributions one might make is to be **vain** (**NE** IV, 3). Since happiness is fulfilled in activity rather than preparedness for activity, possessing virtue should not be treated as the proper function of man. (For more on this attitude, see **vanity** in Chapter 4-A.)

  – **money** also leads one to confuse a means for an end, but this time an external means. A certain amount of money is a necessary means to a happy and active life, but it cannot be the ultimate goal because one can become a miserable human being in the process of acquiring lots of it (**NE** IV, 3 & **Pol** I, 8-11). Since treating the acquisition of money as ultimate can constrain us to give up everything else we love, acquiring money should not be treated as the proper function of man. (For more on this attitude, see Chapter 3.)

  While many people function as though these goals were ultimate, they do so not so much because they have rationally evaluated their effects on their lives but because the life circumstances and ethos of their upbringing habituated them to function as though they were ultimate. Anyone opposed in principle to the imperialistic imposition of one nation's values upon another's must recognize that the principle we are advocating here encourages us to be sensitive to any instance when people are habituated to values and vices which undermine their wishes to develop themselves in the light of their best deliberations about their own interests and resources and to act according to their own choices. Such a positive theory of the principle of self-determination is required if the concept of anti-imperialism is not to protect people from outside coercion while ignoring the fact of domestic coercion within many cultures.

  We must note too that people who feel defeated in pursuing higher wishes for themselves often settle on these alternative goals as a way to compensate themselves for not having been allowed or encouraged to find a way to become who they really wished to be. And insofar as we are under the sway of self-indulgence, excessive ambition, vanity or the greed for money, both our perceptions and feelings are distorted. We focus so much on external sources and standards of goodness that we aren't even trying to be in touch with ourselves and discover what we would consider most important if we felt freer to pursue it.

And in such a state of alienation from ourselves, we aren't very reliable judges of the difference between being really happy and simply being satisfied with secondary compensations or in doing what others expect of us. Rather than revealing our own lack of fulfillment by acknowledging the truth of a higher standard we haven't attained, many of us lower our standards hoping to hide our disappointment even from ourselves. We simultaneously prepare ourselves to ignore the unhappiness and needs of those around us which might otherwise challenge us to grow stronger in order to make a more responsible contribution to them.

In the eyes of many, the idea of being truly happy appears to be purely subjective and as having neither moral nor philosophical content. Easy sex is felt to rival really loving somebody; becoming famous rivals really respecting what one has done with his life; and winning the lottery rivals earning an honest living by doing responsible work and caring for others. How could anyone spot the falsity of these assumptions if his whole form of life led him to focus on the externals and ignore his own inner experience of humanity?

Aristotle's Functional Conception of the Goal of Human Life and of the Nature of Human Development and Happiness. To act rightly and function properly as a mature and happy person, one must wish to know what one feels and thinks about the world in his own right and not simply report what he has been taught. All too many intellectuals do not explore what they think about their experience of a subject so much as try to remember what they have heard or read without regard for their own beliefs. Miles Davis the musician once said, "You have to play a long time before you sound like yourself." But you have to wish and work for that, and emulate people who are already doing it. It doesn't just happen automatically and it's certainly not what everybody means in practice by education.

Being in touch with one's own experience is not easily acquired but is indispensable if one is to succeed in living his or her own life rather than simply perceiving, thinking, feeling and acting as others would have us. So functioning according to a proper wish for ourselves means at the very least, wishing to know our own minds and live our own lives rather than being manipulated by environments which play on our vices. We lose our autonomy whenever we develop vices that lead us to desire or fear things so much that we can't see things realistically and pursue or flee them without regard for their true nature and their effects on us and the happiness and well-being of those we care about.

To grasp the nature and importance of the idea of proper wish, deliberation and choice requires us to take seriously Aristotle's insistence in the **De ANIMA** that like all other animals, humans are governed by their desires and as organisms, or systems of organs and powers, must be integrated and coordinated in their motion. We must thus take care to cultivate these desires which promote our coordination and integration rather than those leading to internal conflict and disintegration. Modern life makes us acutely aware of the temptation to develop conflicting desires and interests and of how unhappy and crippled we become when we can neither fit them together in an integrated and satisfying way nor give any of them up. We must discover what wishes are proper for ourselves, given our talents, responsibilities and life circumstances. But the theory of moral character can provide a framework for doing that much more deliberately for ourselves and for helping others.

Synergism and the Concept of Proper Wish. In contemporary terms, we can say that Aristotle's concept of proper wish is a matter of desiring moral, emotional and cognitive **synergism** rather than **dysergism**. Synergism refers to the state in which disparate things, or parts of things, are actualizing themselves together so as to grow stronger rather than neutralizing and undermining each other. Dysergism, on the other hand, occurs when either disparate things or the internal components of a given system conflict with one another and bring about a net loss of energy in the system. For example, alcohol and one's medication might have a synergistic effect on one another that is nonetheless toxic and dysergistic for one's health.

The proper moral and emotional wish is thus to actualize each of one's moral and emotional powers in ways which make an optimal, synergistic contribution to one's well-being and happiness as a whole. The proper wish should be contrasted with wishing to maximize one's gratification of particular desires or to minimize his pain and exertion without regard to the dysergistic consequences of doing so. The more mature one becomes, of course, the more will this proper wish for synergism and integrity spread beyond one's own needs and interests to include the well-being of others. One accepts responsibility for creating and maintaining social institutions which promote this vision of human development--of community-spirited people deeply drawn to one another's mature individuality and creativity.

Given this conception of mankind's **proper wish** as **synergism**, I have made a point in **OMC** always to note the way a **virtue** or a **vice** in one moral and emotional power affects the proper operation of the other moral powers. Vices build on one another to have a dysergistic effect on our total well-being, while virtues have a complementary effect not only on one another but on our system as a whole. This is the literal truth of the popular conception of a vicious as opposed to a virtuous circle.

Cybernetics and the Concept of Deliberation. Since we have both heads and hearts, proper wish includes the synergistic exercise of our cognitive powers as well as our moral and emotional ones. We must wish to become realistic about what is truly desirable and worthy of our choices and actions. Human synergism requires the development of a feedback mechanism for our self-regulation in harmonizing our various needs in an environment of changing demands on our time and resources. Aristotle's theory of **deliberation** represents just this kind of cybernetic functioning. We learn to be more deliberate in our lives by attending to feedback on how well we are living up to our highest wishes, by formulating plans for self-correction and control and by visualizing and actually acting more effectively in the world. No one can be well-integrated without bringing his head to bear on the full-development of his heart and bringing a strong heart to bear on the exercise of his head.

Deliberation starts from the wish we desire, say helping a friend develop the courage he needs to fulfill his own proper wishes for himself. We must then analyze all we know about the nature and source of our friend's fears and the reasons for his lack of confidence in himself. We must continue this analysis until we find things we can do to encourage him to weaken his fears and build up his confidence. By documenting the general nature of how fear and confidence and the other moral and emotional powers work, **OMC** shows how useful a theoretical science can be for the practical science of promoting human development.

The Decision Principle and the Concept of Choice and Weakness of the Will. It is not enough, though, just to deliberate about how to pursue the proper wish for human integrity and development for ourselves and others. We must also develop the ability to **choose** to act on our own deliberations. The power of choice means desiring to do that which our deliberations tell us we must do in order to live up to our wishes. Choice is thus a decision principle that, as we have seen, reveals what we really wish for in life and not just what we enjoy fantasizing about.

People might wish for fine and important things but not seriously enough to deliberate rigorously on how to attain them or to make the hard choices to act on their own wishes and plans. Moral weakness or weakness of the will (**akrasia**), for example, occurs when our wish is proper and strong-enough for us to picture the right thing to do (F1), but is not strong enough for us to stay focused on that reality. Since our wish to do the good thing is weak, we are easily distracted. A vice or constellation of vices is easily awakened by any excuse and we picture our situation in a way that rationalizes our ignoring what we should be focusing on while triggering our acting on less noble desires. This distorted picture sets us in motion in violation of our more proper wishes and of our realistic assessment of the situation. Moved by our impulsiveness, we lose our self-control and the power of choice in our lives.

Only the person with the virtue in question will be disposed to picture the world realistically, and only he will be disposed to handle the stimulating agent appropriately. He will not take the mere appearance of what he desires or fears as a call to action but will analyze appearances from the desire to ground himself in realities.

The Definition of Moral Virtue. The principle of proper wish, deliberation and choice leads us to focus on whether a person wishes to integrate his life and function on a high level of intelligence and performance or wishes instead for conflicting things which literally disintegrate his cognitive, moral and emotional life. On my interpretation, the judgment of whether a character trait is a virtue or a vice depends on this first principle. A moral and emotional desire should be identified as excessive, deficient or appropriate depending on whether it makes proper wish, deliberation and choice possible. Moral virtue is thus the characteristic disposition to make choices based on one's own deliberations about what is required to promote the proper wish for human development in ourselves and others.

The **virtue** of each of the moral and emotional powers is that material disposition which allows us to function properly in the face of the specific **agents** associated with that power. The **vices** on the other hand distort our functioning in the face of those agents. This means in practice that we identify a person as having a vice of **excess** in a given power only after we have come to expect him to picture the world in the ways associated with triggering a given emotion **more** often than is called for, and to be more often in the states of mind disposing us to that emotion.

Since we are using the concept of proper wish, deliberation and choice as the benchmark for stipulating which character traits should be considered virtues and which should be considered vices, the practical application of the theory depends on our ability to learn to recognize when people are acting impulsively and irrationally without regard to the natural principles governing human development and happiness. When we say "irrationally" in this context we do not mean without reason or explanation. We mean instead that a person is acting against the natural requirements of his own development and happiness as a human being even though it might be perfectly natural and logical that he do so in his circumstances. The racism of lower middle-class whites, for example, must be seen as irrational from the point of view of their own and other people's moral, emotional and cognitive development. But from another perspective we must see their racism as a natural response to their political-economic and cultural histories. A people's way of life can just as readily celebrate or discourage the development of proper wish, deliberation and choice.

The Particular Virtues and Vices Illuminate the Meaning of Proper Wish, Deliberation and Choice in the Face of their Respective Agents. Investigating what it means to have any of the virtues or vices does much to illuminate the nature of proper wish, deliberation and choice. For example, we are **apathetic** (Ch 5) when we don't stand up for ourselves against unjustifiable slights. In investigating this vice, we come to understand the difference between the wish just to get by rather than trying to pursue our own wishes and interests in the face of opposition. We see what it means to fail to deliberate about the costs of surrendering to slights, and to feel we have no choice in the matter. By analyzing how apathy or any of the other vices leads us to betray ourselves, we deepen our appreciation of why proper wish, deliberation and choice is rightly considered the first principle of moral development.

Analyzing Aristotle's descriptions of each of the virtues and vices deepens our understanding of what it means to function on this high level as well as of the particular moral and emotional powers required for us to do so. The heightened consciousness of the self-betrayal and error involved in vicious action actually helps us appreciate the truth and goodness of the virtuous way. Ethical education from this perspective centers on learning to recognize and celebrate when people are functioning according to the wish to integrate their powers on a high level of excellence by proceeding according to their own best deliberations and choices--especially insofar as they are contributing to others doing the same.

It is the desire to get into the flow of being our own person and contribute to others doing the same that leads us to develop the virtues. Knowing this sense of personal integrity and aliveness is perhaps the height of the Western sense of respect for the human personality. Where are the leaders who will help us recognize and value this way of living again?

PHILOSOPHICAL ATTITUDES BLINDING US
TO THE REALITY OF HUMAN NATURE AND CHARACTER

We have now reviewed what I take to be the essential principles and causes in the realist approach to moral practice and development. Morality is not essentially a matter of obeying rules, exercising political rights or expressing our feelings. What is essential is the cultivation of proper wish, deliberation and choice and conducting ourselves so as to promote the development of the moral virtues which makes such functioning possible. Rules, rights, reasoning and feeling must all be evaluated against the measure of the kind of character they promote among the people in question.

The Aristotelian approach centers on acknowledging man to be a potentially rational, political animal whose perfection is not instinctual but requires both institutional encouragement and cultural cultivation. It treats the system of people's gifts and potentials as a fundamental reality but one which can be developed in either virtuous or vicious ways. Human nature from this perspective thus includes all these moral and emotional possibilities and every single human life is equally natural in this sense. The way people develop their character becomes their "second nature" adaptation to the institutional and cultural environments they must learn to handle in one way or another. And again all of these adaptations are equally natural.

But the fact that there is a natural structure and logic discoverable in all these forms of development allows for the possibility of distinguishing between those attitudes and practices that are naturally perfective and those that are crippling and damaged. To the extent that different attitudes and forms of life can be shown to lead to either fuller or more limited and distorted experiences of ourselves and the world, we can say that those which open us more completely to what is within and beyond ourselves are more naturally perfective of our powers than those which must inevitably limit our openness to what is real.

It is distressingly common these days, however, to find that the better educated a person is, the more articulate he becomes in explaining why we can't really know anything about natural standards of value and worthiness. In such a climate of sophisticated ignorance, it is always a special joy to spend time with a connoisseur of almost any subject from wine-tasting to antiques, botany, horses or typesetting to see how much pleasure and comfort he finds in perceiving distinctions and natural hierarchies of value that one totally ignores so long as he refuses to give himself so lovingly to his subject. I want next to identify what I believe to be the central philosophical attitudes and assumptions which contribute to our alienation from our own species nature and to our lack of openness about our place in the natural world. Unless we can transcend these attitudes, we will never become connoisseurs and lovers of humanity.

Philosophy as a Culture's Basic Operating System. In computer language, philosophers can be thought of as masters of competing operating systems upon which the conflicting theoretical and practical programs in all the other special disciplines are based. As the keepers of the first principles of competing approaches to life, philosophers actually have more in common with people in other disciplines who approach life on the same assumptions than with other philosophers whose basic assumptions differ. Philosophers from different traditions enjoy intellectual workouts together, but we seldom convert or even convince one another except on minor technical points so long as our ultimate commitments and purposes differ. Since we more often talk past one another than to one another, the idea of a cumulative growth of knowledge and mastery of method is possible only within a tradition. As a discipline, philosophy thus differs from natural science in that it reflects no consensus on its purpose and thus no moral commitment to evaluating theories according to a shared methodology.

Philosophic operating systems are like CP/M or MS DOS in the computer field. They are system grammars and languages which allow us not only to organize our data bases but to write and run programs for filing, retrieving and correlating what we know. The knowledge explosion we face today is compounded by the spread of competing operating systems, and is made even worse by the fact that these competing systems of philosophical assumptions are insufficiently recognized, investigated and taught in our supposedly pluralistic philosophy departments. Yet there is probably no philosophy department in America where a graduate student could find an organized program tracing any of the three philosophic traditions through its ontology and logic, philosophy of science and nature, philosophy of biology and mind, epistemology and metaphysics, ethics, politics, aesthetics and rhetoric. The political constitution of today's philosophy departments promotes an unprincipled tolerance based more on the denial of differences than on respecting the right of each tradition to celebrate and declare to the world its own unique vision of human experience.

At the level of analysis and abstraction at which philosophers work, mankind has discovered a basically finite set of alternative moves and assumptions. Yet we devote so little energy to exploring the metasystems of these assumptions that many students are not aware of how pervasive they are. Philosophy teachers all too often fail to distinguish between treating a philosopher's work as reflecting a basic attitude toward the world encompassing and possibly refining generic assumptions and methodological principles he shares with others in a tradition (whether he knows it or not) and treating his philosophy as simply his own specific conclusions from having investigated the world at a particular point in human history. With an exclusively situational and individualistic approach, one misses the structural morphology and logic of the different aspects of a philosopher's thought and how his various assumptions might follow from one another in a commonly encountered structure. One then misses not only the person's unique contribution to his tradition, but even the fact that he is expressing an organized system of fundamental attitudes and assumptions displayed by any representative of the rationalist, realist or positivist operating system.

It is crucial to understand that just as with computer operating systems, philosophies are not equally powerful and just because a given program can be run on one system does not mean it can be run on the others. These limitations are important for us because the rationalist and positivist operating systems have dominated modern culture and both of them deny that man has the kind of nature that would make the study of moral character possible. Their system languages simply do not allow us to run practical programs promoting character development because what the realist means by moral character is unthinkable on their assumptions. Their dominance has caused us enormous, unnecessary intellectual and even moral inhibitions against dealing with the character issue. Formal education has largely ignored the moral significance of the intellectual limitations of the rationalist and positivist operating assumptions in theory because it has not tried to train us to think deeply and clearly about moral character in practice.

The Three Philosophical Families. The three great families of philosophical outlook are the rationalist (Plato, Augustine, Kant), the Positivist (Democritus, Ockham and Hume), and the realist (Aristotle and Aquinas). Each has its own view of what is ultimately real (i.e. ontology and metaphysics) and of how we are able to learn about these realities (i.e. epistemology). Randall's three volume **THE CAREER OF PHILOSOPHY**

traces the modern history of these traditions from the perspective of the priority of their epistemologies. I believe, however, that any philosophy's positions in metaphysics and epistemology should be seen as reflecting its prior commitments in practical life (i.e. ethics and politics). Metaphysics and epistemology should be seen as rooted ultimately in ethics and politics because the former express how one experiences and thinks about the world as a result of adopting a given practical attitude toward it.

This means that philosophy should be seen as a social construction arising out of a people's practical life and community practices which habituates them to think about the world in shared ways based on common experiences. Philosophers who share the same moral and political practices as others in their community are unique only in trying to work out the metaphysical and epistemological assumptions of these common attitudes and forms of life. Hegel described this as the philosopher grasping the spirit of his time in thought. (This does not mean, however, that philosophers are necessarily aware of the attitudes and practices which determine the way they experience the world.) Aristotelians speak of the same idea in terms of the primacy of politics and the exigencies of social life in determining what sciences or disciplined ways of thinking, acting and producing will exist in different states and societies (NE I, 1).

The truly important fact today in philosophical circles is that a consensus is developing among representatives from all three great traditions on this assumption about the social construction of philosophical theories. Pragmatists, deconstructionists, existentialists and other positivists affirm it as do neo-Kantians, Wittgensteinians, phenomenologists and other rationalists. Sharing a major premise like this is a rare and wonderful event in the history of philosophy. It can set the stage for overcoming some of the fragmentation of modern thought and for establishing a broader basis of intellectual consensus if representatives of the three traditions battle out their differences in an organized disputation. Since we all share a major premise, we can focus our energies on our respective minor premises and the conclusions we draw from them. Clearly the single most important issue in this struggle concerns the truth of the realist's claims about the possibility of knowing natural structures and norms, particularly those concerning human nature and moral character. (Rorty's celebrated **PHILOSOPHY AND THE MIRROR OF NATURE** has made the most systematic attack on philosophical realism.)

Somehow, both rationalists and positivists seem to believe that since not everyone believes in the realist theory, the realist theory cannot be true. They literally denounce the belief in human nature and in a naturalistic theory of character as what they disdainfully call "essentialism" or "foundationalism" and speak of it as coming from a bankrupt tradition. But why should anyone believing that people's forms of life shape their beliefs expect that a true theory will necessarily be believed by all? That would follow only if we assumed that everyone shared the same form of life and that that form of life focused on trying to discover whether or not there are essential truths about human nature. Only then would their conclusions reflect results drawn from the same experimental conditions.

Realism, on the other hand, teaches one to recognize the fact of differing opinions and attitudes toward life without surrendering our belief in the possibility of acquiring a true knowledge of nature and of our place in a larger frame of reference than that which might be dictated by our individual desires and fears. One of the first things one learns when trying to understand real people is that the desire to discover the truth about oneself and others is a relatively rare accomplishment that we must cultivate in ourselves and not simply assume as a given characteristic of human nature. The love of truth--especially with regard to human nature and character--is by no means promoted in all forms of life. The fact that there is no consensus on the existence and quality of human nature can itself be explained on realist assumptions and in no way entails the conclusion that there is no human nature. Only through effort and experience does the order of knowing come to reflect what is essential in the order of being. True knowledge is the accomplishment of relating ourselves to the world in a spirit of friendly realism and does not follow from just any practice of life.

The philosophical controversy over the existence of things with their own essential properties, natures and norms of perfection and corruption really comes down to a controversy over the existence of differing forms of life with differing ethical attitudes toward nature and reality. This metaphysical and epistemological controversy should alert us to the existence of different ethical and political commitments with regard to respecting and attempting to cultivate the essential natures and ecological balance between living things.

In one sense, of course, everyone is committed to promoting human development. But to content ourselves with that generalization, we must demote human development from the status of being a normative principle with its own specific content to being no more than the generalization that we all affect one another's development in one way or another. My point here is thus the more specific one that insofar as one follows rationalist and positivist assumptions in practice, he cannot wish to promote that form of human development which requires a friendly, realistic assessment of how people's choices and actions affect both their own character and the development of others. One can be decent, hard working, brilliant, honest, sympathetic and well liked--but one's form of life will not reflect the wish to promote human development in this sense.

If the realist theory is true in a worthwhile and important sense, anyone approaching the study of human life with the appropriate attitude, procedures and gifts for scientific analysis should find it confirmed in his or her own experience. Since **ON MORAL CHARACTER** provides the most detailed analysis the realist tradition has had to date of the essential properties of man's moral nature, readers should find ample opportunities to test its claims against their own experience of themselves and others. But for this to be a legitimate test, one must replicate the experimental conditions within which these conclusions are claimed to be confirmable. And far and away the most important of these is one's moral attitude because of its pervasive influence on one's sense of what is real and how we can most truly know reality.

In the next few pages, I want therefore to describe the two moral attitudes which I have found to support those rationalist and positivist assumptions which deny the reality and knowability of human nature and character. These descriptions allow us to see why people can get so angry simply at the idea of human nature and character even when they cannot make a strong case against them in theory. Since their angry denunciation is often enough to make people back off from thinking about moral character in the way proposed here, it is important for students of character to reflect on these moral attitudes and learn how to handle them in both a courageous and compassionate way.

Lest I be accused of providing a merely psychological and not a moral analysis of the compromised forms of life which seem required to make the rationalist and positivist assumptions appealing, I have set in boldface the Aristotelian virtues and vices which are my explanatory principles. I make no claim to having established that these moral attitudes are commensurately universal with rationalist and positivist assumptions, i.e. that every rationalist or positivist acts and feels these ways and that everyone who acts and feels these ways thinks like a rationalist or positivist. To do so, I would have to follow the Aristotelian method of resolution and composition, which Newton taught us to speak of as analysis and synthesis, through at least the major figures of each tradition. I would have to analyze their forms of life to determine the character traits they developed in response to their life circumstances and then argue synthetically that these moral traits were the true causes of the choices they made in formulating their philosophies out of the political-economic and scientific materials of their times. It would also be necessary to to study the thought and character of non-philosophers to see if one found the same causal connections.

With the space available to me here, I wish to do no more than suggest in a general way how the synthetic aspect of this procedure might proceed. Articulating the broad outlines of these competing forms of life and the corresponding operating system assumptions they give rise to should be of practical assistance in freeing the mind to take the realist theory seriously. Its strengths are highlighted when contrasted with the alternative systems. The exercise also brings home the way philosophers simply work out the metaphysical and epistemological implications of forms of life that they share with other people as well.

Rationalism: the Moral Attitude Underlying Its Epistemology and Metaphysics. I have found that people who develop an excessive degree of **self-control, ambition, anger** and **shame** find rationalist assumptions to ring true to how they experience life. They approach the world with a profound sense of self-control animated by the ambition to be thought acceptable in the eyes of authorities for their moral and craftsmanlike intellectual accomplishments. Their moral attitude is one of duty and obedience to rules which requires the development of an angry and self-reproving conscience and tends to stimulate **depression** when they fail at things. One often finds as well a deep **fear** of allowing oneself to be truly close and vulnerable to others. From this constellation of moral traits and the form of life out of which it arises and which it serves to recreate, we can explain why a person would believe in the most common assumptions of rationalist metaphysics and epistemology.

Self-control in the face of the temptations of the flesh is this outlook's greatest virtue. Pursuing it requires one to be obedient to a categorical schema which allows him to ignore anything falling outside his duty and the conceptual framework expressing that duty. The rationalist's practical commitment to a demanding set of ideals thus explains his temptation to substitute ideas for a more direct and exploratory experience of the world--a temptation which is by no means as great for those with a less over-developed sense of duty.

His sense of duty makes him feel he can be truly himself only when he denies natural bodily impulses rather than trying to discipline and cultivate them. In practice this tends to make one rule-bound and bureaucratic, rather than responsive and responsible--lest one's impulses get out of hand. This moral attitude quite naturally supports a two-world, metaphysical hypothesis about the nature of reality. There appears to be a spiritual world of ideals that is divorced from the natural world which man is part of only insofar as he is a fallen, self-indulgent being. The supernatural world of intellect and will tend to exhaust what is essential in the human spirit. Reason and will are exalted to the exclusion of desire and emotion, the head to the exclusion of the heart, the paternal to the maternal principle. Ideals and the categories of one's duty will naturally appear more real than actual things when one's form of life requires that he deny himself the experience of things which might tempt him away from his duty.

His form of life is thus based on striving for an ascetic ideal of perfected duty within a larger moral vision of the need for continual struggle against the temptations of a fallen nature in a jungle-like environment. With such heavy moral expectations, the human spirit must be seen as supernatural rather than as part of nature so as to place it beyond the realm of causality and dependence on one's environment. One could not rationally accept a self-punishing sense of duty unless he felt himself to be unconditioned by his surroundings and free to do his duty at will, regardless of the pleasure and pain involved.

But this attitude also suggests that since man's spirit has no nature, one cannot violate it by pushing too hard for obedience. The rationalist view is thus more arbitrary than developmental and represents a kind of wild-card conception in which we should be able to will any combination of dispositions in ourselves. With no structures and dynamics built into the nature of human character requiring both study and respectful cultivation, all one needs to know is that if he does his duty by accepting a categorical framework handed down to him, he will free himself from the bondage of shameful lower desires and be able to take pride in having lived up to what was expected of him. One can see how such an ontology of spirit both reflects and rationalizes a tendency to ignore how much easier it is for people to develop self-control in some social environments than in others.

Since the whole approach to life is designed to play down and control sensuality in all its forms, we should not be surprised at the way this moral attitude affects a person's epistemology as well as his metaphysics. We have seen why he would be drawn to the notion that we know ideas themselves rather than knowing real things through ideas. But we can also see why it would strike him as foreign that we should try to gain access to the reality of things through reflecting on our sensory experience of them, or that by doing so we should be able to correct and refine the ideas we use to grasp the reality of things. With his great ambition to be accepted for doing his duty in applying the categories given to him, the rationalist strives to fit his experience into the accepted categories and paradigms of his group. From this perspective, he could not be expected to advocate evaluating accepted forms of thinking against the reality of personal experience.

I find that people with such overly strict consciences tend to repudiate the theory and study of moral character out of the fear that it will draw them back into seeing themselves as subjected to the temptations of a fallen natural world. They are uncomfortable with the realist concept that character is something we must work with in the context of the environmental agents impinging on us and that we must get ourselves into better shape over time in the same way we do our bodies. These ideas conflict with their conception of free will and the belief that we ought to be able to change ourselves instantly if we only altered our will and became more obedient to reason and the established rules.

The contrast between their high ideals and inner conflicts makes them fearful that reflection on their own character will reveal their short-comings and that this will trigger their painfully demanding and guilty consciences. They become terribly ashamed and angry at themselves when they feel they have violated their own standards, so they are understand-ably angry when anyone threatens to trigger their doing so.   Friendly realism and encouragement by others is hard for them to recognize be-cause all observations about people's character appear to be marking them out for damnation. The attempt to develop good judgment about people so that one might be more encouraging appears essentially judgmental from their perspective.

The chief block to rationalists taking character seriously thus will always be their self-punishing consciences and a tendency to be vain in their excessive expectations of themselves. Only as such a person comes to believe in the possibility of friendly realism toward himself and with others will he desire greater knowledge of people's moral strengths and weaknesses, his own included. He will accept a naturalistic conception of character in theory only when he desires the guidance it offers in practice for promoting a more forgiving, self-respecting and life-affirming form of human development.

Positivism: the Moral Attitude Underlying Its Epistemology and Metaphysics. I find that people with deficient self-control and a deep fear and anger that authority and even knowledge itself will limit their freedom to have new experiences find positivist assumptions to ring true to how they experience life. Their life solution is to surrender to their feelings, passions and habits rather than to follow the guidance of reason which they fear will justify the repression of their desires through insisting on excessive self-control. If the person's environment permits a pleasing de-gree of indulgence, he will wish to conserve it and rebel against those threatening it; if not, he will desire a more commodious environment to condition him and others in more pleasing and successful ways and rebel against leaders who do not provide it. In either event, he believes it is ultimately the environment which governs and habituates us to our form of life without really believing people should be held responsible for creating and maintaining such an environment.

His moral attitude is one of self-indulgent permissiveness with a conscience governed by the principle of tolerance (except toward rationalists and realists who they tend to confuse with one another) and sympathy toward those rebuked by harsh authority. They replace rules and will with sentiment and habit, and exalt the heart with its governance by pleasure and pain to the exclusion of the head. The paternal demand for obedience and production is replaced by the maternal provision of a supportive and harmonious, if less challenging, environment.

By insisting on going with what feels right and seems to work at the time rather than basing his actions on the implications of his best theoretical analysis, such a person effectively denies interest in knowing the nature of anything. They know, and are interested in knowing, only their own experience and data rather than trying to know the natures, principles and causes of real things through reflecting on our experience of them. They tend to demote reason to the level of mere calculation and treat it as no more than what Hume called the slave of our passions--as though we cannot be passionately interested in knowing the nature of things so that we might act more responsibly toward them.

The whole approach to life is designed to play down the power of reason as a source of truth and authority in preference to its simply helping us calculate how to gain power over the things which will satisfy our desires. Sensory experience and isolated bits of data tend to become the ultimate ontological experience for such a person because he trusts and feels more alive in his body than in his head. This belief that sense data and isolated bits of information are all that we can ever truly trust reinforces both his distrust of reason and his assumption that we can never know the truth of our rational intuitions into natural structures and causes.

Surrendering to the pleasures and pains of environmental conditioning encourages a view of man as part of the natural world and therefore as a fit subject for scientific study. Yet feeling that he must always rebel against authoritative pronouncements that might limit the possibility of new experience, the positivist is obliged to treat whatever is known about the nature, the principles and the causes of things as being no more than mere hypotheses. Causality becomes nothing more than constant conjunction and statistical correlations between atomized data which could in no way reflect the underlying nature of people or anything else. Even the most cherished scientific convictions about nature merely reflect the way we have been habituated to think and could be refuted at any time by a sudden transformation in our experience.

Self-indulgence, the desire for tolerance and the struggle against authoritarian limitations effectively eliminate the moral concept of an ideal of human perfection as a guiding principle in human affairs. For such a person, the only moral ideal he can imagine is the rationalist form of self-denial he rebels against. And along with the rationalist ideal of excessive self-control and satisfaction through duty, the positivist gives up the concept of freedom of the will in attaining it.

How could one believe in free will on the ethical assumption that people self-indulgently surrender to the pleasing stimuli in their environments and flee from the painful ones, exercising little or no self-control and freedom in the process? How could one have faith in the power of reason when he expects himself at any moment to surrender to his environment--no matter what his own reason might lead him to believe was in his own best interests?

People who approach life this way repudiate the theory and study of moral character out of the fear that it will be nothing more than the rationalist outlook they are rebelling against. They are uncomfortable with the notion that we can live a more deliberate and disciplined life when guided by knowledge of the natural consequences of pursuing a given line of action rather than simply doing what one has been habituated to by earlier environments and feels like doing at the time. The concept of moral character and of deliberation based on real knowledge challenges the positivist's rejection of introspection as inevitably excessive and destructive of spontaneity. These ideas go against their desire to treat man's spirit as a black box, the inner workings of which are irrelevant to man's environmentally-determined choices.

Friendly realism and encouragement in developing greater self-control and independence is hard for them to take because all observations about character appear as impositions and the blaming of a victim which they instinctively rebel against. They tend to believe that we can change only when our environment is altered in such a way as to make up for the deficiencies we acquired in the past. They thus ignore the fact that the creation of improved environments always requires establishing higher moral expectations of personal accountability and maintaining a cultural ethos which encourages such standards.

They want a more benign environment but shy away from becoming the kind of person who could challenge others to face their weaknesses and stand on their own two feet to build a better situation for themselves. Any such friendly and realistic approach to other people's character requires that one be willing to hold himself accountable for his own development and well-being as well. And to do that, one must become an authority in his own right, rather than simply rebelling against authority out of the wish that others will provide a more gratifying environment in which to indulge one's impulses.

This view of the human spirit is again more arbitrary than developmental, and suggests that we could condition any combination of dispositions into people since there is no human nature against which the environment is working. And with its preoccupation with how we are determined by immediate gratifications, the outlook ignores any larger sense of human purpose and character development which could give us greater independence in the face of environmental pressures.

The chief block to positivists taking character seriously thus will always be their greediness in desiring more and more experience and data and their fear that all authority and knowledge is unreliable and limiting. With their restlessness and anxiety, they feel no experience will ever be enough to still their doubts about the truth of anything. To recognize themselves as having a given character at a given time appears as a limitation on what they feel is their infinite potential to be anything. They find it hard to imagine how knowledge and realism about one's state might contribute to one's freedom rather than being simply one more limitation and disappointment at the hands of authority. And misperceiving themselves as being limited again in that way makes them understandably angry at the concept of character.

Rationalism, Positivism and Politics. In our own day, the rationalist and positivist attitudes tend to find expression in political conservatism and liberalism respectively--although each of these operating systems has given rise to markedly different political programs depending upon the political-economic circumstances within which different authors wrote and how far their attitudes diverged from the moral mean. On my view, the rationalist ethical attitude leads one to call for a state that makes great moral demands on the character, initiative and sense of duty of its people while providing little in the way of material support and protection from the demanding competition of markets. Its policies are Paternal, individualistic and challenging, animated by a vision of eternal conflict against evil and sloth.

As strange as it might at first appear, libertarians, anarchists and the classical, capitalist liberals of the 19th century all fall in this rationalist camp. Liberty for them is not freedom for self-indulgence but from state interference in the economy. They wish for a paternal state rather than a paternalistic one that would mother and over-protect people. They want a state which, through its laissez-faire policies, will expect people to become tough and inner directed, self-disciplined and capable of surviving in the jungle of life. What greater moral demand could a political party place on its followers than that they be responsible for managing their own affairs without benefit of benign authorities and leaders?

The positivist ethical attitude, on the other hand, calls for a state that makes few moral demands on the self-control and initiative of its people while providing considerable material support and protection from the demanding competition of markets. Its policies are Maternal, communal and supportive, animated by a vision of the desirability of harmony and the acceptance of differences.

As strange as it might at first appear, contemporary liberals are joined in this positivist camp by earlier, more community-oriented conservatives. They tend to treat "liberal" as meaning generous and caring toward others as well as liberty from state interference in areas of personal indulgence. Positivists wish for a Maternal and accepting state to protect people from the social upheaval of unleashed individualism. The conservative positivist rebelled against threats to the traditional society and patterns of indulgence he was habituated to and is comfortable with. The modern liberal also rebels against environments and authorities limiting people's indulgences, but does so with the aim of creating an environment more supportive of a broader base of people and which will habituate them to a better life. In both cases, the state should mother and show people how to fit in and belong without making the paternal demands which would help them take better care of themselves.

Practical Life, Character and Philosophic Belief. No matter how many times their philosophic assumptions might have been refuted in the history of philosophy, people approaching practical life in these ways will return to them again and again because they seem required to make sense of how one experiences the world when approaching it with these attitudes. Yet, as we have seen, the positivist is no more inclined than the rationalist to take the study of human nature and character seriously enough to pass a fair-minded judgment on its truth. Their assumptions cause so many glitches in our thinking that the whole concept of moral character appears largely unintelligible to them and those they influence. The change from a rationalist or positivist metaphysics and epistemology to a realist one is more like a religious conversion in its effect on one's life and actions than it is a matter of simply changing one's mind.

Few people are likely to change their most fundamental attitudes toward life on the basis of even the most philosophically compelling arguments and the dialectical demonstrations of their inconsistencies and untenableness. We can change ourselves only when we recognize how our present attitudes and assumptions create unbearable contradictions and limit our attaining a fuller experience of life. We must then base our choices and actions on a broader understanding of our nature and a higher wish for human well-being and practice. We can change our beliefs and character for the better only when our thought reflects an improved practice of life. Thought and analysis prepare the way and complement such a change but can never substitute for life-transforming action.

Let me add, however, that only when our professed philosophy is sincere and not just an academic veneer does it reflect our practical approach to life and the way we really experience the world. Most people espouse the philosophy they have been taught and do not hold its ideas in this sincere sense. Their philosophies bear no necessary relation to the assumptions they actually base their lives on. Philosophic training in the modern period has not been geared to helping us investigate the assumptions which are actually entailed by the forms of our lives. If it were, philosophical disputation would once again become a high art practiced in public before intensely partisan audiences as it was in the middle ages and during the prolonged beginnings of the modern world. I hope to live to see such a time return when intellectuals will stand up once again for the naturalistic and humanistic principles of the realist tradition.

Realism: the Moral Attitude Underlying Its Epistemology and Metaphysics. I have found that realists can have as many vices as rationalists and positivists but that they differ in their basic faith that even with all one's faults and all that is violent, unjust and unkind in the world, one is nonetheless better off facing the reality than denying painful things or indulging pleasing illusions. They wish to care for and know the world and know they can do so only through developing the individual wholeness and integration that is required if one is to act most responsibly and intelligently toward it. They know, for example, that we simply can't hear what other people are trying to say to us when we are dominated by our own fears, desires for pleasure or anger. Overcoming the distortions of unrealistic attitudes requires a quality of **courage, self-control, high-mindedness** and **friendliness** that is not found in the view of rationalism and positivism suggested above. The realist strives to respect and affirm what is true in the exaggerated assumptions of rationalists and positivists while transcending the limitations of their compromised starting points. In fact, many of us are recovering rationalists or positivists.

Realists in my sense strive to construct a picture of man and the world that is not limited by a distorted and partial experience based on how humanity has been actualized in their own lives and times. One need think only of Hobbes' view of man as a wolf to other men and dominated by the fear of death, Hume's sense of man as having an innate moral sense of sympathy he should simply surrender to without relying on reason to discipline and refine his feelings or Kant's view of man as dominated by a sense of moral duty transcending the wish for earthly happiness to recognize how tempting it is to treat our own politically conditioned experience as though it expressed the essential nature of man rather than a special case of how man can develop for good or ill under different conditions.

For these philosophers to know human nature in this more generic sense, they would have had to know their own experience as not only a special, historically conditioned case of a broader theory of mankind's possibilities but sadly as revealing a less than fully happy or virtuous expression of what mankind could aspire to in their circumstances. They accepted their moral and emotional limitations, but not as limitations--and raised what they should have treated as problems to be overcome to the level of first principles in their philosophies. Instead of helping others overcome the unhappiness and limitations of the rationalist and positivist attitudes, they used their wonderfully brilliant minds to rationalize them as realistic assessments of man's power to grasp the world.

One of the most telling signs of this rationalizing attitude is the way in which the early modern philosophers triumphantly announced to the world their various discoveries for why man can in no way rely on reason to grasp the classical conception of human nature and use that knowledge as a guide in promoting man's development and happiness. Would one not expect such a discovery to lead to a profound sense of loss for anyone who was seriously searching for such knowledge?

Realists know they must try to acknowledge the limitations of their own form of life and personal development in the light of what history and culture show our species to be capable of and the larger picture of possibilities and needs they find around them. Since we can grow and develop, we do not have to be already moral to do the moral thing and stand up for what is right. We become moral by doing finer things than we have done before in the same way that we become wiser by affirming truths we did not know before and get into shape by exercising muscles we have neglected. We must reach to strengthen our grasp.

The realist strives to develop a quality of self-control that allows him a full sensuous experience of the world without surrendering to the illusion that sensuality exhausts our experience of reality. While we are grounded in ontology through our bodies and all knowing arises initially through physical practice, it is the patterns of functioning and natural structures of things that we come to know through analyzing our experience of them. The realist's more balanced moral attitude makes him able to integrate the positivist's insistence on the epistemological priority of empirical experience with the rationalist's insistence on the role of insight and analysis. He affirms the naturalistic assumption that we can learn to recognize the real structures revealed through our empirical experience. He sees the rationalist and positivist as affirming different aspects of what is more properly seen as an integrated cognitive process. Each of them maximizes their own aspect while minimizing the other instead of aiming for the optimum development and coordination of sensuality and thought.

Since he neither denies his own sensuality nor fears the restrictions on that sensuality that authoritative knowledge might threaten, he can strive to find the causal structures within things which explain why we experience them (M) in differing ways (F) under differing experimental conditions (A). And trusting his own body and mind, he believes the rational analysis of his own experience might require him to correct and reform both his practices and the concepts and categories he was trained to bring to his experience. He agrees with the rationalist that all perception and reasoning occurs in the context of our prior experience and knowledge but does not accept the notion that we can never get beyond these structures to new truths which reveal the limitations of our earlier perceptions and thoughts in grasping what really exists in the world beyond our thoughts.

Since the realist does not repudiate his natural, physical desires in his ethics, he is not tempted to treat man's moral spirit and intellect as supernatural and beyond the causal realm in his metaphysics. But by the same token, since he does not self-indulgently surrender to environmental agents, he does not see us as simply determined by environmental factors either. Man is a causal power in his own right. When properly developed, we are capable of responding selectively to the various possibilities latent in our life situations which might allow us to pursue our own wishes and perfect and express ourselves within the bounds of our own talents and resources.

Since environmental and biological factors can go so strongly against us, realists know that there can be no guarantee that virtue will make us fully happy. But we know just as surely that without developing the virtues one has no chance at all to be happy--even when environmental factors are going one's way.

The desire for such perfection and the fullness of life which it makes possible focuses the mind on knowing and appreciating real things and where it's appropriate on coaxing them into assuming the perfection of their own natures. Real things realizing their perfective potentials represent the ultimate natural realities and are celebrated as noble and beautiful wherever they occur: the flowering of an orchid at midnight, a discuss-thrower at the Olympics, Astaire and Rogers on the dance floor, a writer criticizing a President to his face for moral insensitivity or a scientist explaining the wonders of an ecosystem he has reverently studied for years. To attain perfection is possible only for the most gifted, of course, when measured by universal standards of accomplishment. It becomes possible for everyone, however, when measured by the internal standard of what athletes call "playing within one's game," i.e. making the most of one's talents in contributing to a team effort.

The realist also takes a different attitude toward truth, authority and the issue of whether the human spirit can be violated than rationalists and positivists do. He recognizes that we learn about things not only through our experience of them but through the desires and questions we bring to them. Truth thus has an undeniably **pragmatic** dimension to it. But this means for him that any true statement within a given practice of life will in some sense **correspond** with the state of the world as experienced from that perspective and that all the true statements made from that perspective will be **coherent** with one another. As a consequence, realists should thus see rationalists and positivists as making true statements in all three of these senses but as having failed to rise to the level of what modern physicists call the complementarity principle.

The human truth is that we can experience the world in the ways described by all three traditions. But only the realist theory can explain why rationalists and positivists are actually complementary to one another and can be seen as special cases of the generic realist theory. The rationalist speaks the truth when he says that natural physical desires can corrupt a person's reason, but he betrays a lack of knowledge about the experimental conditions under which this truth will be confirmed when he claims that man's physical nature is essentially corrupt. Men and women can be raised to see their physical desires this way and to repress them as corrupt, but we can also be raised to enjoy physical pleasure in a disciplined and self-controlled way that contributes greatly to our love and respect for other living things.

And from the other side, positivists speak truthfully when they say that reason can be used to make people unnecessarily inhibited and self-conscious and to rationalize all sorts of guilt trips when they have not done what they were supposed to. But when they say this, positivists are confusing the particular way they have experienced the use of reason with the very nature of reason itself. Surely some people try to make others guilty of enjoying themselves and try to talk them into doing things they really don't want to do. But one should not confuse the fact of having been treated this way with an exhaustive exposure to the power of reason. Reason can also be seen as most properly applied to serving our happiness and well-being in a life that is both orderly and open to new and deeper experiences.

The whole logic of the rationalist and positivist attitudes suggests a repressed longing for a sense of friendly and realistic authority that would affirm the optimal development of one's desires under the disciplined guidance of humanistic reason. Where the rationalist might long for a less restrictive sense of order, the positivist longs for a more orderly sense of freedom. Each, however, is fearfully reluctant to explore the freeing possibilities of this friendly, realist sense of authority--the first from the fear that they will be overwhelmed by the chaos of their unchecked desires, the second that they will be made to surrender the sweetest indulgences in their lives.

Laboratory and Clinical Training in Moral Character Analysis. Since philosophers in the rationalist and positivist traditions repudiate the possibility of discovering the natural structures within things, it follows quite naturally that they would look with unconcealed disdain on the idea that philosophy should **train** people to see the ontological structures within things. And certainly their conceptions of ethics in no way involve the cultivation of practical judgment. So here too, the idea of practical training and apprenticeship appears unphilosophical from a rationalist or positivist perspective. The picture changes drastically, however, the moment one approaches philosophy on realist assumptions.

We must face the fact that today students and teachers alike come to philosophy without the knowledge and experience of moral character and virtue that educated men and women were exposed to in happier times. As a result, the ordinary language of everyday life no longer expresses a clear focus on this reality. We must therefore create experimental conditions under which people might examine for themselves the truth of this perspective and evaluate the merits of the skeptical assumptions they have understandably acquired through growing up in the modern world.

The paradigm for this experience is a clinical seminar in which people interested in learning to understand the reality of moral character analyze a tape-recorded interview of someone they preferably don't know. The interview is based quite directly on the TABLE OF THE VIRTUES AND VICES. The person is told that the group is interested in how others handle the kinds of things we all have to deal with in life. After guaranteeing the person's anonymity and asking him to sign a standard research release form, the interviewer asks a couple of questions designed to establish rapport with the person and to create a confident and relaxed atmosphere such as When have you felt happiest in your life? and When have you felt strongest? After exploring his answers for a few minutes, the interviewer then says, We all have to deal with painful or destructive things, for example, and we are interested in what things like that come to your mind, what you have learned about how you tend to handle such things and what effect they have had on you. We're especially interested in examples (not so much the person's image of himself, which will come out anyway, but his description of what was actually going on so we can see whether there is any conflict between how he actually saw things and how he wanted or was afraid to see them.)

The interviewer goes right down the list of agents in the first column in the TABLE asking each time, What kinds of thing come to mind in each case and could you give us an example to illustrate what you have in mind. The more familiar the interviewer becomes with each of the moral and emotional powers, the more insightful his follow-up questions will be, although I have found that some people are just naturally intuitive interviewers and do a great job with little or no training. The questioning should be conducted in a friendly and dignified way always respecting the person's wishes to say nothing further on a subject. Many people end the interview after answering all the questions by thanking the interviewer for the opportunity to take an inventory of their own lives and character.

The taped interview is later played back to the study group one question and answer at a time and the group is asked to examine what it reveals about his or her character. One finds immediately how interrelated the moral and emotional powers are and how much we all reveal about ourselves when we talk. Different people will pick up on different things and the challenge soon becomes one of synthesizing the different insights to see how they might all be true because of the moral and emotional conflicts the person is caught up in. But one also comes to see how often we are blind to certain things that others see so much more clearly and quickly than we do, and that there is an ethically significant difference between those who wish others well in a spirit of friendly realism and those who wish to triumph over others. To belittle the person whose answers appear on the tape is a flagrant violation of the whole spirit of the teaching.

The basic concept of such a seminar is to put the theory of moral character to a laboratory test, but also to train people to see others from the perspective of wishing to contribute to their proper wish to become who they most want to be and to their ability to deliberate and choose how best to handle the challenges they must face. Students often tell me that participating in such a seminar and the process of writing up their analysis of the interview in the light of OMC is one of the most rewarding and satisfying experiences they've had at school and that it has very much deepened their knowledge and respect for people. We can use the same approach in analyzing novels and biographies, plays and movies, music lyrics, political speeches, advertisements or any other material that either describes people or tries to touch them.

The basic model for such a seminar can be used for both research and training purposes as well. Teachers at the high school or college level could analyze interviews with students to gain a deeper sense of what issues and practices are affecting the character development of their students and as a basis for deliberating about how to bring out what is best in them. Social work professionals in all fields could do the same as an ongoing part of their staff-development programs. Ministers, counselors, community development workers could all benefit.

We must understand though that this perspective lies at the very core of the Western humanist tradition and is not to be relegated to the supposedly lowly status of an applied technique of some kind. We need desperately to develop teaching resources that would document the central role of moral character in all the disciplines that study man. How could a sociologist teach Max Weber's **PROTESTANT ETHIC AND THE SPIRIT OF CAPITALISM** or Emile Durkheim's theory of collective conscience and social solidarity in **THE DIVISION OF LABOR IN SOCIETY** without treating the theory of moral character as a central explanatory variable? How could

Shakespeare be taught and students leave the course with no no
theory of virtue and vice? How could one appraise Washington a:
cal leader without regard for his moral character and the conflict
characters of the Southern aristocrats and New England Yankees?

Those of us who believe in this perspective must show
brings to life the works of all those men and women who have pei   .ated
to the heart of man and to the age old struggle to create a society worthy
of good men and women. And we must offer redescriptions of the master-
works in all the humanities in the light of this perspective. We must
show in philosophy how dependent the early modern rejection of
philosophical realism about nature and character depended on a now out-
moded model of the universe based on mechanical physics and on the
political economic circumstances of the rise of industrial society.

Modern society has become rather like an alcoholic who denies he
has a problem. The friends of man must now adopt the intervention
strategy recommended by Alcoholics Anonymous. We must gather together
all the documentation we can muster and in a spirit of friendly realism we
must confront this culture with the fact that we have all been denying.
We have a problem with nature and with moral character. Our public spirit
of tolerance has not been based on respect but on indifference to one
another. Our ignorance of man's moral nature is not because it can't be
known but because we haven't cared enough to learn. We're not living up
to the highest ideals of our civilization. It's time we turned that around
and begin once again helping our people see the beauty, goodness and
truth of moral character and the fact that we can best take care of
our interests as human beings by searching for the natural norms and
ecological principles by which we should guide our practice.

BACKGROUND

This analysis of the classical virtues and vices is based on the
experience that comes from five years of training in applying the
psychoanalytic theory of character to the study of the evolving work place
in America, specialized graduate work in the philosophy of science, and
nearly 15 years of teaching and empirical research into the virtues and
vices of hundreds of people in all walks of life. Before beginning the
Ph.D. program in philosophy at Georgetown, I worked for five years under
Dr. Michael Maccoby, on the Harvard Project on Technology, Work and
Character. In addition to following the ancient philosophical maxim that
"The Unexamined Life Is Not Worth Living" through psychoanalysis with
Maccoby, I learned from him the research methodology which he called
socio-psychoanalysis. The approach, inspired by Erich Fromm's pioneering
efforts to integrate psychoanalytic methodology and theory into the larger
perspective of humanistic social science and culture, provided both hands-
on laboratory training and an intellectual focus for my confused political
and cultural longings as a sixties radical.

In this context, working with Maccoby on the Harvard Project on
Technology, Work and Character was the most realistic, practical and
morally moving experience of my life. Fromm's theory and method of investigating the character dimension of the social structures dominating
people's lives provided a form of life focused on tracing the connections
between the effects of politics on ethics and psychology and vise versa.

The Project combined a deep respect for theory with empirical research animated by an unwavering commitment to the promotion of human development. I was later to recognize that it was through participating in this form of life and applying its methodology and theory to myself as well as others that I was able to become a philosophical realist.

It was there that I also recognized the truth of Aristotle's adage that one had to learn first to follow before he could learn to lead. It was often humiliating in our clinical seminars to discover that the picture I had developed of a person whose interview transcript we were analyzing reflected my own prejudices and insecurities and that someone else in the group with different prejudices and insecurities was able to integrate the evidence we had into a more realistic picture. The seminar was not a touchy-feely affair at all, but still one couldn't hide from the way character distorted perception. I will always be grateful for the ethos of friendly realism Maccoby created in these seminars. He taught us all the need to struggle so that the love of truth might win out over vanity and fear. Without realizing he was doing so in these seminars, he showed us too the truth of Aristotle's observation that the most intellectually accomplished person is the one who can comprehend and synthesize all that is true in what is said about a subject.

In learning more about myself and about the character and social relations of the engineers and managers we were studying, I came to appreciate the profoundly important role of authority and leadership in human life. Leaders can create a climate in which people's individuality and creativity flourishes or a climate of sterility, self-seeking and mediocrity. Many of us at the time saw red at the very mention of authority, leadership or management.

Boiling with energy and a gift for insight as a child, but having a totally unguided intelligence, I had felt a profound sense of waste and resentment in the fact that no one expected me to make much of a contribution even if I were properly motivated and disciplined. My sense of neglect was greatly compounded by a physical disability which tended to set me apart from the normal flow of life. Lacking proper direction and any vision of perfection to strive for and vocation by which to be of service, my talents turned to seed through many a season. I used my sensitivity to people as much to manipulate as to understand and encourage them. Gradually my intelligence and other gifts frightened me because of the hurt I knew I might cause if my hostility ever came out.

Striving consciously to be good and to care about society and others in the late sixties and early seventies, I did not realize the despair I felt at not having found a useful function for myself. Not knowing how to make something fine and beautiful with my talents, I found it easy to identify with the Black rage of the times. While I read and thought a great deal, most of it escaped me because I had committed myself to no recognized purpose and form of life and lacked a framework within which to organize my experience and memories. I knew of no tradition or group whose form of life and narrative history I could give my heart and my mind to.

Participating in the ethos of Maccoby's research group and in my own analysis with him gave me a theory and practice of life for facing the limitations in my own character and clarifying my own vocational goals. This work experience along with finding a woman to love gave me a great incentive to change so that I might participate more actively and creatively in the fullness of life. Maccoby helped me see that the basic strategic principle in bringing about such a character change is first to clarify the wishes for a fuller life that one could actually begin pursuing today if it were not for one's own vices. One must cultivate this wish and become ever more realistic about what he should begin doing to pursue it and what it is about himself which keeps him from doing what would otherwise be possible for him. This is ultimately the heart of the process of deliberation in which one starts with his wished for outcome and then pursues a line of analysis back to the first things in his power which he must choose to do if he is to have any chance to change.

Having changed myself in important respects, I developed a deep confidence in the possibility for others to do so too under the right social and cultural circumstances. Being involved in a practice of life committed to contributing what I could to creating such an ethos made me acutely sensitive to how foreign such a conception is to the ruling assumptions and practices of modern life and education.

Having studied political theory at Canada's Carlton University in the late sixties before meeting Maccoby, I knew that the kind of philosophy being taught in North American graduate schools was often used to discredit the very knowledge that I now sought to acquire and make more accessible to people. Professors in the social sciences would seize on whatever philosophical arguments they could use not only to defeat their opponents but to deny them the right to be heard and treated seriously. It was clear that students had no hope to resist an overpowering professor on their own without appealing to a philosophical champion whose outlook and counter-arguments legitimated an expanded conceptual space for alternative approaches.

This was perhaps my first experience of the power of being part of a tradition as I learned how much more respectfully an opinion was treated in class when identified as part of a coherent tradition with well-respected authorities of its own. Professors often showed a deference to the principle of pluralism that was impressive in its own way, even if they were reluctant to fight out a battle between the titans, and it depended a lot on who was in or ought of fashion. The task of trying to re-establish the outlines of the realist operating system by tracing it back to its roots in Aristotle has taken the better part of the last sixteen years, although I did not at first realize that that was the proper way to conceptualize what I was doing.

The need to provide a philosophical defense for what my experience and conscience insisted was important was driven home when I began teaching active-duty police officers at the American University School of Justice in the early seventies. When I began teaching policemen courses on "The Administration of Justice and the Community," "Social Processes and Deviant Behavior," "Humanizing Police Work," "Police Subculture and Character," "The History and Philosophy of Criminology" and "Morality and Justice" it soon became obvious that I must reach out beyond Fromm's important work to a larger philosophical system if I were to bring the importance of character to bear on this broader range of issues.

It was at this point in the early-seventies that I discovered Aristotle's realist philosophy and discovered that he rooted his whole approach to ethics and social leadership in the analysis and development of character and that he and his school had already applied such principles to the whole domain of civilization, albeit at an earlier stage of historical

development and knowledge. I was overjoyed to learn that he and the an-
cients were already thinking in the same terms we were on the Harvard
Project.

In fact Aristotle was actually thinking about character in a more
fundamental way because he integrated the category of character into all
the strains of his philosophy, not just in the **POLITICS**, **ETHICS** and
RHETORIC, but in the doctrine of the **CATEGORIES**, the **POSTERIOR
ANALYTICS**, the **PHYSICS** and the **De ANIMA**. At last I could begin to see
the philosophical principles and methodology that allowed Aristotle, and
his ancient and medieval followers, to take the development of virtuous
character and nobility so seriously.

I would have never discovered how integral a place the theory and
cultivation of man as a natural being has in Aristotle's philosophy had it
not been for my good fortune in studying the Aristotelian philosophy of
science and philosophy of nature perspective which animates this work
under Father William Wallace of Catholic University. He is a leading
figure in that school of the history and philosophy of science which has
convincingly documented the crucial importance for the rise of modern
science of Aristotle's theory of the four causes and of the nature of
causal demonstration. He approaches Aristotle as the father of the form of
intellectual life that gave rise to what is best in modern science. He has
been a tower of strength in refuting the false belief that Aristotle was the
albatross around the neck of modern science that led so many early-
modern intellectuals to lose faith in the philosophic and scientific power
of this tradition.

Wallace and his writings thus gave me the deep experience in applying the theory of causal explanation and Aristotle's methodology for
analyzing the powers of the soul to these texts from the **RHETORIC** and
the **ETHICS**. Wallace served as an external mentor for my doctoral dissertation at Georgetown and greatly honored me by opening my defense by
stating that he believed the dissertation, **THE ANCIENT VIRTUES AND
VICES: Philosophical Foundations for the Psychology, Ethics and Politics
of Human Development** represents a landmark in the history of the tradition. It is my most systematic statement of the realist operating system to
date. I was fortunate too along the way at Georgetown to have studied under Henry B. Veatch and to have been inspired by his championing of
Aristotelian philosophy on many of the same issues that I now take up.

ACKNOWLEDGMENTS

I gratefully acknowledge the proof reading assistance and helpful
textual suggestions offered by Christopher High, who has a rare blend of
philosophical and psychological insight and skill. He has been a loyal
friend to me and to the book. Chuck Sorensen has put in herculean labors
in translating my files from a CP/M monospaced to a DOS proportional for-
mat and reconstructing each page. The effort and achievement involved is
beyond one's imagination unless he has been involved in a similar
project. Jim True has very much improved the overall design of the book
and is largely responsible for its covers. He has been a dear friend
through the final stages of writing and production. Evans Palmour, Jr. and
Cynthia Anderson helpfully proofed much earlier drafts. Laura Chassen
keyed in the first draft of the work and Nan Hannapel-Russell and Claire

Palmour Costello keyed in some of the corrections in later drafts. Eve Silverstone worked with me several times in maintaining computer files and Arnold Kuzmack replaced underlining throughout the text with bold face. Lisina Noel assisted in the design of the TABLE OF CONTENTS and in developing parallelism in headlines.

Many others have provided intellectual, emotional and financial support of one kind or another. The first among these are my family and our family's friends. They include especially my mother, Claire Palmour Costello, and step-father, Paul Costello, Evans Palmour Jr., Eve Silverstone, Mary Palmour Castle, Mr. and Mrs. Evans Palmour Sr., Joe and Carrie Hatfield and John and Martha Jacobs. Vlady and Patrick Kanski have been a special comfort to me and Vlady has been an inspiration to excellence. Leni, Henry and David Stern have been friends and supporters over many years. Rocco Porreco, John Brough, Henry B. Veatch, Dorothy Brown, Tom Gannon and the Woodstock Community, and Wilfried Ver Eecke all at Georgetown have supported me and this work in one way or another—as has Jude Dougherty at Catholic University. Elliot Liebow has been a special friend as have been Brian Downing, Andrea Croce Birch, Sr. Claire Adams, Robert A. Hill, Christopher High, Billy Stott, Kari Poyry, David Crooks and Al and Maria Miller. John Rigby provided a wonderful opportunity to apply this perspective to a management consultant/work-improvement project in a private voluntary organization. Mitchel Optican, Mark Warfel, Joe Schiebler, Jameson Kurasha, Beverly Whelton, Angela Chen, Martha Dudley and Michael Locke have been good companions and have shown me many acts of kindness.

It has become fashionable to bash Kohlberg in recent days. I wish to acknowledge here my respect for his enormous contribution in reawakening national concern with moral education as a legitimate issue for social research and educational policy. It is my belief that Kohlberg and his impressive group of coworkers in the Association for Moral Education are developing their insights into the structure of moral reasoning in ways that will be recognized as more and more obviously complementary with the character perspective. He and they deserve to be treated as much more than simply someone whom Gilligan criticizes. Aristotle, after all, came out of Plato's school and it is surely a mistake to believe that just because one studies reasoning, he must be a rationalist.

I am happily indebted to all of these people, but I am not alone in this debt. It pleases me to think that to the extent I have accomplished anything here of value to the reader that I have thereby put him or her equally in debt to those who made it possible for me to make my contribution.

The texts used in this volume are taken from the McKeon edition of the **THE BASIC WORKS OF ARISTOTLE**, David Ross' translation of the **ETHICS** and W. Rhys-Roberts' translation of the **RHETORIC** with occasional supplementation drawn from translations by Ostwald and Rackham for the former and Freese for the latter.

HINTS TO THE READER

The reader will be helped if he keeps the following pointers in mind. The basic lay-out of the book is a schematic presentation of Aristotle's texts designed to separate them into their various causal components. These are the kinds of agents (A) a given power responds to and the states of mind (M) disposing a person to respond in a given form (F). Sensitivity to these causal annotations should alert the reader to the focus and purpose of the given discussion. Each CHAPTER begins with an INVENTORY of the different factors involved in the operation of its particular moral and emotional powers.

Commentaries follow the presentation of each section of Aristotle's text. If I have divided up and numbered these texts, the commentaries will likewise be divided and numbered. Unless otherwise noted, all quotes in the commentaries are from the text being commented upon and are not separately cited.

I am often able to propose a **formula** or **ratio of factors** involved in the operation of a moral and emotional power. These formulas are designed to express the factors and ratios involved in determining whether a given power is operating in an excessive, deficient or appropriate form. The reader should keep these formulas in mind as he reads a chapter to see if they do not help in appraising the functioning of the power and the difference between its virtues and vices.

SUGGESTED READING

Those interested in reading more about Aristotle will find the following particularly interesting.

ARISTOTLE by John Herman Randall, jr.

INTRODUCTION TO REALISTIC PHILOSOPHY by John Wild

CHAPTER ONE

Handling Painful and Destructive Things

INVENTORY

A. THE POWER TO BE AFRAID AND TO BE CONFIDENT (RH II, 5)

1. FEAR DEFINED

a. The People Arousing Our Fear

1. Spiteful or angry people with power over us
2. Unjust people with power
3. Just people outraged by injustice
4. Powerful people afraid of us
5. Greedy or frightened people, especially those who know we did something wrong
6. People who feel we have wronged them and are looking to get back at us
7. Powerful people afraid of retaliation for their injustice
8. Our rivals in a zero-sum game
9. People who frighten others stronger than we are
10. People attacking others weaker than we are
11. Quiet, dissembling, unscrupulous people we might have wronged
12. Having no chance to retrieve a blunder
13. Not being able to help the situation very easily

b. Our States of Mind When Afraid

1. When we are neither insolent-sadistic, disdainful nor reckless
2. When we still have hope that we might escape a painful or destructive situation

2. CONFIDENCE DEFINED

a. Things Arousing Our Confidence

1. Having the resources to cure or prevent trouble
2. Having nobody around whom we have wronged or by whom we have been wronged
3. Having no strong rivals who are spiteful toward us
4. Having kind and friendly rivals
5. Having the same wishes to protect as the strongest people around us

b. Our States of Mind When Confident

1. Having had many successes and no defeats
2. Believing that people like ourselves or even weaker have nothing to fear
3. Having the resources which make one formidable
4. Having wronged no one
5. Initiating a new project

c. How People Undermine Our Confidence

B. COURAGE, COWARDICE, BOASTFULNESS AND RECKLESSNESS AS THE VIRTUE AND VICES OF THIS POWER

1. THE AGENT THAT BEST REVEALS COURAGE (NE III, 6)

- Divisions made in identifying the best agents for revealing courage

2. THE VIRTUE AND VICES OF THIS POWER (NE III, 7)

a. Courage Must Be Evaluated with regard to Threats within the Bounds of Human Strength
b. Courage as the Virtue
c. Recklessness as the Vice of Deficient Fear
d. Macho-Boastfulness as the Vice of Excessive Confidence
e. Cowardice as the Vice of Excessive Fear and Deficient Confidence

3. ATTITUDES CONFUSED WITH COURAGE (NE III, 8)

a. The Citizen-Soldier and the Conscript
b. The Confidence of the Professional
c. The Confidence of the Angry
d. The Confidence of the Overly-Optimistic
e. The Confidence of Those Ignorant of the Danger

4. COURAGE RELATES TO BOTH PAIN AND PLEASURE (NE III, 9)

a. Painful Means Test Our Wish for a Pleasant End
b. The Virtuous Person Is The Most Pained By Death

A. THE POWER TO BE AFRAID AND TO BE CONFIDENT (RH II, 5)

1. FEAR DEFINED

Aristotle's definition of fear focuses on its painful and disturbing form and the kinds of perception which give rise to it.

Fear may be defined as a pain or disturbance due to a mental picture of some destructive or painful evil in the future...
(1382a 20-1)

He further clarifies the agent causality (A) involved in feeling afraid when he says that our picture must be

Of destructive or painful evils only; for there are some evils, e.g. wickedness, injustice or stupidity, the prospect of which does not frighten us: I mean only such as amount to great pains or losses. And even these only if they appear not remote but so near as to be imminent: we do not fear things that are a long way off: for instance, we all know we shall die, but we are not troubled thereby, because death is not close at hand. (1382a 23-7)

COMMENTARY. As explained in the INTRODUCTION, each of the moral powers governs how we are disposed to see things in its area, and it is the resulting picture we develop which stimulates us to act. In this case, the picture "of some destructive or painful evil in the future" is what causes us the pain which is fear. It causes us pain in the present through leading us to anticipate the pain the impending injury might cause us in the near future. The power of anticipation is particularly well-developed in human beings and leaves a large opening for speculation about the power things might have to cause us harm.

Fearful things must be seen as drawing very near which explains why people who do not see their own deaths as drawing near are not made very afraid by the inevitability of death. But the requirement of nearness might also explain why people are not normally afraid of evils like injustice and stupidity. The assertion would make no sense if we took it to mean unjust or stupid people who clearly can hurt us and who we naturally fear when they are in positions to do so. Aristotle's point is rather that many of us do not fear becoming stupid or unjust because having these two qualities is not necessarily painful, for example, the way being angry is painful to the angry person.

Precisely insofar as we are motivated by unjust passions and are acting stupidly, we are not deliberating about the painful future consequences of doing so. When focusing solely on immediate passions, we do not see the nearness of the painful consequences which often follow from indulging them. We might even say that the ability to fear injustice and stupidity is a sign of a person's having some sense of justice and intelligence, and is restricted to people who have these traits to at least some degree.

Aristotle is most concerned here with the generic agent (A) and form of response (F) of our power to be afraid. Fearful forms of response are painful and disturbed (F) which means that they tend to undermine (Tfa) our powers to wish, deliberate and choose those things which promote human development. Courage lessens the quality of this disturbance while the different vices (M) associated with it aggravate this disturbance. A courageous person can, for example, deliberate with a cooler, more realistic head about what needs to be done than a less courageous person.

The ratio between the following factors explains why we picture things as sources of either fear or confidence. The judgment that something is a threat results from comparing in some sense our own wishes and resources against those of the potentially threatening agent. This determination follows the general causal principle that an agent's power (A), in this case to hurt us, depends on the relation between its nature and that of the material (M) it works on.

We can express the ratio between these factors in the following formula.

$$\frac{\text{the agent's WISHES} \quad X \quad \text{his RESOURCES}}{\text{our WISHES} \quad X \quad \text{our RESOURCES}} = \text{our FEAR/CONFIDENCE}$$

The reader should note that the factors concerned with the potentially threatening agent are found in the numerator while those concerned with what we bring to the encounter are found in the denominator. The reader can easily see that the following sections in the Chapter correspond respectively with the factors involved in the numerator and the denominator of the formula.

There is an inverse proportional at work in the formula. The stronger and more confident we are about our resources and the fixity of our wishes in relation to those of the agent, the less will the agent seem threatening, while the more powerful the agent seems in relation to our resources and wishes, the more threatening it will seem. We see this at work, for example, in Aristotle's later assertion that confidence results from "the nearness of what keeps us safe and the absence or remoteness of what is terrible" (1383a 17). That is, we feel confident when our resources seem large and there seems to be nobody around who both desires and has the resources to harm us.

The key to understanding the formula is to see how our WISHES function to activate RESOURCES in the service of our purposes. Both the potentially threatening agent and the person responding to him or her try to bring their resources into play in pursuing their wishes. The reader will have grasped a central principle in this work when he or she realizes that the strength and integrity of one's wish is perhaps his greatest resource, or more precisely, is the source from which he is able to approach other things as resources.

a. The People Arousing Our Fear

Aristotle focuses first on the factors which make up the numerator of the formula by exploring the various wishes and resources which characterize the people arousing our fear. The basic conception of a fear-arousing agent is

> whatever appears to have great power of destroying us, or of harming us in ways that tend to cause us great pain. (1382a 28-30)

As we have seen, this harm must be seen as impending or about to befall us.

> Hence the very indications of such things are terrible, making us feel that the terrible thing itself is close at hand; the approach of what is terrible is just what we mean by "danger." (1382a 30-2)

Aristotle then lists the kinds of people and situations which he and his students found actually make people frightened. Throughout this work we try to underscore Aristotle's references to those aspects of character and behavior which differentiate each such listing and facilitate the cross-referencing that is so important if one is to understand the interdependence between the various virtues and vices.

Aristotle says we are afraid of

1. The **enmity** and **anger** of people who have power to do something to us; for it is plain that they have the will to do it, and so they are on the point of doing it. (1382a 33-4)

2. Also **injustice** in possession of power; for it is the un-just man's will to do evil that makes him unjust. (1382a 34-5)

3. Also **outraged virtue** in possession of power; for it is plain that, when outraged, it always has the will to retaliate, and now it has the power to do so. (1382b 1-2)

4. Also **fear** felt by those with the power to do something to us, since such persons are sure to be ready to do it. (1382b 3)

5. And since most men tend to be bad--slaves to **greed**, and **cowards** to danger--it is, as a rule, a terrible thing to be at another man's mercy; and therefore, if we have done anything horrible, those in the secret terrify us with the thought that they may betray or desert us. And those who can do us wrong are terrible to us when we are liable to be wronged; for as a rule men do wrong to others whenever they have the power to do it. (1382b 4-10)

6. And **those who have been wronged**, or believe themselves to be wronged, are terrible; for they are always looking out for their opportunity. (1382b 10-2)

7. Also **those who have done people wrong**, if they possess power, since they stand in fear of retaliation: we have already said that wickedness possessing power is terrible. (1382b 12-4)

8. Again, our **rivals** for a thing cause us fear when we can-not both have it at once; for we are always at war with such men. (1382b 14-5)

9. We also fear **those who are to be feared by stronger peo-ple than ourselves**: if they can hurt those stronger people, still more can they hurt us; and, for the same reason, we fear those whom those strong people are actually afraid of. Also those who have destroyed people stronger than we are. (1382b 15-8)

10. Also **those who are attacking people weaker than we are**: either they are already formidable, or they will be so when they have thus grown stronger. (1382b 18-9)

11. Of **those we have wronged**, and of our enemies or rivals, it is not the passionate and outspoken whom we have to fear, but the **quiet, dissembling, unscrupulous**; since we never know when they are upon us, we can never be sure they are at a safe dis-tance. (1382b 20-3)

Aristotle then mentions two things which **intensify** the fear we feel at the sight of threatening things.

12. All terrible things are more terrible if they give us no chance of retrieving a blunder--either no chance at all, or only one that depends on our enemies and not ourselves. (1382b 24-5)

13. Those things are also worse which we cannot, or cannot easily, help. (1382b 25-6)

Finally, Aristotle identifies a **sign** or **indicator** of the things that particular people are likely to be afraid of.

Speaking generally, anything causes us to feel fear that when it happens to, or threatens, others causes us to feel **pity**. (1382b 26-7)

COMMENTARY. Aristotle's list focuses our attention on the kinds of people who are frightening. If we are disposed to be afraid, we will be disposed to see people in these ways even when they are not like this. Which way we distort our perception will reflect the kinds of frightening people we have actually had to face in developing our character. In work-ing with excessively frightened people, it is thus helpful to identify how they see the people they irrationally fear. But the list should also sensitize us to how we might be unnecessarily frightening to others and how some people's life and job circumstances can lead them to live in such fear that they lose confidence in themselves.

Aristotle's list is limited to **people** who scare us and does not include such frightening things as natural disasters, diseases, accidents, etc. The examples involve a confluence of causal factors none of which alone is enough to make us afraid. A person must not only have an **intention** to harm us but must be in a social or physical **position** to do so. As we have seen, we must see him or her as having both the wish and the resources to do us harm before we will be afraid.

We can express this causally by saying that a person's social and/or physical resources must be such that his material disposition or wish (M) to respond to us in a harmful way (F) can actually function (Tfa) as an agent of harm to us (M). For example, if a person wants us fired from a job, his saying so has causal agency only when he can either directly or through others activate the payroll officer to stop writing our pay-checks. If he has no such power to influence others in the organization, we are not as frightened by his wanting us fired. On the other hand, just because someone has the power to fire us does not mean we will be afraid of him. He might like our work and wish us to continue doing it.

We follow Aristotle's principal focus on the (im)moral wishes which make people seem threatening. We are more able to specify what these wishes are, and the situations in which they arise, than we are to specify the social and physical resources which allow people to execute their wishes. Aristotle's list is naturally enough focused on those cases where people truly wish to do things that will be painful or destructive to others.

It is important to realize, however, that an otherwise be-nign wish executed in ignorance of its real consequences can sometimes lead to equally devastating and fearful results. Someone might try to help us by turning on the lights, for example, and in the process electrocute us. Such benign wishes are not frightening in themselves but become so only in the specific context in which they are acted on. As such, it would be impossible to list such fear-arousing benign wishes without regard to the infinite number of detailed situations which actually make them frightening.

The following is a commentary on each of Aristotle's eleven frightening agents and on the two aspects of situations which intensify our fearfulness. The attitudes described can apply as easily to parents with power over their children as to spouses, teachers, managers, political leaders or criminals.

1. **SPITEFUL OR ANGRY PEOPLE WITH POWER OVER US.** We are prop-erly afraid of people with power over us who feel either **envy-spite** or **anger** toward us (**Rh** II, 4 & 10). It can be even more terrible for powerful people to envy and feel spiteful toward us than for them simply to be angry. Anger is not only less destructive than spitefulness in its normal operation, it can also be more easily assuaged. Envy-spite is long-standing and unforgiving, while anger is not necessarily so.

2. **UNJUST PEOPLE WITH POWER.** It is because we want or fear things in ways we should not that we act unjustly and are unjust. Justice and injustice are, after all, expressions of our other virtues and vices. A

person motivated by vices and who has the power to act on them will treat others unjustly and is properly considered a frightening person.

3. **JUST PEOPLE OUTRAGED BY INJUSTICE.** Where in #2 above the frightening person is **unjust**, here he is **just.** Under what conditions is a virtuous person frightening? When he has been "outraged" by an injustice. The reference to "the will to retaliate" against an injustice indicates that we are talking about virtuous **anger** (Rh II, 2 & NE IV, 5) or **indignation** (Rh II, 9). Deficiency in virtuous anger leaves us **apathetic** in the face of injustice and morally and emotionally incapable of standing up for ourselves even when we have the social and physical resources to do so. It means as well that we will not defend just institutions and procedures. People with this virtue are frightening to those wishing to do unjust things.

4. **POWERFUL PEOPLE AFRAID OF US.** When people with power are afraid of us, they are frightening because they might hurt us to escape their fear. Their fear of us breeds our fear and watchfulness toward them.

5. **GREEDY OR FRIGHTENED PEOPLE, ESPECIALLY THOSE WHO KNOW WE DID SOMETHING WRONG.** The American Federalists might well have adopted Aristotle's assertion that "it is, as a rule, a terrible thing to be at another man's mercy" as a leading text for their doctrine of checks and balances. Power is a potentially threatening resource requiring only the wish to abuse it for it to become actually threatening. As Aristotle notes, men are inclined to develop **greed** (NE III, 10-2 & IV, 1) and **fear** (NE III, 6-9) and these wishes lead them to act unjustly toward others. Without countervailing institutional resources for resisting such unjust behavior, the weak are left to the mercy of the strong. They have no appeal to rights, and thus to state and social resources, which might override the latter's power.

Our own wrong-doing can place us at the mercy of such people who acquire power over us because they were either in on our vice or simply learned about it. They "may betray or desert us" and the thought of their doing so is terrifying. We are thus afraid of people who know bad things about us.

6. **PEOPLE WHO FEEL WE HAVE WRONGED THEM AND ARE LOOKING TO GET BACK AT US.** People who "have been wronged" are **angry** like the people in #1 above. The difference here is that the power of these people is not so great as those in #1 since these people are "always looking out for their opportunity" to retaliate instead of being able to do so at will. And like the people mentioned in #11 below, they scare us when we do not know when or where they might attack.

Aristotle also adds the important reminder that it is enough for people to "believe themselves to be wronged" for them to be angry at us and to be frightening to us. This is a major reason why people with power should avoid even the appearance of injustice (as well as behavior that arouses **envy**) lest they encourage people to look for opportunities for revenge or to vent their spite through sabotage, vandalism, etc.

7. **POWERFUL PEOPLE AFRAID OF RETALIATION FOR THEIR INJUSTICE.** If unjust rulers (#2) cause their people to fear injustice from on

high, it is equally true that such rulers must themselves live in the fear that the people will retaliate against them for their injustices.

8. **OUR RIVALS IN A ZERO-SUM GAME. Envious** people are disposed to define situations as zero-sum games in which as "rivals for a thing... we cannot both have it at once" (**R h** II, 2 and 10). We are rightly afraid of envious people because they are likely to be spitefully destructive toward us to avoid the pain they will feel at our enjoying our success. It is sometimes possible, however, to approach rivalry as a non-zero-sum game in which one person's gain is not subtracted from his rival's rewards, and thus to avoid this kind of malignant envy.

9. **PEOPLE WHO FRIGHTEN OTHERS STRONGER THAN WE ARE.** We should fear any one who is actually feared, or should be feared, or who has already destroyed, someone stronger than we are. When someone who is stronger than we are is defeated by a third person, that person will seem frightening to us too.

10. **PEOPLE ATTACKING OTHERS WEAKER THAN WE ARE.** Just because someone is attacking people weaker than we are does not mean that the attacker is weaker than we are. The attacker might gain further resources and a more malignant wish in the process of his conquest, and then turn against us. He is already revealing his threatening intent. Attacking weaker people is characteristic of the **insolent-sadistic** attitude (**R h** II, 4). As the repentant German said, "First they attacked the Jews, and I did nothing because I was not a Jew..." One sees this closer to home whenever anyone makes fun of weaker people whether it be a teacher ridiculing a student or a macho bully humiliating someone on the street. Such people are frightening.

11. **QUIET, DISSEMBLING, UNSCRUPULOUS PEOPLE WE MIGHT HAVE WRONGED.** Not all **angry** (Rh II, 2) or **spiteful** (Rh II, 10) people are equally frightening. The most frightening are the **sullen** ones who are not open and honest about their feelings and who cannot express and get over them. We are more frightened by people who swallow their anger and hostility because we never know when it will come out or how powerful it will be (**NE** IV, 5). This uncertainty not only intensifies our fear, but we live with it for longer periods since such people never get the hostility out of their systems.

Aristotle closes his description of frightening people by indicating two **fear-intensifiers.**

12. **HAVING NO CHANCE TO RETRIEVE A BLUNDER.** Examples of this general principle can be found in a surgeon's fear of operating near life-dependent organs, or a job-applicant's fear that she will have no opportunity to correct a mis-statement in a truncated interview. Playing with fire-arms, driving too fast and doing any number of other dangerous things show us how having no chance to retrieve a blunder makes situations more threatening.

13. **NOT BEING ABLE TO HELP THE SITUATION VERY EASILY.** Terrible things are more terrible the more we would have to do to avert their

destruction. This point is the obverse of a basic strategic principle when one is on the offense. One should design his or her attack in such a way that whatever defensive maneuvers one's opponent employs will themselves cost him dearly. As a result, the very things the defender will be forced to do will increase his fear of the attack.

Finally, Aristotle shows how we can learn what people are afraid of even if we never see them directly frightened when he notes that the things people **pity** (**R h** II, 8) when they happen to others are the same things they are afraid might happen to them or theirs.

b. Our States of Mind When Afraid

Where before we examined the way we see the wishes and resources of other people (A) when we are afraid of them, now we examine the states of mind (M) we are in when capable of being afraid. This is a shift in focus from agent to material causality. To clarify "the conditions under which we ourselves feel fear" (1382b 28), Aristotle examines the contrary ones in which we cannot feel afraid even when we should. He says that

If fear is associated with the expectation that something destruc- tive will happen to us, plainly nobody will be afraid who believes nothing can happen to him; we shall not fear things that we believe cannot happen to us, nor people who we believe cannot inflict them upon us; nor shall we be afraid at times when we think ourselves safe from them. (1382b 29-34)

By reversing the states of mind in which it is impossible for us to feel afraid, Aristotle concludes that

fear is felt by those who believe something to be likely to hap- pen to them at the hands of particular persons in a par- ticular form, and at a particular time. (1382b 34 1383a 1)

Stated causally, people (M) feel afraid when they believe a particular per- son will do a particular thing (A) at a particular time that will destroy them (F) or cause them great pain (F).

There are two extreme states in which we cannot feel fear. The first occurs when we are dominated by vices disposing us to **excessive** confidence, the second when our confidence falls to **zero**.

1. People do not believe this [i.e. that something is "likely to happen to them," etc...] when they are, or think they are, in the midst of great prosperity, and are in consequence **insolent**, **contemptuous**, and **reckless**--the kind of character produced by wealth, physical strength, abundance of friends, power... (1383a 1-3)

2. Nor yet when they feel they have experienced every kind of horror already and have grown callous about the future, like men who are being flogged and are already near dead--if they are to

feel the anguish of uncertainty, there must be some faint expectation of escape. This appears from the fact that fear sets us
thinking what can be done, which of course nobody does when
things are hopeless. (1383a 4-8)

Finally, Aristotle points out how an orator should depict a threatening agent (A) with reference to his audience's confidence in themselves
(M) if he is to put them in a state of mind (Tfm) in which he can mobilize their fears (F) of that agent. The orator must show them that the
threatened harm has

happened to others who were stronger than they are, and is happening, or has happened, to people like themselves, at the hands
of unexpected people, in an unexpected form, and at an unexpected time. (1383a 10-3)

COMMENTARY. Aristotle's remarks cover the continuum between the
vices of excessive and deficient fear. From one extreme to the other, the
person expects either everything or nothing to happen to him, that
everybody or nobody is a threat, that the threat could come in any con-
ceivable form and at any time, or in no form and at no time. Excessive
fear often appears as a kind of objectless anxiety because so many objects prompt it. Radically deficient fear, on the other hand, appears as a
kind of indifference to the world, as we will see below.

1. **WHEN WE ARE NEITHER INSOLENT-SADISTIC, DISDAINFUL NOR
RECKLESS.** "Wealth, physical strength, abundance of friends, power" encourage vices which dispose us not only to feel excessively confident but
to be unrealistic in how we picture the powers others have to hurt us.
The first of these vices is **insolent sadism** or **hubris** which is very in-
adequately translated as "pride". With this character trait, we want to
think of ourselves as more powerful than others and try to confirm this
judgment by causing them pain. The second trait is **contempt** or **disdain**.
With it we are so filled with ourselves and our importance, we think
others are not worth worrying with and overlook potential threats they
might pose. (Both are discussed at **Rh** II, 2.) Finally, **recklessness** disposes us to be insensitive to pain and thus over-confident about the
likelihood of our being hurt or destroyed. (We will soon see that it is the
vice of deficient fear, **NE** IV, 7.)

It is noteworthy that being disdainful is contrary to being insolent-
sadistic. Precisely insofar as the disdainful person is distant and dismissing toward the importance of others, he cannot actively try to build up his
own image through humiliating them. The insolent sadist, on the other
hand, takes his victim's fearful view of the sadist's greater power as a
sought-for confirmation of his own worth and is far from dismissing him
as unimportant. The sadist could not find the confirmation he seeks for
his own worth if he were disdainful toward his victim.

And while a certain behavioral recklessness is often found in
insolent-sadism and contempt-disdain, these character orientations are not
the same as the reckless and excessively spirited character. All three of
these character traits do, however, dispose one to an excessive confidence which distorts one's ability to recognize genuine threats. Such
excess makes the person less able to be afraid than a realistic concern

for his welfare would warrant.

2. **WHEN WE STILL HAVE HOPE THAT WE MIGHT ESCAPE A PAINFUL OR DESTRUCTIVE SITUATION.** The example of the man flogged to the point of death illustrates a general state of mind in which one has "experienced every kind of horror... and... grown callous about the future." While such a person might be in a great deal of **pain**, Aristotle speaks of him as no longer being **afraid**. This applies as much to moral and emotional threats as it does to physical ones. Gifted politicians grasp the fact of this mechanism intuitively whenever they try to mobilize their constituents against threatening agents. They know that if they picture the enemy as too threatening and overwhelming in its power, people will become indifferent and deadened to it because they will feel they have no resources to combat it. They will in that event simply adapt to the threat as a fact of life.

Robert K. Merton reports in **SOCIAL THEORY AND SOCIAL STRUCTURE** that this happened immediately prior to World War II when the U.S. Government mounted its first propaganda efforts to arouse American fears about Nazi successes in Europe. The program back-fired because the government presented the Nazi war machine as such a threat that it seemed invincible. In terms of the formula for fear and confidence, they presented the numerator as being too large for the denominator. The same counter-productive results seem to have happened more recently with the anti-nuclear arms movement in the United States.

What, though, is the mechanism that explains this phenomenon of the perception of threat increasing only up to a certain point after which it drops to zero and no fear is felt? Why do people sometimes lose their fear of things which seem to threaten everything they hold dear? The key to answering these questions is found in the importance of **uncertainty** in causing people to be afraid.

As Aristotle says, "if they are to feel the anguish of uncertainty, there must be some faint expectation of escape." It is painful uncertainty that most stimulates fear. If we are completely confident of either a successful outcome or of a defeat, we are not afraid. It is only when we are between these two extremes that we can be frightened. This explains, for example, the strange relief from fear people gain from giving up something hard they have been trying to do, or from learning even the worst about an anxiously-awaited decision from a college or a prospective employer.

Obviously the escape from the one fear might expose us to many others that follow as a consequence of giving up or having been turned down, but these do not cause so much fear at the time because they are not so impending. The immediate emotion at learning that something bad has happened is often relief from the fear that it might happen. We hurt, but we are no longer afraid.

The basic mechanism here centers on the fact that we are afraid when what we wish for is threatened and we are uncertain about whether we will gain what we want. By losing the hope that we might have what we wish, we lose the fear that we will not have it. The abandonment of the wish is the loss of that which was the internal source of our fears, and simultaneously the loss of the power to perceive the things which threatened that wish as threats.

The central role of confidence and hope in building up our power to perceive threats realistically and to affirm our wishes in the face of these threats is dramatically revealed in the clinical process of overcoming repression. Confidence-building ex-periences with encouraging people (whether they be therapists, teachers, friends, etc.) tend to affirm those **wishes** and interests which people fear are no longer possible for themselves. The reawakening of these wishes tends in turn to promote **deliberation** in making plans for pursuing their wishes even in the face of these threats and to promote the making of one's own **choices** in order to act on these plans.

With newly awakened hopefulness, one gains the power to see how other people might have consciously or unconsciously threatened him in the past into giving up the wish to be himself. Our realistic perception of others is always blocked when they frighten us into surrendering not just our preferred behavior but the very wishes behind that behavior. Having surrendered the wish to be ourselves, we no longer see them as a threat to that wish. And insofar as we see them as a threat, we are still clinging to the wish they threaten even if we are afraid to act on it. The great irony is that gaining renewed confidence in one's wish occurs simultaneously with, and is actually the cause of, an increased and realistic fear of the threats to fulfilling one's wishes.

How does virtue and vice relate to this mechanism of losing fear through the loss of hope for one's wish? Aristotle notes in general that all fear "sets us thinking what can be done, which of course nobody does when things are hopeless." Only the fear rooted in a courageous attitude to life derives from a true judgment about our own wishes and resources and about the challenges actually facing us. And in those crucial mid-range cases where outcomes are in fact uncertain, courage allows us to do our best while living with painful uncertainty.

The power to live with uncertainty allows the courageous person to **deliberate** and **choose** to act on what should be done to pursue one's proper **wishes** in the circumstances. The lack of courage, on the other hand, disposes us to picture more things as threatening than really are so, given our abilities and resources. Cowardice disposes us to see things as excessively threatening and to turn away because we are unable to face them. We can literally run away so that the threat is not in our field of vision, or we can develop such an imaginary way of picturing the world that we do not recognize evil and conflict when we encounter them.

We can become so afraid that we lose the power to make our own **choices** or even to make plans and **deliberate** about what we should do to attain our wishes should opportunities ever open up for us. But neither of these limitations shows the most radical consequence of lacking courage. That arises when we give up the very **wish** to be ourselves which had set us in opposition to the threatening agent in the first place.

People fail to develop the wish to be themselves in large part because they lack people to **emulate** (**Rh** II, 11) who have individuated themselves through doing fine things. But it also comes from actively wishing to be who authorities want us to be so as to avoid the unacceptably painful perception that they are threats to us so long as we have our own wishes for ourselves. Such a strategy of self-betrayal allows us to live with people we feel we cannot escape without the painful sense of facing a constant threat.

People who give up their wishes in the face of threats tend to adopt the threatening agent's wishes for them and to identify themselves with that agent's view of things. This is known clinically as **identifica-tion with the aggressor** and occurs precisely in just those situations in which, as Aristotle says, people "have grown callous about the future" of their own wishes and plans and have lost any "expectation of escape" from the threatening agent. (See Anna Freud, **THE EGO AND THE MECHANISMS OF DEFENCE.**)

By giving up **their own** wishes, people avoid the uncertainty of whether they will be able to act on them. They thus lose the fear that they might not be able to do so. But they escape the sense of threat only at the price of surrendering their identity and integrity. The fearful part of themselves leads them to betray and repress those wishes they lack the courage to act on.

We do not have to repudiate our wishes totally, however, for them to cease being determinate in animating our deliberations and choices. Many such people try to keep their wishes alive by indulging in fantasies about the things they wish to do and be. When such fantasies become a substitute rather than a preparation for reality, they mask from us the real threats and challenges we must confront to act on our wishes. At best such a strategy allows us to pursue our wishes only insofar as they remain fantasies.

Our wishes and values wither and lose power when they are no longer exercised as the first principles animating our deliberations and choices. And with the loss of our true wishes and values, we lose the sense of our own identity, our strength, and our natural vulnerability and spontaneity. Such alienation from one's true wishes has become so characteristic in modern society that the very concept of wish has become fanciful and fickle.

Our analysis of this state of mind when we can no longer perceive threats has obvious significance for explaining the social consciousness and ideology of whole groups of hopeless people. To the extent a class of people feels hopeless to change the social institutions which thwart their wishes, and lacks the courage to hope and plan and work to find opportunities to act on their wishes, they will become more apathetic than afraid. A loss of social perceptiveness will occur at the same rate at which they lose their ability to wish, deliberate and choose for the sake of their own development.

Hopeless people are the least realistic and perceptive when they need to be the most. Anything, therefore, which keeps alive people's highest wishes for themselves and for each other, and which promotes the virtues they need to act on these wishes, will increase their ability to be realistic about the things which threaten them, whether the threat comes from the outside or from within themselves.

Positivist theory and methodology cannot distinguish between a people's free acceptance of just social conditions and its coerced surren-der to unjust conditions. Similarly, progressive political strategists with no eye to the mechanism of fear and confidence will miss the material importance of encouraging whatever social programs develop people's con-fidence in their own powers, even when the programs might not in any way directly confront the explicit political issues which challenge the people's well-being. But by building up people's confidence, one is laying the foundation for their becoming more realistic about the threats they must confront if they are to prosper as human beings.

Finally, Aristotle's remarks about how orators can make people afraid concern both the agent and the material dimensions of causality. Since all forms of response (F) are the product of the interaction between agent (A) and material causes (M), we can make someone afraid either by picturing the agent (A) as being malicious and powerful or by picturing the person we wish to frighten (M) as being weak and lacking in reasons for confidence. Orators wishing to make people afraid can work on the numerator, the denominator, or both the factors in the formula. The most complete attack on someone's confidence would include both. But this is tricky. Orators who explicitly challenge the strong picture people have of themselves risk provoking the **anger** of those who feel slighted by this action (**Rh** II, 2).

Aristotle advises orators to picture the agent as being so powerful that he has harmed people as strong or stronger than those in the audience. The further advice to highlight the unexpectedness of the people causing the harm, its form and timing, all follow the principle that uncertainty is a primary quality of the fear-promoting situation.

Now that we have examined the agents which arouse **fear** and the states of mind in which we are either able or unable to feel it, we turn to an examination of these same issues with regard to **confidence**.

2. CONFIDENCE DEFINED

Aristotle says that confidence is

the opposite of fear, and what causes it is the opposite of what causes fear; it is, therefore, the expectation or hope associated with a mental picture of the nearness of what keeps us safe and the absence or remoteness of what is terrible: it may be due either to the near presence of what inspires confidence or the absence of what causes alarm. (1383a 17-20)

COMMENTARY. Once again we see the importance of how we picture things as the agent stimulating our emotional responses. This has great practical significance when using visualization techniques to build up our own confidence or anyone else's. Picturing the "nearness of what keeps us safe" refers in the formula to our resources and what we can do with them to protect ourselves. By the same token, "the absence or remoteness of what is terrible" refers to a threatening agent with malicious wishes and the resources to act on them. Given the formula's ratio between the agent's wishes and resources and our own, we should not be surprised to find Aristotle saying that confidence comes from either the absence of the first or the presence of the second.

Fear and confidence are "opposite" to one another in the first two of the four senses of opposition described in Aristotle's book the **CATAGORIES** Ch. 10. They are both **relatives** and **contraries** to one another. Aristotle says that "Those things are called relative, which, being either said to be of something else or related to something else, are explained by a reference to that other thing." (6a 35-7) Whether something should be thought frightening, for example, is relative to the confidence one has in his resources for handling it. On the other hand, whether one should be confident of his resources is relative to the potential source of fear. Neither confidence and fear nor their objects can be known without reference to each other.

The second category of opposition is for things to be contraries to one another. "It is possible for relatives to have contraries. Thus virtue has a contrary, vice, these both being relatives; knowledge, too, has a contrary, ignorance." (6b 15) Contraries are such that to the extent one exists in a subject, the other cannot. Contraries do admit of degree and some have intermediaries between them like the continuum of shades between white and black.

The contrary relation between fear and confidence helps make sense of what we saw earlier about hopelessness. As confidence declines to absolute deficiency, fear itself disappears because its being is always in relation to that degree of confidence which creates at least some uncertainty about the outcome. Fear and confidence come into being and disappear together.

a. Things Arousing Our Confidence

In examining the things arousing confidence, Aristotle mentions how we picture both the resources and the wishes of the agents who might threaten us. With this in mind he lists the following.

1. We feel it if we can take steps--many, or important, or both--to cure or prevent trouble... (1383a 20-1)

2. If we have neither wronged others nor been wronged by them... (1383a 21-2)

3. If we have either no rivals at all or no strong ones... (1383a 22-3)

4. If our rivals who are strong are our friends or have treated us well or been treated well by us... (1383a 23-4)

5. If those whose interest is the same as ours are the more numerous party, or the stronger, or both. (1383a 24)

COMMENTARY. It is interesting to see that, just as the formula leads us to expect, the things arousing confidence include not only the wishes and resources of the people who might threaten us, but also the strength of our resources for resisting them. These are the kinds of things we try to think about and direct other people's attention to in building up confidence--and the kinds of things that are lacking in the lives of excessively fearful people, either in fact or as they see things. It should be clear from the list that the better we treat others, the less likely we need fear them.

1. **HAVING THE RESOURCES TO CURE OR PREVENT TROUBLE.** Seeing an agent as something we have the resources to handle easily gives us confidence. In keeping with what we saw above about hopelessness, it is important to distinguish between seeing an agent as not threatening and seeing it as posing a threat we are confident we can handle. An agent

seen as not threatening because it appears to be invulnerable and inescapable will be a source of resignation rather than confidence. Resignation, of course, is not the same as confidence.

2. HAVING NOBODY AROUND WHOM WE HAVE WRONGED OR HAVE BEEN WRONGED BY. If we have not wronged others, we have no reason to fear their angry retaliation. We have no reason to expect they wish to harm us on this account. On the other hand, we have two reasons for confidence if we have not been wronged by them. In the first place, we are confident simply because we are not being wronged. In the second place, if they have not wronged us, we do not have to fear their fearing us and are confident on that account.

3. HAVING NO STRONG RIVALS WHO ARE SPITEFUL TOWARD US. Rivals are frightening when they are **envious**, particularly in explicitly zero-sum contexts, and when they have the resources to act on their spite. Without rivals with such a wish to hurt us, we can be confident on this score.

4. HAVING KIND AND FRIENDLY RIVALS. If we do have rivals, but they are our **friends** (Rh II, 4 & NE IV, 6) or they have been **kind** to us or we have been to them (R h II, 7), we will be confident because they are not likely to wish us harm.

5. HAVING THE SAME WISHES TO PROTECT AS THE STRONGEST PEOPLE AROUND US. We feel confident when the majority or at least the strongest people around share our wishes and interests rather than opposing them. This means they will not only not threaten us themselves, they are likely to be on our side against anyone threatening these common interests. They share our wishes and in a sense become resources for us.

b. Our States of Mind When Confident

Having examined the wishes and resources of the people (A) promoting a sense of confidence, we now examine our own states of mind (M) which incline us to be confident. They involve the perception of both our resources and our wishes. Aristotle observed that

1. We feel confidence if we believe we have often succeeded and never suffered reverses, or have often met danger and escaped it safely. For there are two reasons why human beings face danger calmly: they may have **no experience** of it, or they may have **means to deal with it:** thus when in danger at sea people may feel confident about what will happen either because they have no experience of bad weather, or because their experience gives them the means of dealing with it. (1383a 25–33)

2. We also feel confident whenever there is **nothing to terrify other people like ourselves,** or people weaker than ourselves, or people than whom we believe ourselves to be stronger--and we believe this if we have conquered them, or conquered others who are as strong as they are, or stronger. (1383a 33–5)

3. Also if we believe ourselves superior to our rivals in the number and importance of the **advantages that make men
formidable**--wealth, physical strength, strong bodies of supporters,
extensive territory, and the possession of all, or the most important, appliances of war. (1383a 35-b3)

4. Also if **we have wronged no one**, or not those of whom we
are afraid; and generally, if our relations with the gods are satisfactory, as will be shown especially by signs and oracles. The
fact is that anger makes us confident--that anger is excited by
our knowledge that we are not the wrongers but the wronged, and
that the divine power is always supposed to be on the side of
the wronged. (1383b 3-9)

5. Also when, at the **outset of an enterprise**, we believe that we
cannot and shall not fail, or that we shall succeed completely.
(1383b 9-11)

COMMENTARY. Where earlier we examined external factors affecting
our confidence, here we examine the more internal factors affecting our
morale in the denominator of the formula. These are the kinds of things
we search for in trying to encourage people. There presence or absence
has a big effect on character development in both individuals and whole
groups.

1. **HAVING HAD MANY SUCCESSES AND NO DEFEATS.** Confidence can
come from either the presence or the absence of experience. The first of
these sounds very much like what Aristotle says about the apparent
courage of professional fighting men which will be examined later in this
chapter (N E III, 8). A person in a state of mind in which he is picturing
his past successes and his resources for facing a present challenge is
naturally disposed to being confident. Their past successes, training and
arms give them the resources, i.e. "the means to deal with," the dangers
of war in the same way that the experiences of sailors allows them to
face confidently the dangers of storms at sea. Although Aristotle is explicit that such professional confidence is not the same thing as courage,
the former nonetheless manifests a pragmatic as opposed to a moral virtue
or excellence.

But an inexperienced, unprofessional person can also be disposed to
confidence although of an excessive and unrealistic kind. The lack of
experience and training leaves such a person ignorant of conditions that
actually are threatening. He does not yet know enough to realize how
afraid he should be. It is also true, though, that while ignorance and inexperience can cause excessive confidence, they can also cause excessive fear--as when inexperienced soldiers are frightened by things which
veterans immediately recognize as being no real threat.

2. **BELIEVING THAT PEOPLE LIKE OURSELVES OR EVEN WEAKER HAVE NOTHING TO FEAR.** If we know that people like ourselves have handled a given threat, then we feel confident that we too have the resources to handle it. This seems an extension of the above-mentioned reference to experience, except that here it is not so much a matter of knowing our own experience as knowing the experience of others like ourselves that gives us confidence. We can see here why role models and heroes are so important in building up people's confidence in themselves, and how impoverished those people are who come from families and cultures in which the people like themselves have experienced frequent failure. Coming from cultures of failure, they must work that much harder to gain confidence in themselves.

If somebody weaker than we are is not seriously threatened, then we are not either. The fact that we have conquered people who are not genuinely threatened by something that we must now confront, or we have conquered other people as strong or stronger, leads us to believe that we too have nothing to fear. We use our knowledge of their strength (M) to appraise the strength of the agent (A) they have resisted (F). When we focus our minds on these relations, we feel confident.

3. **HAVING THE RESOURCES WHICH MAKE ONE FORMIDABLE.** "Wealth, physical strength, strong bodies of supporters, extensive territory... all, or the most important, appliances of war" are all resources we can bring to a potentially threatening exchange. They represent extensions of our material power (M) to resist threatening agents (A). They build up the denominator of the formula for fear and confidence. Picturing these things makes us feel "formidable" and confident, and tilts the balance in our favor.

4. **HAVING WRONGED NO ONE.** We feel confident when we feel justice is on our side. Although he does not say so explicitly, Aristotle seems to be talking here about **shame** (**Rh** II, 6 & **NE** IV, 9). If we have wronged others, we feel they have a right to be **angry** at us (**Rh** II, 2 & **NE** IV, 5). Anger is an emotion of confidence in which people feel like justice and the gods are on their side. If, however, we are ashamed of what we have done and feel others are right to be angry at us, we feel justice and the gods are not on our side and we cannot stand up for ourselves whole-heartedly. We are therefore much more confident when we have been wronged than when we feel we have wronged others. In the one case we are divided against ourselves and do not feel we deserve to triumph. In the other, we are at one with ourselves and wish whole-heartedly to succeed.

This mechanism is ironically confirmed by jingoistic war propaganda. In order to make young men willing to fight (and their families willing to sacrifice them), leaders must picture their cause as just even when it is not.

5. **INITIATING A NEW PROJECT.** At first sight it seems strange for Aristotle to say we feel confident "when, at the outset of an enterprise, we believe that we cannot and shall not fail, or that we shall succeed completely." Doesn't it already take confidence to get started in the first place? Yes, but the point to see here is that the very fact of setting out on a project gives us confidence because the active pursuit of a proper

purpose gives us energy and something to fight for. When we have developed initiative and momentum like this, we are more likely to react confidently to anything else that threatens us. This explains, for example, why the unemployed and the bored have less confidence than the actively engaged and the committed.

c. How People Undermine Our Confidence

While Aristotle does not directly address the question of what orators can do either to promote or to undermine people's fear and confidence, we can say the following based on his list of the states of mind in which we feel confident. Orators, parents, teachers, managers, advertisers, etc. can either encourage (literally **en-courage** or put courage into) people or they can undermine people's confidence and make them more afraid. The latter skill is particularly important in unjust regimes and in institutions that motivate people through cultivating their greed and envy. Since courageous and hopeful people are not so envious, any marketing strategy based on envy must undermine people's confidence.

Both **insolent-sadistic** and **spiteful** individuals (**Rh** II, 4) actually aim to undermine others, although they do so in characteristically different forms and for different ends. When one learns to recognize such behavior, he can better protect him- or herself against it.

Reversing each of the above-listed confidence-givers provides the following ways of undermining people's confidence.

1. We can emphasize their failures rather than their successes, remind them of all the things they do not know, and suggest unexpected threats lurking in these areas.

2. We can be preoccupied with stories of how others even stronger than our friends have been defeated and come to nothing.

3. We can constantly denigrate and complain about the inadequacy of the resources available to meet challenges one must face.

4. We can try to make people feel ashamed and believe they are always in the wrong. We can deny them the right to be angry about anything, because that right belongs only to those who have been wronged, not those who have done wrong. We can make them feel that the gods or the powers that be are never on their side.

5. We can throw cold water on all their plans and interfere with their taking any initiative in getting things moving in their lives.

It is important to see, too, that we can undermine our own confidence even more effectively than anyone else can, since we can picture these demoralizing things to ourselves even when we are alone and at any hour of the day or night.

B. COURAGE, COWARDICE, BOASTFULNESS AND RECKLESSNESS AS THE VIRTUE AND VICES OF THIS POWER

1. THE AGENT THAT BEST REVEALS COURAGE (NE III, 6)

In keeping with his focus on fear and confidence that we have just examined from **THE ART OF RHETORIC**, Aristotle now examines the virtuous and vicious ways this power can be developed in **THE NICOMACHEAN ETHICS.** He first asserts that courage

is a **mean** with regard to feelings of fear and confidence... and plainly the things we fear are terrible things, and these are, to speak without qualification, evils; for which reason people even define fear as expectation of evil. (1115a 7-11)

Courage disposes us to respond to threatening situations with a characteristically proper ratio between fear and confidence.

Aristotle's task here, however, is to identify the threatening agents which best reveal whether we have the fullest courage. To do so, he first divides the class of all dangerous things into those people **should** fear and avoid and those we **should face.** In the process, he begins implicitly to show that we often mistakenly identify courage simply with being **fearless** and thus miss the true nature of courage. He says,

Now we fear all evils, e.g. disgrace, poverty, disease, friendlessness, death, but the brave man is not thought to be concerned with all; for to fear some things is even right and noble, and it is base not to fear them--e.g. disgrace; he who fears this is good and **principled**, and he who does not is **shameless**. He is, however, by some people called brave, by a transference of the word to a new meaning; for he has in him something which is like the brave man, since the brave man also is a fearless person. (1115a 11-6)

If we identify courage with **fearlessness**, we would be wrongly led to call a **shameless** person courageous because he seems fearless in the face of **disgrace.**

While there are some dangerous things a courageous person **should** fear, such as being disgraced in front of good people, there are others that he **should face courageously and not fear.** He says, for example, that

Poverty and disease we perhaps ought not to fear nor in general the things that do not proceed from vice and are not due to to a man himself. But not even the man who is fearless of these is brave. Yet we apply the word to him also in virtue of a similarity; for some who in the dangers of war are cowards are **generous** and are confident in face of the loss of money. (1115a 16-22)

We should be afraid about our poverty and disgrace insofar as they are **our own fault**, but should otherwise face them fearlessly in order to combat them.

We have seen that frightening things can be divided into those which we should courageously face and those we should be ashamed of. We should be ashamed of being disgraced in front of good people, but we should courageously face things like the loss of money or disease, although we obviously should not be shameless about these things insofar as they are our own fault. But not even all the things we should courageously face provide pure tests of our courage. Battle, for example, is a better test than the loss of money.

Aristotle offers additional examples to show that courage is not simply a matter of **being confident** and that cowardice is not simply a matter of **being afraid**. He says, for example,

Nor is a man a coward if he fears **insult** to his wife and children or **envy** or anything of the kind; nor brave if he is confident when he is about to be flogged. (1115a 22-3)

A knowledge of true courage would be simple if it required no more than the assumption that courage is a matter of always being fearless while cowardice is simply a matter of being afraid.

Aristotle believes that the **prospect of death** provides a greater challenge to one's courage than do other frightening things. This is his next division.

With what sort of terrible things, then, is the brave man concerned? Surely with the greatest; for no one is more likely than he to stand his ground against what is awe-inspiring. Now death is the most terrible of all things; for it is the end, and nothing is thought to be either good or bad for the dead. (1115a 24-7)

So we must now divide all the threatening things we should face into those that are **life-threatening** and those that are not; and clearly those that are life-threatening require more courage than those that are not.

The problem now becomes one of dividing life-threatening situations into those that are the **noblest** of these and those that are not. And with this division he comes to the end of the line and isolates what he considers the greatest test of courage.

But the brave man would not seem to be concerned even with death in ALL circumstances, e.g. at sea or in disease. In what circumstances, then? Surely in the noblest. Now such deaths are those in battle; for these take place in the greatest and noblest danger. And these are correspondingly honored in city-states and at the courts of monarchs. Properly, then, he will be called brave who is fearless in face of a noble death, and of all emergencies that involve death; and the emergencies of war are in the highest degree of this kind. (1115a 28-34)

He believes that battle normally provides a better test of a person's courage than do death by disease or in a storm at sea because facing such a death is both more noble in itself and more broadly honored.

Aristotle thinks courage can be shown in death by disease and at sea, but is not normally shown so fully in facing these things.

> Yet at sea also, and in disease; the brave man is fearless, but not in the same way as the seaman; for he has given up hope of safety, and is disliking the thought of death in this shape, while they are hopeful because of their experience. At the same time, we show courage in situations where there is the opportunity of showing prowess or where death is noble; but in these forms of death neither of these conditions is fulfilled. (1115a 35-b 7)

So facing death on the battlefield is more noble than facing it simply in disease or for a passenger to face it at sea because battle normally allows a man to show **greater prowess** in fighting against that which threatens him.

COMMENTARY. Except for his extended discussions of **justice** in **NE** V and of **friendship** in **NE** VIII and IX, Aristotle devotes more attention to **courage** than to any other virtue. He is particularly concerned with its differential diagnosis, that is with differentiating true courage from the whole host of things people confuse with it. We will see below that in **NE** III, 8, for example, Aristotle examines six different forms just of battlefield behavior that are confused with courage. It must be realized, though, that Aristotle considers battle to be the **purest** agent (A) for testing the **highest**, but not the **only**, form or manifestaion (F) of courage (M). The reader is advised to note this balanced judgment on the question of battle so as not to assume that his is a romantic, life-rejecting glorification of war.

In the present chapter, Aristotle also examines the claims that examples of **shamelessness, generosity,** or facing death by disease or drowning at sea reveal courage, and finds that while some of them are not courage at all, others do not reveal the heart of courage because they are either admixtures with other virtues or are incomplete.

But saying this raises a problem we must immediately address. People fear a great many different evils and speak of how we handle many of them as being courageous. How are we to tell which ones provide the truest test of what courage is? How can we tell if people are misusing the term, if we cannot determine the situations which best reveal courage? How can we be sure we are defining courage with regard to the best examples of it? We might end up describing something that does require courage but that involves other moral and emotional powers as well. We have to choose our examples very carefully to avoid this problem.

Aristotle bases his examination of the agent(s) that best reveal courage on the methodology of **division** that goes back at least to Plato. He will use the method again most prominently in identifying the best agent for revealing **self-indulgence** and **self-control** (**NE** III, 10). He applies the method in the present chapter by dividing the various things we fear into two different classes which are then examined to determine which provides the clearer and less ambiguous test of a person's courage.

The procedure is then to make a further division within this class and to ask again which of these two provides the clearer test. The procedure is repeated until he finds the best, no longer significantly-divisible class of agents for testing courage. By making further divisions down the line of those frightening things we should face, we will come to the best agents for revealing courage. The criteria discovered along the way for making the various divisions provide the differentia for defining courage itself. This means that in clarifying the best agent (A) for testing the highest courage, Aristotle is simultaneously clarifying the nature of courage itself (M and F).

Two principles from Aristotle's TOPICS are crucial if we are to follow the strategy behind his reasoning and the method of division he employed. First, he tells us that with regard to investigating the meaning of a term like courage that

> when there are more things than one to which the term which is being defined is applicable, you must see whether he has assigned it in reference not to the better but to the worse; for every kind of knowledge and capacity is generally regarded as concerned with the best. (TOP VI, 5, 143a 9-12)

Since Aristotle wants to find the best instances of courage in order to understand what is essential to this virtue, he must find the best agent for revealing when a person is genuinely courageous. To do this, he had to collect the most prominent instances of actions which people think of as brave before using the division procedure to discover which is best for investigating courage.

We must, however, use an additional principle from the TOPICS to reconstruct Aristotle's thought process. He says in this regard that "you will be able to make a **problem** out of any **proposition** by altering the way in which it is stated" (Topics I, 4 101b 35). This means we can take the propositions in the texts we are commenting on and translate them into the problems Aristotle was posing in his search for the best test of someone's courage. With these two principles of looking for the best instances and turning propositions into problems, we can reconstruct his analysis. (See the diagram of these divisions found on below.)

Our basic problem, of course, is to find the frightening things which require the greatest courage. Aristotle's first division is to separate all the things that are potentially frightening into those that we **should face** and those we **should avoid as shameful**. This cut is based on the idea that we should try to avoid some painful things while trying to find the confidence to face the others. Since it takes more courage to face frightening things than to avoid them, those we should face will reveal our courage more than those we should avoid.

People who simply equate courage with fearlessness are like teenagers, for example, who think their peers are brave for acting recklessly with cars or insolently toward authorities. People can be fearless about insults to their families and about the **envy** of their neighbors because they are **apathetic** (**Rh** II, 2 & **NE** IV, 5) about standing up for themselves or because they are **shameless** (**Rh** II, 6 & **NE** IV, 9) about parading their good fortune in front of others. Truly courageous people, on the other hand, are afraid of such insults and other people's envy, and act rightly to try to avoid them.

And just as fearing insult and envy is no proof of cowardice, so too is confidence when one is about to be flogged no sign of courage. A wicked man with no genuinely noble wishes, perhaps a Charles Manson or a Sirhan Sirhan, might go stoically even to their executions. But what would that show about their moral character? At best, it would show that they have enough natural spirit to hide their vulnerability and pain from their enemies. But we will see further below in discussing **N E** III, 8 that having great natural spirit is not the same as having a developed moral virtue. Such behavior might simply be another instance of the wrongdoer's shamelessness in the face of the moral judgment others rightly pass on their wicked conduct, and/or a sign of how little they value their own lives and how unafraid they are to die.

To give another example of how being confident in the face of pain

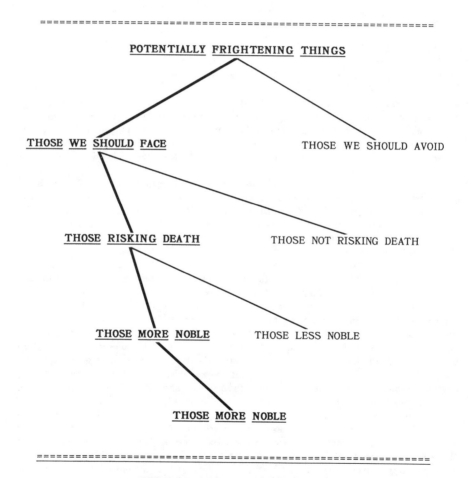

DIVISIONS MADE IN IDENTIFYING
THE BEST AGENTS FOR REVEALING COURAGE

is not always a true test of a person's courage, someone might have the confidence to come back from a significant financial loss, for example, but still be a coward on the battlefield. While we would speak of such a person as having that aspect of **generosity** (**NE** IV, 1) which governs the production of money and the courage not to be destroyed by its loss, we would not think of him as having **courage per se** because of the cowardly way he acted on the battlefield.

Conversely, we would be inclined to say that even though a person might be miserly, exploitative or otherwise vicious when it comes to money, he nonetheless showed a real potential for courage in saving his friends on the battlefield. The difference in how we speak about these two cases reflects the fact that the battlefield is a better agent for testing courage than is the loss of money, although both of them are frightening and both require confidence if one is to face them rightly.

Here we see the need to distinguish between those agents that threaten to kill us and those that do not. Death is the greatest threat, the most "awe-inspiring," the hardest "to stand [one's] ground against," and the elimination of all good and bad things for the person himself. Surely agents **threatening death** call for greater courage than those which do not.

Aristotle mentions disease and poverty as evils not necessarily risking death. Even a non-fatal disease or injury can be very painful and frightening, of course, and we commonly distinguish from among people who suffer such things those who face them bravely and those who do not. And certainly a person could not face an economically challenging future without courage. The reference to such people as being courageous is not so much wrong as it is misleading when it comes to identifying the greatest courage.

The reader should keep in mind, however, that we are not asking whether it is more important to face violent enemies or economic problems courageously. The best answer to this is probably the one Aristotle gave when asked whether a serious disease or tripping is the greater danger to your health. He noted quite simply that it all depended on where you trip. Violent enemies are sometimes the greatest threat to civilization; at other times economic problems are. Economic problems can themselves promote the rise of violent threats as the Depression did with Hitler and poverty does today in inner-cities.

Our focus instead has been simply on the issue of the best test for courage by itself which has led us to the difference between threatening things we should face which could **kill us** and those which by stipulation could not. We must now though make a final division within the class of those threats risking death between those that are **more** and those that are **less noble** for us to face. To Aristotle there was no question that it is more noble to risk dying bravely fighting for one's country than to die bravely facing a disease or a storm at sea.

What is Aristotle's basis for saying this? His first argument appeals to the fact that facing death in battle is commonly "honored in city-states and at the courts of monarchs" for its nobility. The implication is that since brave resignation in the face of fatal diseases and accidents is not so honored, it is not commonly thought to be as brave as risking death in battle.

This conclusion squares with an observation Aristotle made at the beginning of the **ETHICS** when he said that

> The attainment of the good for one man alone is, to be sure, a source of satisfaction; yet to secure it for a nation and for states is nobler and more divine. (NE I, 2 1094b 9-10)

Clearly, facing death for the good of one's country is a noble thing--with the proviso, of course, that one's country is pursuing a noble policy.

We might conclude from this that actions are more noble when they are in the interest of more than just the actor himself. Most people do not face and fight against dying of cancer or other diseases for the sake of other people. The case of death at sea is more complex, however. To grasp Aristotle's point we must distinguish how a brave passenger might respond to such a threat at sea from how a professional sailor might. Aristotle focuses on the threat the sea emergency (A) poses to the traveller (M) and not to the sailor. The threat would seem to offer sailors a greater opportunity for showing their courage because of two factors which distinguish their situation from that of passengers.

In the first place, they have the greater opportunity of showing **their prowess** in facing the threat at sea than do the untrained travellers. Like professionals generally in threatening situations (**NE** III, 8), the sailors "are hopeful because of their experience", their nautical training, equipment, etc. In the second place, precisely because of their prowess, sailors have the travellers' fate in their hands as well. So they can both show their prowess and care for others in a way that is not so accessible to someone simply as a passenger on the ship. The sailors' resources are greater than those of the passengers in relation to the threatening emergency, so it is obviously easier for them to be confident and show their stuff.

Nobility is beautiful human functioning on a high plane of excellence for the protection and promotion of human development and must obviously include showing our prowess in handling terrifying things which disturb most people's ability to function at all.

The travellers might show enormous bravery in other areas where they have the talent, training and resources to face frightening things while helping others. But Aristotle seems to have assumed that the normal Athenian would not be able to do this in an emergency at sea. Aristotle does describe them as having a certain kind of fearlessness even in such situations at sea, but for a totally different reason than the sailors are and in a different way. With little or no resources to master the actual threat, they do not know what to do and "give up hope of safety." And as we have come to expect, they lose their fear with the last of their hope.

Where a brave person feels ennobled by dying while exerting himself for the good of others, the helpless traveller finds nothing to like in "the thought of death in this shape" which denies him both these noble wishes. At best the traveller can be proud that he did not panic from indulging in fantasies of magical escape and lose control of himself. Being free of **self-indulgence** (**NE** III, 10-2), he does not allow himself to fantasize about miraculous rescues which tend simply to heighten uncertainty and promote a sense of panic.

We conclude by summarizing the various differentia Aristotle employed in the divisions that led him to conclude that facing death in battle is the greatest test of courage. Courage is shown more fully in **confidently facing** frightening things than in avoiding the things we should not defiantly face, like shameless things and other people's envy. Courage is shown more fully in **life-threatening** situations than in those that are not. And, finally, courage is shown more fully in facing **noble deaths for the sake of other people** and doing so in ways that allow us to **show our prowess** than in facing those deaths from disease and accidents that do not normally involve these purposes or allow these forms of response.

The differentia of the best agent (A) for testing courage give us at the same time the best examples of courage (M) itself. This analysis thus simultaneously points to courage as a matter of confidently facing life threatening situations (A) for the sake of other people as well as ourselves (T) and doing so in a way which shows our prowess (F).

2. THE VIRTUE AND VICES OF THIS POWER (NE III, 7)

a. Courage Must Be Evaluated with regard
to Threats within the Bounds of Human Strength

Having identified what most fully tests one's courage, we must now differentiate between the virtuous and the various possible vicious developments of our power to deal with threatening things. These character orientations will determine different people's responses to the whole range of possible threats, of course, and not just to physical confrontations.

Aristotle begins this chapter, however, with a further division of fearful things into those that are and those that are not **beyond human strength**. It will be by analyzing people's responses (F) only to those frightening things (A) which are not beyond human strength that we can judge their courage and cowardice (M). He notes that

> What is terrible is not the same for all men; but we say there are terrible things even beyond human strength. These, then, are terrible to everyone--at least to every sensible man; but the terrible things that are not beyond human strength differ in magnitude and degree, and so too do the things that inspire confidence. Now the brave man is as dauntless as man may be. Therefore, while he will fear even the things that are not beyond human strength, he will face them as he ought and as **reason** directs for **nobility's** sake, for this is the end of virtue. But it is possible to fear these **more**, or **less**, and again to fear things that are **not** terrible as if they were. Of the faults that are committed one consists in fearing **what** one should not, another in fearing **as** we should not, another in fearing **when** we should not, and so on; and so too with respect to the things that inspire confidence. (1115b 16-27)

We can identify within this class of terrible things not beyond human strength several different dimensions that allow us to measure how we can go wrong in the area of courage and within which virtue shows its excellence. Fearing **what** we should not is a matter of agent causality and occurs when we fear things we should not fear at all. Fearing **as** and **when** we should not is a matter of formal causality and occurs when our form of response is not as it should be.

COMMENTARY. The great practical significance of the theory of character comes from its ability to help us explain and to some extent predict the way people with different character orientations will respond to stimuli, and the effect on their overall functioning and well-being of developing excessive or deficient orientations. Aristotle's opening remark that "What is terrible is not the same for all men" signals his intent to provide a differential diagnosis of how courage and the various vices associated with it dispose different people to see different things as causes of fear and confidence. These different character traits then allow us to explain **w h y** people who develop their moral and emotional powers in these **different** ways do not respond to the same things in the **same** way.

Aristotle applies a resolutive or analytic procedure to identify these different material dispositions. He works his way down to the identification of these different causal powers (M) from an initial recognition of differences in the syndromes of **agents** (A) which arouse different people's fear and confidence, and differences in their **forms of response** (F) and **purposes** (T). Through this process he identifies the specific virtue of **courage**, and the vices of **excessive spirit, boastfulness** and **cowardice**.

Aristotle distinguishes between the threatening agents that are beyond human strength and those that are not because the latter group has no diagnostic value. Everybody is afraid of them. Since these things are beyond human strength, they fail to distinguish between virtuous and vicious people--or at least they do not do so very well. But what are such threats "beyond human strength"? One clue is his reference to their being beyond human strength--"at least to every **sensible** man." This reference suggests the **excessively-spirited** vice we will discuss further below. At any rate, the man with the excessively-spirited vice is not a legitimate touchstone for what is beyond human strength because he is insensible to legitimate dangers.

A second reference takes us further. At an earlier point in **T H E ETHICS** in establishing the basic difference between **voluntary, involuntary** and **nonvoluntary** actions (**NE** III, 1), Aristotle speaks of cases where a person might be faced with a cruel choice. He says, for example, that a tyrant might kidnap one's parents and children and threaten to harm them if one refuses to do something dishonorable. He compares this cruel choice with that of being at sea and having to choose between jettisoning all one's valuables and allowing the ship to sink. Both alternatives are in themselves involuntary. No one would do either except under duress. Yet, at the actual time of performance, one might well voluntarily do the dishonorable act demanded by the kidnappers or jettison one's possessions overboard.

Aristotle notes that in cases such as the kidnapper's demand, men are **praised** if they accomplish a **noble** thing at the price of taking **base** and **painful** action. On the other hand, they are **blamed** if the **end** for which they acted basely was **ignoble** or **trifling**. He mentions too that there are some actions which are so base that we should not do them even for a noble end. To make up an example of this, we might say that it would be noble to want to protect one's family, for example, but not at the price of telling the Nazi air force how to defeat British radar.

Such situations in which people might act involuntarily clarify the nature of actions "beyond human strength." They involve the following combinations of factors. In each case we have a **base** form of response that is **forced** on the actor. The variations occur in the **nobility** of purpose for which the act was taken and in the consequential **praise** or **blame** accorded the actor.

1- When the purpose (T) of the action is more noble than the coerced form of response (F) is base, the person is praised.

2- When the purpose (T) is ignoble or trivial and the action is base (F), the person is blamed.

3- When his purpose (T) is noble but is less so than the baseness of his action (F), he is also blamed.

The fourth permutation of these factors only occurs among corrupt people who praise others for commiting base actions for ignoble purposes.

BASE AND PAINFUL ACTION	FOR NOBLE /	OR IGNOBLE END
PRAISED	#1	
BLAMED	#3	#2

Aristotle adds a final class of involuntary actions which do not fit on this chart because they go beyond praise and blame when he says that

On some actions praise indeed is not bestowed, but pardon is, when one does what he ought not under pressure which overstrains human nature and which no one could withstand. (1110a 24-6)

Lest this classification become a moral wild-card permitting all kinds of base action, Aristotle admonishes us to remember that some actions are so **base** that **no** noble purpose could justify them, i.e. the #3 case above.

Since "actions beyond human strength" to resist are not **blameworthy**, we can exclude those that are more base than the noble purposes they aim to serve, i.e. #3, because these are blamed. We can also exclude as blame-worthy those in which one's purpose in surrendering to a threat is either ignoble or trivial, case #2. Finally, since a person is not **praised** for surrendering to a threat "beyond human strength," we can assume that his purpose in committing the base act was not particularly noble either, i.e. case #1.

We are thus left with coerced and **involuntary** actions that are neither **overwhelmingly base** in form (F) and **outcome** (T), nor **outstandingly noble** in intent (T). These would be the actions beyond human strength which do not adequately show or test one's real courage because a courageous person might do the same thing as a coward in such a situation even though his inner attitude would be different.

What kinds of action fit this description? They must involve a threat beyond our power of resistance and for which no noble purpose is served by dying. (In some such circumstances we would even betray our moral responsibilities by taking undue risks.) Something like submitting to heterosexual or homosexual rape would seem to fit these requirements

when the assailant intends and has the power to kill you i
and there are no means of escape.

Self-preservation at any cost is not an outstandingly
compared to taking risks for the welfare of others. Neith
demanded act so condemnably base as to require surrendering
rather than submitting to it. (Aristotle does not contradict thi\   ..1s
discussion of **self-indulgence** at **Rh** II, 10 when he says we should fight
against unwanted advances. The case here, by stipulation, is when we
have no power to offer such resistance.) And while one is not blamed for
surrendering to such coercion, neither is he or she exactly praised for it
either--even if he is respected for having his priorities straight in doing
what offered the best chance to save his life.

No doubt there are many other situations which would allow us to
show how a courageous person might respond to agents "beyond human
strength." But the chief point to keep in mind here is that they do not
differentiate very well between how a courageous person handles them and
how a noncourageous person does. While one does not have to be a
coward to surrender to something "beyond human strength," doing so does
not necessarily reveal one to be courageous.

We can now turn to those threatening cases that are within the
bounds of human strength and which do allow us to differentiate between
virtuous and vicious dispositions to fear and confidence. As always in
matters of virtue and vice, we are concerned with matters of "magnitude
and degree"--the magnitude or number of things (A) arousing fear or confidence and the degree to which people are frightened or made confident
by them (F). Aristotle gives us a causal definition of courage in just
these terms.

b. Courage as the Virtue

Drawing on this idea of the limits of human strength, Aristotle concludes,

> Therefore, while he will fear even the things that are not beyond
> human strength, he will face them as he ought and as reason
> directs, for nobility's sake, for this is the end of virtue. (1115b
> 11-13)

He further clarifies the nature of courage when he says that

> The man, then, who faces and who fears the right things and from
> the right motive, in the right way and at the right time, and who
> feels confidence in the corresponding conditions, is brave; for the
> brave man feels and acts according to the merits of the case and
> in whatever way reason directs. Now the end of every activity is
> conformity to the corresponding state of character. This is true,
> therefore, of the brave man as well as of others. But courage is
> noble. Therefore the end also is noble; for each thing is defined
> by its end. Therefore it is for a noble end that the brave man en-
> dures and acts as courage directs. (1115b 18-23)

COMMENTARY. The guiding principle, or telos (T), of courage (M) is to do and to promote what is noble in the face of threatening agents (A). This purpose dictates a certain form of response (F) given the agent (A) one must deal with and the resources that are part of one's own material causality (M). Surprisingly perhaps to some readers, the courageous man's response is fearful when the agent is in fact a threatening one. Just because cowards are afraid even when there is nothing to fear does not mean courageous people are unafraid when there is a real threat. To assume that brave people are unafraid of real threats is to dishonor them by ignoring how confidently they act even when they are afraid and in pain.

Another characteristic of a courageous form of response (F) is that it is a facing of not only the threatening agent (A) but also, by implication, the person's own wish, goal or purpose (T) that is being threatened. It is decisive to emphasize holding on to the larger goals being threatened because otherwise one might simply escape the threatening agent (A) by giving up the wishes (T) the agent threatens. The basic point about courage and all the other virtues is, after all, that they are the material dispositions which allow us to exercise proper wish, deliberation and choice.

Facing what one fears should not be identified with standing and fighting, however, since it is foolish to fight when clearly outnumbered or outgunned. The point is rather that one's response must be based on the true situation. It must be realistic and reasonable in the circumstances.

Facing the situation realistically means no more than that one center him- or herself in the wish being threatened (T), appraise the agent threatening it (A), and then draw on one's resources for dealing with it (M) in such a way as to make the optimal response (F) to it. Sometimes the courageous thing to do is run like crazy or bide one's time until a better opportunity occurs. All that can be said for certain about the form of courageous responses to genuine threats is that they will be painful and that they will realistically face the threat in the light of one's resources and in a way that serves noble purposes.

Aristotle's focus on final causality (T) is of special interest. The insistence on courage being for a noble end has broad implications for the agents (A) that arouse both a courageous person's fears and his confidence. As we saw much earlier, someone can be a threatening agent only insofar as his wishes and resources are such as to harm a goal or end we care about and wish for. The agent must threaten to interfere with our purposes (T) or with those of someone we consider to be part of ourselves. It is therefore our own commitments and purposes (T) which determine what agents (A) will have the power to threaten us (M).

If our purposes are ignoble, we are not courageous even when we stand up to many threats in pursuing what we want. We might have much spirit and guts, but we are not truly courageous. Many criminals and even successful, legitimate professionals, are gutsy in this sense of taking great risks in pursuing their ambitions (NE IV, 4). The courageous man, on the other hand, "faces... and... fears the right things... from the right motive." The single-minded pursuit of wealth, status or fame simply for their own sake is not a noble motive. While one's skill and audacity might be stunning, there is nothing of lasting beauty or goodness about it. One can succeed in acquiring these things and still be a bad person.

Nobility requires that we search for forms of action that embody and encourage the nobility of man in the face of all agents that threaten human well-being. In tragic circumstances this can mean dying. More commonly in industrialized societies it means risking the displeasure of superiors and the uneasiness and rejection of peers whose dominant wish is more to get along than to live according to high standards.

Here is where courage shows its nobility and dignity before hostile, superior powers. The traditional Jewish maxim "to speak truth to power" so as to leave them no room for self-deception about the justice of their actions expresses a lasting truth here. But nobility also calls for one to hold bravely to higher wishes even when he or she cannot express them outright and must search for more subtle ways to keep these wishes alive in himself and others.

This emphasis on courage as always being for a noble end (T) shows us something more about the **form** of a courageous response (F) when risking one's life or career in pursuing **lost** causes and struggles which will not be won in one's own lifetime. How can we explain the fact of people acting bravely even when they will preserve neither their own lives nor see the triumph of the particular cause they are championing? If a courageous response has to be rational and realistic and there really is nothing a person can do to avert the immediate defeat, how can he or she do anything courageous in the circumstances? The answer to this important question helps us see why **noble wishes** give the courageous person confidence even in situations which would otherwise be considered **hopeless**.

The courageous person wishes above all to protect and promote the nobility of mankind by acting nobly himself. While his specific projects, commitments and friendships manifest this wish, they do not exhaust it. So, as much as he cares about each of his specific commitments and as painful as specific losses will be to him, he must guide his life by a purpose that transcends them. Even in defeat, he or she might still affirm his belief in human dignity and in the possibility of just institutions which provide the necessary environment for human development.

Because of his commitment to these overarching values, his particular losses and defeats do not rob him so entirely of what he or she loves. The other people in his life, and humanity as a whole, might have a greater chance for happiness and development because of his or her sacrifice in taking his best shot in the circumstances. There is nobility and beauty in that even when nobody notices. As long as he can keep his eye on this deeper wish, he will less easily surrender to the feeling that any particular loss or combination of losses means he has lost everything of value to him.

A person who loves acting nobly and promoting nobility in others does not live just for himself, and does not find pleasure solely in his own comfort. Ignoble wishes rooted in vices, on the other hand, such as excessive **ambition**, dependent **love**, or **greed** for money, make one more afraid of threats to these desires than one should be. The person, for example, who wishes above all **to be loved** rather than **to love** feels like he risks everything by getting close to someone who might not indulge his deep desire to be taken care of and supported. They are thus inclined to be excessively self-protective and inwardly isolated from others regardless of the appearance they might give of being close to a great many people. The wish, on the other hand, actively to love and befriend others gives one a higher and sustaining purpose to fall back on when particular efforts and commitments do not work out.

c. Recklessness as the Vice of Deficient Fear

Having established the nature of **courage**, we now examine the first of the three **vices** associated with it. Aristotle says that

> Of those who go to excess he who exceeds in fearlessness has no name (we have said previously that many states of character have no names), but he would be a sort of **madman** or **insensible** person if he feared nothing, neither earthquakes nor the waves, as they say the Celts do not... (1115b 24-8)

While Aristotle tells us the Greeks had no name for this character orientation, we will speak of it in English as **recklessness**.

COMMENTARY. The expression "exceeds in fearlessness" is an awkward way of saying that someone is **deficiently fearful.** As we will see below, Aristotle believes the reckless or the excessively-spirited person is better characterized by his **lack of fear** than by his boasting about his **confidence** that he can handle a threat successfully. Even though such excessively-spirited behavior is a **vice**, it is often confused with courage. The Greek terms Aristotle used to describe a person with this trait, translated here as "madman or insensible," provide an important key for understanding this attitude and linking it with what he says at **NE** III, 8, discussed in a later section.

The first of these Greek terms is **"mainomenos"** which means one who is in a rage or furious, one mad with wine or in a frenzy like Dionysius. The English "manic" and "maniac" can probably be traced back to this Greek root. The idea is that being in a frenzy over what one is doing distorts one's perception of how threatening things really are.

The manic aspect of this vice thus implies our having such a strong desire for a goal (T) that we underestimate the threat posed by real conditions (A). One's form of response (F) is then inappropriate to the threatening agent (A) and might not function (T) to handle it properly. Characteristically one throws himself recklessly against the agent when a more circumspect response would not only place the actor in less jeopardy, but would offer a more realistic promise of success in handling it.

Yet to say the person **cares too much** for his goal (T) is misleading and incorrect. This supposed "caring too much" means in practice not caring enough to deliberate about the best course of action and discipline oneself to act accordingly. Surely one's readiness to sacrifice himself without due reflection on his options and longer-range ability to contribute makes one wonder whether the reckless person does not have a secret agenda and wishes that are different from his stated ones. Perhaps the hidden agenda when one is talking about religious zealots, for example, is an excessive **ambition** to become part of an other-worldly elect, and/or a **cowardly** desire to escape painful threats and duties in **this** world?

What is vicious in the excessively-spirited character is thus its failure to fit forms of response (F) to the threatening agent (A) in the way best calculated to bring about the declared purpose (T). We can conclude then that since this attitude does not exercise **c h o i c e** between options laid before it by its own **deliberations**, it is not pursuing a noble **wish**. The excessively-spirited character undermines right wish, deliberation and choice and is thus by definition a vice.

The second Greek word is translated as "insensible" (**analgetos**) and adds another dimension to our explanation of how this character trait "exceeds in fearlessness." The Greek is the root for our "analgesic" which refers to pain-killers like aspirin. Unlike "anaesthesia" (**an-aesthetic** or without sensation), an analgesic deadens our sensitivity only to pain and not to all sensation. Anaesthesia knocks us out and puts us to sleep, while an analgesic allows us to continue functioning in the face of pains that would otherwise stop us.

Our earlier analysis of the mechanism of fear in **R h** II, 5 helps explain why an analgesic or insensible character will be excessively fearless. Put simply, since fear is the anticipation of pain, a person deficiently sensitive to pain will be deficiently afraid and inclined to rush into situations believing he cannot be hurt.

Insensitivity to one's own pain also explains how such a reckless person is inclined to be hard-hearted and ruthless to **others**. The virtues of **generosity, friendliness, pity** and **indignation** are all concerned with the pleasures and pains of others and are obviously impaired if one is insensitive to pain. How can one be responsive to the pain of others when he is insensitive to his own? With a lack of both inner and outer sensitivity, the reckless fanatic loses a major source of knowledge about himself and the world. He can no longer monitor and correct his behavior with reference to the pain and damage he causes and cannot discipline his aggressive impulses very effectively.

What could cause such insensitivity to pain in the first place? In some cases there may be a constitutional deficiency (M), as with psychopathic personalities. In other cases environmental factors (A) might be so powerful as to nurture the attitude even in those not particularly disposed to it. Lest the reader forget that we are talking about the excessive range of a common, normal phenomenon, we remind him, for example, that athletes frequently become so ambitiously involved in a game that they discover only after it is over how painfully they were hurt during it. But one does not have to be an athlete, of course, to become so involved in doing something that he fails to notice when he bruised his leg or scratched his hand.

Biochemists have discovered that the brain produces its own morphene-like analgesics called endorphins. One suspects that the rituals of fiercely fanatical cultures, like the ancient Celts, promoted the kinds of frenzied activity which produce these organic pain-killers. For such a result to occur, it would seem necessary that the fanatic's goal include not only that one sacrifice him- or herself, but that he make no true commitment to the development of specific other people either. Otherwise, they would have to retain and develop their sensitivity to both their own pain and vulnerability and that of others. The fanatic's goal, whether religious, political, or careerist, must be attainable independently of concrete human relations based on sensitivity and caring. Is it any wonder, then, that fanatacism is so characteristically other-worldly?

A kind of fanatacism thus occurs whenever we aggressively pursue goals without reference to their moral-emotional effects on the people involved. We become insensitive to our own experience and inner states (both painful and pleasant) insofar as they do not directly contribute to the success of our ambitions. The vice of **recklessness** is thus causally linked to the vice of **excessive ambition** (NE IV, 4).

Up to a certain point, the more people deaden their sensitivity to themselves and to each other, the more they can throw themselves into the fray. But aggressive, single-minded professionals show the vice of recklessness when they are indifferent to the effects of their careers on their families, their coworkers, and their own moral and emotional development. Career success in no way diminishes the vicious effects of ignoble **aims**, inadequate **deliberation** about more humane life approaches, and the lame excuse of having no **choice** in what one must do to pursue these wishes. Ignoble wishes are defined and characterized by the way in which they impoverish one's deliberation and undermine one's sense of choice.

d. Macho-Boastfulness as the Vice of Excessive Confidence

In contrast to the reckless person's deficient fear which we just described, we now confront the vice found in the person whose confidence is in excess of his actual performance. Aristotle says that

the man who exceeds in confidence about what really is ter- rible is macho. The macho man, however, is also thought to be boastful and only a pretender to courage; at all events, as the brave man IS with regard to what is terrible, so the macho man wishes to APPEAR; and so he imitates him in situations where he can. Hence also most of them are a mixture of macho and cowardice; for, while in these situations they display confidence, they do not hold their ground against what is really terrible. (1115b 28-34)

Here the emphasis is on the excessive quality of the person's claims about his confidence rather than on his being deficient in his fear the way the reckless person is.

Aristotle contrasts this **macho-boaster** character with both the **coward** proper and the **brave** or **courageous** person.

The coward, the macho man, and the brave man, then are con cerned with the same objects but are differently disposed toward them; for the first two exceed and fall short, while the third holds the middle, which is the right, position; and macho men are precipitate, and wish for dangers beforehand but draw back when they are in them, while brave men are keen in the moment of ac- tion, but quiet beforehand. (1116a 4-9)

The coward is most noteworthy for the way he **exceeds in fear** while the macho-boaster appears to **fall short**.

COMMENTARY. The reader can best picture the present vice by thinking of the **macho** or **bully** character who loves to talk big until he is actually put to the test. The true macho combines **boasting** about his courage with **insolent-sadism** toward weaker people as described at **Rh** II, 2. These vices can, however, occur separately. While most boasters are actually cowards, some are courageous when the chips are down.

The macho character is a complex one. We can distinguish the following vices as implied in Aristotle's account of the macho-boaster's character starting with his implicit **purpose** (T). By pretending to courage, the macho-boaster acts in a form (F) that brings him a kind of **honor** and **respect** which he has not earned and does not deserve (T). This desired honor implies the vices of excessive **ambition** and the **vanity** of needing to maintain an image in his own eyes as well.

Aristotle distinguishes between those macho-boasters who are cowards and those who are not. When a macho person who has courage boasts about it, his vice would seem to be in his **vanity** or **ambition** rather than in his fear and confidence proper. As such his particular character flaw would not constitute one of the vices associated with **courage**. But such cases mask the essential lack of confidence and self-assurance that drives one to boast in the first place, and suggest that it would be more accurate to say that such a person lacked faith in his or her own considerable potential for courage.

Aristotle's focus here is precisely on the macho-boaster's **cowardice** which underlies the **untruthfulness** and exaggeration associated with this kind of **vanity** and excessive **ambition**. They wish to satisfy their excessive ambition and vanity to be thought brave (T) more than to act nobly in the face of danger. Their ignoble goal can actually be detected in the quality of the macho-boaster's responses (F) to the threat. Careful observation reveals him to be a **pretender**--"as the brave man IS with regard to what is terrible, so the macho man wishes to APPEAR." His actions are imitations without the intent and spirit of the courageous people they imitate. The form of their behavior (F) does not fit the function (T) it should serve. The macho-boaster has a secret plot (T) and wishes only to **appear** brave, not to be so.

The macho-boaster's timing permits him to pose as having confidence in excess of his or her real feelings. This becomes apparent with the changes that come over him when the danger actually draws near and he is challenged to prove himself. The ambitious fantasies he had sought to indulge must then be abandoned when the time for action finally arrives.

What is vicious in this attitude? In the first place, it represents an **improper wish** to gratify our excessive ambition while avoiding the painful risks involved in trying to act nobly. We act in an unseemly manner, and at the very least mislead and demoralize others about our reliability. In doing so we betray the people and purposes we should protect. Second, as a result of this improper wish, we **deliberate** about what will make us **look good** rather than about what noble purposes (T), the threat (A) and our resources (M), call upon us to do (F). Finally, we are unaware of the **choices** we should be making in the circumstances, instead of merely surrendering to our ambitious fantasies about how we want others to see us.

e. Cowardice as the Vice of Excessive Fear and Deficient Confidence

Finally, Aristotle comments on the third vice associated with courage, **cowardice** proper.

> The man who exceeds in fear is a coward; for he fears both what he ought not and as he ought not, and all the similar circumstances attach to him. He is lacking also in confidence; but he is more conspicuous for his excess of fear in painful situations. The coward, then, is a despairing sort of person, for he fears everything. The brave man, on the other hand, has the opposite disposition; for confidence is the mark of a hopeful disposition. (1115b 34-1116a 4)

While cowardice shows itself most markedly by an excess of fear, it also reveals itself by a despairing lack of confidence in one-self and a lack of hope about what one can accomplish and endure. We have been led to expect this relation, of course, by what we learned earlier about the interdependence of fear and confidence.

Aristotle next alerts us to the fact that unless we pay careful attention to the motives behind people's actions we can confuse courage with what is in fact a suicidal fleeing from life which is sometimes confused with courage. He thus observes,

> As we have said, then, courage is a mean with respect to things that inspire confidence or fear, in the circumstances that have been stated; and it chooses or endures things because it is noble to do so, or because it is base not to do so. But to die to escape from poverty or love or anything painful is not the mark of a brave man, but rather of a coward; for it is softness to fly from what is troublesome, and such a man endures death not because it is noble but to fly from evil. (1116a 10-4)

Courageous people sacrifice their lives only for noble purposes and out of a love for life, not to flee from it.

COMMENTARY. As always, we see the decisiveness of wish, purpose and intentionality (T). Just because a person is willing to die in battle or otherwise commit suicide does not make him brave. The courageous person makes the best of painful economic and love situations rather than wishing to die because of them. He is enabled to overcome such problems by developing the virtues of making and using money, i.e. **generosity** (NE IV, 1), and of **friendliness** and **love** (Rh II, 4 & NE IV, 6).

Like any other man, the generous, friendly and loving person will be greatly hurt by losses in any of these areas, and may well need an extended mourning period for recovery. But just as his original attitude toward the things he has lost was rooted in virtue, so too his ability to love other people and to generate the money he needs exists as a need and telos (T) within himself (M). This ongoing, life-sustaining wish allows him to transcend the particular losses he has suffered.

We thus see clearly how **courage** underlies the virtues of **generosity** and **love**. If **any** man or woman can handle such losses, it will be the courageous person who has the other virtues appropriate for the task. People without courage, on the other hand, are characteristically over-whelmed when their love relationships do not work out the way they wish or when they suffer financial reverses. They become afraid to love again or to risk new economic initiatives, and begin to dry up inside.

The formula for determining fear and confidence has as its **denominator** the person's own **wishes** times his **resources** for re-sponding to the threatening agent. Cowardice introduces such a weak wish for noble action into the equation that the cowardly person utilizes nowhere near his true resources. Cowardice occurs in those situations where a person has the resources, for example, to take care of himself economically or to make new friends and love other people. But the cowardly person does not do the things he could because of his or her excessive fear. We can thus see very clearly that higher level virtues such as generosity and love depend on courage and collapse with it.

Aristotle's comments about the interaction between **h o p e** and **despair** also show how courage is related to other virtues and vices. Hopeful and despairing dispositions (M) give rise respectively to confident or fearful forms of response (F). We can see, for example, that when the **envious** person (**Rh** II, 10) shows excessive pain at another's good for-tune and despairs about his own well-being and prospects, he is also showing his lack of courage.

The **emulous** man (**Rh** II, 11), on the other hand, shows his courage when he responds hopefully and confidently to the pain he feels at not at-taining what he sees that others have accomplished and what he knows he is capable of. This hopefulness and confidence allows him to go out and emulate them rather than being eaten up with envy and reacting to their success with spite and impotent rage.

What then is vicious about cowardice? In the first place, it turns us away from the **w i s h** to act nobly both for ourselves and for others. The wish to love, create and accomplish truly fine things requires a deep faith in our resources and firmness in holding to our purposes. We must be strong and abiding in our purposes, resilient in response to set-backs, and prepared to sacrifice to remain true to a noble purpose. Cowardice erodes the very foundation of such purposiveness by replacing it with the contrary wish for safety and security above all.

With its despairing disposition, cowardice undermines our con-fidence and demoralizes our **deliberation**. We are paralyzed and do not search for alternate responses to the threat since these too might expose us to painful risks. Our estimation of the threat and how best to deal with it is not true to its reality, to our resources and our highest wishes. We underestimate our resources while exaggerating the malignant intent and power of threatening agents. Seeing things as more threatening than they are, and seeing more things as threatening, we live in needless pain and suffer a paralysis of perception, planning and spontaneous learning.

Cowards feel compelled to flee the threats they perceive and effec-tively surrender the power to **choose** how they will live. Their life options are more and more circumscribed by the things they must avoid and to which they must adjust their deepest wishes and all their plans accord-ingly. Proper wish, deliberation and choice are thus deeply compromised by cowardice.

3. ATTITUDES CONFUSED WITH COURAGE (NE III, 8)

After differentiating courage from the various **vices**   that are associated with it, Aristotle then carefully distinguishes courage from attitudes that are often **confused with it**. As he says by way of transition,

> Courage, then, is something of this kind, but the name is also
> applied to five other kinds. (1116a 15)

Just as in Aristotle's time, people today still commonly call all sorts of
things courageous that really are not. As we saw earlier, Aristotle concluded that battle provides the clearest test of courage. But even in
response to this one kind of threat, he found the following kinds of attitude commonly confused with courage. Many of them are found in non-
battle situations as well of course.

a. The Citizen-Soldier and the Conscript

Aristotle begins by making a careful distinction between courage
and two attitudes commonly found in citizen armies. The first is that of
the **citizen-soldier**.

> First comes the courage of the citizen soldier; for this is most
> like true courage. Citizen-soldiers seem to face dangers because
> of the penalties imposed by the laws and the reproaches they
> would otherwise incur, and because of the honors they win by
> such action; and therefore those peoples seem to be bravest
> among whom cowards are held in dishonor and brave men in
> honor. This is the kind of courage that Homer depicts, e.g. in
> Diomede and in Hector: "First will Polydamus be to heap reproach
> on me then"; and "For Hector one day 'mid the Trojans shall utter
> his vaulting harangue: 'Afraid was Tydeides, and fled from my
> face'." This kind of courage is most like that which we described
> earlier, because it is due to virtue; for it is due to **s h a m e** and
> to **desire of a noble object** (i.e. honor) and avoidance of dis-
> grace, which is ignoble. (1116a 16-29)

The second is that of the **conscript**.

> One might rank in the same class even those who are compelled
> by their rulers; but they are inferior, inasmuch as they do what
> they do not from **shame** but from **fear,** and to avoid not what is
> disgraceful but what is painful; for their masters compel them, as
> Hector does: "But if I shall spy any dastard that cowers far from
> the fight,/ Vainly will such an one hope to escape from the

dogs." And those who give them their posts, and beat them if they retreat, do the same, and so do those who draw them up with trenches or something of the sort behind them; all of these apply compulsion. But one ought to be brave not under compulsion but because it is noble to be so. (1116a 30-b 2)

These two together constitute the first of Aristotle's list of five attitudes confused with courage.

COMMENTARY. Neither of these two attitudes is fully courageous because neither is animated by the proper noble wish (T). Rather than courage, **shame** (**Rh** II, 6 and **NE** IV, 9) and **ambition** (**NE** IV, 4) explain the **citizen-soldier's** response. He wishes to be thought well of by others and fears being shamed in their eyes. This is honorable, of course, but he actually cares more about what they think of him than he does about acting rightly for its own sake.

The highest sense of acting for the sake of nobility comes from one's own love of proper action, even if no one else learns of it, and not from a concern for what others will think. The ethical wish must be genuinely internalized if one is to have moral and emotional independence in the face of one's environment. (A genuinely wicked person is also independent from what others think of him, but his wishes are ignoble.)

Like shame, the wish to **emulate** others and earn their respect and love is essential to human development, both individually and socially. But it must be no more than a transitional wish if it is not to limit people to established patterns of appropriate behavior that might become inappropriate in changed circumstances. Should the wish to be honored by the best of the established authorities be elevated to an ultimate principle, narrow fashion could eventually replace the love of the truth in judging what is noble in the event that less noble people come to power.

At some point, morally-gifted people must follow their own judgement beyond what others **have** seen and perhaps even beyond what they are **capable** of seeing at the time. While courageous action might be congruent behaviorally with what one's fellows expect in a courageous society and when issues are well defined, it is never **essentially** a matter of what others expect. Courageous action can even be opposed to their expectations when a more noble person sees beyond them.

The wish for honor and the ambition for a decent standing among our fellows can help us withstand painful threats when we lack courage's wish for noble action. The citizen-soldier's attitude thus represents a development beyond the **conscript's** indifference to what others think. The conscript's greater fear undermines such **ambitions** (NE IV, 4) and **friendly** concern for others' pains and pleasures (**Rh** II, 4 & **NE** IV, 6). The conscript might still fight, but it would be from the wish to flee the painful consequences of what **his own side** will do to him if he does not, rather than from his wish to keep their respect. The conscript example shows again how one can act from cowardice even when he stands and fights. He is simply more afraid of his **leaders** than of the **enemy**.

Such coercion will no doubt always occur in war and in other cases in which people are mobilized to fight against threats to their well-being or simply against their leaders. But it is important to see that it is not courage which is motivating their involvement in the conflict. Of the two attitudes we have just considered, that of the citizen-soldier is the more nearly courageous.

b. The Confidence of the Professional

Professionals are also often thought to be courageous. Aristotle focuses here on the battle situation, but his remarks clearly have a broader significance for all professionals.

> Experience with regard to particular facts is also thought to be courage; this is indeed the reason why Socrates thought courage was knowledge. Other people exhibit this quality in other dangers, and professional soldiers exhibit it in the dangers of war; for there seem to be many empty alarms in war, of which these have had the most comprehensive experience; therefore they seem brave, because the others do not know the nature of the facts. Again, their experience makes them most capable in attack and in defense, since they can use their arms and have the kind that are likely to be best for attack and for defense; therefore they fight like armed men against unarmed or like trained athletes against amateurs; for in such contests too it is not the bravest men that fight best, but those who are strongest and have their bodies in the best condition. Professional soldiers turn cowards, however, when the danger puts too great a strain on them and they are inferior in numbers and equipment; for they are the first to fly, while citizen-forces die at their posts, as in fact happened at the temple of Hermes. For to the latter flight is disgraceful and death is preferable to safety on those terms; while the former from the very beginning faced the danger on the assumption that they were stronger, and when they know the facts they fly, fearing death more than disgrace; but the brave man is not that sort of person. (1116b 3-23)

COMMENTARY. While Aristotle describes an attitude here that characterizes the confidence of professionals in many fields, it is perhaps misleading in the modern context to apply the term "professional soldiers" to this attitude. Aristotle's reference is actually to what we would call **mercenaries** rather than professional soldiers **per se.** Today's military professionals are more apt to be motivated by the fear of acting shamefully and by the desire for honor which Aristotle attributed to the **citizen-soldiers** of his time. Modern military culture shows an exaggerated preoccupation with **shame** and **honor** as the organizing motivation at the professional level.

Freud teaches us to see how this exaggerated sense of honor and formality is over-determined by a second function (T) it performs. The military function requires soldiers to cultivate their capacity for violence and hate against enemies against whom they feel no personal anger. The shaming insults to a soldier's independence and self-respect which the culture inflicts actually helps cultivate the inner violence required to carry out the military's function. The culture's exaggerated formality then serves to control the very anger it helps to bring into being. The emphasis on **honor** and **shame** is thus central to this subculture's mission of carrying out the military's function regardless of the nobility of the cause it serves.

At present, though, we are talking about Aristotle's analysis of "mercenaries." The confidence they bring to threatening situations nicely illustrates the difference between one's **wishes** and his **resources** in the denominator of the formula for fear and confidence. Our wishes constitute the **moral power** with which we are able to use the resources available to us. Our **resources**, on the other hand, determine only the potential range of response (F) we could make if we used our full potential.

The virtue of courage is that it allows us to make optimal use (F) of our resources (M) relative to our purposes (T) and the challenge posed by the threatening agent (A). It would be just as foolish, for example, to work at full capacity at inappropriate times the way the fanatic does, as it would be to surrender a well-fortified and well-provisioned position just because one could not stand the tension of an approaching fight.

The **mercenary** shows us someone with great resources to draw on, who nonetheless lacks the strong sense of moral purpose required for using them properly. His **weapons** extend his material power beyond that of his opponents just as his training and experience extend his physical and cognitive powers beyond theirs. And his greater cognitive virtue in the ways of war heightens his awareness and allows him to see the intent and resources of the enemy more accurately than a less well-trained soldier can.

These advantages in his cognitive resources increase the **denominator** while tending to diminish the **numerator** in the formula for his fear and confidence--which makes him afraid of fewer things. But it would be a mistake to attribute to his **moral** virtue and motivation what is actually a result of his **cognitive** virtue and his superiority in other **resources**. He is less afraid not because he is more **courageous**, but because he has a more developed capacity to know what he is facing, and has the additional resources we have mentioned. A less experienced but more courageous person would actually be more afraid in the same circumstances because he would be naturally inclined to misjudge his enemy's immediate intent and capacity.

This example illustrates how important it is to understand the dynamic relation between the **moral** and the **intellectual** virtues and vices, and the need to identify where a problem lies in assessing the moral and emotional significance of anyone's behavior. Is the problem simply cognitive or is it rooted in a moral and emotional vice that characteristically distorts the person's perceptions? The importance of the complex mechanism of their interaction signals again the inadequacy of a **positivist** methodology that would be content to know only whether someone was afraid (F) without discovering the underlying causality (M) of his or her response.

The mercenary shows he was not fighting for the sake of nobility when he runs away from his cause in the face of unexpected defeat. Flight seems neither cowardly nor a real betrayal to the mercenary because he was never morally committed to the cause which he now abandons. He was there in a professional and not in a personal capacity. The brave man, on the other hand, does not run away when doing so would betray a noble wish that he lives for and is willing to die for.

Finally, by distinguishing between motive and resources, Aristotle is breaking with the much older Homeric conception that identified courage with dominance and success. Since one man's resources might be greater than another's, the stronger man with the greater resources can dominate an exchange even though his moral strength was actually much less than that of the man he triumphs over. The effect of this differential in resources explains Aristotle's observation that "it is not the bravest men who fight the best."

c. The Confidence of the Angry

Courage is also confused with having an **angry, excessively-spirited** or **passionate** temperament.

> Passion also is sometimes reckoned as courage; those who act from passion, like wild beasts rushing at those who have wounded them, are thought to be brave, because brave men also are passionate; for passion above all things is eager to rush on danger, and hence Homer's "put strength into his passion" and "aroused their spirit and passion" and "hard he breathed panting" and "his blood boiled." For all such expressions seem to indicate the stirring and onset of passion. (1116b 23-9)

Aristotle then differentiates various ends which passion or anger might pursue.

> Now brave men act for **nobility's** sake, but passion aids them; while wild beasts act under the influence of pain; for they attack because they have been wounded or because they are afraid, since if they are in a forest they do not come near one. Thus they are not brave because, driven by pain and passion, they rush on danger without foreseeing any of the perils, since at that rate even asses would be brave when they are hungry; for blows will not drive them from their food; and lust also makes adulterers do many daring things. (Those creatures are not brave, then, which are driven on to danger by pain or passion.) The "courage" that is due to passion seems to be the most natural, and to be courage if choice and motive be added. (1116b 30 - 1117a 4)

And finally he contrasts courage with anger.

> Men, then, as well as beasts, suffer pain when they are angry, and are pleased when they exact their revenge; those who fight for these reasons, however, are pugnacious but not brave; for they do not act for nobility's sake and according to **reason**, but from strength of feeling; they have, however, something akin to courage. (1117a 5-8)

COMMENTARY. The Greek term here is **"thume"** which means anger, spirit and passion, as can be seen by its various references at different points in the text. We have already encountered it to some extent in examining the vice of **recklessness** or **excessive spirit**. In the present context, though, Aristotle's focus is not on its character as a vice but on its being confused with courage.

Aristotle identifies several purposes (T) excessive spirit or passion can pursue. One is **anger's** wish for revenge against the source of an injury (**R h** II, 2 & **N E** IV, 5). Another is the desperate effort to flee pain. Finally, there is **lust**'s desire for food or sex. This is a matter of **self-indulgence** (**NE** III, 11). In all these cases, the desire is strong enough for the person or animal to withstand great pain and fearful threats in order to attain a goal. None of these desires necessarily aims at what is noble, however.

Aristotle's point is to show the error of confusing courage with the great passion shown by those who are angry, by cowards when they are cornered, or lustful people when they are aroused. They show little or no **choice** and **deliberation**, and certainly none motivated by noble **wishes**. Yet anyone with such a high level of energy would surely be quite courageous if he ever came to love noble action and learned to deliberate and make his own choices, instead of just reacting wildly to things based on uncultivated feelings.

Elsewhere Aristotle speaks of such spiritedness as a kind of **natural courage**, a constitutional disposition or gift for courage that **can** be cultivated to something very valuable. We might add, too, that if their gift of passion is not given a noble direction and objective, what could have been a great gift for both its possessor and for society can become a terrible curse and threat. A significant number of inner-city criminals, for example, display just this waste of great human spirit. Unfortunately, less highly spirited people tend to be threatened by displays of passion and deep feeling and lead young people to think of their forcefulness in negative terms instead of motivating them to make something wonderful out of it.

d. The Confidence of the Overly-Optimistic

People also confuse a false sense of optimism and omnipotence with courage.

> Nor are sanguine people brave; for they are confident in danger only because they have conquered often and against many foes. Yet they closely resemble brave men, because both are confident, but brave men are confident for the reasons stated earlier, while these are so because they think they are stronger and can suffer nothing. (Drunken men also behave in this way; they become sanguine.) When their adventures do not succeed, however, they run away; but it was the mark of a brave man to face things that are, and seem, terrible for a man, because it is noble to do so and disgraceful not to do so. Hence also it is thought the mark of a braver man to be fearless and undisturbed in sudden alarms than to be so in those that are foreseen; for it must have proceeded more from a state of character, because less from preparation; acts that are foreseen may be chosen by calculation and rule, but sudden actions must be in accordance with one's state of character. (1117a 9-21)

COMMENTARY. The Greek for sanguine or optimistic is **"euelpides."** The "eu-" shows up in words like "eulogy" and "euphoria" and signifies something like "being well-situated with respect to..." Here it refers to a person who is expectant that things will turn out well, the way somebody who has had too much to drink feels when he is about to undertake something. While Aristotle speaks of these people as having been victorious in the past, his emphasis is not on the experiences that would give them the professional's confidence but on their generally optimistic attitude. His point is more moral and emotional than a matter of the resources they bring to the encounter.

These overly-optimistic people think they are stronger than anyone else and cannot be hurt. In short, they are **vain** (NE IV, 3) or narcissistic. They have the courage of their narcissism but only until they realize that they have misjudged the situation. Lacking noble purpose there is nothing to hold them to the task in the face of their fearful discovery.

Aristotle seems to be saying, too, that like men who get drunk, this type person has to work himself up into a state of confidence. He talks himself into thinking he is stronger than anybody and cannot be hurt. He is not so brave, however, when faced with sudden, unexpected threats. And it is these that are the best test of one's character. We must add, though, that **morally-strong**, as opposed to fully **self-controlled** people might also react poorly when first confronted with a challenge. But morally-strong people find their strength when they have thought it through.

e. The Confidence of Those Ignorant of the Danger

Finally, people can appear courageous when actually they are simply acting in ignorance of the real threat.

> People who are ignorant of the danger also appear brave, and they are not far removed from those of a sanguine temper, but are inferior inasmuch as they have no self-reliance while these have. Hence also the sanguine hold their ground for a time; but those who have been deceived about the facts fly if they know or suspect that these are different from what they supposed, as happened to the Argives when they fell in with the Spartans and took them for Sicyonians. (1117a 21-8)

COMMENTARY. The Greek here is **"agnoonetes"** which provides the root for our "agnostic" (**a-gnosis**). The type under discussion feels confident when he does not know who he is really fighting and underestimates his opponent's strength. This is a mistake concerning the numerator in the formula for determining fear and confidence, i.e. the opponent's intent and capacities. Mercenaries, vain narcissists, and the simply ignorant all run away when they recognize how they have underestimated their opponent, because they have no higher motive to keep them in the fight. But they do so for different reasons.

We can distinguish the mercenaries from the other two by their having special training and resources which realistically build up their confidence. They see the situations they are in very clearly and leave when the odds turn against them. Vain optimists, on the other hand, want so much to believe in their own superiority that it takes them a while to see the extent to which reality is not living up to their expectations. Aristotle caught this fact by noting that they "hold their ground for a while," but it might be a little misleading to speak of this as "self-reliance." The last case seems to be lacking in emotional motivation and to be simply a matter of misperception, perhaps through the enemy's trickery.

4. COURAGE RELATES TO BOTH PAIN AND PLEASURE (NE III, 9)

a. Painful Means Test Our Wish for a Pleasant End

Aristotle's next task is to establish the way in which courage is more concerned with **fear** than with **confidence**.

> Though courage is concerned with feelings of confidence and of fear, it is not concerned with both alike, but more with the things that inspire fear; for he who is undisturbed in face of these and bears himself as he should toward them is more truly brave than the man who does so toward the things that inspire confidence. It is for facing what is painful, then, as has been said, that men are called brave. Hence also courage involves pain, and is justly praised; for it is harder to face what is painful than to abstain from what is pleasant. Yet the end which courage sets before it would seem to be pleasant, but to be concealed by the attending circumstances, as happens also in athletic contests; for the end at which boxers aim is pleasant--the crown and the honors--but the blows they take are distressing to flesh and blood, and painful, and so is their whole exertion; and because the blows and the exertions are many the end, which is but small, appears to have nothing pleasant in it. And so, if the case of courage is similar, death and wounds will be painful to the brave man and against his will, but he will face them because it is noble to do so or because it is base not to do so. (1117a 27-b 9)

COMMENTARY. While cowards are afraid even of things that pose **no real threat**, and courageous people are confident before these same things, such confidence is not a very good mark of courage. Courage shows itself much better when there really is something to be afraid of in the light of the person's resources. Fear is painful, and the courageous man is most noted for his ability to work well even when in pain. Pain does not make him give up his highest **wishes** or lose his ability to **deliberate** and **choose** well; and because he chooses well, he acts well in confronting such threats.

The thought of satisfying his goal (T) is pleasant to the courageous person, but this does not mean that all the forms of response (F) he must make to a threatening agent (A) are pleasant. Yet he must endure this pain to attain the objective which will give him a higher pleasure and happiness. The person who cannot resist fleeing painful stimuli loses the power to pursue any wish that requires him or her to do so.

The coward does not deliberate about his options nor make choices about how best to pursue his highest goals. These are replaced by the one wish to avoid pain--and that wish leaves him controlled by a painful environment that robs him of his freedom. When men are controlled by the immediate calculus of pleasure and pain and have no eye to higher pleasures, they are determined **by their environment** and lose the power of **self**-control. This shows that the human spirit is not born free but must develop its freedom through the development of courage and the other virtues.

We can add to the impact of **cowardice** the way a **self-indulgent** attitude toward pleasure (**N E** III, 10-2) compounds the loss of freedom before the environment. A person who is only somewhat cowardly yet seriously self-indulgent might hold to his higher purposes (T) in the face of a **threatening** agent (A), but lose his freedom through being seduced by **pleasant** temptations (A). The opportunity for pleasure, no matter how trifling, can distract him from a higher wish. Gratifying his self-indulgence is especially tempting to such a person because it would take his mind away from both the higher goals being threatened and the **shame** he would otherwise feel at betraying them.

This is the basic manipulative principle of the carrot and the stick, Mutt and Jeff police interrogation, an iron hand in a velvet glove, etc. Considerable virtue is required to resist the cowardly temptation to escape frightening responsibilities by hiding in pleasing diversions and fantasies.

b. The Virtuous Person Is The Most Pained By Death

Contrary to what is commonly thought, courageous people are actually **m o r e** pained than others by having to face serious threats. Aristotle says of such a person,

> And the more he is possessed of virtue in its entirety and the happier he is, the more he will be pained at the thought of death; for life is best worth living for such a man, and he is knowingly losing the greatest goods, and this is painful. But he is nonetheless brave, and perhaps all the more so, because he chooses noble deeds of war at that cost. It is not the case, then, with all the virtues that the exercise of them is pleasant, except insofar as it reaches its end. (1117b 9-17)

Still, attaining victory by no means **constitutes** courage.

> It is quite possible that the best soldiers may be not men of this sort but those who are less brave but have no other good; for these are ready to face danger, and they sell their lives for trifling gains. (1117b 17-9)

COMMENTARY. We saw earlier that cowards who lack virtues such as a **generous** ability to support themselves (**N E** IV, 1) or the power to make **friends** and stimulate love in others (**Rh** II, 4 and **NE** IV, 6) can actually **wish** to die to escape from the pain these failures cause them. Death does not threaten their happiness so much as it promises relief from their suffering. With no larger aim in view, they surrender to this reasoning.

The noteworthy implication of this logic is that a truly virtuous, brave person will actually be more afraid of a genuine threat than will a less virtuous person who does not love life so much. The more we love something the more painful it is to think of losing it. The pleasurable fantasy of a noble death can even seduce a person who does not love his own life into reckless sacrifices that a more life-affirming person would reject.

The person who places little value on his life actually can have a competitive edge in some circumstances, however. His deficient sense of self-preservation can allow him to go all-out in fanatically using his resources. He is, after all, risking something he does not care very much about. But this only shows again the need to distinguish success in isolated aspects of life from success at being a good human being. Biographies record countless lives of people who risked everything of moral value to attain great wealth, power, and status--only to die unhappily because the vices developed in pursuing these goals made it impossible to enjoy them once they were attained.

CHAPTER TWO

Handling Eating, Drinking, Sex and Drugs

Inventory

A. THE AGENT THAT BEST REVEALS SELF-CONTROL (NE III, 10)

- Divisions made in identifying the best agents
  for revealing self-indulgence

B. SELF-CONTROL, SELF-INDULGENCE, AND DEPRESSION AS THE VIRTUE AND VICES OF THIS POWER (NE III, 11)

1. NATURAL AND IDIOSYNCRATIC APPETITES

2. SELF-CONTROL CONCERNS PAIN AS WELL AS PLEASURE

3. SELF-INDULGENCE AS THE VICE OF EXCESSIVE PLEASURE

4. DEPRESSION AS THE VICE OF DEFICIENT PLEASURE

5. SELF-CONTROL AS THE VIRTUE

C. THE DEVELOPMENT OF SELF-CONTROL (NE III, 12)

1. VOLUNTARY AND INVOLUNTARY RESPONSES
   TO PLEASURE AND PAIN

2. THE ANALOGY BETWEEN CHILDHOOD IMMATURITY
   AND ADULT SELF-INDULGENCE

3. THE NEED FOR A RULING PRINCIPLE
   TO DISCIPLINE DESIRE DURING THE PROCESS OF DEVELOPMENT

This chapter examines the central moral and emotional power corrupted in alcoholism, drug addiction and sexual promiscuity. Interestingly, the power to find pleasure in physical experience is not examined in **THE ART OF RHETORIC**. The book's silence about how to arouse an audience's **self-indulgent** impulses speaks volumes about the difference between contemporary commercialized societies and ancient Greece since so much of modern advertising rhetoric is geared to this vice along with that of **extravagance** described in the next chapter.

Where the **RHETORIC's** strategy is always to examine 1) how we must picture an **agent** in order to be afraid of him, angry at him, or to pity him, etc. and 2) the **states of mind** we must be in to be disposed to see agents in these ways, the **ETHICS** requires us to isolate the **clearest agent** for determining whether a given moral power functions in a virtuous rather than a vicious manner. The present chapter thus starts with the same issue as that found in the examinations of **courage, generosity** and **high-mindedness.**

A. THE AGENT THAT BEST REVEALS SELF-CONTROL (NE III, 10)

Aristotle identifies **self-control** as the virtuous form of development of our power to deal with pleasurable things and **self-indulgence** as the vice of excess.

Self-control is a mean with regard to pleasures (for it is less, and not in the same way, concerned with pains); self-indulgence also is manifested in the same sphere. Now, therefore, let us determine with what sort of pleasures they are concerned. (**NE** 1117b 24-7)

Aristotle once again pursues the classical method of division to determine which pleasures are most properly associated with self-control. He identifies those things which give people pleasure and then divides them into different classes searching for the best test of whether people are self-controlled or indulgent. The first division he makes is between the pleasures of the **soul** and those of the **body**. These are agents (A) which arouse and give pleasure either to our higher **moral** and **intellectual** powers (M) or to our five **sensory** powers (M).
Aristotle distinguishes between them by saying that

We may assume the distinction between **bodily** pleasures and those of the **soul**, such as love of **honor** and love of **learning**; for the lover of each of these delights in that of which he is a lover; the body being in no way affected, but rather the soul; but men who are concerned with such pleasures are called neither self-controlled nor self-indulgent. Nor, again, are those who are concerned with the other pleasures that are not bodily; for those who are fond of hearing and telling stories and who spend their days on anything that turns up are called **gossips**, but not self-indulgent, nor are those who are pained at the loss of **money** or of **friends**. (**NE** 1117b 27-36)

While we can obviously go wrong in the love of honor or learning, gossip, money or friends, the vices in each of these powers have their own names and are not called **self-indulgence.**
Among the **bodily** pleasures, Aristotle first examines the power of **vision** (M) and its objects (A) to see if people are rightly considered self-indulgent because of some excess in this power.

Self-control must be concerned with **bodily** pleasures, but not all even of these; for those who delight in objects of **vision**, such as colors and shapes and painting, are called neither self-controlled nor self-indulgent; yet it would seem possible to delight even in these either as one should or to excess or to a deficient degree. (1118a 1-7)

His fuller reflections on the pleasures of sight and the other senses will emerge below.

Hearing and its objects are likewise dismissed as primary cases of self-indulgent or self-controlled behavior.

> And so too is it with objects of **hearing**; no one calls those
> who delight extravagantly in music or acting self-indulgent, nor
> those who do so as they ought self-controlled. (1118a 7-8)

While we can indulge to excess in watching and listening to soap-operas, for example, doing so is not the most straightforward sign of being self-indulgent.

With **smell**, Aristotle introduces an important distinction between a sense functioning for the pleasure of **knowing its own object** versus being used to **arouse pleasure in another sensory power.**

> Nor do we apply these names to those who delight in **odor**, unless
> it be incidentally; we do not call those self-indulgent who delight
> in the odor of apples or roses or incense, but rather those who
> delight in the odor of unguents or of dainty dishes; for self-
> indulgent people delight in these because they remind them of the
> objects of their **appetite**. And one may see even other people,
> when they are hungry, delighting in the smell of food; but to
> delight in this kind of thing is the mark of the self-indulgent
> man; for these are objects of appetite to him. (1118a 8-16)

Delight in the **smell** of food or perfumes is self-indulgent when it is used to arouse appetites that were not otherwise pressing at the time. This is markedly different from already being hungry and delighting in the smell of food.

Aristotle insists that man is unique in finding pleasure in smell, hearing and sight not only through their association with the **desire to eat or have sex** but as sources of **discrimination and knowledge in their own right**. This is broadly speaking the sense of **beauty** and the love of truth. Aristotle observes,

> Nor is there in animals other than man any pleasure connected
> with these senses, except incidentally. For dogs do not delight in
> the scent of hares, but in the eating of them, but the scent told
> them the hares were there; nor does the lion delight in the lowing
> of the ox, but in eating it; but he perceived by the lowing that it
> was near, and therefore appears to delight in the lowing; and
> similarly he does not delight because he sees "a stag or a wild
> goat," but because he is going to make a meal of it. Self-control
> and self-indulgence, however, are concerned with the kind of
> pleasures that the other animals share in, which therefore appear
> slavish and brutish; these are touch and taste. (1118a 18-27)

The self-indulgent person is thus functioning like the lower animals when he regresses to this attitude. Finding genuine pleasure in hearing, sight, and smell means opening ourselves to the reality of things in their own right. This is a uniquely **human** power, or at least one that functions at a qualitatively higher level in us than in other animals.

Taste too can be used to discriminate and know its object in its own right as opposed to being used to satisfy other powers. Self-indulgent people subvert this power's mature functioning in the same way they do the others.

> But even of **taste** they appear to make little or no use; for the business of taste is the discriminating of flavors, which is done by wine-tasters and people who season dishes; but they hardly take pleasure in making these discriminations, or at least self-indulgent people do not, but in the actual enjoyment, which in all cases comes through touch, both in the case of food and in that of drink and in that of sexual intercourse. This is why a certain gourmand prayed that his throat might become longer than a crane's, implying that it was the contact that he took pleasure in. (1118a 27-35)

Touch is thus the primary sensory power in which self-indulgence and self-control occur because it bends the operation of the others to its own satisfaction.

Self-indulgence is blameworthy because it leads us to approach the agents (A) of our experience not as mature, developed human beings (M) but on the same basis as animals (M). The self-indulgent person wishes to know and experience things as **objects of physical gratification** rather than as sources of delight in knowing them for their own sake.

> Thus the sense with which self-indulgence is connected is the most widely shared of the senses; and self-indulgence would seem to be justly a matter of reproach, because it attaches to us not as men but as animals. To delight in such things, then, and to love them above all others, is brutish. For even of the pleasures of touch the most liberal have been eliminated, e.g. those produced in the gymnasium by rubbing and by the consequent heat; for the contact characteristic of the self-indulgent man does not affect the whole body but only certain parts. (1118b 1-7)

Self-indulgence thus cripples our uniquely human power to know and enjoy the world.

COMMENTARY. While Aristotle's examination might appear rather technical, it will nonetheless allow us to penetrate quite deeply into the heart of the self-indulgent person and gain a more practical understanding of what self-control is and how it is developed. The main theme will be that self-control can only occur when we have developed higher order wishes for ourselves according to which we make our deliberations and choices. Lacking such dominant wishes, we will be controlled not by ourselves but by whatever pleasing temptations and distractions present themselves. The self-indulgent person is literally controlled by such rewards in his environment and seems to be the kind of centerless character envisioned by the cruder forms of behaviorism.

Our interpretation of Aristotle's analysis of this moral power is influenced by Freud's **THREE ESSAYS ON THE THEORY OF SEXUALITY** and by Ernest Schachtel's **METAMORPHOSIS: On the Development of Affect, Perception, Attention, and Memory**. Freud argued--in a way that is easily assimilable to Aristotle's theory--that a too early stimulation of a person's **sexual** power can make it so dominant in the field of his or her **other** moral powers that he will be unable to develop mature interests in the world. This premature arousal leaves the still-developing young person so preoccupied with sex that he becomes incapable of developing and taking delight in his other powers.

In Freud's rather awkward terminology and theory, such a person is unable to **sublimate** his **sexual** energies into other, culturally more acceptable forms. In Aristotelian terms, on the other hand, we are not talking about some kind of **transformation of energy** from one form to another but about the **dominance** of one moral power and the **recessiveness** and limited development of others.

Schachtel carries the same insight about the threat of self-indulgence into the **cognitive** realm in explaining the transition from what he calls the **auto-centric** to the **allo-centric** orientation. He argues that the ability to discipline one's desires for physical indulgence is a moral and emotional prerequisite to realistic perception and the development of our attention span and memory. When restlessly worried about gratifying ourselves, we are impatient and distracted, unable to attend to the needs, interests and complexities of other people and things, and thus not very affected by or thoughtful about them. Self-control is thus a key to developing many other virtues, and as we will see, depends in its own right on developing them.

We must add, however, that if taken too far, a self-controlled refusal of pleasures competing with one's single-minded ambitions can lead to a cognition distorting preoccupation with one's own categorical schema of what is important. Such a duty-bound ethic cuts us off from the world just as self-indulgence does, but this time so that one sees only what he is supposed to see. An overly controlled person becomes irresponsible in the technical sense of refusing to respond to anything which is not part of his or her defined duties. Rather than wishing to respond maturely to whatever might present itself, he wishes instead to live up to a **vain** (NE IV, 3) image of himself and/or to satisfy an excessive **ambition** (NE IV, 4) to please demanding authorities.

While Freud and Schachtel deserve more than this passing mention of their views on the importance of self-indulgence in human development, we must return to Aristotle's examination of the best agent for revealing self-indulgence. The most striking point here is Aristotle's anticipation of the recent scientific discovery of the great importance of the sense of touch in human (and mammalian) development and the life-long craving and unhappiness steming from either its overstimulation or frustration.

Aristotle followed the process of division in concluding that self-indulgence is primarily concerned with food, drink, and sex (A), and, therefore, with the power of **touch** (M). As always, identifying the proper **agent** (A) for evaluating the virtuous or vicious operation of a moral and emotional power will simultaneously clarify the nature and definition of the power (M) as well. He starts with the classical distinction between the pleasures of the **body** and those of the **soul**.

He lists the following as pleasures of the **soul**: what our translator calls "love of honor" (literally in Greek **philo-time**) is what we speak of today as **ambition** (NE IV, 4); love of learning, the love of stories and of gossip Aristotle speaks of elsewhere with respect to **high-mindedness** and **vanity** (NE IV, 3); the love of **money** (NE IV, 1) and **friends** (NE IV, 6 & **Rh** II, 4).

The pleasure given by these is not necessarily centered in our bodies. The fact that someone honors us must, of course, be physically communicated if we are to be pleased by it, and is to that extent physical. There is a physical substrate to all pleasure in this sense. But the pleasure of satisfying our ambitions, vanity, the love of money and friends requires no direct bodily contact the way eating, drinking and sex do. One can find great pleasure in learning about things he will never have direct bodily contact with. Stories of people long since dead, or fictional characters, can please or pain our moral sensibilities even though we will never touch these people physically.

While **sexual** gratification and physical affection might provide people with their most acute and supportive sense of pleasure, it by no means exhausts the pleasure we take in our loved ones and friends. And unless one adopts Freud's rather wild-card like theory that all of the higher moral pleasures motivating the creation of civilized life are really sublimations of sexual pleasure, then most of the goals and relations people have are of this spiritual, non-bodily kind.

Even the pleasure we take in **money** is not necessarily in physically possessing it or the things it can buy so much as in satisfying our ambition for a certain standing in the eyes of others and in gaining the confidence that we can pursue our plans for the future. In other words, money is only a means to the exercise of these higher powers.

People do seem to lose self-control when they indulge in **extravagant** desires to spend money (NE IV, 1), when they encourage people to flatter their **vanity** (NE IV, 3) or further their **ambitions** (NE IV, 4), or when they vent their **anger** (NE IV, 5) or show excessive **wit** (NE IV, 7). Yet, while self-indulgence underlies these various vices, they do not give us the heart of self-indulgence (M). We must conclude then that the pleasures of the **soul** do not give the essence of self-indulgence. Aristotle returns to the five **bodily** senses.

Having excluded these so-called "pleasures of the **soul**," self-indulgence and self-control must be states of one of our five **sensory** powers, i.e. the five senses. Aristotle examines each of them (M) to determine whether it can be self-indulgent in its particular area. This leads to the discovery that self-indulgence in the power of touch can distort the functioning of all the others.

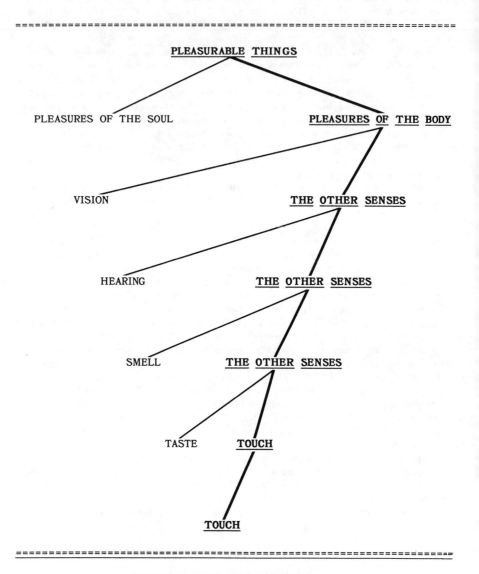

**DIVISIONS MADE IN IDENTIFYING
THE BEST AGENTS FOR REVEALING SELF-INDULGENCE**

It is mankind's ability (M) to focus his sensory response (F) on things (A) **for the sake of knowing and taking pleasure in them in their own right** (T) that provides the standard for judging a self-indulgent response. Self-indulgent people are so hungry and self-centered they are not genuinely interested in the world. Self-indulgence knows things simply for the sake of gratifying the knower, but not **as a knower**. When self-indulgent, we focus not on the world but on our desperate desire to be satisfied by the world. Aristotle's examples clarify these points. We can line up the **animal** illustrations alongside the **human** ones, since his point is that when self-indulgent we do not act according to the capacities which differentiate our species from the other animals.

Starting with **vision**, we see that the lion is pleased at the sight of a stag and the self-indulgent man is pleased at the sight of food or of a woman--not because they find these things visually beautiful but because the food and the female arouse the pleasing fantasy and hope that they can be consumed. The self-controlled man, on the other hand, is free to find pleasure simply in a woman's beauty and grace.

When the lion **hears** the lowing of an ox, or a self-indulgent man hears sexually arousing music or speech, their pleasure is not in what they hear but in what they associate with the sound. They are not taking pleasure in the sound at all, but are focusing auto-centrically on satisfying their own desires for eating and sex. When the dog **smells** a rabbit and a self-indulgent man smells perfume or dainty dishes, the pleasure they take in these is in the anticipatory satisfaction of the **completely different power** of eating and sex.

Aristotle is clearest on this point when he discusses the power to **taste**. He offers no animal example of the power of taste--experimentation would have been required to say anything about this. But his example of the self-indulgent **man** illustrates the point again that even in the sense of taste, his real interest lies in satisfying the dependent desire to be touched through eating, drinking or sex. He does not delight in the discriminating knowledge of different flavors the way wine tasters and gourmands do who enjoy knowing their object as much as, or more than, they enjoy consuming it. Connoisseurs do not glut themselves with food or rush to inebriate themselves. As Schachtel says, they go beyond an auto- to an allo- (or "other") centered orientation and are interested in the being of their object.

The self-indulgent person (M) is not interested in any of the individuating aspects of the agent (A) to which he responds (F). He responds to things (A) only in so far as they satisfy his desire (M) to be touched and filled up. His pleasure is not in actively knowing and responding (F) to things (A) but in being pleased and comforted by them. Schachtel speaks of this as "embeddedness-affect"--as though one's highest wish were to remain in a hot bath or in a warm bed on a cold morning. When a person's greatest pleasure lies in responding to this class of agents, all of his senses are turned away from a more active knowing and responding to the world. In a way presaged by Aristotle, both Schachtel and Freud argued that man must develop a taste for the pleasures of the higher moral and intellectual powers if he is to grow out of the infant's natural auto-centrism and desire to feel embedded in a supporting and protective environment that does not challenge him to develop and enjoy himself.

In an important sense, we all start as self-indulgent and have to grow out of it through establishing more allo-centric relations with the world. So the real problem is not so much how to explain self-indulgence--it will occur naturally enough if we do not develop self-control. The key to self-indulgence must be sought in the explanation of how people develop self-control. The failure of this development leaves us in the self-indulgent state which, as a given, requires no explanation.

B. SELF-CONTROL, SELF-INDULGENCE, AND DEPRESSION AS THE VIRTUE AND VICES OF THIS POWER (NE III, 11)

1. NATURAL AND IDIOSYNCRATIC APPETITES

Having identified the proper agents for testing self-control and indulgence, Aristotle now seeks to differentiate the virtue and vices of this power. He begins by dividing people's appetites into those that are **common** to most people and those that are **idiosyncratic**.

Of the appetites some seem to be common, others to be peculiar to individuals and acquired; e.g. the appetite for food is natural, since everyone who is without it craves for food or drink, and sometimes for both, and for love also (as Homer says) if he is young and lusty; but not everyone craves for this or that kind of nourishment or love, nor for the same things. Hence such craving appears to be our very own. Yet it has of course something natural about it; for different things are pleasant to different kinds of people, and some things are more pleasant to everyone than chance objects. (1118b 8-15)

Within this division between common and idiosyncratic responses, Aristotle first analyzes the vice of **excessive degree** associated with the common or natural appetites.

Now in the natural appetites few go wrong, and only in one direction, that of excess; for to eat or drink whatever offers itself till one is surfeited is to exceed the natural amount, since natural appetite is the replenishment of one's deficiency. Hence these people are called belly-gods, this implying that they fill their belly beyond what is right. It is people of entirely slavish character who become like this. (1118b 16-22)

With these **common** things, the most natural way to go wrong is by going to excess beyond what is required for one's replenishment. Pursuing such things in this way results from failing to be one's own master.

Aristotle then considers appetites for peculiar or **idiosyncratic** things. We can go wrong in three different ways with these things beyond just wanting too much of something perfectly natural for us to desire.

But with regard to the pleasures peculiar to individuals many people go wrong and in many ways. For while the people who are "fond of so and so" are so called because they delight either in the wrong things, or more than most people do, or in the wrong way, the self-indulgent exceed in all three ways; they both delight in some things that they ought not to delight in (since

137

they are hateful), and if one ought to delight in some of the things they delight in, they do so more than one ought and than most men do. (1118b 22-8)

Here we can go wrong not only by wanting things too much or too little, i.e. in degree, but by wanting things we shouldn't want at all. Where before the focus was on an improper form of response (F), here it is on an improper agent (A).

COMMENTARY. In the preceding section we identified food, drink and sexual objects (A) as the primary focus for self-indulgent people (M). We should include drugs under drink as having analogously inebriating effects. Our purpose now is to prepare the way for defining the virtue of **self-control**, the vice of **self-indulgence** and the as yet unmentioned vice of deficient pleasure in such objects which we will call **depression**.

People can respond to potentially pleasurable things 1) in too strong a **degree** by wanting something too much, and 2) in the **magnitude** of their response by having too much of a given thing, and finally 3) by wanting things they should **not desire at all**. Self-indulgent people err in one or all three of these ways depending on whether the appetite in question is one that is **common** to mankind or one that is idiosyncratic. Aristotle means by these "peculiar appetites" those that later came to be called the **perversions** in both sexual activities and eating. (See Kraft-Ebbing.)

The lay reader might be amazed to learn how enslaved men and women have become throughout history to the pleasures acquired from sexual or other contact with animals, children, clothing, corpses, excrement, physical abuse (actively administered or passively suffered), etc. People have eaten, drunk, or otherwise ingested through their nostrils or veins, everything from airplane glue, to paint-thinner, and the bodies of their enemies. These are things that one goes wrong by enjoying at all, not by enjoying too much or too often.

The fact of enjoying these things at all is already a sign that something is drastically wrong in the whole system of a person's moral powers. A kid who sniffs glue lacks the **hope** and **courage** he needs to face life. He probably has no noble person before whom he feels **emulation** (Rh II, 11) or **shame** (Rh II, 6 & NE IV, 9) at his own self-betrayal. Such a youth will be so lacking in perspective about the possible development of his life that he or she can glibly risk everything to indulge a trifling pleasure. Barring the development of higher, competing interests, the desire for immediate, reassuring pleasure will dominate his life and he or she will indulge in the activity again and again.

There are, of course, disagreements about what agents fall into the class of things that are by their very nature destructive to a person's well-being. Aristotle's own approach to the question is a **functional** one. Agents should be counted in this proscribed class when they give pleasure only to those whose sensibilities reflect a larger loss of the powers of proper wish, deliberation and choice, i.e. those seeking pleasure indiscriminately as compensation for defeat, fearfulness and unfulfillment.

On the other hand, the moral rejection of somethings like oral-genital sexuality among heterosexual married couples is more likely to come from **spite** (Rh II, 10) than from a legitimate assessment of their dysfunctional consequences in people's lives. While many instances of

homosexual relations are grossly self-indulgent, it is simply not true for all such relations. There appears to be an organic or developmentally-based sex-identity confusion behind some cases of homosexuality which neither arise from nor give rise to moral and emotional vices. Not all homosexuals are sexually excessive to the point of corrupting their other moral powers.

To accept wrongly frowned-upon activities as legitimate agents of pleasure does not mean, however, that self-indulgent people cannot take **more** pleasure in such practices than is commensurate with a noble life, or indulge **more often** than they should. It is simply to say that finding pleasure in them can be an appropriate human activity--one that does not by itself undermine the fundamental principles and causes of human development and happiness. And on these grounds they cannot be ruled out as immoral.

The most common way of going wrong with things that are in principle alright is to have **too much** of them. Aristotle's comments on food are particularly interesting in this respect. He says the self-indulgent attitude is to "eat or drink whatever offers itself till one is surfeited." The basic self-indulgent aim is always to stuff or fill oneself up in order to **combat a sense of emptiness** and lack of fulfillment in one's life. Aristotle's observation of the lack of discrimination in consuming "whatever offers itself" characterizes the self-indulgent attitude toward sex and drugs as well as eating and drinking.

Insofar as a person is self-indulgent, he or she does not genuinely wish and work for his own physical and moral well-being or that of others. If he were more self-controlled, he would look to his larger purposes and what he needs both physically and spiritually when determining his responses to pleasurable things. The self-indulgent person does not listen to his body to determine how much he needs to eat and drink, nor is he truly attentive to his sexual frustrations and urges. Such a person looks for ways not just to **satisfy,** but to **arouse,** his appetites. He or she starts from a **psychological** and not a **physical** sense of emptiness and then tries to arouse and satisfy their hunger, thirst or sexual drive in order to provide a sense of psychological fullness and completion.

They are trying to solve what is, in fact, a psychological and moral problem of emptiness and lack of fine purpose and activity in their lives through a merely physical means. By doing so, they actually strengthen the dominance of their self-indulgent attitudes over their desire to exercise their other powers. They allow to lie fallow the very powers which could pull them out of their despair and make their lives more fulfilling, i.e. full-filling.

2. SELF-CONTROL CONCERNS PAIN AS WELL AS PLEASURE

While the powers to deal with **pain** and with **pleasure** are **distinct,** they none the less **interact** with one another. Aristotle notes that

> Plainly, then, excess with regard to **pleasures** is self-indulgence
> and is culpable; with regard to **pains** one is not, as in the case
> of courage, called self-controlled for **facing** them or self-indul-
> gent for not doing so, but the self-indulgent man is so called be-
> cause he is pained more than he ought at not getting pleasant

things (even his pain being caused by pleasure), and the self-controlled man is so called because he is not pained at the absence of what is pleasant and at his abstinence from it. (1118b 28-35)

Self-indulgent people are excessive in their desire for **pleasure** and are excessively **pained** when they do not get it. So, in a certain sense, both **courage** and **self-control** concern pain. The difference is that people are said to be courageous for **facing** painful things properly, while self-control and self-indulgence concern whether our wishes are so excessive as to make us too disposed to be pained by their frustration.

COMMENTARY. The fact that self-indulgence and self-control are revealed in the **pain** people feel at not having what they want provides a nice illustration of how the virtues and vices of different moral powers interact with one another. While **courage** and **cowardice** control how we handle threats and work with the fact of pain, self-control and indulgence control what we will see as threats to our proper or excessive desires and how painful their frustration will be to us.

Self-indulgent people are **too hurt** if they do not get what they want on the spur of the moment. Pain rooted in self-indulgence is in this sense **self**-inflicted. It is because we want to indulge ourselves that we are so hurt at not getting what we want. This pain sorely compromises our ability both to make and to act on long-range plans.

This excessive pain at frustrated desire raises the stakes in all our endeavors and provides a further explanation of why self-indulgence is a vice. Since wanting things too much can make us too afraid to take the risks involved in actively pursuing what we wish, the wish to develop and integrate ourselves must inevitably become ineffective in guiding our lives. Unless we can gain greater self-control, we will be ruled by the fear generated by these excessive desires as much as by the desires themselves.

If one doubts this relation between **self-indulgence** and **cowardice**, he need only observe the face of a self-indulgent person when he learns there is no more food, alcohol, sex or drugs available to him or her for an extended but not unreasonable period. Panic is common in such circumstances. In contrast, the self-controlled and courageous person takes not only similar frustration in stride but can even accept the possibility of his or her own death in serving a noble cause. He thus gains the **freedom** to wage his very life on the contests he believes in while the self-indulgent person is characterized by the **loss of freedom** in the face of even trivial temptations.

Courage is a matter of the strength of our wish to pursue a fine goal in the face of threats. It would seem thoroughly legitimate then to speak of a self-indulgent person as showing courage when he begins facing the pain involved in gaining self-control through resisting self-indulgent wishes. But to be courageous in this sense we must always develop higher goals than simply pursuing whatever pleasures, and fleeing whatever threats, happen to appear before us.

This is where **generosity, high-mindedness, ambition,** and **friendliness** come in. These moral powers determine our higher goals, what they mean to us, how much pleasure gaining them will give us, and how much pain abandoning them will cause us. These more individuated powers issue the goals and marching orders, so to speak, which our courage and self-control allow us to pursue.

3. SELF-INDULGENCE AS THE VICE OF EXCESSIVE PLEASURE

Aristotle observes that

> The self-indulgent man, then, craves for all pleasant things or those that are most pleasant, and is led by his appetite to pursue these at the cost of everything else; hence he is pained both when he fails to get them and when he is merely craving for them (for appetite involves pain); but it seems absurd to be pained for the sake of pleasure. (1119a 1-5)

Self-indulgence (M) thus disposes one to be moved by an excessive number of pleasures (A) in such a way as to undermine everything else in one's life (T) and to lead one to feel pain in both the excessive desire itself and its frustration (F).

COMMENTARY. As always, the key to understanding a character trait is its purpose or final causality (T). The self-indulgent person aims for pleasure **above all** and "at the cost of everything else." This leads to an expansion of the **kinds** of agents (A) he finds pleasurable (e.g. the perversions), or of the **quantity** of the legitimate agents he consumes (e.g. of food or drink or sexual partners), or of the **frequency** of his consumption. Self-indulgence thus starts with the desire for pleasure as its conscious intention, but has as its not necessarily intended outcome the causing of great pain.

Since the self-indulgent person responds to pleasurable agents at the cost of all others, we must add to the list of agents (A) **affected** by self-indulgence, all the painful but important challenges (A) which might lead to higher pleasures and happiness later on. Self-indulgent people do not find projects requiring deferred gratification as worthwhile and attractive as those offering a quick fix.

Since it is painful to desire things we do not have (A), and self-indulgent people have excessive desires (M), their desire for pleasure leaves them both too pained and too often in pain (F). This is the painful feeling of **emptiness** that follows naturally from being so centered on gratifying **oneself** that one fails to develop the higher moral powers that open us to **the fullness of life** and **the richness of the world** around us. With no developed virtues linking us to the world, we collapse in on ourselves.

Self-indulgence clearly undermines the three principles of human development which the virtues alone make possible. When a pleasing opportunity comes along, the self-indulgent person goes for it without reference to any higher **wish** for a noble life of integrated functioning. He does not **deliberate** about how best to live a better life and so he does not examine how going after this immediate pleasure (A), or refusing to face something painful (A), might effect his higher purposes (T). His instinctive pursuit of pleasure is thus not a **choice** at all because the dominance of his self-indulgent wish robs him of the power to make his own choices.

Self-indulgence comes down in the final analysis to the wish **to be indulged**, i.e. to be held, fed, supported and stimulated rather than wishing to be active and noble in one's own right. When the self-indulgent wish becomes truly excessive, the person becomes deeply regressive and dependent. Self-indulgent wishes often become so frightening that the person must deny consciousness of his own wish in order to avoid feeling the fear, shame and anger generated by such a demanding sense of dependency. The more one wishes to be indulged rather than to actively indulge oneself, the more passive and afraid he or she becomes. The **ultimate** fear here is quite simply that by no longer wishing to discover and be oneself, one will lose the integrity and independence of one's whole personality.

People by and large cannot allow themselves to be conscious of having such a deeply self-indulgent goal because they would then have to live with the awareness of how empty and unsupported they feel, and of how they are their own worst enemy in driving people away from them. Where the effort to pursue his wish **in practice** might lead a person to discipline and moderate his self-indulgent desires, sullenly hiding these wishes allows them to luxuriate and become ever more dominant in his **fantasies**. Only to the inexperienced will it appear paradoxical that the person who sleeps with a large number of different people can actually be **less** emotionally self-indulgent than someone whose desires are more excessive and dependent, leaving him afraid of all initiative and all possibility of rejection.

4. DEPRESSION AS THE VICE OF DEFICIENT PLEASURE

Aristotle observes that

> People who fall short with regard to pleasures and delight in them less than they should are hardly found; for such insensibility is not human. Even the other animals distinguish different kinds of food and enjoy some and not others; and if there is anyone who finds nothing pleasant and nothing any more attractive than anything else, he must be something quite different from a man; this sort of person has not received a name because he hardly occurs. (1119a 6-11)

COMMENTARY. Such a deficiency makes one insensible to the world and less able to discriminate between and enjoy different kinds of foods and other pleasures. As such this state (M) disposes one to respond to fewer agents of stimulation (A) and to do so in a form that lacks pleasure and appreciation for differences (F). Such a person is lacking then in the natural human motivations and goals (T).

Aristotle does not mention any sense of the finality (T) that might be involved in this attitude. His focus is rather on its agent (A) and formal (F) dimensions. The person Aristotle has in mind finds a deficient **number** of things (A) pleasant (F), and even when they are pleased, they are **less so** than they should be (F). This diminished pleasure is associated with a lessened power of discrimination, or "insensibility," in response to things.

What might this trait be in contemporary terms? **Mourning** and **melancholia** or the general state of **depression** come to mind most prominently. Mourning is that condition in which one has lost an agent (A) he was so closely tied to that, with its loss, he temporarily loses the capacity to respond to other things with discriminating interest and pleasure. Freud spoke of melancholia, on the other hand, as not so much a response to the loss of a loved one as the sense of having lost something about **oneself** without which he can never again be loved or feel fully alive. Melancholia is a character trait and a vice, while mourning is a natural process of healing from a profound injury to one's happiness. The latter can turn into the former, however, if carried on too long.

The **HANDBOOK OF PSYCHIATRY** provides the following account of **depression** which allows us to link it very closely to Aristotle's description of deficient appetite and the dynamics of several other moral and emotional powers as well.

> **Depression** rivals **anxiety** as the most important and inclusive category in psychopathology... Mild depression manifests itself largely by a **loss of pleasurable interest** in the usual affairs of life. Spontaneity is gone. Everything requires effort and provides less gratification than before... Realistic worries and ordinary bodily discomforts are prominent in awareness, while **encouraging memories, hopes,** and **plans** are hard to keep in mind... **Sexual disinterest** or **incapacity** ("loss of libido") is described as a classical symptom. To put it briefly, the 4 major appetites are impaired. Modern psychodynamic formulations emphasize **dependency** as a primary issue in people prone to depression. Such people have exaggerated needs for **nurturing, support,** or **approval.** Some require **special foods** and **bodily attentions** from **specific other people.**
>
> A very dependent person is always vulnerable to disappointment. Since **he needs too much,** he can never get enough. Because his needs are chronically unfulfilled, he has feelings of frustration and **anger.** Such a person is in a serious bind because expressing his anger will drive away or make hostile the very people he is dependent on. Therefore, he must hold in his anger, which seems to eat away at his insides, leading ultimately to feelings of **helplessness** and **self-reproach...** The vicissitudes of anger and hostility remain part of every dynamic account of depression. It usually comes as a surprise to discover how angry the patient is, because superficially and consciously he blames no one but himself. (Philip Solomon, MD & Vernon D. Patch, MD, eds., Lange Medical Publications: Los Altos, 1971, pp. 58-60)

An Aristotelian apologist could not have written a more confirmatory account of the existence of a vice of deficiency associated with our power to respond to pleasurable things. With their reference to **anxiety,** these psychiatrists also seem to share Aristotle's implicit judgment that **courage** and **self-control,** and the vices associated with them, are the principal moral powers underlying man's whole moral and emotional development. These two respond to all agents in so far as they involve pain and pleasure which involves them in the operation of all of the other moral powers. It is common today, however, to add the category of **sub-**

stance abuse to that of anxiety and depression as a third great class of disorders, but that simply rounds out our account by including self-indulgence proper along with depression and the lack of courage.

The text also confirms our earlier observation that the vice of **excess**, i.e. self-indulgence, when taken to great extremes, ends in the corresponding vice of **deficiency**, i.e. depression. To explain this process further, we must focus on how self-indulgence dominates and inhibits the exercise and development of the other moral powers.

As we have seen, self-indulgence undermines our interest in the world. None of our **other** sensory powers can know and enjoy its own object when dominated by our overwhelming desire to be held, sensually-gratified, and touched. It inhibits the spontaneous expression of what we're doing and feeling, because exposing our real intentions would tend to diminish other's desire to satisfy and take care of us. The loss of **spontaneity** in any of our powers results from its being dominated by the vice in another power such as excessive ambition, vanity, or greed. By leading us to focus on ulterior motives, such vices make us indifferent to what is going on right in front of us. Having an **ulterior** motive causes us to hide our **real** motives from others and even from ourselves.

In the case of depression, we are so dominated by self-indulgent wishes that we do not really wish for the pleasure of exercising our higher powers. With our interest focused on more primitive gratification to salve painful feelings of emptiness and dependency, we really are not interested in other things, and must make ourselves do them. We are auto-centric and become conscious of every little discomfort and pain. These discomforts would not attract our attention if we were actively interested in anything other than our own unsatisfied and repressed longing to be held and fed.

Since our desire to do things for ourselves is so small, worries about being able to accomplish anything loom large in our lives. We cannot keep "encouraging memories, hopes, and plans... in mind" because they are not in the service of our self-indulgent wishes. Being so afraid that we cannot do for ourselves, we cannot deliberate and plan at all effectively.

The psychiatric reference to the depressed person's requiring "special foods and bodily attentions from specific other people" suggests what we saw earlier about the desire for idiosyncratic pleasures. The reference here, however, is not necessarily to these as perversions so much as to their marking the depth of the person's dependent and demanding nature and insistence that others take care of him. He wants to be indulged by this special person and in his own special way.

The dynamics of depression's **vicious** circle tend to drive the self-indulgent person to make ever greater demands and sink into deeper depression. There is, for example, no check on his **anger** (Rh II, 2, 3 & NE IV, 5) at people who do not give him the one thing he wishes for in life, to be taken care of so he won't have to work to develop himself. By dominating the development of the higher powers, the self-indulgent wish leaves him with no emotionally satisfying alternative to wanting his regressive desires satisfied. His anger when they cannot gratify his excessive desires cannot then be offset by **friendly** (NE IV, 6 & Rh II, 4) or **kind** (Rh II, 7) wishes for their welfare which at the least would make him more sensitive to what is just and fair to expect from others. As he is, he really does not care whether his demands are **fair**. How could he care about others, when his primary wish is for them to take care of him? Excessive **anger** is thus a natural consequence of having self-indulgent desires. Witness how upset babies are when they are not fed and held when they wish to be! But anger creates an enormous conflict as one grows older. The frustrated rage that was so effective in infancy in stimulating nurturing behavior becomes for the adult the greatest single **threat** to having others take care of him. Infants have little or no capacity for the friendliness and justice that adults are expected to have. The self-indulgent person must thus repress the expression of his unjust anger--exercising excessive self-control in the process, and using up a tremendous amount of scarce energy and attentiveness.

Ironically, to carry out this repression, he must deny to himself that the agent is slighting his deepest wish. To protect his wish he must pretend he does not have it. His anger would expose his selfishness and drive others away. Yet, if he cannot acknowledge even to himself that his primary goal is self-indulgence, how can he deliberate and make choices to satisfy his wish the way less excessively self-indulgent Don Juans and nymphomaniacs do? He is caught in a conflict that leaves him ever more passive, dependent and afraid.

The only way out of this syndrome is through the development of the person's higher moral powers and wishes. But this can never happen, of course, so long as his primary wish is self-indulgent. And it is not exactly a matter of choice either. A person does not **choose** between wishes, because wish is the principle upon which choice itself is based. There is, however, a dominant/recessive struggle between wishes which comes into play whenever people become aware of their conflicting wishes.

The choices we make build up the dominance, or the recessiveness, of our different wishes, so every time we make a choice we strengthen the wish the choice is based on. And since our plans and choices arise from, and aim to satisfy, our wishes, a wish that does not activate deliberation and choice is not so much a real wish as a whim. This is true by definition because we mean by a person's wish the desire which actually animates his or her deliberations and choices. It follows, too, from this that we can learn to recognize our potentially conflicting wishes through observing more carefully the otherwise unconscious deliberations and choices we make which reflect them.

The awakening of a person's powers of generosity, high-mindedness and friendliness can give him a foothold on a path that might lead to his greater self-control, human development and happiness. But it is only a foothold. The depressed person does not know that his primary wish is self-indulgent. The hope is that his desire to pursue these higher wishes will give him the courage to face the painful fact of his wishing for harmful things which keep him from enjoying the real possibilities for a fuller life that lie before him.

He must thus discover that self-indulgent wishes lie behind the choices which cause him so much suffering. His only hope is that, by seeing both the real happiness becoming possible for him through these awakening powers and the pain caused by his self-indulgence, he will become more frightened by the self-indulgent wish than by the fear of its frustration. This fear might lessen his indulgent desires sufficiently for him to come to value even more the pleasures of exercising the higher powers which had given him the courage to see his self-indulgence in the first place.

His success will obviously depend in large part on finding friends and socio-political conditions which cultivate these higher wishes. In many cases, it will have been the absence of such opportunities which weakened the person's wish for a higher, more active life in the first place. The absence of such stimulation to develop one's powers leads many of us to regress to the self-indulgent wish from which we all started as infants.

5. SELF-CONTROL AS THE VIRTUE

Aristotle thought that

The self-controlled man occupies a middle position with regard to these objects. For he neither enjoys the things that the self-indulgent man enjoys the most--but rather dislikes them--nor in general the things that he should not, nor anything of the sort to excess, nor does he feel pain or craving when they are absent, or does so only to a moderate degree, and not more than he should, nor when he should not, and so on; but the things that, being pleasant, make for health or for good condition, he will desire moderately and as he should, and also other pleasant things if they are not hindrances to these ends, or contrary to what is noble, or beyond his means. For he who neglects these conditions loves such pleasures more than they are worth, but the self-controlled man is not that sort of person, but the sort of person that right reason prescribes. (1119a 12-21)

COMMENTARY. The self-controlled person wishes for (T) "things that, being pleasant, make for health or for good condition," for what is noble and not "beyond his means," and for what is according to right reason. These goals then determine what agents he will respond to and in what form. He simply does not find pleasurable some of the agents self-indulgent people are so attracted to. Of the other agents, he does not find them so dominantly pleasurable that he thinks only of them--which allows him to devote his time and energy to higher things. Since these sensual things are not so dominantly pleasurable to him and are not his principal wish, he is never particularly pained by the frustration of not having them.

The self-controlled person assumes pleasure to be a good thing. But because his or her primary wish is for a good life, he always deliberates (even if he can do so instantaneously) about how surrendering to an opportunity for pleasure will affect his highest wishes. This gives him the freedom always to choose for himself how he will respond rather than being manipulated and controlled by his immediate environment. This is why the virtue of this power is rightly called "self-control". Without it, we are controlled by whoever or whatever offers us pleasure.

The person who controls himself excessively and takes deficient pleasure in the world, on the other hand, denies the basic goodness of human desires and replaces friendly self-discipline with harsh repression. In the process, he gives self-control an undeservedly bad name.

146

C. THE DEVELOPMENT OF SELF-CONTROL (NE III, 12)

1. VOLUNTARY AND INVOLUNTARY RESPONSES TO PLEASURE AND PAIN

In explaining the development of self-control, Aristotle first contrasts the degree of **voluntariness** involved in becoming **self-indulgent** with that involved in becoming **cowardly**.

> Self-indulgence is more like a voluntary state than cowardice. For the former is actuated by pleasure, the latter by pain, of which the one is to be chosen and the other to be avoided; and pain upsets and destroys the nature of the person who feels it, while pleasure does nothing of the sort. Therefore self-indulgence is more voluntary. (1119a 20-4)

The self-indulgent person appears obviously to be doing more what he wants than does the cowardly person whose behavior seems coerced and unwanted. Since it is easier to refuse a pleasure than to stand up to a pain, becoming self-indulgent is more voluntary, i.e. more nearly under our own control, than becoming cowardly is.

In addition to its greater intrinsic ease, we also have many more opportunities to learn self-control in responding to pleasurable things.

> Self-indulgence is more a matter of reproach; for it is easier to become accustomed to its objects, since there are many things of this sort in life, and the process of habituation to them is free from danger, while with terrible objects the reverse is the case. (1119a 25-8)

Because self-indulgence is more voluntary, it is also more blame-worthy.

Having distinguished self-indulgence from cowardice on the basis of the voluntariness and pain involved in acquiring them, Aristotle uses the same criteria to distinguish between individual **acts** of cowardice and self-indulgence, on the one hand, and the cowardly and self-indulgent **character traits** on the other.

> But cowardice would seem to be voluntary in a different degree than its particular manifestations; for it is itself painless, but in these we are upset by pain, so that we even throw down our arms and disgrace ourselves in other ways; hence our acts are even thought to be done under compulsion. For the self-indulgent man, on the other hand, the particular acts are voluntary for he does them with craving and desire, but the whole state is less so; for no one craves to be self-indulgent. (1119a 28-33)

While cowardly acts are thought to be less voluntary than cowardice as a character trait, self-indulgent acts are thought to be more voluntary than a self-indulgent character.

COMMENTARY. Voluntary actions come from one's own wishes and will, while involuntary ones are done under compulsion effected through pain or the threat of it. Cowardice is manifested in just such involuntary situations when we act ignobly from fearing a painful threat which a more courageous person would not surrender to. Self-indulgence, on the other hand, in pursuing pleasure, acts much more voluntarily. Cowardly acts--as opposed to wicked, opportunistic ones taken on purpose for an ulterior motive--thus appear to be involuntary and against the person's wishes to do something more noble. Unlike the courageous person, the coward cannot live with pain, or in the anticipation of it. His higher functions of proper wish, deliberation and choice are undermined by the fact that "pain upsets and destroys the nature of the person who feels it."

These points allow Aristotle to establish whether self-indulgence or cowardice is the more blameworthy. Based on the assumptions that voluntary actions are more blame-worthy than involuntary ones and that people wish to pursue their indulgences regardless of the pain, Aristotle concludes that self-indulgent people are more blame-worthy for their situations than cowardly people. We normally have many more opportunities (A) for developing self-control (F) than we do for developing courage (F), and they are less painful and threatening to practice with, making self-control easier to acquire.

Self-indulgent people must learn to use every opportunity to exercise and develop self-control by saying yes to things which strengthen their higher interests and powers and no to things which threaten to take control of them by feeding their wish to be indulged.

There is an interesting difference, however, between the voluntary nature of self-indulgence and cowardice when considered as individual acts rather than as character traits. The point to remember here is that a form of response (F), in this case an individual action, is not the same as the material disposition (M), or character trait, which gives rise to it. While a person voluntarily takes a self-indulgent act (F), he becomes a man or woman with a self-indulgent character (M) much less willingly. The consequences of having a self-indulgent character are considerably less pleasant than the acts leading up to it.

The consequences of having a cowardly state of character, on the other hand, are less acutely painful than the frightening acts leading to it. But this means too that the individual **act** of cowardice is more **involuntary** than the development of the cowardly state of character. The fact that a person failed to use his time to develop a stronger sense of purpose and the resources for facing threats seems more **voluntary** than any individual act of running away. The person seems not to want to become more courageous. In the safety of nonthreatening conditions, he neglected those activities which would have allowed him to build up a more courageous character.

So, if it is true to say that individual **acts** of self-indulgence are more **voluntary** than a self-indulgent **character**, it is also true that individual **acts** of cowardice are more **involuntary** than a cowardly **character**.

Does it follow, then, that the more voluntary the act or the condition, the more **blame-worthy** it is? This would make a self-indulgent act more blame-worthy than a self-indulgent character, while a cowardly character would be more blameworthy than a cowardly act. The practice in our culture seems to bear out these judgments. We tend to feel sorry for an alcoholic, for example, but to blame him for having another drink. We are understanding about his condition, but demanding about his particular actions.

On the other hand, the individual act of fleeing from pain seems to us, too, more understandable and forgivable than a person's having failed to develop a more courageous character. What seems blameworthy is a person's not using his or her time, when not immediately exposed to threatening situations, to prepare himself to handle them better.

2. THE ANALOGY BETWEEN CHILDHOOD IMMATURITY AND ADULT SELF-INDULGENCE

Aristotle observed that

> The name self-indulgence is applied also to childish faults; for they bear a certain resemblance to what we have been consider-ing. Which is called after which, makes no difference to our present purpose; plainly, however, the later is called after the earlier. The transference of the name seems not a bad one; for that which desires what is base and which develops quickly ought to be kept in a chastened condition, and these characteristics belong above all to appetite and to the child, since children in fact live at the beck and call of appetite, and it is in them that the desire for what is plea-sant is strongest. (1119a 34-b 6)

COMMENTARY. The Greek **"akolasia"** is translated here as "self-indulgence" to show its relation to "self-control." Translated literally it would be "unpunished" or "undisciplined." Aristotle's point here is to show the cultural wisdom embodied in the Greek term. But what is wonderful to the modern student of psychology is his penetration in seeing how closely related the adult trait is to the natural childhood state. It is a character-istically Aristotelian insight to recognize the way an attribute that is natural and fitting at one stage of development can become greatly dys-functional at another.

A tendency to excessive indulgence in physical pleasure is in an important sense a given in human life and can lead to all the unhappiness we have discussed unless people are disciplined and "chastened" in grow-ing up. As Nietzsche says somewhere, "Pleasure wants eternity, deep, deep eternity." Yet what kind of punishment or discipline is required? In the first place, it is decisive to distinguish between a disciplinary practice which cultivates a person's responsible openness to the world and one that imposes a dutiful set of categories upon it. The first uses discipline to help people grow stronger, more independent in their judgment, and more committed to the proper wish of promoting human development. The second tends to break people's backs, so far as independence is con-cerned, and promotes a tendency toward the depression associated with dependency, excesssive **ambition** to please authorities, and **envy** toward those more fully alive.

3. THE NEED FOR A RULING PRINCIPLE TO DISCIPLINE DESIRE DURING THE PROCESS OF DEVELOPMENT

Aristotle concluded that

If, then, it is not going to be disciplined and subject to the ruling principle, it will go to great lengths; for in an irrational being the desire for pleasure is insatiable even if it tries every source of gratification. The exercise of appetite increases its innate force, and if appetites are strong and violent they even expel the power of reason. Hence they should be moderate and few, and should in no way oppose the rational principle--this is what we call a disciplined and chastened state--and as the child should live according to the direction of his tutor, so the appetitive element in a self-controlled man should harmonize with the rational principle; for the noble is the mark at which both aim. The self-controlled man craves for the things he ought, as he ought, and when he ought; and this is what reason directs. (1119b 6-19)

COMMENTARY. We see here Aristotle's fundamental ethical commitment to the development of people's power of self-direction, or self-control in the larger sense of the term. The principle of discipline must ultimately become the inner one of proper wish, deliberation and choice, rather than the fear of punishing authorities. Yet it should be clear from our earlier analysis why the child is initially dependent on **external** discipline. He or she must first build up his higher moral powers and reason before he can use these powers to discipline his own appetites in a healthy way. Yet, he cannot do this so long as he is dominated by his self-indulgent desires. The child's way out is through obeying authorities who will guide him with friendly discipline and realism toward a more generous, self-respecting and loving openness to the world.

The child's overpowering desires will tend to persist, on the other hand, and even grow stronger if parents, teachers and other authorities neglect and/or indulge the child's undisciplined impulses. Psychoanalytic case studies show that such indulgent desires become dominant in people's lives when they have been either **excessively** or **deficiently** satisfied in childhood. Mothers and fathers can be too affectionate and giving, or too little so. This latter clinical observation, while puzzling to some, is fully comprehensible in the light of Aristotle's theory that virtue is the mean or appropriate response between extremes of excess and deficiency.

And as we have seen, appetites are self-indulgent when they lead us to want things more than they are worth, given the functional outcome of one's pursuing them without regard to the cost of doing so. The basic idea that desires should not oppose reason is therefore not derived from an overly **cerebral** conception of human life, so much as it is an admonition to practice self-control if one is to take care of his true interests as a human being. What is reasonable is simply a matter of doing those things that promote human development and happiness, and avoiding those that undermine them.

CHAPTER THREE

Handling Money and the Things It Will Buy

INVENTORY

A. MONEY ON A PERSONAL SCALE (NE IV, 1)

1. THE POWER TO GENERATE, GIVE, KEEP, TAKE AND RECEIVE MONEY

- Virtue as a mean in any one of the three dimensions
  of giving, taking, and receiving reflects our level
  of productiveness or generativity
- The more pronounced our investment in any one
  of these dimen-sions, the more our other traits fit
  into the same mold and form an inegrated constellation
- These constellations of character traits are
  adaptations to modes of work and production

2. THE EQUIVOCAL USE OF "EXTRAVAGANCE"

3. ARGUMENTS FOR SPENDING AND GIVING AS THE PROPER USE OF MONEY

a. Virtue is more a matter of using money well
   than of acquiring and possessing it well
b. Virtue is more a matter of acting rightly with money
c. The greater gratitude and praise accorded proper giving
   than that accorded proper taking reflects its greater
   virtue
d. By being harder to do, giving shows it is
   the greater virtue
e. Linguistic usage associates "generosity"
   with proper giving, "justice" with proper taking
f. Their giving makes the generous the most useful
   and therefore the most loved

4. GENEROSITY AS THE VIRTUE

a. Generosity finds pleasure in proper giving
b. Generosity concerns generating money
   and not just giving, receiving, taking and keeping it
c. The generous help those who wish to help themselves
d. The generous tend to leave too little for themselves
   but not in a small-minded way
e. The degree of one's generosity is relative
   to one's resources
f. Those with inherited wealth tend to be more generous
g. The generous are careful about where, when and how much
   they give so as not to waste their resources for giving
h. Gifts are no longer generous when they are too high
   relative to our resources
i. While generosity requires one to attain the mean in all
   in the same person
j. The generous person is only moderately pained
   by spending money wrongly
k. The generous person is more afraid of failing to make
   a right expenditure than of making a wrong one

5. EXTRAVAGANCE AS THE VICE OF EXCESSIVE GIVING

6. HOARDING AS THE VICE OF DEFICIENT GIVING

    a. Hoarding combined with a love of justice
       and a proper sense of shame
    b. Hoarding combined with deep fearfulness

7. EXPLOITATIVENESS AS THE VICE OF EXCESSIVE TAKING

    a. Exploitativeness combined with recklessness
    b. Exploitativeness combined with flattery
       and/or contentiousness

8. HOARDING AND EXPLOITATIVENESS ARE WORSE THAN EXTRAVAGANCE

B. MONEY ON A CIVIC SCALE (NE IV, 2)

1. MAGNIFICENCE, NIGGARDLINESS AND VULGARITY
   AS THE VIRTUE AND VICES OF THIS POWER

2. MAGNIFICENCE AS THE VIRTUE

    a. Magnificence shows its artistry in spending large sums
       to create a fitting effect for worthy purposes
    b. Magnificence wishes to create beautiful objects
       and occasions which inspire the noble wish
       for friendliness and human development
    c. The magnificence of a creation is not found in its cost
       but in the grandeur and admirableness
       of the effect achieved
    d. Magnificent expenditures are made for public affairs
       and ceremonies, for religion and the arts,
       and for the construction of inspiring public spaces
    e. Magnificent expenditures should fit both the resources
       of the producer and the effect sought
    f. Magnificent expenditures are also made
       for special private occasions
    g. A certain magnificence is appropriate
       in a wealthy person's home
    h. Magnificence leads one to do what is both great
       and fitting, whether on a small stage or a large one

3. VULGARITY AS THE VICE OF EXCESSIVE DISPLAY

4. NIGGARDLINESS AS THE VICE OF DEFICIENT DISPLAY

5. THE STATUS OF VULGARITY AND NIGGARDLINESS AS VICES

A. MONEY ON A PERSONAL SCALE (NE IV, 1)

1. THE POWER TO GENERATE, GIVE, KEEP, TAKE AND RECEIVE MONEY

Aristotle begins by clarifying the proper agent of this power.

Let us speak next of generosity. It seems to be the mean with regard to **wealth**; for the generous man is praised not in respect of military matters, nor of those in respect of which the self-controlled man is praised, nor of judicial decisions, but with regard to the **giving** and **getting** of wealth, and especially in respect of giving. Now by "wealth" we mean all the things whose value is measured by **money**. Further, **extravagance** and **meanness** are excesses and defects with regard to wealth; and meanness we always impute to those who care more than they ought for wealth... (1119b 23-31)

COMMENTARY. While **courage** and **self-control** are the most fundamental virtues, in the sense that they are required for the development of all the others, it is the way we develop the power to acquire and use money and the things it will buy which most affects the particular shape of our character and our relations with others. On a day to day practical level in working with people and trying to bring out what is best in them, there is no more important knowledge than to recognize whether their fundamental orientation tends to be **receptive-extravagant, exploitative, hoarding** or **generous**. As interpreted here, it is the virtue of generosity which allows us to be fully responsible in handling money, not only when it comes to getting and keeping it but in using it to promote the fullness of life as well. Generosity allows us to take money and work very seriously as preconditions for human development without allowing them to be ends in themselves. It is only when we develop our basic strategy of survival on a generous foundation that we can keep from treating money as the first principle in our lives.

Like all the other moral and emotional powers, the psychic power we are about to examine is differentiated by the specific class of agents to which it responds. This power does not deal with military matters, physical pleasures, issues to be litigated, or any of the other things to which the other moral and emotional powers or technical skills respond. Here we are dealing with our power to deal with **wealth**, or more generically, **money** and the things it will buy.

At this stage of his analysis Aristotle speaks of the **giving** and the **getting** of money as the basic focus of his analysis, and of **generosity** as the virtue, **extravagance** as the vice of excess and **meanness** as the vice of deficiency. We will soon see, though, that he greatly refines this analysis as he proceeds.

We must begin by making several points about terminology in translating Aristotle's ideas about this power into English. The discussion of the modes in which we handle money is one of the few times in this book in which English seems to provide a more articulate vocabulary than Aristotle had access to. The move from Greek to English here is rather like trying to translate an English discussion of snow conditions into an Eskimo language or of camel behavior into Arabic. We are moving from a less to a more articulate vocabulary.

We translate Aristotle's term "eleutheriotes" as "generosity" instead of the older term "liberality." While the Greek denoted the quality of how one handles money, it also had a broader association with being a "free" and "independent" person. The Latin "liberalitas," on the other hand, had the same connotations about liberty, but lacked the direct reference to how one handled money. The Greeks thus implicitly saw more clearly how one's ability to generate and use money properly lays the foundation for one's general freedom as a person. If we are dependent on others for money, or become enslaved by the obsessive desire for it, we lose the independence required for the free exercise of our other powers.

In addition to its vagueness, "liberality" has the further shortcoming of sounding quaint to American ears where "generosity" does not. "Generosity," on the other hand, has the merit of directing our attention to the **generative** processes by which money and the things it will buy are produced, as well as to being generative in our giving so as to promote the development of others so that they too might become more generative and productive.

In understanding the moral and emotional powers (M), we must always clarify the class of agents (A) each power deals with (F) and how it functions to show its particular virtue or excellence (T). Generosity shows its nature most fully in dealing with **money** and the **things it will buy.** We must thus try to understand the different aspects of how we can deal with the general issue of handling money.

Aristotle begins his account of how we handle money by making a division between how we **give** it and how we **get** it. Following the translator Rackham, we note that the Greek term, "lambanein," which Aristotle used as the contrary of give, means in other contexts either "receive" or "take." "To get" is thus the generic contrary of "to give," but getting itself can be divided into "receiving" and "taking" as two specific forms in which we might get money from others.

This terminology highlights Aristotle's characteristic method of division. He first divides the handling of money into **giving** it and **getting** it, and then further divides **getting** it into **receiving** it and **taking** it. The first of these latter attitudes (the receptive) wishes **to be given** things, the second (the exploitative) **to take** them. "Meanness" also raises a terminological problem. Taken generically it is a **deficiency** in **giving.** But there are two specific forms of not giving properly; one found in simple **miserliness** (hoarding), the other in **excessive taking** (exploitativeness).

These two sets of divisions isolate three dimensions in which to evaluate whether our power to deal with money is **deficient, appropriate,** or **excessive,** as shown in the TABLE below. We can make excessive, deficient or appropriate responses to money in **giving, receiving,** and **taking** it. **Hoarding,** the fourth basic character orientation to money, is best treated as the deficiency of **giving** rather than as a separate dimension the way **receiving** and **taking** are.

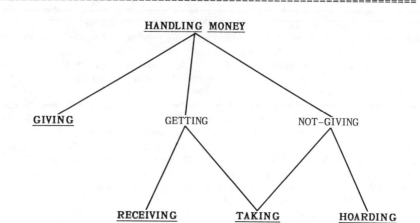

DIVISIONS MADE IN IDENTIFYING THE DIMENSIONS INVOLVED
IN THE VIRTUE AND VICES OF THE POWER TO HANDLE MONEY

    Having identified these basic dimensions in handling money, we can be much more precise in assessing people's strengths and weaknesses in this area. The following table displays the virtue and the vices of excess and deficiency associated with each dimension. The virtue and the three vices are listed according to the forms of bahavior most characteristic of each. Generosity requires one to handle all three dimensions appropriately.

    Each of them will be discussed more fully below, but it will be helpful first to make several concluding observations about the importance of this moral and emotional power in shaping the development of our whole moral character. By drawing out implications from the thought of Freud, Fromm and Marx we will be able to provide a significant advance in the integration of the Aristotelian theory and in accentuating its importance for explaining both individual and social development.

    We saw in analyzing **self-indulgence** in the last chapter that Aristotle had already grasped aspects of Freud's later discovery of the profound consequences for human development of failing to discipline our sexual and other pleasurable desires in a proper way. In the present chapter, we can see how Freud provides similar confirmation and elaboration of Aristotle's analysis of the various modes of our power to deal with money. To see this, we must once again pare away Freud's clinical **descriptions** from the Procrustean bed of his sexual **theory**, and from the outmoded metaphysics of his metapsychology. Erich Fromm has taken the lead in doing this with his theory of the **four basic modes of assimilation**. (See Erich Fromm, **MAN FOR HIMSELF**, and especially Fromm and Michael Maccoby, **SOCIAL CHARACTER IN A MEXICAN VILLAGE**.)

	EXCESSIVE	APPROPRIATE	DEFICIENT
GIVING	Extravagant	Generous	Hoarding
RECEIVING	Extravagant	Generous	Hoarding
TAKING	Exploitative	Generous	

**TABLE SHOWING THE THREE DIMENSIONS OF HANDLING MONEY
AND THE NAMES OF THE VIRTUE
AND THE VICES OF EXCESS AND DEFICIENCY IN THIS POWER**

Careful textual analysis shows that what Aristotle called the "generous" man, Freud referred to as the "genital" character, and Fromm called the humanly "productive" person. Aristotle's "miserly" character is Freud's "anal retentive" and Fromm's "hoarding" character. Aristotle's "piratical" or "excessively taking" character is Freud's "oral-sadistic" and Fromm's "exploitative" character. Aristotle's "extravagant" character is a particular form of development of Freud's "oral-receptive" and Fromm's "receptive" character. The table below lays out these relationships more graphically.

Our terminological convention is to use generosity for the virtue and Fromm's hoarding, exploitative and receptive for the vices except in the latter case where the context requires extravagance. The psychoanalyst Eric Ericson lends support to our usage of generosity with his important concept of the "generative stage" of human development in which people strive to promote the development of younger generations. (See "The Eight Ages of Man" in **CHILDHOOD AND SOCIETY.**)

Several points are worth noting about the contribution of these later thinkers to our understanding of the importance of this moral power in the development of the whole system of our other moral and emotional powers, and how it helps explain more precisely why man is a social and political being.

VIRTUE AS A MEAN IN ANY ONE OF THE THREE DIMENSIONS OF GIVING, TAKING, AND RECEIVING REFLECTS OUR LEVEL OF HUMAN PRODUCTIVENESS OR GENERATIVITY. Aristotle's theory that virtue is a "golden mean" or disposition to responses that are neither excessive nor deficient finds its immediate counter-part in Fromm's speaking of more or less "humanly productive" forms of each of these traits. Fromm does not reserve "receptive, hoarding and exploitative" just for the markedly or extremely vicious forms of this moral power. In Aristotelian terms, we would speak of more or less **generous** forms of the hoarding character, the exploitative and the receptive character. Fromm is using an alternative formulation to describe the same reality that Aristotle refers to with the doctrine of the mean.

ARISTOTLE	FREUD	FROMM
GENEROUS	GENITAL	PRODUCTIVE
MISERLY	ANAL	HOARDING
PIRATICAL	ORAL-AGGRESSIVE	EXPLOITATIVE
EXTRAVAGANT	ORAL-RECEPTIVE	RECEPTIVE

TABLE SHOWING THE RELATION
BETWEEN THE FOUR CHARACTER TRAITS
TO WHICH ARISTOTLE, FREUD AND FROMM GAVE DIFFERENT NAMES

This parallel is borne out by Fromm's further recognition that the more **productive** each of these various character types becomes, the less difference there is between them. In Aristotelian terms this means that the more productive a **hoarding** character is, the more **generous** he becomes. The more productive a **receptive** person becomes, the more he can **save** and **give** and **take** appropriately, and therefore the more generous he becomes, etc. Wilhelm Reich referred to the same reality with the somewhat misleading idea that the healthier a person becomes, the less character he has because his actions are governed by the requirements of the situation and not by his own characteristic dispositions.

Fromm's concept of "level of productiveness" is thus his way of indicating that the receiving, taking, giving or keeping at issue in any given instance is appropriate to the situation and is meant to promote human development. And this, after all, is what Aristotle meant by the **mean** or **virtuous** response.

THE MORE PRONOUNCED OUR INVESTMENT IN ANY ONE OF THESE DIMENSIONS, THE MORE OUR OTHER TRAITS FIT INTO THE SAME MOLD AND FORM AN INTEGRATED CONSTELLATION. People can often be spoken of as being either receptive, hoarding, exploitative or generous in a general way that gives coloring and shading to their whole personalities. Still other people show blends of these various orientations and present a much less sharply defined character. Investing our moral and emotional energy predominantly in one of these dimensions represents a commitment to a whole strategy of life affecting not only what Fromm calls our mode of **assimilation** but our mode of **relatedness** to others as well. Our moral, emotional and intellectual responses come to be integrated around the common purpose of giving, receiving, taking or keeping. In short, how we work and how we love, at least when we are free to be ourselves, will express the same aims and approach to life.

We can express Fromm's theory of a systemic development of moral powers in terms of Aristotle's theory of the various possible forms of our powers to handle **money**, on the one hand, and of **friendliness** and **love** (**NE** IV, 6), on the other. More particularly, Fromm's theory leads us to expect that there would be a strong correlation between the various vices of our approach to money and to other people. And this is precisely what we find, as seen in the following TABLE.

We can take the goal of each mode of assimilation to be the cause for each correlation, and in doing so can explain something of the way in which the developmental direction of the powers of generosity and friendliness runs like an axis through the center of our whole character development.

```
===============================

Generous           Friendly
-------------------------------

Hoarding           Contentious
-------------------------------

Exploitative       Flattering
-------------------------------

Receptive          Obsequious
===============================
```

**TABLE CORRELATING THE VIRTUES AND VICES IN HANDLING MONEY
WITH THOSE IN RESPONDING TO THE PAINS AND PLEASURES OF OTHERS**

When our basic approach to the world is **receptive**, for example, we do not so much wish to generate what we need as to receive it from others. With such a wish with regard to things, is it any wonder that we would tend to be **obsequious** with regard to people to gain their affection and support, and even **extravagant** in spending money to impress them? All of our other attitudes will likewise be colored by this basic, strategic assumption that the only way we can have the things we want is by receiving them from others--by being given them, not by creating, earning or taking them.

When predominantly receptive, we are **afraid** of being unsupported and unprovided for, and tend to be **self-indulgent** in our thoughts and actions, **small-minded** in what we expect of ourselves, **unambitious** and lacking in drive, **apathetic** in not standing up for ourselves but **angry** or **depressed** when not fed and supported. We are inclined to be somewhat **shameless** and unprincipled when violating our own standards to find pleasure.

If our basic approach is **hoarding**, on the other hand, we start from a strategic assumption of both physical and emotional scarcity, a sharp distinction between what is ours and what belongs to others, and a generalized sense of needing to keep an eye on our own and protect our things from anything which might harm them. With such a hoarding and private wish, is it any wonder that we would tend to be **contentious** and indifferent to the pleasure and pain we cause others, especially to those outside the circle we call our own?

When predominantly hoarding, we are **afraid** of scarcity, that things will fall apart, and that others will take what is ours. We are excessive in **self-control** and allow ourselves deficient pleasure, are inwardly **vain** and proud of our self-denial, **ambitious** to have control over our own work and space, although often dependent on others to assign our duty. We tend to be **sullen** and secretive in our anger, hold tightly to **friends** from the past and reluctant to let new people inside. We hold ourselves responsible for everything and are **ashamed** when we do not live up to demanding standards.

If our basic approach is **exploitative**, we start from a strategic assumption that life is a jungle divided between predators and prey, takers and the taken. We see people and things as potential resources to be enlisted in our projects, some of which might even be designed to defend our people from other predators. With such an exploitative wish, should we be surprized by the tendency to be **flattering** toward others in order to convince them to do what we want?

When predominantly exploitative, we are inclined to treat ourselves as a resource as much as the rest of the world. So we develop whatever sides of our character are required to cut deals in the circumstances. This makes the exploitative character less patterned than the receptive and hoarding orientations. But clearly, with this orientation we will be **afraid** of being swallowed up and devoured unless we become strong enough to take the things we need. We will be **vain** enough to feel we are worthy of doing so and **ambitious** enough to want others to honor our wishes. In addition to **flattery** we will be inclined to **insolent-sadism**, in the same way that **hoarding** characters are inclined toward **spite**.

Finally, if our basic approach is **generous** or **generative**, we start from a basic assumption of strength and abundance. We start always from our own power to create and share the good things of life with others, most importantly the power to become a creator and source of goodness in their own lives. With such a productive wish, there is no surprise in finding that such a person is also **friendly** and inclined to acquire the other virtues as well. Maccoby has noted, for example, that the more productive the receptive person becomes the more he is inclined to be a **helper**, the more productive the exploiter, the more he is a **defender**, the more productive the hoarder, the more he is a **craftsman**.

THESE CONSTELLATIONS OF CHARACTER TRAITS ARE ADAPTATIONS TO MODES OF WORK AND PRODUCTION. While Freud correctly **described** these basic orientations, and showed their pervasive influence throughout the whole system of our **other** character traits, he diminished their importance by reducing them to dependant variables, mere stages in the development of the sex drive, instead of being the forms of development of a separate power of generating and using the things we need. He therefore naturally failed to identify them as adaptations to the modes and relations of production available to people during different stages of their development, at any one of which they might become fixated depending on environmental circumstances and constitutional dispositions. And failing to make these connections, Freud's sex-centered theory tended to isolate human development from the political-economic context in which it occurs. He therefore could not adequately **explain** the social factors shaping psychological development nor the psychological factors shaping social development.

If Freud is the master student of **self-indulgence** through his focus on the power of sexuality, Fromm became the master of the moral power of dealing with the production and use of **money** and the things it will buy through building on Freud's insight into the four basic character orientations, and combining that insight with Marx's philosophical anthropology. We can now bring such modern insights back into the context of Aristotle's ancient wisdom on the virtues and vices.

Fromm contributed the major insight that the requirements of one's work or social function tend to determine how **hoarding, receptive, exploitative** or **generous** people become. He argued that this **socio-economic** factor explained ever so much more about the pathways of human development than Freud's **libido** theory with its emphasis on toilet training and fixations on different erogenous zones. With his theory of **social character** Fromm was able to explain how the **modes of production,** or more generically the modes of organizing life functions in society, indirectly affect all of our relations to society and nature through their direct influence on the development of our power of generativity.

2. THE EQUIVOCAL USE OF "EXTRAVAGANCE"

In keeping with his concern to differentiate very carefully between traits often confused with one another, Aristotle examined the difference between **extravagance** and **self-indulgence.** He says that

> we sometimes apply the word "extravagance" in a complex sense; for we call those men extravagant who are self-indulgent and spend money on self-indulgence. Hence also they are thought the poorest characters; for they combine more vices than one. Therefore the application of the word to them is not its proper use; for 'extravagant' means a man who has a single evil quality, that of wasting his substance; since an extravagant person is being ruined by his own fault, and the wasting of substance is thought to be a sort of ruining of oneself, life being held to depend on possession of substance. (1119b 31-1120a 3)

COMMENTARY. If we are to talk effectively further below about the specific vice of **extravagance,** we must carefully distinguish it from **self-indulgence.** Since they are rooted in different moral and emotional powers, they respond to different agents and they do not necessarily occur together. Self-indulgence responds to eating, drinking and sex while extravagance responds to money and the things it will buy. The person who has both vices spends his money wastefully for the sake of indulging in physical pleasures.

While we will have to wait until later to examine the wishes of the extravagant person, we should at least note from this text that rather than wishing to take care of himself and his resources, he spends so much money that he ends up being "ruined by his own fault." The Greek **"asootos,"** translated here as **extravagance,** literally means being "in a desperate case" or being "not saved."

3. ARGUMENTS FOR SPENDING AND GIVING AS THE PROPER USE OF MONEY

Aristotle makes the following six arguments for why the quality of a person's **giving** should be taken as the surest sign of his having the virtue associated with **using** money well,

a. Now the things that have a use may be used either well or badly; and riches is a useful thing; and everything is used best by the man who has the virtue concerned with it; riches, therefore, will be used best by the man who has the virtue concerned with wealth; and this is the generous man. Now spending and giving seem to be the using of wealth; taking and keeping rather the possession of it. Hence it is more the mark of the generous man to give to the right people than to take from the right sources and not to take from the wrong. (1120a 5-12)

b. For it is more characteristic of virtue to do good than to have good done to one, and more characteristic to do what is noble than not to do what is base; and it is not hard to see that giving implies doing good and doing what is noble, and taking implies having good done to one or not acting basely. (1120a 13-15)

c. And gratitude is felt towards him who gives, not towards him who does not take, and praise also is bestowed more on him. (1120a 15-6)

d. It is easier, also, not to take than to give; for men are apter to give away their own too little than to take what is another's. (1120a 17-8)

e. Givers, too, are called generous; but those who do not take are not praised for generosity but rather for justice; while those who take are hardly praised at all. (1120a 19-20)

f. And the generous are almost the most loved of all virtuous characters, since they are useful; and this depends on their giving. (1120a 21-2)

COMMENTARY. So many people today focus on getting money without ever reflecting on what they would like to use it for. Generosity, on the other hand, is the virtue required for the excellent handling or virtuous **use** of money. But what does it mean to use money rightly? Since Aristotle distinguished between the **giving** and **keeping** of money, and between the **receiving** and **taking** of it, he had to establish which of these displays the most characteristic aspect of the generous person's use of money. All six of his arguments end in the conclusion that **proper giving** is the best mark of the virtue involved in handling money well.

a. **VIRTUE IS MORE A MATTER OF USING MONEY WELL THAN OF ACQUIRING AND POSSESSING IT WELL.** Aristotle first divides **useful** things into those handled **well** and those that are handled **badly** and identifies money as a useful thing. Virtue lies on the side concerned with using things **well**, and generosity is identified as the virtue in using money well.

Aristotle next makes the division between **using** and **possessing**. The problem now is to determine from among the various attitudes toward money the one best characterized as using it. The **extravagant-receptive**, **exploitative** and **hoarding** attitudes are all classed under the category of possession because they aim either to get or keep it. **Spending** and **giving** money fall just as obviously under the contrary heading of use.

There would be nothing unusual in finding someone who takes or receives money from only the right sources and refuses to take it from the wrong ones, who is nonetheless an **ungenerous person** who is thought not to use his or her money very well. People who do not take from the wrong sources are thought to be **just** rather than generous. Proper giving therefore is a truer mark of the generous character because it illustrates the proper use of money more clearly than does its proper possession or acquisition. By focusing on possession rather than use, we would fail to distinguish between those who are merely honest and those who are genuinely generous. Honest people lacking in generosity are not fully virtuous when it comes to money.

b. **VIRTUE IS MORE A MATTER OF ACTING RIGHTLY WITH MONEY THAN OF ACCEPTING IT RIGHTLY.** This argument turns on the division between the categories of **action** and **passion**, used here in the sense of passivity or the state of being acted upon. Aristotle divides passion into the two classes of **having something done to oneself**, and **inaction through refusing to act basely.** And he believes that the virtuous man will both allow others to do good things for him (**high-mindedness**, NE IV, 3) and will refrain from ignoble **action**. Passion in these senses is a vital part of the good man's life. While virtue governs both proper **action** and **passion**, generosity is better characterized by the proper activity of giving and doing good, than by the proper passivity of having good done to us and of refusing to do evil.

c. **THE GREATER GRATITUDE AND PRAISE ACCORDED PROPER GIVING THAN THAT ACCORDED PROPER TAKING REFLECTS ITS GREATER VIRTUE.** Gratitude and praise reflect what people think is more virtuous. They are given more to the man who **gives** than to the man who **refuses to take** improperly.

d. **BY BEING HARDER TO DO, GIVING SHOWS IT IS THE GREATER VIRTUE.** Within the division between **harder** and **easier** things to do, virtue falls on the side of the harder, especially when one is developing a virtue. Most people find it harder to **give** to others than to **take** or **receive** from them. They are more apt to be stingy than to be dishonest. If it were not more difficult, more people would give properly. This greater difficulty is one of the reasons why people are grateful to the generous and honor them.

e. **LINGUISTIC USAGE ASSOCIATES "GENEROSITY" WITH PROPER GIVING, "JUSTICE" WITH PROPER TAKING.** When people see someone refusing to take from the wrong person, they call him **just**, not **generous**. We might add here that when a person refuses to receive from the wrong person, e.g. from someone who has even less or from someone who acquired his money unjustly, we think of him as having a proper sense of **shame** (**Rh** II, 6 & **NE** IV, 9) or as being **high-minded** or self-respecting (**NE** IV, 3). We do not call this generosity, even if we do recognize the way a person's ability to generate the money he needs contributes to his ability to act rightly in such matters.

f. **THEIR GIVING MAKES THE GENEROUS THE MOST USEFUL AND THEREFORE THE MOST LOVED.** Being useful to others tends to stimulate **love** and **friendliness** (**Rh** II, 4). The fact that generous people are "perhaps the most loved of all virtuous characters" attests again to the priority of giving, since it is their giving that makes them most useful.

4. GENEROSITY AS THE VIRTUE

Aristotle offers the following observations on the nature of generosity as the virtue of this power and on how the generous person functions. Aristotle says,

> a. Now virtuous actions are noble and done for the sake of the noble. Therefore the generous man... will give for the sake of the noble, and rightly; for he will give to the right people, the right amounts, and at the right time, with all the other qualifications that accompany right giving; and that too with pleasure or without pain; for that which is virtuous is pleasant or free from pain--least of all will it be painful. But he who gives to the wrong people or not for the sake of the noble but for some other cause, will be called not generous but by some other name. Nor is he generous who gives with pain; for he would prefer the wealth to the noble act, and this is not characteristic of a generous man. (1120a 23-31)

> b. But no more will the generous man take from **wrong sources**; for such taking is not characteristic of the man who sets no store by wealth. Nor will he be a ready asker; for it is not characteristic of a man who confers benefits to accept them lightly. But he will take from the **right sources**, e.g. from his own possessions, not as something noble but as a necessity, that he may have something to give. Nor will he neglect his own property, since he wishes by means of this to help others. (1120a 32-b2)

> c. And he will refrain from giving to **anybody** and **everybody**, that he may have something to give to the **right people**, at the right time, and where it is noble to do so. (1120b 2-3)

> d. It is highly characteristic of a generous man also to go to **excess in giving**, so that he leaves too little for himself; for it is the nature of a generous man not to look to himself. (1120b 4-5)

> e. The term "generosity" is used relatively to **a man's substance**; for generosity resides not in the multiplicity of the gifts but in the state of character of the giver, and this is relative to

the giver's substance. There is therefore nothing to prevent the man who gives less from being the more generous man, if he has less to give. (1120b 6-9)

f. Those are thought to be more generous who have **not made** their wealth but **inherited** it; for in the first place they have no experience of want, and secondly all men are fonder of their own productions, as are parents and poets. It is not easy for the generous man to be rich since he is not apt either at taking or at keeping, but at giving away, and does not value wealth for its own sake but as a means to giving. Hence comes the charge that is brought against fortune that those who deserve riches most get it least. But it is not unreasonable that it should turn out so; for he cannot have wealth, any more than anything else, if he does not take pains to have it. (1120b 10-20)

g. Yet he will not **give** to the **wrong people**, nor at the wrong time, and so on; for he would no longer be acting in accordance with generosity, and if he spent on these objects he would have nothing to spend on the right objects. (1120b 21-3)

h. He is generous who spends according to his substance and on the right subjects; and he who exceeds is **extravagant**. Hence we do not call despots extravagant; for it is thought not easy for them to give and spend beyond the amount of their possessions. (1120b 24-27)

i. Generosity, then, being a mean with regard to the **g i v i n g** and **taking** of wealth, the generous man will both give and spend the right amounts and on the right objects, alike in small things and in great, and that with pleasure; he will also take the right amounts and from the right sources. For, the virtue being a mean with regard to both, he will do both as he ought; since this sort of taking accompanies proper giving, and that which is not of this sort is contrary to it, and accordingly the giving and taking that accompany each other are present in the same man, while the contrary kinds evidently are not. (1120b 7-35)

j. But if he happens to spend in a manner contrary to what is right and noble, he will be **pained**, but **moderately** and as he ought; for it is the mark of virtue both to be pleased and to be pained at the right objects and in the right way. (1121a 1-5)

k. The generous man is easy to deal with in money matters; for he can be **got the better of**, since he sets no store by money, and is more annoyed if he has not spent something that he ought than pained if he has spent something that he ought not, and does not agree with the saying of Simonides. (1121a 6-9)

COMMENTARY. It is not easy to tell when we are being either extravagant or too tight. There are many factors involved. The basic formula for generosity includes both the **needs** and **deserts** of the agent (A) who stimulates our desire to help (M) as well as our other **w i s h e s** and

resources. Our own wishes are obviously affected by the weight and direction of our prior commitments and the resources we have available for helping others after meeting these prior responsibilities.

We can state the formula for the ratio between these factors this way.

$$\frac{\text{The agent's NEEDS X his DESERTS X our GIFT}}{\text{Our WISHES X our RESOURCES}} = \text{our GENEROSITY}$$

When the ratio is right between these agent (A) and material (M) factors, the act is **generous,** when improper, our act is **extravagant, miserly** or **exploitative.**

We can see how these various factors come into play by examining the following points Aristotle made about the **generous** character.

    a. **GENEROSITY FINDS PLEASURE IN PROPER GIVING.** The giver's motive is often revealed by the **pleasure** or **pain** he takes in his action. A generous response (F) is pleasant and free from pain. Finding pain in the act of giving is a sign that the act is not being done in a generous spirit. Such pain signals a sense of loss and indicates that **possession** was preferred to **using** one's money to act nobly. We are not talking, of course, about cases in which money is withheld because one has other ethically legitimate commitments, but about people who give without the primary wish to act nobly by being helpful.

When people do not give from a **noble wish** (T), they are not thought generous. Drug dealers, for example, give away drugs hoping to get people hooked on them. Prostitutes are also called "hookers." Although the term is thought to derive from the provisioning practices of General Hooker during the American Civil War, "hooked" is an apt fishing metaphor because of its oral and exploitative reference.

    b. **GENEROSITY CONCERNS GENERATING MONEY AND NOT JUST GIVING, RECEIVING, TAKING AND KEEPING IT.** Unlike the **extravagant** person, the generous person is not excessive in giving his resources away. He must in fact husband and develop his resources if he is to have anything with which to be generous to others. The English "generous" conveys this idea nicely with its root meaning of generation. On our interpretation, this power to generate what we need not only gives us the confidence required to give ourselves and our things away, but also makes us creative givers in recognizing where our gifts can be most generative.

Since the **possession** of money is not a dominant wish with him, it will not lead him to excesses or deficiencies in any of these other dimensions. His **taking** from others and exploiting money-making possibilities will not be **vicious** and he will not take from the wrong **people,** or take the wrong **amounts,** or at the wrong **times,** etc. He will not ask for or want to **receive** excessively from others, either, since his basic orientation is as a giver and not as an **asker** or **petitioner.** (See **high-mindedness,** NE IV, 3). He will not be an extreme **hoarder,** either, but will draw from his own resources when it is necessary to help the right people.

c. **THE GENEROUS HELP THOSE WHO WISH TO HELP THEMSELVES.**
The more committed the generous man is to noble purposes (T), the more
focused he will be on determining **to whom** (A) he should give.   If he
gives money to the wrong people, he will have none for the right people.
The right people are those who genuinely **wish to help themselves** and
to contribute to others.

d. **THE GENEROUS TEND TO LEAVE TOO LITTLE FOR THEMSELVES
BUT NOT IN A SMALL-MINDED WAY.** The dominance of his wish to help
others (T) disposes the generous man (M) to be forgetful (F) about himself
(A), the outcome of which (T) is that he sometimes does not leave enough
for his own needs.   This is an empirical description of how generous
people behave and shows again that Aristotle is not constructing a mere
idealization of the virtuous.   It is important to realize though that a
genuinely **generous** person must also be **high-minded** and self-respecting.
The kind of self-forgetting Aristotle describes here differs from the **small-
minded** person's self-sacrifice which most often turns out to be an
extravagant giving of oneself designed to win the affection and respect
one does not really feel he or she deserves.

e. **THE DEGREE OF ONE'S GENEROSITY IS RELATIVE TO ONE'S
RESOURCES.**   The **quality** of a person's generosity cannot be determined by
the **amount** of his gift seen in isolation from his resources and the other
legitimate demands being made on those resources.   The **right amount** of
a gift (F) is relative to both agent (A) and material (M) factors.
Aristotle's concern here is with the material factor of one's own resources
and commitments (M) rather than with the nature of the person needing
help (A).   His specific concern is to show that the degree of one's
generosity is relative to one's "substance" or resources.

If we hold the agent (A) and the form of response, i.e. the gift, (F)
constant between **two** generous men (M), the one with **less** resources will
have been the more generous even though he gave the same amount.   This
relation between the size of one's resources and the degree of his
generosity (all other things being equal) holds even when one gives **less**
so long as one **had less to draw from.**

f. **THOSE WITH INHERITED WEALTH TEND TO BE MORE GENEROUS.**
Within the division between people who **made** and those who **inherited**
their money, Aristotle finds that those who made their money normally
have two attitudes which tend to make them **less** generous. In the first
place, having initially suffered from being without money, they are likely
to be more afraid to give some of it up. Secondly, like poets and other
craftsmen, they enjoy keeping their money around as both a product they
have made and as a sign of their potency and ability to make it.

If people who make a lot of money do not easily become generous,
the reverse is true as well. The generous man does not easily **become**
rich either because accumulating money is not his primary aim nor the
determining factor in his decisions. He or she does not specialize in the
taking and keeping which great accumulation requires, but in the giving
and using of money to help others.

These points suggest that the people who could **use** money most
productively to help others will tend not to have as much of it as those
who do not wish or know how to use it generously for mankind's welfare.

This is a prime reason why it is so important to honor and encourage the virtue of **magnificence** (NE IV, 2) which we examine further below in this chapter.

g. THE GENEROUS ARE CAREFUL ABOUT WHERE, WHEN AND HOW MUCH THEY GIVE SO AS NOT TO WASTE THEIR RESOURCES FOR GIVING. Aristotle here reiterates the admonition not to give to the wrong people, at the wrong time, etc. so as to have money to give to the right ones. See item c. above.

h. GIFTS ARE NO LONGER GENEROUS WHEN THEY ARE TOO HIGH RELATIVE TO OUR RESOURCES. One of the ways an **extravagant** person is distinguished from a **generous** person is by giving **beyond** his means or resources. This is in keeping with the general formula for generosity. In extravagance the ratio is not right between the gift, the deserts of the recipient, and our resources. It is not proper to give that much of our resources to such a recipient.

Aristotle believes too that this relation between one's resources and the size of one's gift explains why despots were not spoken of as being extravagant even though they gave away huge sums of money. Despots or tyrants (or other fabulously wealthy people) **do not undermine their economic security** so long as their lavish gifts are not high relative to their resources.

i. WHILE GENEROSITY REQUIRES ONE TO ATTAIN THE MEAN IN ALL THREE DIMENSIONS OF GIVING, TAKING AND RECEIVING, THE VICES IN THESE AREAS ARE NOT READILY FOUND IN THE SAME PERSON. The generous person acts rightly in giving, keeping, taking and receiving and does so with pleasure. A single generous person embodies the norm in all three dimensions (keeping is not-giving). But the contrary to this one virtue fractionates into three **separate** vices that are not necessarily found in the same person. It is a rare person who displays extreme hoarding, exploitativeness, and receptiveness.

j. THE GENEROUS PERSON IS ONLY MODERATELY PAINED BY SPENDING MONEY WRONGLY. Having said earlier that the generous person feels **pleasure** when he acts rightly about money, Aristotle now addresses the issue of **pain**. Unlike the **hoarding** person especially, a generous man will be only moderately pained if he **spends money wrongly**, e.g. by buying something he did not really need or by paying too much for something. Such excessive pain indicates an improper attitude toward money.

k. THE GENEROUS PERSON IS MORE AFRAID OF FAILING TO MAKE A RIGHT EXPENDITURE THAN OF MAKING A WRONG ONE. In that the generous person is more oriented to **using** money than to **possessing** it, he is more pained by **not** making a right purchase or gift than by the possibility of making a **wrong** one. But the fact that he is not so pained by making a mistake makes him less **afraid** of being taken advantage of which unfortunately makes him more vulnerable to being taken advantage of in questions of finance.

5. EXTRAVAGANCE AS THE VICE OF EXCESSIVE GIVING

Aristotle compares and contrasts **extravagance** with the **generous,** **exploitative** and **hoarding** characters. He notes to start with that

> The **extravagant** man errs in [the same respects] as the **generous** man, i.e. more annoyed at not buying what he should than at buying what he shouldn't; for he is neither pleased nor pained at the right things or in the right way... Extravagance exceeds in giving and not getting, and falls short in getting, while **mean-** **ness** falls short in giving, and exceeds in getting, except in small things. (1121a 8-15)

He thus starts with the way extravagance is **like** generosity and **unlike** meanness, i.e. hoarding and exploitativeness.

Aristotle thinks the pure extravagant trait is quite rare because of the way it exhausts people's resources and undermines its own foundations. He also believes that this vice is ethically superior to the two types of mean character. He observes that

> The characteristics of extravagance are not often combined; for it is not easy to give to all if you get from none; private persons soon exhaust their substance with giving, and it is to these that the name of extravagant is applied--though a man of this sort would seem to be in no small degree better than a mean man. For he is easily cured both by age and by poverty, and thus he may move towards the middle state. For he has the characteristics of the generous man, since he both gives and refrains from taking, though he does neither of these in the right manner or well. Therefore if he were brought to do so by habituation or in some other way he would be generous; for he will then give to the right people, and will not take from the wrong sources. This is why he is thought not to have a bad character; it is not the mark of a wicked or ignoble man to go to excess in giving and not taking, but only of a foolish one. The man who is extravagant in this way is thought much better than the mean man both for the aforesaid reasons and because he benefits many while the other benefits no one, not even himself. (1121a 16-28)

The pure type of extravagance quickly runs up against the objective limits on the person's resources which either cures him of his extravagance or leads him to be corrupted still further through acquiring the other vices associated with excessive **getting**. Rehabilitation and further corruption explain why pure extravagance is found so rarely.

The next problem is to explain how extravagance can so naturally decline into either improperly **receiving** or **taking** from others.

> But most extravagant people... also take from the wrong sources, and are in this respect mean. They become apt to take because they wish to spend and cannot do so easily; for their possessions soon run short. Thus they are forced to provide from some other source. At the same time, because they care nothing for honor, they take recklessly and from any source; for they have an ap-

petite for giving, and they do not mind how or from what source. Hence also their giving is not generous; for it is not noble, nor does it aim at nobility, nor is it done in the right way; sometimes they make rich those who should be poor, and will give nothing to people of respectable character, and much to flatterers or those who provide them with some pleasure. Hence also most of them are self-indulgent; for they spend lightly and waste money on their indulgences, and incline towards pleasures because they do not live with a view to what is noble. (1121a 29-b 10)

Extravagance is thus an unstable character trait which tends to expand into excessive **receptiveness** and/or **exploitativeness** in order for the person to replenish the resources he must draw upon in his giving.

Since there is a better prognosis for **extravagance** than for **meanness**, Aristotle thought it important to try to correct the former before it degenerates into the latter.

The extravagant man, then, turns into what we have described if he is left untutored, but if he is treated with care he will arrive at the intermediate and right state. But meanness is both incurable (for old age and every disability is thought to make men mean) and more innate in men than extravagance; for most men are fonder of getting money than of giving. It also extends widely, and is multiform, since there seem to be many kinds of meanness. (1121b 11-8)

The declining powers of old age and disability make us less confident about our ability to **generate** what we need, and thus disposes us toward hoarding or exploitativeness.

COMMENTARY. The extravagant character is no doubt more common today given the affluence of so many households and the lack of well-defined, more generous uses of people's money, a point discussed more fully with regard to **magnificence** later in this chapter. The extravagant man is **like** the generous man or woman in being orientated more to **giving** than to **keeping,** as shown by his **pain** at not buying what he should. But the extravagant person is excessive both in his giving and the pain he feels at not giving or spending. On the other hand, the extravagant person is **unlike** the exploitative and hoarding characters with their strong orientation toward **getting** and **keeping.** These mean characters fall short in **giving** and go to excess in **getting,** while the extravagant person does the reverse. He is excessive in giving and deficient in getting.

Aristotle is intent to explain that extravagance by itself is not as bad a vice as **hoarding** and **exploitativeness.** One reason for this judgment is the natural tendency to grow out of it through running out of resources to give away. The other reason is that the extravagant person is after all oriented toward giving to rather than taking from others. While misguided, such people are sometimes genuinely helpful to others.

If a person ceases his extravagant ways, he can become either **hoarding** and tight with whatever resources he has left, or more genuinely **generous** and appropriate in his giving. The person who is extravagant without being **self-indulgent** is the more able to reform himself short of running through all of his posessions and simply tightening up and hardening himself this way. He or she can do so through acquiring a genuinely generous wish and a clearer recognition of the proper people to give to. The giving orientation which makes this transformation possible explains why extravagant people are commonly thought better than people with miserly and exploitative characters. Hard times and friendly counsel in right giving would seem to promise considerable improvement.

In understanding the **wish** which underlies extravagance, we must start from the fact that the trait does not "aim at nobility." This is supported by the way extravagant people are indifferent to whether people are of good character and are deserving of help and will make something of it. They often give, on the other hand, to people who do not really deserve help which suggests that their real motive is to encourage "flatterers or those who provide them with some pleasure."

Instead of supporting and encouraging people of virtuous character who are trying to do ethically worthwhile things, when we are extravagant we give to **flatterers** (NE IV, 6) who satisfy our **vanity** (NE IV, 3) without regard to the corrupting effect it might have on the recipient. Children are spoiled, for example, when excessive gifts encourage their **self-indulgence** and **vanity**. Ultimately, such giving plays on the vices of others at the same time that it deepens our own vices.

Aristotle's reference to **flattery** suggests too that extravagance is a compensation for feeling **small-minded** about oneself and incapable of stimulating real friendship through one's own **friendliness** and **love**. Extravagant people normally feel unworthy of being loved and respected in their own right and develop a somewhat desperate need to be flattered and appreciated to make up for this deficiency.

Excessive giving becomes a way to stimulate the flattery and reassurance they crave in order to salve and compensate for their painful small-mindedness. At best, this is only a quick fix, allowing temporary relief without really solving the problem through becoming more genuinely friendly and interested in people's development, their own included. Indeed, the whole strategy is based on the small-minded assumption that the only way they could be loved is by giving their money, not truly themselves.

The fact that extravagance tends rather naturally to end up in one of the two forms of meanness and/or in self-indulgence, provides a nice example of the interaction between the various moral and emotional attitudes. If he is always giving his money away and spending it lavishly on others, he will soon run out--unless he is fabulously wealthy. This tendency to run out of money poses a fundamental choice for the extravagant person. If he is to continue his extravagant behavior, he has only the two alternatives of exploitativeness and receptiveness for replenishing his resources. We can exclude generating his own money as a third alternative since extravagance is by definition a matter of giving and spending beyond what one can generate through one's own means. And we can also exclude hoarding in that its focus on keeping tends to run counter to extravagant spending and giving.

The first alternative means to replenish his resources is to become more receptively dependent on others to give him the things he will then squander in his own extravagance. This can take the form of making others feel sorry for him and encouraging them to feel good about helping him even though they might actually be worse off than he is. The attitude is also common, for example, among husbands who take from the family budget in order to make a big impression where they drink.

The aggressively receptive and dependent approach often dances right up to the line of exploitativeness but crosses over only when the person wishes to take from others rather than to be the recipient of their gifts and be taken care of by them. The exploitative person wishes to be a predator while the receptive person wishes to be provided for and protected. With the first, the extravagant person becomes a flatterer to take from others, while with the second he becomes obsequious so as not to offend someone from whom he wishes to receive much.

The pathway of extravagance leading to exploitativeness is found in a particularly striking way today, for example, among some homosexuals. They develop such a strongly self-indulgent and extravagant life-style based on showing off their posssessions and buying things for their friends that they feel the only way they can maintain their social standing is through incredibly lucrative criminal activities such as selling drugs and even robbing people outright.

These observations suggest why extravagance undermines the principles of proper wish, deliberation and choice. Given his or her excessive desires for reassurance, the extravagant person tends to feel he has no **choice** in giving excessively to others. If he does not do so, he fears they will ignore and abandon him. He does not **deliberate** about how to live a more virtuous and noble life simply because in his desperation to be loved and admired he does not truly **wish** noble things such as caring for others and working to be himself at his best.

6. HOARDING AS THE VICE OF DEFICIENT GIVING

As we have noted, Aristotle recognized two different forms of meanness, one of which is a deficiency in **giving**, the other an excess in **taking**. He makes this explicit when he says that meanness

> consists in two things, deficiency in giving and excess in taking, and is not found complete in all men but is sometimes divided; some men go to excess in taking, others fall short in giving. (1121b 18-20)

So a person can be hoarding without being exploitative and vice versa.

In the present section he describes the **hoarding** or miserly orientation and shows that there are two different types of hoarding character depending on the other motives involved.

> Those who are called by such names as "miserly," "niggardly," "close", "stingy", all fall short in giving, but do not covet the possessions of others nor wish to get them. In some this is due to a sort of honesty and avoidance of what is **disgraceful** (for some seem, or at least profess, to hoard their money for this reason, that they may not some day be forced to do something disgraceful; to this class belong the cheese parer and everyone of the sort; he is so called from his excess of unwillingness to give anything); while others again keep their hands off the property of

others from **fear**, on the ground that it is not easy, if one takes the property of others oneself, to avoid having one's own taken by them; they are therefore content neither to take nor to give. (1121b 20-9)

COMMENTARY. The reader should always remember that the particular quality of a given vice is always determined by how far it is removed from the virtuous mean and how it is caught up in constellations of other virtues and vices. Failing to see how a vice operates in the context of a person's whole character and life situation allows one to slip easily into moralism and to lose sight of the living reality of who people are. Aristotle distinguishes in the present case between two wishes by which people justify their **hoarding** responses. And while neither one is fully noble, they nicely illustrate the qualitative difference between people who have taken the same vice to a greater or lesser extreme and the general idea of people having developed themselves to different levels of human productiveness and virtue.

a. **HOARDING COMBINED WITH A LOVE OF JUSTICE AND A PROPER SENSE OF SHAME.** The most productive wish people can have for their hoarding is actually a syndrome of attitudes involving other moral and emotional powers. Here the wish to be **honest** and **just** (**NE** V) and the fear of being forced to act **shamefully** (**Rh** II, 6 & **NE** IV, 9) leads them to hoard their money. This constellation of traits involves a less extreme degree of hoarding and is closer to the generative and generous response.

Fromm has taught that such people can be relatively productive and not terribly far from the mean. They can be greatly concerned about justice with an acute sense that "what is mine is mine and what is yours is yours." While they are not cheats, they are not particularly generous either. Greatly concerned about their independence, they see their store of goods as the means of maintaining that independence. Being dependent on others seems both shameful in itself and an invitation to do shameful things. They have a strong sense of right and wrong and do not like being told what to do.

Freud added to this description of the hoarding orientation such aspects as a preoccupation with cleanliness, orderliness and punctuality. More importantly for our purposes here is Fromm's recognition of the hoarding orientation's role in the spirit of craftsmanship. The more productive it becomes, the more the hoarding attitude shows the craftsman's virtues of skill, discipline, self-control, patience and a profound respect for standards. On the other hand, the more extreme the hoarding attitude, the more rigidly orderly, punctual, and preoccupied with cleanliness it is and the less open the person is to learning anything new.

b. **HOARDING COMBINED WITH DEEP FEARFULNESS.** This group of hoarding people is less productive and farther from the mean. They are more afraid and are marked by their lack of **courage** (**NE** III, 6-9). A vicious circle ensues. With the elevation of the wish to hoard as the dominant motivation one actually becomes more afraid that other people will take one's things. Where in the first case hoarding is somewhat moderated by being in the service of the higher powers of **justice** and **high-mindedness**, here there is no check against acting out the fear of losing everything. Hoarding becomes a goal in and of itself.

In such cases the person inhibits his wish to take from others, but does so only to lessen his fear they will take from him. Expediency rules with no regard for the wish to act justly and nobly for their own sake. This seems to have been the fear and the wish upon which Hobbes called for a Leviathan of a state to protect people's property and lives from one another. But the more hoarding and withdrawn he becomes, the more he severs his relations with others and the more isolated and afraid he becomes. This dammed-up and walled-in state is then a fertile breeding-ground for **envy** and **spite**.

7. EXPLOITATIVENESS AS THE VICE OF EXCESSIVE TAKING

In describing the **exploitative** orientation, Aristotle once again identifies different forms of the vice based on the vices in other moral powers which become involved in this vice's operation. In contrast to hoarding people, he observes that

> Others... exceed in respect of taking by taking anything and from any source, e.g. those who ply sordid trades, pimps and all such people, and those who lend small sums and at high rates. For all of these take more than they ought and from wrong sources. What is common to them is evidently sordid love of gain; they all put up with a bad name for the sake of gain, and **little** gain at that. For those who make **great** gains but from wrong sources, and not the right gains, e.g. despots when they sack cities and spoil temples, we do not call mean but rather wicked, impious, and un-just. But the gambler and the robber belong to the class of the mean, since they have a sordid love of gain. For it is for gain that both of them ply their craft and endure the disgrace of it, and the one faces the greatest dangers for the sake of the booty, while the other makes gain from his friends, to whom he ought to be giving. Both, then, since they are willing to make gain from wrong sources, are sordid lovers of gain; therefore all such forms of taking are mean. (1121b 30-1122a 13)

COMMENTARY. Again we must keep in mind this crucial idea of level of productiveness if we are to approach people with the exploitative trait in a spirit of friendly realism. Aristotle himself pictures here only the more excessively exploitative and vicious character, a practice in keeping with his intent to highlight the vices relative to generosity. In contrast, Fromm's clinical understanding of the exploitative trait highlights as well people who are more productively exploitative, i.e. those closer to the mean. He sees this trait in **entrepreneurial** characters who are capable of drawing people and resources together for common purposes, whether they be economic, political, cultural or scientific.

Productively exploitative entrepreneurs are capable of making demands on others and acting boldly to create new enterprises and start new initiatives in society. Obviously, some entrepreneurs are more ethical and just than others, but this is a difference within the fact that their economic function calls for exploitative attitudes in this technical sense. The whole range of possible examples of the exploitative character, from the productive entrepreneur to the most vicious armed robber, displays forms of development of the single moral and emotional power to take money and the things it will buy. In each case the **taking** dimension has become dominant and has affected, and been affected by, the development of the person's other moral and emotional powers although at crucially different degrees away from the virtuous and generous disposition. Maccoby has spoken of this character as having the qualities of a junglefighter, but notes that the more virtuously it is developed, the more the person becomes a defender of the innocent against social predators.

Following his usual method of division, Aristotle distinguishes here between taking on a large scale and on a smaller one, and within this class of takers on a smaller scale he distinguishes between those who face great dangers in doing so and those who take from their friends. Just as he distinguished the extravagance of a common man from the excessive giving of tyrants and the fabulously wealthy, he distinguishes different forms of exploitativeness according to their degree of excess beyond the norm. If a man was an exploiter on such a large scale that he sacked cities and spoiled temples, he was not called mean but "wicked, impious, and unjust."

The sordid love of gain is the principal aim of the exploitative character, at least in its extreme form. This character seeks gain even at the expense of destroying the person's reputation and of his **high-minded** desire to be worthy of honor and respect (**NE** IV, 3). This indifference to one's own moral worth implies **shamelessness** (**NE** IV, 9 and **Rh** II, 6) which in turn implies a deficient love for a good person before whom one would be ashamed for his exploitativeness. Michael Maccoby observed in describing what he called "The Junglefighter," in **THE GAMESMAN**, that exploitative characters typically have demanding, ambitious mothers and weak fathers who they do not emulate--where in other terms we would say that the mother's ambition is more greed and vanity than a true desire to be honored by others.

Aristotle distinguishes between two groups of exploiters according to the other vices involved in their pursuit of sordid gain.

a. **EXPLOITATIVENESS COMBINED WITH RECKLESSNESS.** This group includes robbers and dope-dealers. They show the vice of **recklessness** or excessive spirit (**NE** III, 7) in risking their lives for money. It takes great spirit or guts to face such danger, but of course this is not so much moral **courage** as energy and daring in the pur-suit of greed. The tragedy is that the great natural endowments many criminals have in these areas might have been committed to more noble purposes if they had had finer people to emulate and a more morally inspiring upbringing.

b. **EXPLOITATIVENESS COMBINED WITH FLATTERY AND/OR CONTENTIOUSNESS.** This group includes gamblers, usurious money-lenders and pimps, all of whom show a desire to take from their friends. This implies either a deficiency of **friendliness** and concern which we term **contentiousness**, and/or the **flatterer**'s calculatingly excessive concern for the pleasure of others (**NE** IV, 6). None of the types in this class shows a generous interest in the well-being and development of the friends they exploit.

8. HOARDING AND EXPLOITATIVENESS
ARE WORSE THAN EXTRAVAGANCE

Finally, Aristotle explains why the two forms of meanness are thought to be more contrary to true generosity. He says that

it is natural that meanness is described as the contrary of generosity; for not only is it a greater evil than extravagance, but men err more often in this direction than in the way of extravagance as we have described it. (1122a 14-6)

COMMENTARY. Aristotle thought extreme forms of **exploitativeness** and **hoarding** are more evil than **extravagance** because they involve more active harm to others and because they are more commonly adopted. He could have offered a more satisfactory comparison, however, if he had not contrasted these extreme vices with a more moderate instance of the **receptive** character. His doing so explains why he would speak of this character as tending toward generosity, but not the other two. What is needed to make a more proper comparison is an equally extreme and therefore vicious degree of receptive dependence on others.

Such excessive receptiveness brings in its train a broader array of other vices than Aristotle mentions with regard to the form of extravagance which, as he describes it, is closer to the mean. One thinks immediately, for example, of the anger and even physical violence extremely receptive people often indulge in when they feel abandoned by those they expect to provide for them. The **macho** and **insolent-sadistic** attitude is often associated with this kind of demanding receptiveness combined with **exploitativeness**.

The point for now, though, is simply to note the need to evaluate instances of the different vices of receptiveness, hoarding and exploitativeness only when they are equally far removed from the mean, the virtue of generosity. (For Fromm's disagreement with Freud over the ranking of the power of the three orientations to undermine mental health, see **THE HEART OF MAN.**)

B. MONEY ON A CIVIC SCALE (NE IV, 2)

1. MAGNIFICENCE, NIGGARDLINESS AND VULGARITY
AS THE VIRTUE AND VICES OF THIS POWER

Magnificence entails generosity but differs in the scale of both the agents (A) to which it responds and the form (F) of its response. It also differs by dealing only with giving, and not taking or receiving. Aristotle says that magnificence

> also seems to be a virtue concerned with wealth; but it does not like generosity extend to all the actions that are concerned with wealth, but only to those that involve spending and giving; and in these surpasses generosity in scale. For, as the name itself suggests, it is a fitting expenditure involving largeness of scale. But the scale is relative; for the expense of equipping a trireme [a war-ship] is not the same as that of heading a sacred embassy. It is what is fitting, then, in relation to the agent, and to the circumstances and the object. The man who in small and middling things spends according to the merits of the case is not called magnificent (e.g. the man who can say 'many a gift I gave the wanderer'), but only the man who does so in great things. For the magnificent man is generous, but the generous man is not necessarily magnificent. (1122a 20-30)

There are three varieties in how this power can be developed. **Magnificence** is the virtue, **vulgarity** the vice of excess, and **niggardliness** the vice of defect.

> The deficiency of this state of character is called niggardliness, the excess vulgarity, lack of taste, and the like, which do not go to excess in the amount spent on right objects, but by showy expenditure in the wrong circumstances and the wrong manner... (1122a 31-4)

COMMENTARY. With this power we are talking about how people with considerable money and power use it to create a certain spirit and atmosphere in communities and organizations. The range of potential application is from architecture and urban planning to interior decoration and the staging of parties, ceremonies, celebrations and the like. It is an absolutely fundamental aspect of leadership on the highest level because it sets the tone and inspires the spirit of whole organizations and communities.

The vices associated with this virtue make it clear that it is possible to do these things according to what is either more or less fitting and in good or bad taste. We will soon see why it is so important for

177

leaders to develop an aesthetic sensibility in cultivating the morale of their followers. Just as **high-mindedness** (NE IV, 3) is a matter of squaring what we believe we deserve with what we actually deserve and doing so on a high level of moral accomplishment, so too **magnificence** is a relative matter of squaring our expenditures with the requirements of an occasion of high social significance.

Magnificence is distinguished from generosity in several ways, the first of which is by its focus simply on **giving** and **using** instead of on how one takes, receives and keeps money as well. Secondly, it refers to the virtuous giving and expenditure of money on a **large** scale. This usage restricted the virtue to rich people. While a strong argument can be made for singling out the rich in this way, Aristotle also says important things about this virtue which apply to anyone in a managerial and leadership position.

One might feel it improper for Aristotle to single out as a virtue an attitude and character trait which requires considerable wealth for its exercise and development. Doing so tends to violate the democratic sensibilities of modern intellectuals. But consider the alternatives. Are we to pretend there is no difference in the financial resources people either own outright or control as managers and administrators? And that this difference in resources and power creates no difference in people's moral opportunities and obligations?

The view that people with special privileges, resources and talents have thereby no special responsibilities stems from at least two sources. On the democratic side, it comes from the fear that acknowledging any significant difference between us means surrendering the belief that we have an equal right to develop ourselves. On the oligarchic side, it comes from the desire to act as though money and status were their own rewards and those striving for and attaining them owed nothing to others.

Together these two attitudes supplanted the ancient and medieval view of **noblesse oblige**, i.e. that those with outstanding qualities and rank, "noble" in this sense, were obligated to be noble in the moral sense used throughout this book. As a people we seem to have lost the sense that those with the gifts of intelligence, drive, physical beauty, money and position should use them to create institutions and a cultural environment which promotes human development and the respect of man and nature. The virtue of magnificence is the character trait which disposes people who control the expenditure of large sums to do so wisely and well. While we might no longer consciously recognize this virtue, the American public has shown a great hunger and appreciation for it in the past few years.

2. MAGNIFICENCE AS THE VIRTUE

The following passages reveal various aspects of the functioning of magnificence touching on all four aspects of its causality.

a. The magnificent man is like an artist; for he can see what is fitting and spend large sums tastefully. For ... a state of character is determined by its activities and by its objects. Now the expenses of the magnificent man are large and fitting. Such, therefore, are also his results; for thus there will be a great expenditure and one that is fitting to its result. Therefore the result should be worthy of the expense, and the expense should be worthy of the result, or should even exceed it. (1122a 34-b 3)

b. And the magnificent man will spend such sums for the sake of nobility; for this is common to the virtues. And further he will do so gladly and lavishly; for nice calculation is a niggardly thing. (1122b 6-8)

c. And he will consider how the result can be made most noble and beautiful and most becoming rather than for how much it can be produced or how it can be produced most cheaply. It is necessary, then, that the magnificent man be also generous. For the generous man also will spend what he ought and as he ought; and it is in these matters that the greatness implied in the name of the magnificent man--his bigness, as it were--is manifested, since generosity is concerned with these matters; and at an equal expense he will produce a more magnificent work of art. For a possession and a work of art have not the same excellence. The most honored possession is that which is worth most, e.g. gold, but the most honored work of art is that which is great, noble and beautiful (for the contemplation of such a work inspires admiration, and so does magnificence); and a work has an excellence--viz. magnificence--which involves magnitude. (1122b 9-17)

d. Magnificence is an attribute of expenditures of the kind which we call noble, e.g. those connected with the gods--votive offerings, buildings, sacrifices--and similarly with any form of religious worship, and all those that are proper objects of public-spirited ambition, as when people think they ought to equip a chorus or a trireme, or entertain the city in a brilliant way. (1122b 18-22)

e. But in all cases... we have regard to the agent as well, and ask who he is and what means he has; for the expenditure should be worthy of his means, and suit not only the result but the producer also. Hence a poor man cannot be magnificent, since he has not the means to spend large sums fittingly; and he who tries is a fool, since he spends beyond what can be expected of him and what is proper, but it is right expenditure that is virtuous. But great expenditure is becoming to those who have suitable

means to start with, acquired by their own efforts or from ancestors or connections, and to people of high birth or reputation, and
so on; for all these things bring greatness and prestige. (1122b
23-35)

f. Of private occasions of expenditure the most suitable are those
that take place once for all, e.g. a wedding or anything of the
kind, or anything that interests the whole city or the people of
position in it, and also the receiving of foreign guests and the
sending of them on their way, and gifts and counter-gifts; for the
magnificent man spends not on himself but on public objects, and
gifts bear some resemblance to votive offerings. (1123a 1-7)

g. A magnificent man will also furnish his house suitably to his
wealth (even a house is a sort of public ornament) and will spend
by preference on those works that are lasting (for these are the
most noble and beautiful, and on every class of things he will
spend what is becoming; for the same things are not suitable for
gods and for men, nor in a temple and in a tomb. (1123a 7-11)

h. And since each expenditure may be great of its kind, and what
is most magnificent absolutely is great expenditure on a great object, but what is magnificent here is what is great in these circumstances, and greatness in the work differs from greatness in
the expense (for the most beautiful ball or bottle is magnificent
as a gift to a child, but the price of it is small and mean)--
therefore it is characteristic of the magnificent man, whatever
kind of result he is producing, to produce it magnificently (for
such a result is not easily surpassed) and to make it worthy of
the expenditure. (1123a 12-18)

COMMENTARY. Anyone in a leadership position, or who is trying to
involve the wealthy in community affairs, must develop an acute sense of
this virtue. And anyone with money and power who lacks such artistry
himself should find someone who has it to handle these things for him.

a. MAGNIFICENCE SHOWS ITS ARTISTRY IN SPENDING LARGE SUMS
TO CREATE A FITTING EFFECT FOR WORTHY PURPOSES. Aristotle's emphasis throughout is on the artistic quality of the person with the virtue of
magnificence and his or her ability to do what is fitting and tasteful in
making great expenditures for community and organizational purposes. Here
he is declaring the general causal principle that the magnificent man's
form of response and expenditure (F) should be appropriate to the function
and object (T) for which it is intended, and vice versa. This means on the
one hand, not spending a lot of money on what is only a vulgar display,
and on the other hand, not scrimping on something that could be very inspiring in bringing a community, institution or organization together around
shared purposes.

The man or woman with the virtue of magnificence has a deep sensitivity to community feelings and to what people need by way of encouragement at a given time. They have an eye and an ear and a palette
for what is fitting. If a wealthy or powerful person lacks this virtue, he
should take his lead from someone who has it--even if they lack money

or power of their own.

b. **MAGNIFICENCE WISHES TO CREATE BEAUTIFUL OBJECTS AND OCCA-SIONS WHICH INSPIRE THE NOBLE WISH FOR FRIENDLINESS AND HUMAN DEVELOPMENT.** We will see more precisely further below the kinds of expenditures involved in magnificence. Aristotle's point here is that the magnificent person is animated by the same proper **w i s h** as found in all of the other virtues. He or she will give "for the sake of nobility" and "will do so gladly and lavishly." We take this to mean that he conducts all of his public affairs with an eye to inspiring a communal spirit of friendliness and concern for human development and the respect for human dignity.

c. **THE MAGNIFICENCE OF A CREATION IS NOT FOUND IN ITS COST BUT IN THE GRANDEUR AND ADMIRABLENESS OF THE EFFECT ACHIEVED.** The artistic purpose of the magnificent person is to create something which "inspires admiration" not because of its monetary value but for its greatness and nobility. He or she does things which inspire a love and admiration of nobility, and can do so only because of his own sense of beauty and nobility. The effect created is not just from the fact of great expenditures, because with an equal amount of money, the magnificent person creates a more magnificent result. It takes a **generous** spirit to be magnificent, but just because one is generous does not mean he will have the gift of creating just the right spirit in public celebrations and projects even if he has a huge budget for the occasion.

d. **MAGNIFICENT EXPENDITURES ARE MADE FOR PUBLIC AFFAIRS AND CEREMONIES, FOR RELIGION AND THE ARTS AND FOR THE CONSTRUCTION OF INSPIRING PUBLIC SPACES.** The traditional focus of magnificent actions was in providing for the celebration of religion, of the arts, to provide expensive military equipment and all manner of public spaces and ceremonies. To contribute such things was the object of the public-spirited ambitions of wealthy citizens. Today we would add to the list things like the endowment of research institutions.

e. **MAGNIFICENT EXPENDITURES SHOULD FIT BOTH THE RESOURCES OF THE PRODUCER AND THE EFFECT SOUGHT.** The expenditure or form of response (F) must obviously be in keeping with the means of the person (M) making it. If he spends more than he has, the person would be foolish, and no virtuous man is a fool. As we have stressed before, a person must be in an appropriate position to draw on his or her institutional resources in order to be magnificent on a grand scale. If he spends less than he could afford on an appropriate expenditure, he shows the vice of niggardliness.

f. **MAGNIFICENT EXPENDITURES ARE ALSO MADE FOR SPECIAL PRIVATE OCCASIONS.** Interestingly, Aristotle thought that magnificence was also appropriate for private celebrations of what we would call "once in a lifetime" events rather than for regular affairs, which would be **vulgar**. These special occasions include weddings, private affairs which nonetheless concern the whole community or its leaders, the entertainment of foreign dignitaries, etc. But even when there is a guest list, and only certain people are invited, the expenditures of a magnificent person have a public and not a private and personal object in view. They are to create a sense of communal spirit and shared human values.

g. **A CERTAIN MAGNIFICENCE IS APPROPRIATE IN A WEALTHY PERSON'S HOME.** Even the magnificent person's home will reflect his or her values and sense of community responsibility, since it too is a kind of "public ornament." One thinks for example of Mount Vernon or Monticello. His sense of quality means he will buy things of lasting beauty and nobility, not cheap, trendy things. (After twenty centuries and more, we still admire the taste of some of these ancient peoples.) Magnificent people contribute to the flourishing of art through their appreciation and support, in a way that **vulgar** rich people lack the cultivation for. But as in everything else the magnificent person will do what is fitting. He will not build a vulgar temple to himself.

h. **MAGNIFICENCE LEADS ONE TO DO WHAT IS BOTH GREAT AND FITTING, WHETHER ON A SMALL STAGE OR A LARGE ONE.** The magnificent man's most striking feature is his ability to do what is both great and fitting in the circumstances whether it be in small things like giving a gift to a child, arranging a dinner party or for the large events we have described. There is a sense of things he does being larger than life in a way that draws attention not to him but to the value in things we commonly ignore.

3. VULGARITY AS THE VICE OF EXCESSIVE DISPLAY

Aristotle notes that

The man who goes to excess and is vulgar exceeds... by spending beyond what is right. For on small objects of expenditure he spends much and displays a tasteless showiness; e.g. he gives a club dinner on the scale of a wedding banquet, and when he provides the chorus for a comedy he brings them on to the stage in purple as they do at Megara. And all such things he will do not for nobility's sake but to show off his wealth, and because he thinks he is admired because of these things, and where he ought to spend much he spends little and where little, much. (1123a 18–27)

COMMENTARY. Vulgarity is used here to denote the tendency to make large, tasteless expenditures designed to draw attention to the giver rather than to inspire admiration for shared communal values and purposes. To that extent, the attitude cheapens the quality of even the greatest expenditures by being self-promoting rather than transcendent. Once again, we see how the vices of one power such as those of **vanity** and **excessive ambition** (NE IV, 3 & 4), can distort the operation and development of another power. This example shows too the crucial difference between doing things for the sake of their intrinsic nobility versus doing them for the sake of being honored. Vulgarity is effectively the vice of **extravagance** on a larger scale.

4. NIGGARDLINESS AS THE VICE OF DEFICIENT DISPLAY

Aristotle says

The niggardly man on the other hand will fall short in everything, and after spending the greatest sums will spoil the nobility
and beauty of the result for a trifle, and whatever he is doing he
will hesitate and consider how he may spend least, and lament
even that, and think he is doing everything on a bigger scale
than he ought. (1123a 28-31)

COMMENTARY. Niggardliness shows the effect of extreme **hoarding**
on the operation of this power. It is a dramatic and pitiful result of this
trait when people spoil what would otherwise be a beautiful effect to save
nothing more than a "trifle." Calculating always on how to cut costs,
lamenting and exaggerating every expenditure, these are all the marks of
someone who cares more about possessing his or her money than about
using it wisely and well.

5. THE STATUS OF VULGARITY AND NIGGARDLINESS AS VICES

Aristotle concludes that

These states of character, then, are vices; yet they do not bring
disgrace because they are neither harmful to one's neighbor nor
very unseemly. (1123a 32-3)

COMMENTARY. We can see how these two are vices insofar as they
undermine one's **wish** to do fine and noble things for his community, distort his **deliberations** and lead him to make unsound and narrowly self-
serving **choices**. But even so, as described here, they do not involve
genuinely evil choices and are more sins of omission than commision.
Even the niggardly character gives something to community projects--just
not in a very tasteful and noble way. Nonetheless both vulgarity and niggardliness have a more or less subtly demoralizing influence on people's
ability to set aside self-seeking in the name of larger shared interests.
    While even less wealthy people can have the magnificent person's
artistic flair for making occasions grand and inspiring, the Greeks were
right to hold people with greater wealth and power to a higher standard of
public-spirited ambition so that even those who cannot yet wish for
nobility proper will at least try to appear as though they do.

CHAPTER FOUR

Handling Self-Respect and Status

Inventory

A. ACTION AND HONOR ON ISSUES OF GREAT IMPORTANCE (NE IV, 3)

1. HIGH-MINDEDNESS, SMALL-MINDEDNESS, AND VANITY
   AS THE VIRTUE AND VICES OF THIS POWER

2. AGENTS WHICH BEST REVEAL HIGH-MINDEDNESS

3. OUR STATES OF MIND WHEN HIGH-MINDED

   a. Generous and properly ambitious
   b. Being socially privileged
   c. Courageous but not reckless
   d. Generous and kind in serving others
   e. Neither arrogant toward the meek
      nor subservient to the mighty
   f. Properly ambitious rather than trendy
   g. Truthful and courageous about love and hate
   h. Friendly and neither obsequious nor flattering
   i. Gentle and neither excessively angry nor apathetic
   j. Talking properly about oneself and others
   k. Self-reliant rather than dependent
   i. Loving things of beauty

4. THE VICES OF SMALL-MINDEDNESS AND VANITY

B. ACTION AND HONOR ON A MORE PERSONAL SCALE (NE IV, 4)

1. AMBITION, LACK OF AMBITION, AND EXCESSIVE AMBITION
   AS THE VIRTUE AND VICES OF THIS POWER

2. AMBIVALENCE ABOUT AMBITION

   - deficient ambition can reflect either small-mindedness or
     vanity
   - excessive ambition limits us to what others will honor,
     while vanity strives to maintain a given image in our own
     eyes
   - proper ambition seems ambivalent as a virtue because
     sometimes it takes the form of having no ambition
     for a bad temptation

A. ACTION AND HONOR ON ISSUES OF GREAT IMPORTANCE (NE IV, 3)

1. HIGH-MINDEDNESS, SMALL-MINDEDNESS, AND VANITY AS THE VIRTUE AND VICES OF THIS POWER

Aristotle defines high-mindedness with reference to the ratio between what one believes he deserves and what he is actually worthy of.

Now the man is thought to be high-minded who thinks himself worthy of great things, being worthy of them; for he who does so beyond his deserts is a fool, but no virtuous man is foolish or silly. (1123b 1-3)

But high-mindedness is not simply having a one-to-one ratio between what one believes he deserves and has a right to claim from others and what he is actually worthy of.

For he who is worthy of little and thinks himself worthy of little is **self-controlled**, but not high-minded; for high-mindedness implies greatness, as beauty implies good-sized body, and little people may be neat and well-proportioned but cannot be beautiful. (1123b 4-7)

One must be worthy of great things in order to be high-minded. Just because a person of little worth refuses to indulge in pleasing fantasies does not make him high-minded even if it does show his or her self-control.

Vanity, on the other hand, occurs when one's beliefs and claims are greater than his real worth. Aristotle says

He who thinks himself worthy of great things, being unworthy of them, is vain; though not everyone who thinks himself worthy of more than he is really worthy of is vain. (1123b 7-8)

We will explain further below the kind of person who can exaggerate his worth without being vain.

Finally, small-mindedness occurs when one's beliefs and claims are less than his real worth.

The man who thinks himself worthy of less than he is really worthy of is small-minded, whether his deserts be great or moderate, or his deserts be small but his claims yet smaller. And the man whose deserts are great would seem most small-minded; for what would he have done if they had been less? (1123b 9-12)

High-mindedness occurs when one's beliefs and actual worth are in a one to one ratio and one's worth is great.

The high-minded man... is an extreme in respect of the **greatness** of his claims, but a mean in respect of the **rightness** of them; for he claims what is in accordance with his merits, while the others go to excess or fall short. (1123b 13-4)

Like all the other virtues, high-mindedness is an extreme with respect to its goodness, but a mean with respect to the ratio between these expectations and claims and his or her true merits.

COMMENTARY. The ratio of factors involved in determining one's high-mindedness can be expressed in a rather straightforward formula.

$$\frac{\text{CLAIMS ON OTHERS \& BELIEFS ABOUT OURSELVES}}{\text{WHAT WE ARE TRULY WORTHY OF}} = \begin{array}{c} \text{HIGH-MINDED,} \\ \text{SMALL-MINDED,} \\ \text{OR VAIN} \end{array}$$

Our claims on others and beliefs about ourselves are the numerator in the formula while our actual worth is the denominator. We must now clarify the nature of these factors, especially the question of how we might determine what we are truly worthy of.

It is important first, though, to see that high-mindedness concerns what we expect from ourselves as well as others. It is from initially developing improper expectations and claims on others that we later develop distorted beliefs about ourselves. Our distorted view of ourselves is then used to justify and explain our continuing to have improper expectations toward others.

This causal relation between what we expect from others and our view of our own worth explains, for example, the common occurence of vanity arising as a compensation for having been treated as unimportant. Such a person can come to feel that the only way he could be thought worthy of respect would be through exaggerating his merits. Such a person will then vacillate between small-mindedness and vanity. Another person might have always been spoiled by family attention to the point that he never outgrew his or her childhood vanity and expects other people to treat him in the same way as well.

The basic idea is that our view of our own worth has two sides to it: what we expect and claim from others and what we expect from ourselves. What we expect from ourselves is in the service of the claims we try to make on others and what our history has led us to expect from them. While our claims about ourselves arise in the context of what we must believe in order to pursue the claims we wish to make, it is equally true that these beliefs about ourselves serve to consolidate the kinds of relations we will accept with others. No relation is fully acceptable that does not sanction our already established belief about our own worth, whether it be high-minded, small-minded or vain.

To determine whether our estimation of our own worth is virtuous or vicious, we must see whether these claims and expectations have been distorted by vices in our other moral and emotional powers so that they are not true to the reality. Aristotle's statement that a high-minded person "thinks himself worthy of great things, being worthy of them" means that

188

the person's claims square with what his character, talent and skill really are as borne out by what he has actually done. They are the ground of our expectations about ourselves. It is because we have shown ourselves to be of good character through the fine things we have done, or at least tried to do, that we feel we deserve to be treated honorably by others. And with regard to ourselves, when we are high-minded, we believe we are worthy of taking noble actions in the face of challenging circumstances and are not **ashamed** of trying to do so. The high-minded person bases his or her claims about how others should treat him on this realistic judgment about what he has actually done and expects of himself in the future.

We can put this causally in the following way. The high-minded man thinks he (M) both has responded and will continue to respond to important things (A) in a virtuous way (F). He also believes that virtuous actions and character traits (F) should stimulate (Tfa) the respect (F) of other people (M) because such nobility is the most important thing for human beings to learn to value.

We should not assume though that someone is vain just because he thought he was worthy of doing a fine thing that proved beyond him. He might simply be over-extending himself trying to rise to a crisis. While this is an error in judgment, it can nonetheless show a strong high-minded impulse which could mature into the real thing under the proper training and experience. Vanity is more self-serving than simply trying to do more than one is capable of. While all vain people make exaggerated claims, not all exaggerated claims are signs of vanity.

As a general rule, the greater the difference between a person's real ability and accomplishments and his personal expectations and public claims, the more vain or small-minded he is. But just because a disjunction between claims and realities constitutes vice does not mean that a simple identity between them constitutes high-mindedness. Only their identity on a high level of accomplishment and virtue is high-minded. Identity on lower levels is called **self-control** in the generic and not the specific sense of the term.

This relation between high-mindedness and self-control is more than simply a verbal one. Self-indulgence in physical pleasures spills over to encourage vain people to indulge in pleasing fantasies about their own worth and about the satisfaction of their claims on others. Depression, on the other hand, by diminishing the pleasure one finds in life leads to a diminished sense of self-worth and expectations about the future. Such a state is small-mindedness.

The high-minded man or woman makes great claims about his worth, but does so without arrogating to himself more than his due. He or she makes these claims not because he has a particularly strong love of being honored, but because he loves nobility and wishes and expects others to honor it as well. A high-minded person would betray what he most loved if he did not expect others to respect the noble things he has done and which he gives every reason to believe he will continue to do in the future.

When a good person insists on being treated with respect, he is standing up for far more than just his own ego. When people do not respect those who do and strive to do noble things, they do not respect nobility itself and reveal and tend to spread their own ignobility to others.

2. AGENTS WHICH BEST REVEAL HIGH-MINDEDNESS

The Greek term for high-mindedness is **megalopsychea** which means literally "great-souled" or "large-minded", and implies a person's concern with things of **great importance**. Aristotle observed that

> High-mindedness seems even from its name to be concerned with great things; what sort of great things is the first question we must try to answer. (1123a 33-5)

In that it deals with things of great importance, we must expect that this virtue will provide exceptional insight into the meaning of proper wish, deliberation and choice, into synergism, cybernetics and decision-making.

Aristotle argues that high-mindedness is the virtuous development of our power (M) to handle other people's either honoring or dishonoring us. Speaking about what the high-minded person expects from others, he says

> If... he deserves and claims great things, and above all the greatest things, he will be concerned with one thing in particular. Desert is relative to **external** goods; and the greatest of these, we should say, is that which we render to the gods, and which people of position most aim at, and which is the prize appointed for the noblest deeds; and this is honor; that is surely the greatest of external goods. Honors and dishonors, therefore, are the objects with respect to which the high-minded man is as he should be. And even apart from argument it is with honor that high-minded men appear to be concerned; for it is honor that they chiefly claim, but in accordance with their deserts. (1123b 15-23)

We will soon see how handling other people's respect or disrespect improperly can distort the development of our whole character.

COMMENTARY. Since our study assumes that each moral power (M) is defined with regard to a specific class of agents (A) to which it responds (F), we must determine the agents with which high-mindedness is concerned. Aristotle's problem here is the same as that encountered in identifying the best agents for testing courage, self-control and generosity in our first three chapters. Starting from the assumption that high-mindedness concerns how we handle the greatest things we can expect from others, he strives to identify what these things are by determining 1) what is given to the highest beings such as the gods, 2) what men of high position most aim at, and 3) what is accorded to people who perform the finest and most noble actions.

Honor and **respect** satisfies all three requirements and thus seems to be the highest thing we can expect from others. It is with regard to his or her response (F) to honors and dishonors, and more generally the respect and disrespect of others, (A) that the high-minded man (M) shows himself to be "as he should be." He (M) responds rightly (F) when either honored or dishonored (A) and neither undervalues himself nor allows honors to go to his head. As a result, he is not devastated by disrespect either.

The high-minded man or woman expects people (M) to respond to virtuous actions and virtuous people (A) as being worthy of honor and respect (F). He expects them to honor him and anyone else like him in nobility and virtue since expecting this from them tends to promote their love of nobility and virtue too. By signalling what he feels is most worthy, the high-minded person indicates what he believes people should aim for, what he will not countenance their abusing, and what he will respect them for achieving. This ancient attitude of expecting respect for one's virtue is in marked contrast with the contemporary assumption that a truly moral person should not care about what others think of him.

The high-minded person does not aim at honor above all, however. That would elevate what others think of us above what we think of ourselves, above the inner sense of goodness and rightness that can only come through acting nobly. It would be to pursue the excessive **ambition** of finding favor in the eyes of others rather than developing the power to believe in ourselves.

In shaping their characters, children of course must depend on what other people honor in their attitudes and behavior. How could they not do so given their undeveloped state, their inexperience, and their need for guidance? But for an adult to depend so much on other's approval is to foresake the exercise of his own moral powers and to leave himself dependent on the changing fashions of what his peers respect. If everyone pursued external approval above all, no one could rise above the moral understanding of his society, and mankind would be incapable of checking and correcting itself. Social progress requires high-minded Archons who become sources of moral guidance through articulating the contemporary requirements for human development they discern in themselves, their circumstances and those they care for.

It is noteworthy in closing that since this power determines our general sense of what we deserve from others, it will be implicated in all our other powers insofar as they involve some sense of the **justice** of our own actions or those taken by others. For example, an excessive or vain estimation of our worth will dispose us to excessive **anger** by increasing our belief that others are **unjustified** in slighting us. This applies as well to how we handle **money** and the **good** and **bad fortune of others.**

3. OUR STATES OF MIND WHEN HIGH-MINDED

Aristotle begins his analysis with the general principle that

Now the high-minded man, since he deserves most, must be good in the highest degree; for the better man always deserves more, and the best man most. Therefore the truly high-minded man must be good. And **greatness in every virtue** would seem to be characteristic of a high-minded man. And it would be most unbecoming for a high-minded man to fly from danger, swinging his arms by his sides, or to wrong another; for to what end should he do disgraceful acts, he to whom nothing is great? If we consider him point by point, we shall see the utter absurdity of a high-minded man who is not good... Honor is the prize of virtue, and it is to the good that it is rendered. High-mindedness then, seems to be a sort of crown of the virtues; for it makes them greater, and it is not found without them. Therefore it is hard to be truly high-minded; for it is impossible without nobility and goodness of character. (1123b 28-1124a 4)

It is the high-minded person's **other** virtues which make him or her deserve the greatest honor.

He goes on to examine how the honor and respect of others can function as the agent to which high-mindedness responds.

> It is chiefly with honors and dishonors, then, that the high-minded man is concerned; and at honors that are great and conferred by good men he will be moderately pleased, thinking that he is coming by his own; for there can be no honor that is worthy of perfect virtue, yet he will at any rate accept it since they have nothing greater to bestow on him; but honor from casual people and on trifling grounds he will utterly despise, since it is not this that he deserves, and dishonor too, since in his case it cannot be just. (1124a 5-12)

How a person handles (F) the honor and respect (A) others either bestow on or deny him gives us the clearest insight into his high-mindedness (M).

Aristotle lists the following virtues as components of the state of mind (M) in which we are able to respond to the world (A) in a high-minded way (F). Sometimes he is explicit about the virtue(s) in question, other times we must infer the virtue (M) from his reference to the agent (A) with which it deals.

The reader should note both the way in which having the other virtues lays the foundation for having self-respect, and the way in which having the **high-minded** ability to handle properly what other people think helps us develop these other virtues in the first place. With high-minded self-respect, we are not inclined to do bad things merely to impress others.

> a. The high-minded man is concerned with honors; yet he will also bear himself with moderation towards **wealth** and **power** and all good or evil fortune, whatever may befall him, and will neither be over-joyed by good fortune nor over-pained by evil. For not even towards honor does he bear himself as if it were a very great thing. Power and wealth are desirable for the sake of honor (at least those who have them wish to get honor by means of them); and for him to whom even honor is a little thing the others must be so too. Hence high-minded men are thought to be **disdainful**. (1124a 13-9)

> b. The goods of fortune are also thought to contribute towards high-mindedness. For men who are **well-born** are thought worthy of honor, and so are those who enjoy power or wealth; for they are in a superior position, and everything that has a superiority in something good is held in greater honor. Hence even such things make men more high-minded; for they are honored by some for having them; but in truth the good man alone is to be honored; he, however, who has both advantages is thought the more worthy of honor. But those who without virtue have such goods are neither justified in making great claims nor entitled to

the name "high-minded"; for these things imply perfect virtue. **Disdainful** and **insolent**, however, even those who have such goods become. For without virtue it is not easy to bear gracefully the **goods of fortune**; and, being unable to bear them, and thinking themselves superior to others, they despise others and themselves do what they please. They imitate the high-minded man without being like him, and this they do where they can; so they do not act virtuously, but they do despise others. For the high-minded man despises justly (since he thinks truly), but the many do so at random. (1124a 20-1124b 6)

c. He does not **run into trifling dangers**, nor is he **fond of danger**, because he honors few things; but he will face great dangers, and when he is in danger he is unsparing of his life, knowing that there are conditions on which life is not worth having. (1124b 7-8)

d. And he is the sort of man to **confer benefits**, but he is **ashamed of receiving them**; for the one is the mark of a superior, the other of an inferior. And he is apt to confer greater benefits in return; for thus the original benefactor besides being paid will incur a debt to him, and will be the gainer by the transaction. They seem also to remember any service they have done, but not those they have received (for he who receives a favor is inferior to him who has done it, but the high-minded man wishes to be superior), and to hear of the former with pleasure, of the latter with displeasure; this, it seems, is why Thetis did not mention to Zeus the services she had done him, and why the Spartans did not recount their services to the Athenians, but those they had received. (1124b 8-17)

e. It is a mark of the high-minded man also to ask for nothing or scarcely anything, but to give help readily, and to be **dignified** towards people who enjoy **high position** and **good fortune**, but **unassuming** toward those of the **middle class**; for it is a difficult and lofty thing to be superior to the former, but easy to be so to the latter, and a lofty bearing over the former is no mark of ill-breeding, but over humble people it is as vulgar as a display of strength against the weak. (1124b 18-23)

f. Again, it is characteristic of the high-minded man not to aim at the things **commonly held in honor**, or the things in which **others excel**; to be sluggish and to hold back except where **great honor** or a **great work** is at stake, and to be a man of **few** deeds, but of great and notable ones. (1124b 23-7)

g. He must also be **open** in his **hate** and in his **love** (for to conceal one's feelings, i.e. to care less for **truth** than for **what people will think**, is a **coward's** part), and must speak and act openly; for he is free of speech because he is **disdainful** and **contemptuous**, and he is given to telling the truth, except when he speaks about himself ironically to the common people. (1124b 27-31)

h. He must be unable to make his life revolve around another, unless it be a **friend**; for this is **slavish**, and for this reason all **flatterers** are servile and people lacking in self-respect are flatterers. Nor is he given to admiration; for nothing to him is great. (1125a 1-3)

i. Nor is he mindful of **wrongs**; for it is not the part of a high-minded man to have a long memory, especially for wrongs, but rather to overlook them. (1125a 4-5)

j. Nor is he a **gossip**; for he will speak neither about **himself** nor about **another**, since he cares not to be **praised** nor for others to be **blamed**; nor again is he given to praise; and for the same reason he is not an evil-speaker, even about his **enemies**, except from **haughtiness**. (1125a 6-9)

k. With regard to (the need for) necessary or (even) small favors he is least of all men given to **lamentation** or the **asking of favors**; for it is the part of one who takes such matters seriously to behave so with respect to them. (1125a 10-12)

l. He is one who will possess **beautiful** and **profitless** things rather than profitable and useful ones; for this is more proper to a character that suffices to itself. (1125a 12-3)

Finally, Aristotle mentions three **physical traits** which characterize the behavior of high-minded people.

A slow step is thought proper to the high-minded man, a deep voice, and a level utterance; for the man who takes few things seriously is not likely to be hurried, nor the man who thinks nothing great to be excited, while a shrill voice and a rapid gait are the result of hurry and excitement. (1125a 13-6)

COMMENTARY. We have seen that the formula for high-mindedness includes in its denominator what we truly deserve, i.e. what we can realistically expect from ourselves and have a right to claim from others. In its numerator are what we claim from others and believe about ourselves. We will now see how all these factors reflect the state of our other virtues and vices. Since high-mindedness concerns the truth of our high claims about our actions and character, it is impossible without having the other virtues which allow us to act rightly. The high-minded person accepts being honored by people who genuinely value the virtues in the areas of his accomplishments. But he disdains honors bestowed by those who do not love noble action and who honor him on such trifling grounds as the fact of his being famous. And he rejects ever being treated dishonorably since he deserves better than this. Such treatment is unjust both to him and to the principles he stands for.

High-mindedness determines both the source (A) of the honor and respect such a person wishes to receive and the reasons (T) for which he wishes to be honored. Unlike the **vain** person, high-minded men and women do not take excessive pleasure in other people's opinions of them, nor do they feel dependent on anybody else's judgment of their worth. They have a deep confidence in themselves and in their having earned the right to be respected.

It is through their having developed the other virtues that high-minded people have such a self-respecting state of mind. Seeing the respect of good people as the highest tribute, they do not feel their good actions and accomplishments entitle them to other rewards such as money or sexual favors.

Aristotle gives a detailed treatment of the virtues he thought are particularly required for one to be high-minded. He returns repeatedly to the many ways in which believing in ourselves frees us to handle other agents properly and develop the other virtues as well. He also touches on common misperceptions which less morally-developed people often have about high-minded people. We see how people at one character extreme tend to see people who are actually at the mean as though they were at the opposite extreme. In this case, small-minded people see high-minded people as vain.

a. **GENEROUS AND PROPERLY AMBITIOUS.** The high-minded person must be **generous** (NE IV, 1) and properly **ambitious** (NE IV, 4) since he handles himself well not only about **honor**, but also **money** and **power**. Good fortune in these areas will not give him a big head, and bad fortune will not destroy him. The reason is simple enough. Many men and women have done **shameful** things when it comes to money and power which destroyed their self-respect and made high-mindedness impossible. Excess in ambition and in taking or keeping money is after all defined at least in part as having acted in ways one cannot genuinely respect in pursuing these things.

Yet if being excessive in our desires for money and power can make us small-minded and lacking in self-respect, it is also true that being small-minded can lead us to feel we need great power and money to bolster our self-image. Aristotle shows his sharp clinical eye with the observation that most people are more concerned with their status and honor in other's eyes than they are with these things **per se**. They want them to bolster their self-esteem. Feeling we need these external supports can also promote great vanity both as a compensation to wounded self-esteem and as a justification for the excessive demands we make on others in attempting to acquire them.

The key implication is that a person with genuine self-esteem is simply not so tempted to mishandle money and power through trying to impress other people. The down side is that high-minded people with this sense of proportion are rather inevitably thought of as **disdainful** (Rh II, 2 and 11) toward the very things many people value the most.

Just as with **self-indulgence**, if an excessive desire for wealth and power is awakened and grows strong in a young person's character before the wish for noble action can grow to dominance, these lesser wishes will keep high-mindedness from developing to its full potential.

b. **BEING SOCIALLY PRIVILEGED.** Like wealth and power, being born into social privilege can have a mixed effect on people by promoting either a high-minded state of mind or **insolent sadism** and unwarranted **disdain**. Those who are well-placed in these respects are commonly honored simply because of their social position without regard for their moral virtue. Some such people, however, feel they must live up to the responsibilities which come with their social standing by doing noble things and becoming virtuous. Anyone combining the external signs of good fortune with nobility of character will be honored more than people having only one or the other of these qualities. One thinks for example of the public images of Franklin Roosevelt and John Kennedy. In truth, though, virtue and nobility of character is the only thing worthy of the highest honor. The other good things of life merely extend our resources for right action.

Wealth, power and privilege are extremely potent agents, however, and unless they work to further virtuous development, they tend to make the otherwise fortunate person **insolent-sadistic** or excessively **disdainful** (See **Rh** II, 2). Believing themselves superior in all respects without being morally so, they become disdainfully indifferent to other people's needs and even sadistic toward them. Their great temptation is to think they can do anything they want and that they need only play as if they were high-minded.

Unlike genuinely virtuous people, they disdain others on the basis of indulgent whims and not from moral insight into what deserves to be rejected. Most people, and not just the rich, are disdainful without really being superior to the things they look down on. Only the high-minded person shows virtuous and genuinely noble disdain, a point established in discussing **indignation** in the final chapter of this work.

c. **COURAGEOUS BUT NOT RECKLESS.** Because the high-minded person does not need to impress others with his or her **courage**, he does not act from a **reckless** state of mind (**NE** III, 7). He loves life, has a developed sense of ongoing moral responsibilities, and has no cheap sense of having to maintain a reputation before ignoble people. His deliberations about how to handle dangerous situations are not distorted by nervously looking over his shoulder at what other people are thinking about him.

As a result, he is not tempted to rush into dangerous situations lightly. But he will face serious threats to the possibility of living a noble life, since he is committed to acting nobly and promoting nobility. When he does risk his life, he is merely displaying his willingness to lose it for the sake of the values and goals for which he lives it.

d. **GENEROUS AND KIND IN SERVING OTHERS.** The high-minded person is **generous** (**NE** IV, 1) and **kind** (**Rh** II, 7). He believes it is better to give than to receive, and that the person who characteristically gives is superior to him who characteristically receives and depends upon others. He prefers that they benefit more from his kindness than he benefit from theirs. It is a source of **s h a m e** (**R h** II, 6 & **NE** IV, 9) for such a person to receive benefits from people on whom he should be conferring them.

Aristotle shows the decidedly empirical nature of his observations when he notes that this preference to be the giver tends to make the high-minded person's memories selective in his own favor. His wish to be genuinely helpful (and not just to appear so the way **vain** people do) makes him more likely to remember the good he has done than the help or kindness others have shown him. He is pleased by reports of the former and pained by those of the latter.

Aristotle is describing the best men he and his students knew rather than generating a theoretical model through abstract deductions from first principles. Even the best men have failings, in this case the difficulty of admitting the degree to which they have been beneficiaries rather than benefactors. To a certain extent this is an inevitable consequence of the noble wish to be a benefactor rather than primarily a beneficiary.

But it can be taken beyond this inevitable degree to the point where it becomes a real vice. This would show not only a failing of self-knowledge and **truthfulness** (NE IV, 7), but also a lack of **friendliness** (NE IV, 6). It is unfriendly to make others always the inferior, passive beneficiary by refusing to acknowledge when they have been active and generous and kind. The refusal to acknowledge a subordinate's contributions is actually damaging to his or her development. It promotes **small-mindedness, anger** (Rh II, 2 and NE IV, 5) and even **envy** (Rh II, 10) by making the person feel impotent to make a contribution and acquire the honor and recognition he or she deserves.

e. **NEITHER ARROGANT TO THE MEEK NOR SUBSERVIENT TO THE MIGHTY.** The high-minded man is more insistent on being treated as he deserves by the wealthy and powerful than by those who are less influential and less threatening. Rumi, the Persian Sufi, captured this idea with his observation that "Even when the wise man visits the Prince, it is the Prince who is visiting the wise man." As we saw in item a. above, the high-minded man is not overly impressed by wealth and power and insists that respect be shown more for what is noble and virtuous than for things which do not necessarily show their owner's own excellence.

His insistence is not **insolent** or **sadistic** (Rh II, 2), however, because it does not aim at trying to compensate for **small-mindedness** through humiliating and hurting others. The high-minded man shows his freedom from this attitude, for example, through his easy manner with people without great wealth and power. He does not search for pretexts to throw his weight around.

f. **PROPERLY AMBITIOUS RATHER THAN TRENDY.** The high-minded man is not overly **ambitious** (NE IV, 4) to be like all the others. Just as he is not seduced by wealth and power, neither is he caught up in the narrow fashion of his own time. This kind of small-mindedness is found among people who wear clothing fashions, for example, which make them look ridiculous because of not being compatible with their body type or age, even though they could look quite attractive if they respected their own best features.

The point is to determine a proper wish for oneself in keeping with one's natural endowment, talents, stage of development and life circumstances. The high-minded person chooses carefully where he or she can best integrate his powers to make the greatest contribution. He concentrates on a few things he can master instead of dabbling in many things where he will remain a dilettante and second-rate. He exercises strategic judgment in committing himself to selected projects rather than self-indulgently spreading himself thin on too many.

g. **TRUTHFUL AND COURAGEOUS ABOUT LOVE AND HATE.** The high-minded person is naturally **truthful** (NE IV, 7) about what he loves and hates because he lacks the fear of what others think which causes **cow-**

197

ards (**NE** III, 6-9) to speak and act falsely. When we are cowardly, we come to care more about what others think, and how we are expected to talk and act, than we do about what we think is true and noble. Is it any wonder that such people often do not know what they love and hate, or what they think is real and good and important? The high-minded man's rightful **disdain** (**Rh** II, 11) for what is ignoble shows he is free to tell the truth. In dealing with common people, however, he is not disdainful but tends to speak with ironical **self-depreciation**. (See item e. above.)

h. **FRIENDLY AND NEITHER OBSEQUIOUS NOR FLATTERING.** High-minded people are **friendly** (**NE** IV, 6) without being either **flatterers** or **servile** and **obsequious**. The high-minded man's proper sense of priorities about what others think allows him to "revolve around another" without losing his or her self-respect when that person is his friend and they share the common aim of developing themselves. Unlike **small-minded** people who characteristically admire others as greater and more capable of doing good than themselves, the high-minded person is able to see himself as a source of good because he is generous and loving and therefore independent. He does not admire others as being so great that to be worthwhile he must receive or take good things from them.

Such mutuality is not possible for those with either of the two vices of excessive concern for another. The vice of **obsequiousness** or **servility** assumes our inferiority and dependence and makes us revolve around others as the source from which alone we might **receive** some sense of goodness about ourselves. We are led to betray ourselves in the futile effort to make them make us feel better about ourselves. Feeling this way, we obviously cannot function as a source of goodness in our own right. In modern parlance, the combination of small-mindedness, obsequiousness and anger turned inward is called **masochism**.

Flattery is a second form of excessive desire to please others. But contrary to how it might appear, it is not emotionally servile but wishes to **take** what is thought good through manipulating an outside source. It often masks a **sadistic** attitude toward its object. In neither flattery nor obsequiousness can a person act with true self-respect.

i. **GENTLE AND NEITHER EXCESSIVELY ANGRY NOR APATHETIC.** The high-minded person is **gentle** and not disposed to excessive **anger** (**Rh** II, 2 and **NE** IV, 5). He does not hold grudges and is not hyper-sensitive to slights. He is calm rather than touchy. Vain people show the fragility of their self-esteem by nursing the memory of slights, while the small-minded show theirs by failing to see the injustice when they are slighted and being **apathetic**. Having self-respect both contributes to handling anger rightly, and reflects one's power to do so.

This insistence on the high-minded person's gentleness might appear to contradict his aforementioned readiness to rise up in anger when dishonored. But many slights are not worthy of such exertion, and it is especially with regard to them that high-minded self-assurance disposes one to be understanding and forgiving.

j. **TALKING PROPERLY ABOUT ONESELF AND OTHERS.** The high-minded man is not a gossip. Lacking the vices of **vanity** and **boastfulness** (**NE** IV, 7), he does not like to talk about himself nor to encourage others to praise him. He is not prone to excessive admiration and praise for others (item h. above), but neither is he **envious** and **spiteful** (Rh II, 10) toward them. He is not interested in tearing people down and even has respect for his enemies, although he might be haughty toward them in a confrontation to rally those he leads through showing he is not intimidated.

k.   **SELF-RELIANT RATHER THAN DEPENDENT.** Because the high-minded man is **courageous**, he is not excessively pained by small misfortunes nor does he lament about them. Because he is **g e n e r o u s**, he does not tend to look for others to help him when he can generate what he needs himself. And because he wishes for and has his eye on more noble things, he sees small matters in a broader perspective than those who wish for nothing higher than the immediate gratification of trifling things. Playing "poor me" to win the support of others is not a high-minded state of mind nor can it win one genuine honor in their eyes.

l.   **LOVING THINGS OF BEAUTY.** Aiming for more than money, power and status, the high-minded person is not preoccupied with these things and is free to cultivate his or her love of beauty. He wishes to live among beautiful things--because he loves them, not because they have status in other people's eyes. The love of beauty is part of his love of nobility and excellence, and when he is in touch with beautiful things he is rooted in values supporting his self-respecting way of life. We often learn of a person's depth and cultivation by seeing the beautiful things they live among, even if they are magazine photographs taped to the wall.

Finally, with regard to his physical bearing, Aristotle notes that the high-minded person will be self-assured and calm. Since he or she sees things in a true light, he does not get all excited and agitated about them. This shows up quite naturally in his or her physical mannerisms. His movements are not frantic, but well-paced and purposive. His voice is not strained, high-pitched and sing-song, but low and even. (This applies as much to women as to men.) He is not hurried and excited, but resolute and intent.

4. THE VICES OF SMALL-MINDEDNESS AND VANITY

We have seen in the above list examples of how developing vices in our other powers leads to **small-mindedness** and/or **vanity** in this power. We must now examine these latter vices more directly in their own right. Aristotle says that they "are not thought to be bad (for they are not malicious), but only mistaken" (1125a 18). This does not mean they **do** no harm, only that in themselves they **intend** no harm.

Small-mindedness   illustrates an improper ratio between our claims on others and beliefs about ourselves, and what we are truly worthy of. Aristotle says that

> The small-minded man, being worthy of good things, robs himself
> of what he deserves, and seems to have something bad about him
> from the fact that he does not think himself worthy of good
> things, and seems also not to know himself; else he would have
> desired the things he was worthy of, since these were good. Yet
> such people are not thought fools, but to be rather unduly retir-

ing. Such a reputation, however, seems actually to make them worse; for each class of people aims at what corresponds to its worth, and these people stand back even from noble actions and undertakings, deeming themselves unworthy, and from external goods no less. (1125a 19-27)

The small-minded person is deficient in his expectations toward both himself and others relative to his real worth and ability to do fine things. This kind of humility affects not only his or her desire to be honored, but his wish to contribute what he could. He just does not expect enough of himself as a moral and emotional being.

If small-mindedness is the vice of deficient expectations, vanity is the vice of excessive ones.

Vain people, on the other hand, are fools and ignorant of themselves, and that manifestly; for, not being worthy of them, they attempt honorable undertakings, and then are found out; and they adorn themselves with clothing and outward show and such things, and wish their strokes of good fortune to be made public, and speak about them as if they would be honored for them. (1125a 28-33)

While true of both these vices, Aristotle emphasizes the foolish lack of self-knowledge vain people show about themselves.

In comparing the two vices, Aristotle says somewhat surprisingly that

small-mindedness is more opposed to high-mindedness than vanity is; for it is both commoner and worse. (1125a 34)

He believes it more common to under- than to overestimate what we expect from ourselves and others.

COMMENTARY. Aristotle always attempts to show how each virtue and vice operates with respect to the others. We will see later, for example, that **envious** and **spiteful** people (**Rh** II, 10) are identified with respect to their small-minded expectations of what they might accomplish and be worthy of on their own. But it does not follow from this that small-mindedness is essentially envious. While all envious people are small-minded, only some small-minded people are envious.

This observation allows us to explain why vanity and small-mindedness are not considered malicious and evil. Surely an exploitative burglar is vain in thinking he deserves money we worked hard for. A spiteful person, on the other hand, is small-minded in allowing himself to feel so badly when seeing our happiness, but vain in destroying something we love. These are undeniably evil attitudes and practices. But the harm caused in each instance comes from a vice other than vanity or small-mindedness, i.e. **exploitativeness** or **spite**, that specifically aims to do harm to others. Vanity and small-mindedness by themselves do not. While these extremes of exploitativeness and spite require vanity and small-mindedness, the latter do not require the former.

Aristotle's treatment of small-mindedness focuses on the way this vice undermines our ability to actualize our capacities. We see this, for example, if we examine its effect on **cowardice** (NE III, 7). Having low expectations, aims and standards means we will tend to have a diminished picture of the worth of the resources we bring to any challenge. But small-mindedness will also keep us from developing the higher wishes which give us a reason to find our courage in the first place.

Small-minded people do not hold themselves accountable for using their talents to accomplish fine things, nor do they hold others accountable for showing respect toward noble actions and the virtues which make them possible. By betraying higher standards, they allow society to decline into mediocrity and disrespect. A person lacking self-respect is hardly in a position to stand up for people and principle.

Small-mindedness makes functioning according to proper wish, deliberation and choice quite impossible. It is a vice because it undermines the **wish** to act nobly through exercising one's gifts on a high plane of excellence. As a result, one's power of **deliberation** is corrupted in both its goal and in the assessments one makes about one's resources for achieving it. And as always in the weakened state that is vice, the small-minded person feels he has little or no **choice** in what he can do.

Aristotle's account of the vain man shows him claiming to be able to do things he cannot and being easily found out in his exaggerations. His pretensions are often revealed in the way he dresses and shows off. (See **Buffoonery** for how vanity's desire to show off affects the power of **humor**, NE IV, 8.) Vain people look for anything to use in acquiring the honor they crave and know neither themselves nor the way others react to them. We see ignorance of **envy** (Rh II, 10), for example, in their belief that bragging about good fortune will lead others to honor rather than spite them.

Vanity, on the other hand, distorts proper **wish** by leading us to love our image more than the reality of doing good and growing strong. Since we are not really trying to respond to the life around us and the challenges it poses, our **deliberations** are always distorted. Our plans protect appearances more than promoting real development. Finally, such a preoccupation with our image takes on a life of its own and robs us of the power of **choice** about how we wish to live.

Aristotle thought small-mindedness was a greater vice than vanity because many more people undervalue their abilities and hold back from acting nobly than make falsely grandiose claims about themselves or try to do things beyond their power. He also thought it was worse in itself. This is an interesting judgment suggesting a real cultural difference between ancient Greece and the modern world. Outside of aggressively ambitious circles, people today are more likely to feel that being vain is worse than being small-minded. As a result, the fear of being thought vain contributes greatly to many people's becoming small-minded about their own thoughts and creativity.

In a society prone to conformity and envy, small-minded people will be inclined to see as vanity what is actually a high-minded person's effort to act according to his own proper wish, deliberation and choice. The very wish to think maturely and responsibly for oneself will be thought vain, with creative people suffering more than others.

As noted in an earlier chapter, we all start in a sense disposed toward self-indulgence, and depression can be explained as a deficiency resulting from inhibited indulgence. Now we can see how we are in a similar sense naturally disposed to vanity and that small-mindedness can be explained as a deficiency resulting from frustrated vanity. Tendencies toward indulgence and vanity are givens not requiring explanation. The problems to be explained are how people manage to become 1) **self-controlled** or **depressed** and 2) **high-minded** or **small-minded**.

Just as the infant's natural tendency to self-indulgence is overcome, and self-control is developed, only through acquiring the other virtues which require that we be self-controlled, so too natural childhood vanity is overcome, and high-mindedness is developed, only through acquiring the other virtues. Like self-indulgence in adults, vanity is maintained into adulthood only when the virtues which would draw us out of childhood's natural ego-centrism are not developed.

People tend to vacillate back and forth between small-mindedness and vanity. For example, people often become small-minded because they are frightened at the prospect of working without the support, or against the opposition of authorities. They then rather naturally shy away from fulfilling the promise of their talents. When the otherwise small-minded man feels confident and less afraid, he can just as naturally feel he is worth more than he is treated as being and becomes angry about being slighted. But since he has not actually refined his expectations by doing the work which would test his skill and reveal where he stands among his fellows, he will more than likely have excessive expectations about his actual accomplishments at the time. And that is what vanity is. Small-mindedness thus always occurs against a backdrop of a kind of vanity.

We do not become more high-minded by worrying so much about ourselves, but by working to become more generous, friendly, gentle, etc. toward others. For the vain, this means directing our attention not only toward others but toward what we must do in reality to accomplish the things we had wished for only in our fantasies. For the small-minded, it means believing in and actually using our talents for good and standing up for ourselves and what is worthy of honor in life.

Doing so requires becoming more aware of the ways we miss the mark (F) by aiming at vain, small-minded or ignoble goals (T). But such negative feedback about our mistakes (A) must serve the wish (M) of responding rightly (F) for a noble object (T), and not of confirming a negative judgment about ourselves (T). The proper wish to improve inclines us to turn from our errors, not to punish ourselves for them. A virtuous attitude trains the eye to focus on the noble goal and leads to immediate efforts at self-correction in pursuing the target. This is the **cybernetic** dimension of proper wish, deliberation and choice.

Small-mindedness is often combined with anger toward ourselves, however, leading us to seek opportunities for self-castigation and belittling whenever we miss the mark. Such hostility in treating ourselves as being worthy of very little ironically reveals suppressed vanity in expecting perfection. At the same time, it shows great indifference to our external goals in that we would never demoralize ourselves this way if we really wanted to accomplish something fine. This is where friendly realism is as important in appraising ourselves as in understanding others.

B. ACTION AND HONOR ON A MORE PERSONAL SCALE (NE IV, 4)

1. AMBITION, LACK OF AMBITION, AND EXCESSIVE AMBITION AS THE VIRTUE AND VICES OF THIS POWER

Aristotle distinguishes ambition from high-mindedness on the basis of the scale and importance of the agents to which each responds. In doing so he notes an interesting parallel between the relation of these two virtues and that already noted between **generosity** and **magnificence**.

> There seems to be in the sphere of honor also... a virtue which would appear to be related to high-mindedness as generosity is to magnificence. For neither of these has anything to do with the grand scale, but both dispose us to what is right with regard to moderate and small objects; as in getting and giving of wealth there is a mean and an excess and defect, so too honor may be desired more than is right, or less, or from the right sources and in the right way. (1126b 1-8)

The parallel is that ambition stands to high-mindedness in the same relation as generosity stands to magnificence. Both ambition and generosity respond to "moderate and small" opportunities rather than to things on a "grand scale."

COMMENTARY. We gain a key to understanding the difference between high-mindedness and ambition from the etymologies of the Greek terms. As we have seen, high-mindedness comes from **megalopsychea**, meaning great-souled. Ambition, on the other hand, comes from **philotime**, meaning the love of honor. This signals a shift away from the love of nobility in doing fine things to trying to win honor and status in the eyes of others for things which do not necessarily have much intrinsic worth. Ambition is not concerned with actions and honors on a "grand scale" of moral excellence but with "moderate and unimportant objects."

Aristotle provided in the last section a long list of the kinds of virtuous and noble actions that high-mindedness is concerned with, and which illustrated how the Greeks were more moved by mankind's possibilities for moral grandeur than by the narrow and passing fashions of what we would probably call status. No wonder they developed so many people whose accomplishments are still thought immortal. At any rate, it would seem that ambition involves other issues that do not demand so much of our moral powers and where we are being honored or have some sense of standing among our fellows for less important things. These issues are what we would probably mean by "status", things like whether we are promoted or elected to a position, or more prosaically, what we wear or drive or otherwise possess that might bring us increased standing in a certain group.

There is no contradiction in saying that a particular person is high-minded when confronted with large ethical challenges, but not particularly ambitious when it comes to worldly honors such as money, power or status. In this perspective, the big questions are the ethical ones that show either our high-mindedness, vain pretension, or small-minded fear we cannot live up to doing fine things.

Our concern here in other words is with our power to desire a certain status in other people's eyes without any necessary regard to whether it is compatible with high-minded self-respect and the development of the other virtues. Nonetheless, like sexuality and friendliness, the development of ambition or its underdevelopment is often determined by our other virtues and vices. Seen from this perspective, even an attitude such as sado-maschochism embodies a striking element of the vice of excessive ambition.

The sadist desparately desires the masochist to honor him for his cruel power and dominance while the masochist desires the honor of being associated with such an impressive personage and of being corrected by him. The sadistic and masochistic character types exemplify an excessive desire for honor that is not only excessive but is desired in a wrong way and from the wrong source. While trapped in this attitude, neither party wishes for their own development or for each other's, nor to face the parasitic nature of their relationship.

An excessive concern to be honored almost always masks small-minded fears about one's worth. These fears can then lead to a **reckless** (NE III, 7) willingness to risk everything else one loves to gain or keep the honor which authorities or groups might bestow. It is thus behind many people's sense of duty and explains how ruthless and irresponsible dutiful people can be in pursuing their sense of morality. Rather than trying to respond personally and creatively to the needs of a real person before them in a high-minded and independent spirit, the dutiful person is always looking over his shoulder at what the authorities or the community expects. His goal is not to deliberate about what needs to be done to support and promote the development of individual people facing differing environmental challenges, but to avoid trouble by imposing a set of cognitive and behavioral categories so successfully as to win honor in the eyes of people with influence.

We see this, for example, in the stereotype of the bureaucratic attitude when clerks show no human response to our problem and no high-minded, friendly or kind feeling for our distress even when we acknowledge the limitations on what their job might permit them to do. By thinking only of his or her duty, and what their supervisor will praise or blame them for, they allow their ambition to overwhelm the development of these virtues. Ironically, we see a similar kind of excessive ambition in reactionary or even traditional cultures when, for example, mothers and fathers are willing to sever all relations with children who marry into a different sect or commit some other offence that while not genuinely evil in a moral sense is nonetheless treated as a source of dishonor for the whole family.

The upshot of this analysis is that when we praise someone for having been very **ambitious** in creating something new or taking the lead in an innovative project, we might well be misspeaking. It might have been precisely because he was willing to do without significant status in other people's eyes and trusted his own judgement of what is worthy of being honored that he was able to make a break-through in going beyond what they previously honored.

In assessing someone's ambition, we must distinguish what they desire for its own sake out of a high-minded love for it, as in mastering an art or craft, from what they do for the sake of being honored for it. And obviously what might have started out as a matter of ambition can take on a life of its own and become an ingredient of his high-mindedness. It is equally true that when a person shows no self-respecting interest in developing his or her skills and appears to be lacking in ambition, he can actually be excessively ambitious about being accepted by people who are not wishing for his development and thinking about what he might contribute if he truly matures. Is this not what we see when peer pressure makes teenagers afraid to appear intelligent and concerned?

2. AMBIVALENCE ABOUT AMBITION

Already for the Greeks there was something morally ambiguous about ambition. They seem to have had the same kind of mixed feelings about it as many of us do. We both praise and blame it. Aristotle lists the following things people either blame or praise about ambition.

> We blame both the ambitious man as aiming at honor more than is right and from wrong sources, and the unambitious man as not willing to be honored even for noble reasons. (1126b 9-11)

We can go wrong either through excess or deficiency when it comes to ambition.

> But sometimes we praise the ambitious man as being manly and a lover of what is noble, and the unambitious man as being moderate and self-controlled... (1126b 12-3)

So we praise both the "ambitious" and the "unambitious" person depending on the circumstances. Aristotle resolves the ambiguity by saying that

> Evidently, since "fond of such and such an object" has more than one meaning, we do not assign the term "ambition" or "love of honor" always to the same thing, but when we **praise** the quality we think of the man who loves honor more than most people, and when we **blame** it, we think of him who loves it more than is right. (1126b 13-6)

The virtuous mean between excessive and deficient ambition is, however, without a name of its own.

> The mean being without a name, the extremes seem to dispute for its place as though that were vacant by default. But where there is excess and defect, there is also an intermediate; now men desire honor both more than they should and less; therefore, it is possible also to do so as one should; at all events this is the state of character that is praised, being an unnamed mean in

respect of honor. Relatively to ambition it seems to be unambitiousness, and relatively to unambitiousness it seems to be ambition, while relatively to both severally it seems in a sense to
be both together. This appears to be true of the other virtues
also. But in this case the extremes seem to be contradictories
because the mean has not received a name. (1126b 17-25)

COMMENTARY. It is noteworthy that we have the same trouble
speaking of the moral worth of ambition in English as the ancient Greeks
did. It is easier for us too to say what excessive and deficient ambition
are than what virtuous ambition is. After clarifying the two vices of
excess and deficiency, we will explain why it is so much harder to be
clear about the virtue of ambition than of high-mindedness. What is most
noteworthy, initially, is the fact that Aristotle felt the need to devote so
little attention to it when so many people today consider it the key to the
greatest human accomplishments. But is this not explained by his recognition that high-mindedness rather than ambition is the key to human
creativity and accomplishment, and that if anything excessive ambition is
often the greatest threat?

**– EXCESSIVE AMBITION LIMITS US TO WHAT OTHERS WILL HONOR,
WHILE VANITY STRIVES TO MAINTAIN A GIVEN IMAGE IN OUR OWN EYES.**
As explained in the INTRODUCTION, we lose our independence, to say nothing of our self-respect, when we treat what others feel about us as more
important than what we feel about ourselves and wish to contribute from
our own fully-developed powers. Yet it is being in this state that constitutes one's ambition being excessive. People are excessively ambitious
when their desire to be honored is so strong that they do not care about
the moral worth of the people who they wish to honor them or about the
things they must do to be honored. This leads them not only to do things
that are outright ignoble but to neglect opportunities and responsibilities
for more noble actions in one's family, work and community.

It is helpful to see why an excessively ambitious person is not
necessarily vain, even if he or she might be ego-centrically indifferent to
others. The excessively ambitious man does not necessarily have an exaggerated image and make false claims about his moral superiority and worthiness of the higher honors due a good man. His fault is rather in recklessly going after those less morally significant honors which contemporary society treats as more important such as organizational titles,
memberships in associations, designer fashions and other marks of social
status.

Moral and intellectual vanity can actually interfere with excessive
ambition. Vanity distorts one's perception by trying to fit everything into
an image of oneself as the world's center and tends to provoke **anger** and
spiteful put-downs by others annoyed by their disdainful assignment to the
periphery. Excessively ambitious people, on the other hand, who are
successful at it tend to manage their relations with the coolest calculation about how others react and what they honor. So if vanity tends to
make one **contentious**, in the broadest sense of being insensitive to the
pleasure and pain of others, excessive ambition tends to make us a **flatterer** (NE IV, 6).

This points back to Aristotle's earlier comment that vain people
seem foolish in not knowing themselves, their limitations and worth, and

in not really perceiving how others react to them. We can see on the other hand, however, that excessive ambition must normally be pursued with a very careful sensitivity to other's opinions as an essential part of its strategy for advancement.

The problem about excessively ambitious people's **deliberations** is not so much that they are unrealistic as that they reflect a truncated sense of what is worth **wishing** for and **choosing**. Of course an excessively ambitious man or woman can also be vain and vice versa. But they are distinct attitudes with no essential relation to one another.

- **DEFICIENT AMBITION CAN REFLECT EITHER SMALL-MINDEDNESS OR VANITY.** Aristotle says the deficiently ambitious person is "not willing to be honored even for noble reasons." We can see this in at least two ways. First, there is the person who refuses to pursue even those social honors which would place him in a better position to act nobly and possibly be of help to others. This might be a shy person, for example, with great artistic, athletic or scientific talent, who does not like people making a fuss over his abilities and achievement, does not wish really to be honored by them. This shyness becomes a true vice when it leads the person to abandon the cultivation of his talent or refuse to accept a position of public trust where his skills are needed. Such cases tie the vice of deficient ambition to that of **small-mindedness.**

There would also seem to be a deficiency of ambition associated with extreme vanity. One thinks, for example, of an extremely **spiteful** person (**Rh** II, 10). The good fortune and happiness of others triggers his small-minded dissatisfaction and resentment about the lack of fulfillment in his life. This bursts the bubble of his self-contained image which otherwise allows him to ignore his own reality. Lacking both genuine **friendliness** and **ambition**, there is little to hold him back from destroying the good fortune of the people whose happiness shattered the vain image of his own well-being.

- **PROPER AMBITION SEEMS AMBIVALENT AS A VIRTUE BECAUSE SOMETIMES IT TAKES THE FORM OF HAVING NO AMBITION FOR A BAD TEMPTATION.** So far we have focused on the vices and the reasons why we blame people for being excessive or deficient in their ambitions. But we also praise people for being more ambitious than others in pursuing noble things. Of course, some people today praise ambition even when it is thoroughly self-seeking and has no noble goal beyond personal advancement. They support even ignoble action so long as it bears the markings of social success. The philosophical situation is made complex by the fact that on other occasions people are praised for being unambitious, "moderate and self-controlled." In the contemporary setting, we might think of someone giving up a prestigious and lucrative career which did not touch their deepest wishes about the kind of person they longed to be, or refusing to follow their blind ambitions, whether this be to the commission of crimes in the White House or advancing unscrupulously up the corporate or academic ladder.

When used as a virtue, "unambitious" refers to a state in which one's high-mindedness is stronger than his ambitions for tempting but ultimately cheap honors not worth their moral cost. We saw this for example among creative people who feel they must disassociate themselves from the opinions they desire to transcend and correct. This explains why it is so hard to pin down "ambition" as a virtue because there are times when the virtuous response to an opportunity for advancement is ironically an unambitious one.

Where high-mindedness is a matter of expecting ourselves to act with moral virtue and others to honor us for doing so, ambition is a matter of expecting ourselves to attain certain social positions and others to honor us for these more external attainments. Yet clearly, different social positions and responsibilities are not equally appropriate for all people (and of course some are appropriate for none). One's gifts, interests and responsibilities have a great bearing on what ambitions any given person should pursue or shun. No matter its sphere, virtuous action is always relative to the capacities and situation of the person in question.

CHAPTER FIVE

Handling Unjustifiable Slights Against Ourselves

INVENTORY

A. THE POWER TO BE ANGRY (Rh II, 2)

1. ANGER DEFINED

2. OTHER PEOPLE'S ATTITUDES AROUSING OUR ANGER

    a. Contempt and disdain
    b. Spite and hate
    c. Insolence and sadism

3. OUR STATES OF MIND WHEN ANGERED

    a. High-minded, small-minded or vain
    b. Self-controlled, self-indulgent or depressed
    c. Generous, receptive, exploitative or hoarding
    d. Courageous, cowardly or macho
    e. Friendly, obsequious, flattering or contentious

4. PEOPLE AND BEHAVIOR AROUSING OUR ANGER

    - MARKS OF INSOLENCE AND SADISM

    a. People acting like buffoons
    b. People behaving for neither retaliation nor profit

    - MARKS OF CONTEMPT AND DISDAIN

    a. People attacking our high-mindedness, ambition and courage
    b. Friends attacking us, triggering obsequiousness and apathy
    c. People who have honored us in the past
    d. People to whom we have been kind
    e. People of no account
    f. Friends showing insensitivity to us
    g. People acting like buffoons
    h. People treating us worse than they do others
    i. People forgetting our name

    - MARKS OF SPITE AND HATE

    a. People who rejoice at our misfortune
    b. People who are indifferent to the pain they cause
    c. People who are preoccupied with our weakness and misfortune

    - PEOPLE WITH REGARD TO WHOM WE FEEL EVEN MORE SLIGHTED

    a. Those before whom we feel shame and emulation
    b. Those for whom we feel responsible

B. THE POWER TO BE CALM (Rh II, 3)

    1. CALMNESS DEFINED

    2. PEOPLE WHO CALM OUR ANGER

        a. Those who did not mean to slight us
        b. Those who treat us the same as they do themselves
        c. Those who are ashamed of what they have done
        d. Those who are afraid of us
        e. Those who take us seriously
        f. Those who have been kinder to us than we have been to them
        g. Those who are small-minded and beg for mercy
        h. Those who are high-minded and slight others
           only when justified
        i. Those who scare us or earn our respect
        j. Those who are angry at us
        k. Those who wish to emulate us

    3. OUR OWN STATES OF MIND WHEN CALM

        a. Self-controlled, friendly and witty
        b. Generous and properly ambitious
        c. Courageous and self-controlled
        d. After the passage of time, except for those who hate
        e. After our anger is spent against someone else
        f. Friendly and feeling pity
        g. Ashamed and high-minded
        h. Realizing we cannot make our anger known to the person
           slighting us

    4. HOW TO CALM PEOPLE DOWN

C. GENTLENESS, EXCESSIVE ANGER AND APATHY (NE IV, 5)
   AS THE VIRTUE AND VICES OF THIS POWER

    1. GENTLENESS AS THE VIRTUE

    2. APATHY AS THE VICE OF DEFICIENT ANGER

        - Apathy rooted in hopelessness and identification
          with the aggressor
        - Apathy rooted in depression

    3. TYPES OF EXCESSIVE ANGER

    4. EXCESSIVE ANGER IS MORE VICIOUS THAN APATHY

    5. FINDING THE LINE BETWEEN GENTLENESS AND THE VICES

A. THE POWER TO BE ANGRY (Rh II, 2)

1. ANGER DEFINED

Aristotle begins with a general definition of anger.

Anger may be defined as an impulse, accompanied by pain, to a real or apparent revenge for a real or apparent slight directed without justification towards what concerns oneself or toward what concerns one's friends. (1378a 30-2)

He goes on to qualify this definition with reference to the agents (A) arousing anger when he says that

it must always be felt toward some particular individual, e.g. Cleon, and not "man" in general. It must be felt because the other has done or intended to do something to him or one of his friends. (1378a 3-b 1)

And finally, he clarifies the form (F) and function (T) of an angry response.

It must always be attended by a certain pleasure--that which arises from the expectation of revenge. For since nobody aims at what he thinks he cannot attain, the angry man is aiming at what he can attain, and the belief that you will attain your aim is pleasant... It is also attended by a certain pleasure because the thoughts dwell upon the act of vengeance, and the images then called up cause pleasure, like the images called up in dreams. (1378b 1-9)

Interestingly, anger is thus both painful and pleasant, a fact we will explain further below.

COMMENTARY. How could "vengeance" and "the expectation of revenge" make a virtuous person happy? How could he or she aim for such a thing in good conscience? The answer is found in the distinction between the virtue of appropriate and the vice of excessive anger which people often confuse with it. Anger functions in a virtuous way when it gives us the power to resist being slighted and treated as though we and our friends were "obviously of no importance." Although we are not normally taught to recognize this, the maintenance of human rights and **high-minded** self-respect (**NE** IV, 3) depends on the virtuous development of the power of anger so that we can defend ourselves and those we love. (See also **Indignation Rh** II, 9 with regard to standing up for people to whom we are not so close.)

What though is the moral function of revenge? Virtuous anger aims at causing only that amount of pain required for stopping, and possibly correcting, a person's slighting behavior toward us and of affirming our own powers and rights in the face of such threats. As such, anger is a necessary mechanism for setting limits   in social relations, clarifying mutual expectations and enforcing systems of justice. People denied the right to be angry are denied the right to consider their wishes and efforts, indeed their very personhood, as being of any importance. Legitimate, properly proportioned anger is thus a central feedback mechanism in pursuing social relations that respect and promote the development of virtuous personality.

The fact that so many people today tend to look upon anger as essentially wrong suggests how much we have lost our belief that human dignity is something we must stand up for and that we must find the self-confidence to resist those who treat people's self-respect as unimportant. **Apathy** is the vice of deficiency in this area, **excessive anger** or **irascibility** is the contrary vice, and **gentleness** is the virtue.

We understand more fully the nature of virtuous anger when we see its synergistic relation to the other moral powers, as revealed for example in the fact that anger is "accompanied by pain." This immediately suggests that **courage** (NE   III, 7) is required for one to be appropriately angry since we must overcome our fear of the   slighting agent and gain the confidence required to fight back. We can be so afraid of the consequences of being angry   that we lose the power to express our legitimate interests. Just as we saw in the first chapter that a person can become so hopeless he no longer feels afraid, so too one can become so afraid he no longer feels his or her anger.

This connection with courage also helps clarify the way in which anger is both painful and pleasant. Just as in responding to any other threatening agent, an angry response (F) is painful even though picturing and attaining the end aimed at (T) is pleasant. We saw this earlier at NE III, 9 when Aristotle spoke of the boxer's pain at the blows and exertion of a fight, yet also of the pleasure he finds in victory and in anticipating it. There is no contradiction involved in saying that anger (M) is painful as a formal cause (F) in response to the slight (A), but that it is pleasant as an anticipation and fantasy (F) of the striking back which is its final cause (T).

In a sentence that could have been drawn from Freud's theory of dreams as wish-fulfillment, Aristotle says that the mind dwells "upon the act of vengeance," "the images" of which "cause pleasure like the images called up in dreams." Anger's pleasure comes not so much from the simple fact of this outcome, however, as from believing that our own powers (M) and response (F) will bring it about. As Aristotle says, "the belief you will attain your aim is pleasant." And this is where the relation between anger and confidence becomes most apparent. Anger entails confidence in our powers, and confidence and self-esteem are pleasurable.

The pleasure virtuous anger gives comes from feeling we can hold our own and not be overwhelmed by others. There is nobility in standing up for what is right and in stopping and correcting those who treat us wrongly. At the same time, angry exertion is itself painful, as is hurting the other person and suffering his or her anger in return. In our everyday relations, we all too often stop trying to be friends with people just because we are unwilling to go through all the exertion involved in getting angry to set our relation with them on a better track. Apathy with regard to slights spreads to include apathy with regard to love as well.

If we are unwilling to face this pain, we must surely weaken our **wish** to be our own person and to stand up for what is right. Without the ability to get appropriately angry, how can we make our own **choices** based on our own best **deliberations**? How can we strive to live in a just and righteous community?

For an agent to arouse us to anger, it must be seen as slighting us and doing so without justification. We must focus on the person's individual responsibility for the slight rather than on his or her membership in a class or group we hate. (See **Envy** and **Spite, Rh** II, 10.) Technically, our response should not be called anger if we are aroused simply by the fact that we hate a person's class, race or sex, even though they have done nothing personally to slight us or ours. This is the difference between **anger** and **hate** or **spite**--a major point examined below in this chapter and at **Rh** II, 4.

The reader might well ask, though, whether we don't sometimes get mad just because things frustrate us without our attributing any such slighting motive to them. Surely such frustration is commonly believed to cause anger by itself. This view is not supported by the evidence, however, as shown by the well-known fact of early childhood autocentrism. Young children can often be observed scolding inanimate objects, for example, for having purposely caused an accident. A broom might have fallen and caused a knock on the head and the offending object is then punished for having been bad. The child's anger seems explicitly caught up with picturing the object as having moral responsibility for its behavior. In later life, adults unconsciously make the same assumption when they are angered by what are actually no more than frustrations caused by morally neutral, natural processes.

The angry adult actually pictures the physical frustration as a symbol or result of other people's disdain, insolent-sadism, or even hate toward him. Greek mythology canonized this assumption when it attributed all manner of misfortune to the anger of the gods. (In the history of philosophy, Lucretius and Spinoza have been the great critics of such superstitions.) We are always able to calm our anger in such frustrating situations by focusing on the natural causes of our frustration and seeing that they embody no ill-will toward us. This of course requires a deep wish to embrace and be guided by reality and is not simply a cognitive operation.

FORMULA. The various factors involved in making us either angry or calm seem to be expressible in the following formula.

$$\frac{\text{AGENT'S WISHES, RESOURCES, RELATION TO US X HIS BEHAVIOR}}{\text{OUR WISHES, RESOURCES AND EXPECTATIONS}} = \frac{\text{ANGRY}}{\text{or CALM}}$$

The factors in the numerator refer to the qualities and actions of the person arousing our anger. The factors in the denominator refer to the wishes with respect to which we are being slighted, our resources for resisting them and the expectations we have of the slighting person with regard to those wishes. Being **calm** in this context is simply the contrary of being **angry.**

214

The operation of anger always involves the ratio between three basic sets of judgments. There is first a judgment about the attitudes or **wishes** of the people who anger us (A). Second, there is a complex judgment about who (M) has these motives, i.e. their **relation to us**, and the forms of **behavior** (F) which embody the motives (M) making us angry. This is especially important because we get angrier at intimates who slight us than we do at people we don't care about.

Finally, there is a complex judgment we make about ourselves. This concerns the importance we place on the **w i s h e s** being slighted, our **resources** for pursuing them, and the **expectations** (M) we have both toward ourselves and the agent (A) slighting us. It is not enough that the agent slight our wishes for us to be angry at him. He or she must do so in a way which seems **unjustified**, given our expectations of ourselves and of him. This last judgment constitutes the person's state of mind coming into the situation where someone might arouse his or her anger. We can see from these factors that vices of excess and deficiency must inevitably distort our perceptions of ourselves as well as of others.

We examine each of these judgments below starting with OTHER PEOPLE'S ATTITUDES AROUSING OUR ANGER, OUR STATES OF MIND WHEN ANGERED, and PEOPLE AND BEHAVIOR AROUSING ANGER.

2. OTHER PEOPLE'S ATTITUDES AROUSING OUR ANGER

Aristotle believes that all anger-arousing behavior is in the form of a slight and that

> slighting is the actively entertained opinion of something as obviously of no importance. We think bad things, as well as good ones, have serious importance; and we think the same of anything that tends to produce such things, while those which have little or no such tendency we consider unimportant. (1378b 10-4)

All slighting behavior takes the form of treating the wishes of another as having no importance.

There are three basic wishes which cause people to slight others and which make a big difference when it comes to figuring out how to handle the slighting person. It is really these attitudes and not the person's behavior which angers us. Aristotle says

> a. **Contempt** or **disdain** is one kind of slighting: you feel contempt for what you consider unimportant, and it is just such things that you slight. (1378b 14-5)

> b. **Spite** is another kind; it is a thwarting of another man's wishes, not to get something yourself but to prevent his getting it. The slight arises just from the fact that you do not aim at something for yourself: clearly you do not think that he can do you harm, for then you would be afraid of him instead of slighting him, nor yet that he can do you any good worth mentioning, for then you would be anxious to make friends with him. (1378b 16-23)

c. **Insolence** is also a form of slighting, since it consists in doing and saying things that cause shame to the victim, not in order that anything may happen to yourself, or because anything has happened to yourself, but simply for the pleasure involved. (Retaliation is not "insolence," but vengeance.) The cause of the pleasure thus enjoyed by the insolent man is that he thinks himself greatly superior to others when ill-treating them. That is why youths and rich men are insolent... One sort of insolence is to rob people of the honour due them; you certainly slight them thus; for it is the unimportant for good or evil, that has no honor paid to it... (1378b 22-30)

COMMENTARY. All three of these attitudes are important in understanding why we get angry at people. At a practical level they help us understand more fully the attitudes of the people who make us angry and to assess more carefully whether actual behavior warrants the picture we have developed of them. If we tend to excessive anger we are prone to seeing people as feeling one or the other of these ways toward us (depending on how we perceived the character of the formative people in our background) even when they do not. If on the other hand we are apathetic, we will be deficient in recognizing when people really do feel this way toward us.

In working with someone whose anger is excessive, it is always helpful to recognize the particular pattern of their misperception when they get angry at others. Such recognition illuminates the particular areas of their sensitivity and what we must do to make it harder for them to see us as slighting them. We must learn whether they are angry because they perceive others as disdainfully indifferent, or as hating them because of their sex or race, or as sadistically toying with and humiliating them? Knowing how people either exaggerate or are blind in these areas is a great aid in becoming more deliberate and helpful in working with the problem of anger. (There is a whole section on calming anger further below.)

The reader must make a special effort to understand the difference between insolence-sadism and spite-hate since they are so often confused with anger itself. We must remember too that Aristotle is describing here the motives which lead to unjustified slighting. Not all slighting behaviour causes anger because we sometimes feel an agent is justified in putting us in our place. Insolence-sadism and spite-hate, however, are by their nature unjustified slights against other people.

Disdain, on the other hand, is morally neutral in that it is sometimes justifiable. For example, a student might give a teacher a term paper which he spent very little time preparing and which he knows to be worth very little. For his teacher to show disdain and treat such work as being of "no importance" in fulfilling the assignment and in showing what the student is capable of doing can actually reassure the student that the teacher is a serious authority who takes the student seriously as well. We would feel betrayed by a teacher who did not encourage us to aspire to a higher standard and who actually corrupts us to expect less of ourselves.

Such a case offers a nice example of how the formula for anger and calmness works. The student's **wish** to perform on a higher level, his positive judgment about his **resources** for doing so, and his **expectation** that a teacher should hold him accountable for doing so, all fall under the **denominator** of the formula. The fact that the person **behaved** by giving him the undeservedly high mark while **relating** to him as a teacher with the **resources** to hold him to higher standards showed a disdainful **wish** toward him. All these factors fall under the **numerator**. The high-minded wish to develop ourselves would justify anger in such a situation--especially if we felt we could get through to the teacher.

Understanding a person's wish is always the key to moral analysis. The angry person wishes for something else than the **disdainful, spiteful-hateful** or **insolent-sadistic** person. As we have seen, when we are virtuously angry we take pleasure in the confidence we feel in asserting our just interests against someone who has slighted them. We find pleasure too in punishing the person for his offense in such a way as to uphold what is right and contribute to his or her doing what is right. The pleasure comes not so much from the pain or harm caused the offender as from the proper wish to exercise our moral powers for the protection and development of man. Doing so is a legitimate source of high-minded pride.

a. CONTEMPT AND DISDAIN. As we have noted, contempt or disdain is more morally neutral than is commonly thought and can reflect either a virtuous or a vicious disposition. The vicious person relishes a delicious feeling of contempt for others from an unjustified feeling of moral superiority. The virtuous person, on the other hand, finds contempt and disdain an unwanted, painful feeling at encountering something reprehensible. Disdain is forced on a virtuous person, sought by the vicious; warranted in the first case, unjustified in the second. Modern usage, however, tends to treat this attitude as essentially unjustifiable. Does this not reflect a loss of faith in values which should cause us to feel contempt or disdain toward those who willingly violate them? Proper disdain is discussed briefly at **R h** II, 11 as the response a good person makes to bad things which he would not wish to **emulate.**

If, for example, we value genuine hospitality and graciousness, we are not likely to appreciate mere affectations but will keep our distance and be disdainful toward such behavior. It is always with regard to upholding such a higher standard that Aristotle speaks of contempt and disdain in a positive way.

In this section, however, his focus is on **unjustified** contempt or disdain. His point is that we are made angry when we see someone as looking down on us in an unjustifiable way because he or she has an excessive view of his own importance. (See **Vanity, NE** IV, 3.) Disdain is rooted in a straightforward wish to think of ourselves as superior in our own right, and is revealed by the sweetness we find in ignoring the importance of others. The precise quality of this attitude will become clearer when distinguished from the other two discussed below and in discussing further below the behaviors which reveal this attitude. Aristotle seems to have felt it was the most common source of slights.

b. SPITE AND HATE. This attitude is a matter of taking pleasure in the undeserved bad fortune of others. Its motive is to undermine or destroy their good fortune, not so that we can gain it for ourselves, but so that we can eliminate a source of pain at not having accomplished or acquired things for ourselves. Unlike anger proper, spite's pleasure has nothing to do with the confident belief in our power to pursue our interests and stand against those who slight us. It is rather a cold satisfaction in the undoing of others who we irrationally see as somehow the source of our unhappiness. The attitude is treated more fully at **Friendship** and **Enmity** (Rh II, 4) and **Envy and Spite** (Rh II, 10).

Spite is rooted in **envy** and reflects the loss of **confidence** and **courage** required to **emulate** (Rh II, 11) the accomplishments and happiness of others. Lacking this courageous hopefulness, their accomplishments, possessions and happiness represent a painful insult that triggers our impotent rage and the desire to do away with the agent making our unhappiness so apparent. The spiteful person bases his life on a strategy of trying to feel better through destruction and does not really wish to live a happier life by doing the fine things which would make that possible. By undermining the proper wish for integrated human development, spite attacks the first principle of the morally developed person.

Spiteful people destroy and devalue things not because they are genuinely competing for them, but because they take pleasure in preventing the enjoyment others find in actively pursuing their wishes. Spiteful people throw cold water on other people's enthusiasms, find fault with the things they love, and in the most blatant cases actually harm or destroy them through sabotage, vandalism, back-biting, etc.

By treating the wishes, aspirations and feelings of others as worthless, they act as though others are worthy of being neither feared nor cultivated for the good they might do. The attitude is based on hopelessness and the fear that the genuinely hopeful possibilities found in other people's happiness might reveal our own lack of courage. Spite is a hateful, cold and demoralizing attitude well worth being angry at.

c. INSOLENCE AND SADISM. This is the attitude the Greeks called **hubris**, interpreted today most often as simply excessive pride or **vanity**. Hubris or insolence, however, is actually what we now call "sadism," after the 19th century Marquis de Sade. We see this, for example, when Aristotle insists that such a person causes others pain not "because anything has happened to [him], but simply for the pleasure involved." Vanity is, of course, involved in sadism but it is not its essence.

When insolent and sadistic, we cause others to feel **a s h a m e d** by dishonoring, abusing and toying with them in front of other people. The insolent strategy is to take **pleasure** in causing them **pain** because their fear gives us confidence in ourselves. We do not desire to retaliate for a real slight they might have caused us so much as to prove our dominance of them. We find pleasure through building ourselves up by putting them down. The fear in their eyes reflects an enlarged image of ourselves. Aristotle observes that youths and rich people are especially tempted to be insolent like this to build up their self-esteem.

Compared to insolent sadism, disdain and spite are both colder, more distant and unrelated to their objects, and do not feed off them in this way. Insolence is hot, personal and involved, preferably with **masochistic** people looking for strong authorities who will discipline them and give them a sense of belonging. Insolence is rebellious against authorities unless they can bring about a role reversal in which the insolent person becomes masochistic toward the authority in exchange for the right to draw on his status in acting sadistically toward others. Sadism is a component of the **macho** vice associated with cowardice (NE III, 7) and reflects a specific form of **excessive ambition** (NE IV, 4). It is a failed attempt to make up for a **small-minded** lack of faith in our own powers through a desperate effort to have others help us maintain a **vain** image of ourselves.

In sum, anger, disdain, spite and insolence have different aims and seek different kinds of pleasure and satisfaction. **Anger** finds pleasure in our confidence in the legitimacy of the interests that have been violated and in our power to stand up against and punish those who have violated them. **Disdain** finds pleasure in the vanity of acting superior to others but not necessarily in actively causing them pain or destroying what makes them happy. **Spite** finds cold satisfaction in the harm befalling a rival whether or not the spiteful person caused it. **Insolent sadism** is pleased by seeing its power to humiliate.

Aristotle perceptively notes that our waking thoughts and fantasies function the same way dreams do to give us pleasure. They are, after all, daydreams. We must expect then that anger, disdain, spite, and insolence-sadism will also differ in their fantasies. The **angry** man will fantasize a personal confrontation in which his interests are vindicated, the offender acknowledges his slight and accepts his punishment. The **disdainful** man will fantasize doing things like moving through and above faceless crowds deferring to his superior worth. The **spiteful** man will fantasize something destructive befalling his enemies without necessarily picturing himself as its cause. And the **insolent sadistic** man will picture himself humiliating others in such a way as to make himself seem wonderfully powerful and cruel.

Whenever people are unjustifiably **disdainful**, **spiteful** or **sadistic** toward us or ours, we should be angry. But whether we will perceive them this way and actually get angry will depend on our state of mind.

3. OUR STATES OF MIND WHEN ANGERED

So far we have analyzed the **attitudes** of **agents** who we see as slighting us. Now we examine the factors which constitute our state of mind when angered. These include the **wishes** others might slight and our **resources** and **expectations** relative to the people who slight us. Aristotle focuses first on our expectations when he observes that

> A man expects to be especially respected by his inferiors in birth, in capacity, in goodness, and generally in anything in which he is much their superior: as where money is concerned a wealthy man looks for respect from a poor man; where speaking is concerned, the man with a turn for oratory looks for respect from one who cannot speak; the ruler demands the respect of the ruled, and the man who thinks he ought to be ruling demands the respect of the man whom he thinks he ought to be ruling... a man looks for respect from those who he thinks owe him good treatment, and these are the people whom he has treated or is treating well, or means or has meant to treat well, either himself, or through his friends, or through others at his request. (1378b 34- 1379a 8)

The list suggests that our **expectations** are rooted in our **resources** like our wealth or family lineage, personal talents such as speaking skill, and even favors owed us in return for earlier good treatment.

The states of mind affecting our anger are not limited, however, to what we expect from others. Slights are painful because they always interfere with something we are aiming at or **wishing** to do.

> The state of mind is that in which any pain is being felt. In that condition a man is always aiming at something... Each man is predisposed, by the emotion now controlling him, to his own particular anger. (1739a 10-1 & 1739a 22-3)

This recognition of **wish** provides the last component in the **denominator** of the formula.

The agent arousing our anger can do so either through his **active opposition** to our wishes or through his **passive refusal** to help.

> Whether, then, another man opposes him either directly in any way, as by preventing him from drinking when he is thirsty, or indirectly, the act appears to him just the same; whether some one works against him, or fails to work with him, or otherwise vexes him while he is in this mood, he is equally angry in all these cases. (1379a 12-5)

Aristotle lists the following examples of needs and wishes that can be slighted to arouse our anger.

> People who are afflicted by sickness or poverty or love or thirst or any other unsatisfied desires are prone to anger and easily roused: especially against those who slight their present distress. Thus a sick man is angered by disregard of his illness, a poor man by disregard of his poverty, a man waging war by disregard of the war he is waging, a lover by disregard of his love, and so throughout, any other slight being enough if special slights are wanting. (1379a 16-21)

COMMENTARY. In learning to handle anger better ourselves or to help others with it, it is essential to understand the states of mind disposing us to it. A slighting agent (A) triggers our anger (F) only by first frustrating the operation of another moral power (M) such as our desire for physical pleasure. It is the frustration (F) of this latter power which then functions as the proximal agent (Tfa) actually stimulating our power to be angry (M). This section clarifies these other moral powers (M) which constitute our state of mind when agents (A) make us angry.

We see here the synergism and dysergism involved in the interaction between the virtues and vices. Vices in the other powers promote either excessive anger or apathy in this power. Excessive or deficient desires are identified as excessive and deficient precisely because they have this dysergistic effect in corrupting other areas of our lives. Virtues in the other powers work in the opposite, synergistic, manner to help us handle anger properly. An examination of Aristotle's examples establishes this important point.

With certain qualifications to be noted later, we can make the following correlations listed on the table below. We do not include the virtue of generosity in the table because its accompanying vices do not

EXCESSIVELY ANGRY	GENTLE	APATHETIC
vain	high-minded	small-minded
self-indulgent	self-controlled	depressed
macho	courageous	cowardly
contentious	friendly	obsequious

TABLE SHOWING HOW CERTAIN VIRTUES AND VICES
DISPOSE US TO EXCESSIVE ANGER, GENTLENESS OR APATHY

show so pronounced a tendency to either excessive anger or apathy as those listed.

   a. HIGH-MINDED, SMALL-MINDED OR VAIN. Since agents arousing anger must be seen as treating us as though we were unimportant, our disposition to anger will reflect the state of our power of self-respect which governs what we expect both from ourselves and from others. This judgment stems from whether we are high-minded, small-minded, or vain (**NE 3**).
   Small-minded people, for example, feel they deserve less than they actually do, and so they tend not to picture behavior as slighting even when it is. **Vain** people, on the other hand, have an exaggerated sense of their own importance, so they picture things as slights even when they are not. It is only the **high-minded** attitude which allows us to judge correctly whether another's behavior is slighting. This attitude disposes us to a proper estimation of our merits and to confidence in our powers. High-mindedness in turn is made possible only by possessing the virtues of each of the other moral powers. Vices in any of them, particularly strong vices, lead us to confuse a judgment concerning what we **wish** with a judgment about what we **deserve**, as is revealed in the following items.

   b. SELF-CONTROLLED, SELF-INDULGENT OR DEPRESSED. Aristotle mentions **thirst** and **love** (**eros**) as examples of moral powers that can be slighted in our efforts to find satisfaction. How we handle these desires is governed by whether we have developed **self-control, self-indulgence** or **depression** in our power to enjoy physical pleasure (**NE III, 10-2**). Both self-indulgent and depressed people are much more disposed to anger than are properly self-controlled ones, although as we saw in Ch. 2 depression's apathy covers a raging anger underneath. Since the self-indulgent person has both excessive desires for himself and excessive expectations toward others, he or she will tend to see others as unjustified in frustrating his right to indulge himself.

      c. GENEROUS, RECEPTIVE, EXPLOITATIVE OR HOARDING. Aristotle also mentions **poverty** as disposing us to anger. Poverty is a morally neutral term denoting frustration in acquiring and using money (**N E** IV, 1) without regard to whether the difficulties arise primarily from internal (M) or external (A) causes. Yet how we handle or respond (F) to an impoverished situation is a moral matter governed by how we have developed our power to acquire and use money.

      When this power is virtuously developed it is **generous**. When it is viciously developed, it is the disposition to **passive receptiveness** and **extravagance, hoarding** or **exploitativeness.** Clearly, each of these three vices has a different aim and disposes us to see others as slighting us in different ways. A viciously receptive person is angered when others fail to give him the support he wants, a hoarding person when he fears they will take what he desperately wants to hold on to, and an exploitative person when others interfere with his taking what he desires. Sometimes, however, receptiveness combines with obsequiousness to produce apathy, a hoarding person can be so private and controlled as to keep his anger bottled-up and hidden, and an exploitative person can swallow lots of insults as part of his flattering strategy.

      d. COURAGEOUS, COWARDLY OR MACHO. Struggling against sickness and waging war are painful endeavors challenging our **courage** (NE III, 6-9) and making us touchy and inclined to anger. When caught up in a fight, we are more tempted to see others as unjustifiably slighting our efforts. Being absorbed in our own problems makes it doubly difficult to see others realistically. If we are **macho** and insecure, yet need to boast about our courage to maintain a **vain** image of ourselves, we will be most vulnerable to seeing others as slighting us and therefore most disposed to anger. The smallest suggestion that our self-image is exaggerated will appear to be an unjustifiable slight. If we are **cowardly** pure and simple, we will be afraid to stand up for ourselves and thus disposed to apathy rather than anger. We sacrifice our most proper wishes for ourselves and those we love to flee from pain at any cost.

      Courage is the state of mind which allows us to get anger right insofar as pain is involved. When confident, we can perceive the motives and needs of others more clearly and are not irrationally afraid of being slighted. Believing we have the resources to handle the situation, we do not have to launch pre-emptory strikes to frighten off potential threats to our self-confidence. Courage gives us the power, at the same time, to stand up for principles and rights even in the face of overwhelming odds.

      e. FRIENDLY, OBSEQUIOUS, FLATTERING OR CONTENTIOUS. When we show love and friendliness toward others, we are quite disposed to anger if we are disregarded by them. In fact, insofar as we expect more from them, we are more inclined to be angry with them, as will be explained more fully in the next section. In this and other ways, friendliness and love have a profound and complex effect on the operation of anger (**NE** IV,

6 as well as all of VIII & IX, & **R h** II, 4). This power is implied in the very definition of anger with its reference to slights directed not only against us but "toward what concerns one's friends."

Being **just** requires us to discover the proper ratio between our own and other people's rights in apportioning burdens and rewards (**N E** V and **R h** II, 8-11). To do this properly, we need a friendly and realistic interest in understanding them which will help us discipline and calm our anger while searching for an explanation of why they might have slighted us. Friendliness disposes us to minimize the harm someone has done us, to feel compassion for him, and to see the justice of his actions.

If we are **obsequious,** on the other hand, we are inclined to believe other people's wishes and feelings are more important than our own and this makes us apathetic when they slight us. They seem justified in doing so because we see them as being so much more important than ourselves. If however we are exploitative **flatterers,** our anger will be determined by what is to our advantage in the circumstances. This will tend to minimize at least the expression of our anger so long as it does not fit into our strategy. If we are unfriendly or **contentious,** we will be the least sensitive to others and will be the most inclined to excessive anger toward them.

The way we develop our power to be friendly determines the range and depth of our friendly feelings toward others. Having many friends expands the number and quality of the interests agents will be capable of slighting in our eyes. So while friendliness minimizes our tendency to be excessive by making us more understanding, it also makes us angrier and more sympathetic when others who we care about are being unjustifiably slighted. The nature of our friendships thus determines not only the quality of our anger when friends are abused but also of our **indignation** (**Rh** II, 9) and **pity** (**Rh** II, 8) when similar things happen to people who we identify with at a distance.

4. PEOPLE AND BEHAVIOR AROUSING OUR ANGER

As we have just seen, we are particularly inclined to be angry with people we are close to because we expect more from them. This follows the general rule that

> we are angered if we happen to be expecting a contrary result:
> for a quite unexpected evil is especially painful, just as the
> unexpected fulfillment of our wishes is specially pleasant. (1379a
> 23-5)

But we can be even more explicit about the kinds of people and behavior that are most likely to arouse our anger. Aristotle divides them according to the three basic motives which provoke us to anger.

- MARKS OF INSOLENCE AND SADISM

a. The persons with whom we get angry are those who **laugh, mock,** or **jeer** at us, for such conduct is insolent. (1379a 28-29)

b. Also those who inflict injuries upon us that are marks of insolence. These injuries must be such as are neither retaliatory nor profitable to the doers: for only then will they be felt to be due to insolence. (1379a 29-32)

- MARKS OF CONTEMPT AND DISDAIN

a. Also those who speak ill of us, and show contempt for us, in connection with the things we ourselves most care about: thus those who are eager to win **fame** as philosophers get angry with those who show contempt for their philosophy; those who pride themselves on their appearance get angry with those who show contempt for their appearance; and so on in other cases. We feel particularly angry on this account if we suspect that we are in fact, or that people think we are, **lacking** completely or to any effective extent in the qualities in question. For when we are convinced that we excel in the qualities for which we are jeered at, we can ignore the jeering. (1379a 32-b 2)

b. Again, we are angrier with our **friends** than with other people, since we feel that our friends ought to treat us well and not badly. (1379b 2-4)

c. We are angry with those who have usually treated **us** with **honor** or **regard**, if a change comes and they behave to us otherwise: for we think that they feel contempt for us, or they would still be behaving as they did before. (1379b 4-6)

d. And with those who do not return our **kindnesses** or fail to return them adequately, and with those who oppose us though they are our inferiors: for all such persons seem to feel contempt for us; those who oppose us seem to think us inferior to themselves, and those who do not return our kindnesses seem to think that those kindnesses were conferred by inferiors. (1379b 7-9)

e. And we feel particularly angry with **men of no account** at all, if they slight us. For, by our hypothesis, the anger caused by the slight is felt towards people who are not justified in slighting us, and our inferiors are not thus justified. (1379b 9-12)

f. Again, we feel angry with **friends** if they **do not speak well of us** or **treat us well**; and still more, if they do the contrary; or if they **do not perceive our needs**... for this want of perception shows that they are slighting us--we do not fail to perceive the needs of those for whom we care. (1379b 14-8)

g. Also with those who reply with **humorous levity** when we are speaking seriously, for such behavior indicates contempt. (1379b 30-2)

h. And with those who **treat us less well** than they treat **everybody else**; it is another mark of contempt that they should think we do not deserve what everyone else deserves. (1379b 33-4)

i. **Forgetfulness**, too, causes anger, as when our own names are forgotten, trifling as this may be; since forgetfulness is felt to be another sign that we are being slighted; it is due to negligence, and to neglect us is to slight us. (1379b 35-8)

- MARKS OF SPITE AND HATE

a. Again, we are angry with those who **rejoice** at **our misfortunes** or simply keep cheerful in the midst of our misfortunes, since this shows that they either hate us or are slighting us. (1379b 17-8)

b. Also with those who are **indifferent** to the pain they give us: this is why we get angry with the bringers of bad news. (1379b 18-20)

c. And with those who **listen to stories about us** or keep on **looking at our weaknesses**; this seems like either slighting us or hating us; for those who love us share in all our distresses and it must distress any one to keep on looking at his own weaknesses. (1379b 21-4)

- PEOPLE WITH REGARD TO WHOM WE FEEL EVEN MORE SLIGHTED

Aristotle observed that we feel particularly angry when someone unjustifiably slights us before

a. (1) our rivals, (2) those whom we admire, (3) those whom we wish to admire us, (4) those for whom we feel reverence, (5) those who feel reverence for us: if any one slights us before such persons, we feel particularly angry. (1379b 25-8)

b. We feel angry with those who slight us in connection with what we are as honorable men bound to champion--our parents, children, wives, or subjects. (1379b 28-9)

COMMENTARY. We will now examine the kinds of behavior which characterize the three attitudes arousing anger. The list is of practical importance in helping us recognize when our own behavior or someone else's embodies one of the three slighting motives which naturally make people angry. By helping us see how we might unconsciously slight others, this discussion can help us become more deliberate in treating people with respect. We see more clearly what it means to act according to the proper wish to promote human development.

- MARKS OF INSOLENCE AND SADISM

a. PEOPLE ACTING LIKE BUFFOONS. When laughing is **insolent** and **sadistic** it is in the form of mockery and jeering, is aimed **at** the person and intends to shame and belittle him. When a sadistic person characteristically uses humor in this way, he or she is a particular kind of **buffoon** (the vice of **excessive wit**, NE IV, 7). Such people make us angry because they try to make themselves feel big by making us seem small, incompetent, unattractive, etc.

We also get angry at **disdainful** laughter, but it lacks this mocking and jeering quality and is not aimed at humiliating the person it offends. Its offence is rather in the disrespect it shows by making jokes while someone is trying to be serious. (See item g. below.) It is noteworthy that humor is not listed as one of the ways **spiteful** people make others angry. When spiteful, we tend to be humorless.

b. PEOPLE BEHAVING FOR NEITHER RETALIATION NOR PROFIT. We have a clear case of insolence or sadism only when a person humiliates us without our having given him cause and without his gaining anything from doing so beyond feeling superior. To the extent an angry person is retaliating against us for wronging him or someone is disdainfully pursuing his own **profit** at our expense, we do not accuse him of insolence or sadism. He or she must wish to hurt us for his own gratification to be considered sadistic.

A person might have a right to be angry at us, however, and still use the occasion to belittle and humiliate us. In such a case we would be right to get angry at his or her sadism, but not at their legitimate anger at us. Their retaliation for our wrong is not the same as their being sadistic in taking advantage of us. Someone's taking an unjustifiable profit at our expence will make us angry for the disdain shown for our interests, but not because it is a mark of sadism.

- MARKS OF CONTEMPT AND DISDAIN

a. PEOPLE ATTACKING OUR HIGH-MINDEDNESS, AMBITION AND COURAGE. It is natural to be angry at someone showing contempt or disdain toward our philosophy, physical appearance or any other area of our striving to make a contribution. When Aristotle says "those who are eager to win fame as philosophers get angry...", he is referring to a slight not only against our cognitive virtue but our **ambition** (NE IV, 4) as well. When he speaks of "those who pride themselves on their appearance," he is referring to a slight against our **vanity** (NE IV, 3). Finally, his saying that "when we are convinced that we excel in the qualities for which we are jeered at, we can ignore the jeering," he is referring to **courage** (NE III, 6-9) which gives us confidence in our powers and helps keep us from becoming **small-minded** (NE IV, 3) and touchy about our worth.

b. FRIENDS ATTACKING US, TRIGGERING OBSEQUIOUSNESS AND APATHY. We noted above the general principle that the frustration of **expectations** arouses anger. Since we have higher expectations for our friends, we are that much angrier when they are disdainful of us. We expect them to be friendly to us as we have been to them. If, however, we are **obsequious** (NE IV, 6) and lack faith in our power to stimulate friendship through being a friend, our expectations toward others will be reduced, and we will be more inclined to apathy than to anger when they let us down. Whether friends make us angry depends on our state of mind as much as on them.

c. PEOPLE WHO HAVE HONORED US IN THE PAST. The withdrawal of previously given **honor** and **respect** attacks our power of **high-minded-**

ness (or vanity) (**NE** IV, 3), and through appearing to be a sign of disdain, activates our anger. The person's disdain robs us of a pleasure we expected and thought we deserved.

d. PEOPLE TO WHOM WE HAVE BEEN KIND. People get angry when someone does not return their **kindness** (**Rh** II, 7), but this should not be thought to imply that kindness aims at helping another person to put him in our debt. There is no contradiction in saying, "I did not help you in order to force you to reciprocate, but I am nonetheless angry that you will not show similar kindness to me." (See **Indignation, Rh** II, 9.) The slighting person in such situations seems to picture the earlier kindness as an act of servitude rather than as having been done by a good person who is worthy of being helped in return. This is clearly an anger-arousing slight.

Aristotle considers the failure to return a kindness as a mark of considering someone an inferior. People to whom we have established our superiority in a given area treat us in the same demeaning way when they oppose us in that area.

e. PEOPLE OF NO ACCOUNT. People with less worth and right on their side have the greatest potential to anger us because their demands will all the more readily appear as **unjustified** slights against us. People who don't carry their own load, for example, yet criticize those who do, are like this. As we have seen, though, our own state of mind or character determines whether we are inclined to see others as worth more or less than they actually are.

f. FRIENDS SHOWING INSENSITIVITY TO US. Having established that we get angrier at friends, Aristotle adds here that we expect them not only to speak well of us and treat us well, but also to be perceptive of our needs. A gracious perceptiveness about another's needs, especially those the person cannot put into words himself, signals one's caring for that person as a friend (**Rh** II, 4). The lack of perceptiveness is a sign of the weakness of our caring and of how little we value the person. Such indifference is a mark of a disdainful character and a legitimate cause of anger.

But ignorance of others' needs can also be attributed to a lack of education in understanding human motivation. In culturally divergent or emotionally complex situations, exceptional gifts and training in understanding character might be required to figure out what is going on. Even if we care a great deal, we cannot be responsive to needs we have not been taught to recognize.

g. PEOPLE ACTING LIKE BUFFOONS. See item a. under **INSOLENCE AND SADISM** above for the distinction between humor rooted in disdain and that rooted in insolence.

h. PEOPLE TREATING US WORSE THAN THEY DO OTHERS. Disdainful people enjoy feeling superior to others, but they do not actively seek to shame people in doing so. Their sense of vanity does not have this pointed and hurting edge. And unlike spite and hate, disdain's air of superiority is to put a person in his or her inferior and segregated place rather than to destroy him or his happiness. Such contempt nonethelsss makes us angry.

i. PEOPLE FORGETTING OUR NAME. With a little effort we can learn to remember the names of people who have some importance in our lives and for whom it would be unjustifiable for us not to be more thoughtful. If we neglect to do so, we are signalling that we do not consider them worth the effort, and that is a slight. We only neglect those things we consider unworthy of our attention.

- MARKS OF SPITE AND HATE

a. PEOPLE WHO REJOICE AT OUR MISFORTUNE. Spite is the pleasure **envious** (**Rh** II, 10) people take in (causing) the bad fortune of the objects of their envy. People "who rejoice at our misfortunes or simply keep cheerful in the midst" of them are showing their spitefulness and hate for us. They treat our wishes and feelings as unimportant and are genuine sources of anger.

b. PEOPLE WHO ARE INDIFFERENT TO THE PAIN THEY CAUSE. It might be thought that being "indifferent to the pain they give us" is more characteristic of a disdainful than a spiteful person. Aristotle says, though, in talking about **enmity** at **Rh** II, 4, that unlike sadistic insolence, spite aims not so much at causing pain as at doing away with the offending person. In this sense, spite can be said to be indifferent to the pain it causes.

Spiteful people appear emotionally dead on the inside and indifferent, when not outright hostile, toward the vitality, pleasure and suffering of others. On the other hand, not all "bringers of bad news" are spitefully indifferent to the pain they cause. Perhaps the point is that bearers of bad news appear spiteful when they do not suffer with us because they are ignorant of the meaning of the message they carry.

c. PEOPLE WHO ARE PREOCCUPIED WITH OUR WEAKNESS AND MISFORTUNE. Spiteful and hateful people are destructive. They are drawn to whatever bad fortune they can find because it seems to free them from rising to the challenge of becoming more alive and fulfilled through their own creative activity. It is thus with a certain relish that they will "listen to stories about us or keep on looking at our weaknesses." In this way they try to do away with the painful perception that other people are happier than they are and that hard work could pay off for them too. While friends share in our distress and are pained by it, spiteful people enjoy hearing of it (**Rh** II, 4).

- PEOPLE WITH REGARD TO WHOM WE FEEL EVEN MORE SLIGHTED

Aristotle concludes by explaining the way these three types of people can make us even angrier by vexing us in front of particular **third parties.** These people are

a. THOSE BEFORE WHOM WE FEEL SHAME AND EMULATION. These are people such as our rivals and people we admire and who we wish to feel the same about us. We get particularly angry at someone who slights us before such people because we fear these others might also come to think of us as unimportant. (See **Shame, Rh** II, 6 & **Emulation, Rh** II,

11.)

We have seen that insolent sadists seek to shame and humiliate people. Does this mean that all slights before such people are done with the **insolent-sadistic aim** of causing us shame? No. To assume that would be to confuse teleology as conscious purpose with teleology as functional outcome. The fact that we feel shame when slighted before these people does not mean that the agent sadistically aimed to cause us shame to build himself up. A person might simply be so disdainful or spiteful as not to care what we feel. Whatever the motive, though, being slighted in front of people we respect makes us more angry than the same slight in private.

b. THOSE FOR WHOM WE FEEL RESPONSIBLE. There are certain people we are honor-bound "to champion--our parents, children, wives or subjects," and **high-minded** people do so (**NE** IV, 3). To belittle them, or our ability to stand up for them, is a slight against us because it assumes we lack the capacity and character to retaliate and protect our own. It is a most common source of anger and explains why, for example, in lower class communities the world over, attacks on the character of a man's mother or sister so often lead to fights and even killings.

B. THE POWER TO BE CALM (Rh II, 3)

1. CALMNESS DEFINED

Having learned about the nature of anger, we now consider the factors affecting our ability to calm anger in ourselves and others. Aristotle observed that

> Since growing calm is the opposite of growing angry, and calmness the opposite of anger, we must ascertain in what states of mind men are calm, towards whom they feel calm, and by what means they are made so. Growing calm may be defined as a settling down or quieting of anger. (1380a 5-8)

COMMENTARY. This section provides further guidance in handling anger properly and covers much of the same ground just examined except this time with regard to PEOPLE WHO CALM OUR ANGER, OUR OWN STATES OF MIND WHEN CALM, and HOW TO CALM PEOPLE DOWN. Calmness disposes us not to see behavior as a slight and thus functions to keep us from retaliating. It is plain then that the agents who make us **calm** (A) will be pictured (F) differently from those making us **angry** (A). Our perception of someone (F) can change even when there is no change in his objective behavior and intent (A) simply by putting ourselves in a different state of mind (M). Either the agent or the material cause or both can change to bring about this different response and any serious effort to calm excessive anger will work on both fronts. These different possibilities are spelled out below.

2. PEOPLE WHO CALM OUR ANGER

Aristotle lists the following attitudes as having the power to calm our anger. When trying to calm down an angry person, we rather instinctively assume one or other of these postures ourselves if we are being attacked or try to picture whoever is being attacked in one of these ways. Aristotle says

> a. We get angry with those who slight us; and since slighting is a voluntary act, it is plain that we feel calm toward those who do **nothing of the kind,** or who do or seem to do it **involuntarily.** Also toward those who intended to do the opposite of what they did do. (1380a 8-11)

> b. Also toward those who treat **themselves** as they have treated **us**: since no one can be supposed to slight himself. (1380a 12-3)

c. Those who **admit their fault** and are **sorry**: since we accept their grief at what they have done as satisfaction, and cease to be angry. The punishment of servants shows this: those who contradict us and deny their offence we punish all the more, but we cease to be incensed against those who agree that they deserve their punishment. The reason is that it is **shameless** to deny what is obvious, and those who are shameless towards us slight us and show their contempt for us: anyhow, we do not feel shame before those of whom we are thoroughly contemptuous. (1380a 14-21)

d. Those who humble themselves before us and do not gainsay us; we feel that they thus admit themselves our inferiors, and inferiors feel **fear**, and nobody can slight anyone so long as he feels afraid of him. That our anger ceases towards those who humble themselves before us is shown even by dogs, who do not bite people when they sit down. (1380a 22-6)

e. Those who are **serious** when we are serious, because then we feel that we are treated seriously and not contemptuously. (1380a 26-7)

f. Those who have done us more **kindnesses** than we have done them. (1380a 27)

g. Those who pray to us and beg for mercy, since they **humble** themselves by doing so. (1380a 28)

h. Those who do not insult or mock at or slight **any one at all**, or not any worthy person or any one like ourselves. (1380a 29-30)

i. In general, the things that make us calm may be inferred by seeing what the opposites are of those that make us angry. We are not angry with people **we fear** or **respect**, as long as we fear or respect them: you cannot be afraid of a person and also at the same time angry at him. (1380a 30-3)

j. Again, we feel no anger, or comparatively little, with those who have done what they did through **anger**; we do not feel that they have done it from a wish to slight us, for no one slights people when angry at them, since slighting is painless, and anger is painful. (1380a 33-7)

k. Nor do we grow angry with those who **reverence us**. (1380b 1)

COMMENTARY. Skill at calming people down is most acutely needed in crisis intervention, but is invaluable whenever disputes might arise and people must negotiate about the distribution of burdens and rewards. Leaders must be particularly sensitive to these issues if things are not to get out of hand. The strategic point in trying to calm people down is to remember that they must see someone as having either a disdainful, insolent-sadistic, or spiteful-hateful attitude toward them in order to be angry at him. We are calmed down by seeing that he did not have one of these attitudes even if he might have slighted us in some way. When our character is an excessively angry one, we have a hard time imagining someone in these calming terms. When we have an apathetic character, we are inclined to see people in these terms even when they are not that way at all. The list again deepens our understanding of how we appear to others and what we can do to deepen trust and mutual respect between people.

a. **THOSE WHO DID NOT MEAN TO SLIGHT US.** The most obvious defense against our anger is "I didn't mean to do it." We naturally calm down whenever we picture a person as not having intended to slight us. Involuntary acts are those that are not intended and that one repudiates when he becomes conscious of what he has actually done (**NE** III, 1). But this does not mean we necessarily accept what a person claims about his own intentions. He must show remorse at what he did as a sign that it was not his true intent.

b. **THOSE WHO TREAT US THE SAME AS THEY DO THEMSELVES.** People who "treat themselves as they have treated us" do not make us angry because they do not seem to be treating us as less important than themselves. We see this, for example, with leaders who succeed at maintaining unusually high standards by demanding as much of themselves as of their coworkers. Where such leaders tend to calm people's anger, those who expect more from others than from themselves tend to provoke it.

This is not always the case, however. The key seems to be whether people have a common interest (whether financial or moral) in the outcome of such sacrifices. We will hardly be impressed when we cannot in some way identify with a purpose which would appear to give dignity to a sacrifice. Take, for example, the case of an **envious** and unfulfilled person who feels he must deny himself pleasures like sex, drinking or dancing, and who **spitefully** demands the same sacrifices of us. Insofar as this appears to be the **universalization** of **spite** and **envy** and simply a rejection of other people's life-affirming pleasures, he will be a source of anger and therefore an exception to the rule. But insofar as we are able to see it as a universalized rule he applies first to himself as a result of his harsh conscience, it tends to calm our anger by evoking our compassion or pity.

c. **THOSE WHO ARE ASHAMED OF WHAT THEY HAVE DONE.** When people "admit their fault and are sorry," they show us that they acted against what they really value and wish for and that they do not really feel we are worthless. (See **Shame, Rh** II, 6 & **NE** IV, 9.) And as we saw in item a. above, their not meaning the slight is enough by itself to calm our anger. But Aristotle shows here a further reason why such a person has a calming affect on us. Since the offender's grief is painful to him, it also tends to satisfy our desire for retaliation.

It is appropriate to feel pleasure at a person's acknowledging not only that he has violated our rights but that he is pained at having done so. We are pleased both by his honoring our rights and by the prospects for his virtuous development shown by this painful acknowledgement. Leaders wishing to help others turn away from harmful behavior must cultivate a non-sadistic pleasure in causing such painful remorse.

On the other hand, if the offending person refuses to acknowledge what he has obviously done, he adds insult to injury by showing he is so **disdainful** that he will **shamelessly** lie to our faces. If he respected us, he would be ashamed of what he has done. If he genuinely wished to do right, he would feel he deserved an appropriate punishment. Those who act rightly in these respects, not only calm our anger but make us proud of their righteous sense of shame.

d. **THOSE WHO ARE AFRAID OF US.** When someone is humble and afraid of us, even if they are not ashamed of what they have done, they are not treating us as being unimportant. By humbling themselves and not contradicting us, they act in some sense inferior to us. Such behavior takes away our feeling of being slighted. Aristotle illustrates this with the example of how we can calm down an angry dog by stopping in our tracks and "humbling" ourselves before him.

One cannot be simultaneously slightful and afraid of the same person, in the same respect. But being afraid of a person in one respect can lead us to slight and belittle him in others. We see this, for example, in the way envy leads us to be pained by the good fortune of others and thus to be afraid of seeing them happy. This cowardly fear can then lead us to do spiteful things to undermine others in order to try to feel better ourselves (**R h** II, 10). Slighting behavior is a common means some people use to try to deny the fear that they cannot be fully alive themselves.

e. **THOSE WHO TAKE US SERIOUSLY.** Obviously when someone is taking us seriously and listening to our complaints against them, he will tend to calm us down because we no longer see him treating us as unimportant. It is not sufficient, however, for someone to appear to take us seriously; they must try to right the wrong as well. For the distinction between insolent and disdainful laughter when we are trying to be serious, see item a. under MARKS OF INSOLENCE AND SADISM in section A, 4 above.

f. **THOSE WHO HAVE BEEN KINDER TO US THAN WE HAVE BEEN TO THEM.** We are less inclined to be angry at someone who has been especially **kind** to us than at others who commit the same slight (**kindness, R h** II, 7). We are excessively disposed to seeing people this way when we are **small-minded** (NE IV, 3) and do not feel we are worth very much. Simple civility then appears as great kindness, while we minimize our own goodness.

g. **THOSE WHO ARE SMALL-MINDED AND BEG FOR MERCY.** To pray and beg for mercy shows a great loss of **high-minded** self-respect (NE IV, 3). Such small-mindedness is **pitiful** (Rh II, 8) in so far as it is sincere and is hardly the mark of someone treating us as unimportant. Seeing it this way has a calming influence unless, of course, we are **sadistic** and turned on by the sense of power their attitude gives us. Seeing their begging as **flattery,** on the other hand, will seem still another mark of their disdain and not calm us at all.

h. **THOSE WHO ARE HIGH-MINDED AND SLIGHT OTHERS ONLY WHEN JUSTIFIED.** People with a reputation for justice and for slighting no one, especially no honorable person or no one like ourselves, will have a calming effect on others. We know we are not likely to be slighted by them and this gives us the confidence to relax and try to deal with the situation in a calmer way.

   i. **THOSE WHO SCARE US OR EARN OUR RESPECT.** We have already seen that we cannot be angry at people in so far as we are **afraid** of them. The same applies to people we **respect.** We cannot be angry at somebody for doing something we respect, but we can be angry at him in some other respect. We always respect and fear things in a given place, at the proper time, etc. So while we might feel this way about a friend's piano playing, for example, and would never get angry at him for doing something so beautifullly, we are nonetheless angry at him for playing next door to our bedroom at 3 o'clock the morning before a comprehensive exam. The point here is the issue of focus. When we focus just on the thing we respect in isolation from the factors which slighted us, we are calmed.

   j. **THOSE WHO ARE ANGRY AT US.** Interestingly, we feel "comparatively little" anger at people who feel slighted and are angry at us. This holds, however, only insofar as we remember the distinction between legitimate anger and contempt-disdain, insolence-sadism and spite—all of which do make us angry, as does excessive and illegitimate anger. Aristotle notes two reasons why we calm down when others are angry. First, they show us they take us seriously and are not slighting us in that respect. Since the agent cause of anger is always a slight, anger cannot be a cause of anger. Second, when their "anger is painful" to them and they do not like being angry with us, they are not trying to build themselves up at our expense and do not seem to be slighting us on that account either.

   k. **THOSE WHO WISH TO EMULATE US.** The fact that people **honor** us tends to keep us calm both because we have no fear that they will slight us and because we wish to keep their respect and are afraid our anger might jeopardize it. (See **Emulation, Rh** II, 11.)

3. OUR OWN STATES OF MIND WHEN CALM

   Having seen the kinds of people (A) who tend to calm our anger, we now examine the states of mind (M) which dispose us to be calm. The general principle is that any state of mind inclining us to remain calm is "plainly the opposite to that which makes [people] angry" (1380b 2). Aristotle says people feel calm and tend not to be angry

   a. ...when they are amusing themselves or laughing or feasting (1380b 3)

   b. ...when they are feeling prosperous or successful or satisfied (1380b 4)

   c. ...when, in fine, they are enjoying freedom from pain, or inoffensive pleasure, or justifiable hope. (1380b 5)

   d. ...when time is passed and their anger is no longer fresh, for time puts an end to anger. (1380b 6)

e. ...vengeance previously taken on one person puts an end to even greater anger felt against another person. Hence Philocrates, being asked by someone, at a time when the public was angry with him, "Why don't you defend yourself?" did right to reply, "The time is not yet." "Why, when is the time?" "When I see someone else calumniated." For men become calm when they have spent their anger on somebody else. This happened in the case of Ergophilus: though the people were more irritated against him than against Callisthenes, they acquitted him because they had condemned Callisthenes to death the day before. (1380b 7-13)

f. ...men become calm if they have convicted the offender; or if he has already suffered worse things than they in their anger would have inflicted upon him; for they feel as if they were avenged already. (1380b 14-7)

g. ...if they feel that they themselves are in the wrong and are suffering justly (for anger is not excited by what is just), since men no longer think then that they are suffering without justification; and anger, as we have seen, means this. Hence we ought always to inflict a preliminary punishment in words; if that is done, even slaves are less aggrieved by the actual punishment. (1380b 17-21)

h. ...if we think that the offender will not see that he is punished on our account and because of the way he has treated us. For anger has to do with individuals. This is plain from the definition. Hence the poet has well written: "Say that it was Odysseus, sacker of cities," implying that Odysseus would not have considered himself avenged unless the Cyclops perceived both by whom and for what he had been blinded. Consequently we do not get angry with anyone who cannot be aware of our anger, and in particular we cease to be angry with people once they are dead, for we feel that the worst has been done to them, and that they will neither feel pain nor anything else that we in our anger aim at making them feel... The poet has well made Apollo say, in order to put a stop to the anger of Achilles against the dead Hector, "For behold in his fury he doeth despite to the senseless clay." (1380b 22-9)

COMMENTARY. The following states of mind affect our power to calm our anger. The practical implication here is that by doing the things which put us in these calmer frames of mind, we will improve our ability to handle excessive anger. Obviously we can apply the same approach in working with others as well. Indeed, the leadership of organizations and communities can be seen to set a general tone for doing so among their members.

a. SELF-CONTROLLED, FRIENDLY AND WITTY. When amusing ourselves, laughing and eating together in appropriate ways, we are disposed more to calmness than to anger. We are inclined to remain calm in the face of things that would otherwise make us angry. The dominance of pleasurable emotion--so long as it is not excessive--means that our iras-cible or angry emotions are recessive at that time. Wishing to have fun, we do not want our anger to spoil a good time.

It is important to note though that if we are **self-indulgent** in our desires for pleasure, we might well be more inclined to anger than to calmness, as anyone knows who has lived around people who drink too much. If we are **contentious** or a sadistic **buffoon** we are also more in-clined to anger than to calm. (For more on how these virtues and their corresponding vices affect our disposition to anger, see **Self-control**, NE III, 10-12, **Friendliness**, NE IV, 6 and **Rh** II, 4, and **Wittiness**, NE IV, 8.)

b. **GENEROUS AND PROPERLY AMBITIOUS.** The confident feeling that we are prosperous and successful, satisfied with where we are at a given time and able to generate what we need, allows us to remain calm when others act as though we were not important. We try to preserve the pleasurable feeling of such satisfaction and to avoid spoiling it by getting all worked-up and angry. In such a state, we do not doubt ourselves so much and are not so threatened by other people's attitudes. We are not stretching to the breaking-point, worried that any interference might mean we will not make it.

c. **COURAGEOUS AND SELF-CONTROLLED.** Without **courage** (NE III, 6-9) and **self-control** (NE III, 10-2), people are less able to "enjoy freedom from pain, or inoffensive pleasure, or justifiable hope." These two virtues dispose us to remain calm. "Justifiable hope" springs from courage, while unjustifiable hope comes from cowardice and self-indulgence. The latter tends to leave people touchy in th[e face of anything that might burst the bubble of their illusions. Cowards are too afraid of too many things and live in fear. And as we have seen, struggling with painful things disposes us very strongly to anger.

Both self-indulgence and depression's excessive self-control under-mine our ability to enjoy the calming influence of inoffensive pleasures. Depression leaves us furious at our inability to enjoy ourselves, while self-indulgence leaves us greedy and undisciplined, prone to anger at the slightest frustration. Neither the frightened, the self-indulgent nor the depressed can be calm because of their agitated desires respectively to flee, to gratify themselves, or flee from the excessive desire to gratify themselves.

d. **AFTER THE PASSAGE OF TIME, EXCEPT FOR THOSE WHO HATE.** Time heals old wounds and the mere passage of time is often the best way to put one in a calmer state of mind. This is not the case, however, when one has become embittered toward life itself. While "time puts an end to anger," it has no such effect on hatred. (See **Enmity**, **Rh** II, 4.) Anger will calm down given the chance to cool off, hatred and spite will not. This is why the strife in Northern Ireland and the Middle East is so intractable. The different sides are not just angry; they hate one another.

e. **AFTER OUR ANGER IS SPENT AGAINST SOMEONE ELSE.** Forcefully expressing anger normally leaves us depleted and calm. This suggests then the strategy of postponing dealing with someone's anger against us until after he has really given it to somebody else. This only seems to work, however, when the person is genuinely angry and neither spiteful nor insolent-sadistic. While "men become calm when they have spent their anger on somebody else," insolence and especially spite seem to feed on themselves.

f. **FRIENDLY AND FEELING PITY.** We cannot both befriend (or pity) someone and be angry at them at the same time and in the same respect. This is why it is a good strategy in trying to calm our anger to focus on the suffering the offender has undergone as a result of his offence, including that resulting from our anger toward him, or that might have led him to it in the first place. But this fact also implies that the very act of our punishing someone can change our attitude toward him and put us in a different state of mind toward him. There is a self-correcting and dampening mechanism at work here, at least among the virtuous, as compassion and pity are called into play to put a check on anger so that it does not consume us and the people we care about enough to get angry at. The person's suffering satisfies and spends whatever vengeance we desired, while stimulating our **friendliness** (Rh II, 4 and NE IV, 6) or **pity** toward him (**R h** II, 8). Knowing this increases our confidence to uphold our principles and try to instill respect for them.

g. **ASHAMED AND HIGH-MINDED.** Since anger is caused by picturing something as an **unjustified** slight, it calms down when we see the justice of a person's action. This is why people should always be told the reason for their being punished. Without an explanation, we take punishment itself to be an unjustifiable slight, react angrily to it and miss the lesson punishment should teach. To avoid this outcome, we must of course accept the justification for the punishment; just announcing a rationalization is not enough. Our ability to respond to such explanations and criticism is governed by our sense of **high-mindedness** (NE IV, 3) and **shame** (Rh II, 6 & NE IV, 9).

If we have the vices of being **excessively ashamed** and **small-minded**, our state of mind inclines us to feel others are right to treat our wishes as unimportant. We will remain calm, but it will be the calm of the **apathetic** rather than of a self-respecting and just person. If on the other hand, we are **vain** and/or **shameless** about our own actions, we are prone to anger. We find it difficult to see the justice in anyone else's position, and are seldom calm. Such self-centeredness makes it difficult for other people to get through to us when we have no right to be angry.

h. **REALIZING WE CANNOT MAKE OUR ANGER KNOWN TO THE PERSON SLIGHTING US.** If we see we cannot get through to the person to let him know how we feel about what he has done to us, our anger tends to calm. Aristotle mentions the way Odysseus wanted the Cyclops to know who blinded him, and the way our anger subsides against the dead whom we cannot reach. But I believe this principle applies as well when we are angry at people about things we realize they just do not see. Feeling they cannot understand us and the reasons for our anger, we tend to calm down--but often at the cost of becoming apathetic and indifferent toward them.

While **insolence** shares anger's personal focus, **spite** is impersonally directed against whole classes of people and against individuals only because they are members of a hated class such as authorities, the rich, etc. A spiteful person is content with anonymous and wanton destructiveness as seen in vandalism, for example. Unlike anger, **hatred** is not assuaged by recognizing we cannot personally get through to the offending party. The only thing that matters is that his happiness be destroyed.

4. HOW TO CALM PEOPLE DOWN

Now that we know the kinds of people who have a calming influence on us, and the states of mind disposing us to be calm, we can understand the wisdom of Aristotle's advising speakers to

> put your hearers into the corresponding state of mind, and represent those with whom they are angry as formidable, or as worthy of reverence, or as benefactors, or as involuntary agents, or as much distressed at what they have done. (1380b 31-4)

COMMENTARY. Aristotle's advice covers both how the audience should be led to view themselves, i.e. the state of mind they should be put in, as well as how they should picture the person they might otherwise be angry at. He does not review all of these factors, and we need not comment on them again here since they can all be readily found in sections 2. and 3. above.

C. GENTLENESS, EXCESSIVE ANGER AND APATHY (NE IV, 5) AS THE VIRTUE AND VICES OF THIS POWER

1. GENTLENESS AS THE VIRTUE

So far we have learned the basic principles of how anger operates and how it can be calmed down. Our final task will be to characterize the difference between virtuous and vicious anger in terms of their effect on our power to function according to **proper wish, deliberation** and **choice.** Aristotle identifies the virtue and vice this way.

> **Gentleness** is a **mean** with respect to anger; the middle state being unnamed, and the extremes almost without a name as well, we place gentleness in the middle position, though it inclines towards the deficiency, which is without a name. The excess might be called a sort of **irascibility.** For the passion is anger, while its causes are many and diverse. (1125b 27-31)

Further below Aristotle distinguishes several different forms of **irascibility** or **excessive** anger and explains that **apathy** is the vice of **deficiency,** but first he clarifies the way in which **gentleness** is the virtuous disposition which allows us to function properly.

> The man who is angry at the right things and with the right people, and further, as he ought, when he ought, and as long as he ought, is praised. This will be the gentle or good-tempered man, since gentleness is praised. For the gentleman tends to be unperturbed and not to be led by passion, but to be angry in the manner, at the things, and for the length of time, that reason dictates; but he is thought to err rather in the direction of deficiency; for the gentle man is not revengeful, but rather tends to make allowances. (1125b 32-1126a 3)

COMMENTARY. It is interesting that the Greeks had as great a problem naming the virtue and vices of the power of anger as we do. (We saw the same problem earlier with the power of **ambition**.) As with the other virtues, the goodness and appropriateness of anger always depends on the fit between the circumstances and our response to them, so we cannot say that anger is either good or bad in any simple way. With so much variation in circumstances and appropriate responses, we have no broadly used term for all the cases in which we are inclined to handle anger appropriately. "Gentleness" will have to do for the disposition to such responses.

The first two factors in which we can go wrong in getting angry concern the agent (A) which arouses our anger. We can go wrong 1) in misjudging his form of response (F) to us by thinking he is slighting us when he is not, or 2) by holding one person responsible for what someone else has done. The other factors concern our form of response (F). The first of these is the appropriateness of our response, i.e. of what we actually say and do. Some things might be appropriately said in response to one slight but not to another. A given response might also be appropriate in response to a slight at one time but not another. This is the temporal dimension of our response. The virtuous person responds not only how but when he should. Sometimes the right time to be angry is when the slight occurs, other times doing so might disrupt more important things. A person can also be angry for too long or too short a time. People who respond rightly on all these scores are praised as being gentle.

Like all the other virtues, gentleness is a possibility condition for proper wish, deliberation and choice. We see this when an excessively angry person flies off the handle and acts against his own higher **wishes**, for example, to be **friendly** (NE IV, 6 & Rh II, 4). In doing so, he acts irrationally by going against what his own **deliberations** might have warned him against doing. We see it when he suffers the shameful feeling of having lost the power to **c h o o s e** how he will respond to the challenging times when he all too often feels other people are slighting him or getting ready to do so. Such an angry character orientation can cripple our whole enjoyment of life and undermine our faith that we will ever be able to give our best. Apathy, as the contrary vice of deficient anger, can be equally destructive of proper wish, deliberation and choice, as we will see immediately below.

Gentleness creates the necessary emotional room for acquiring **friendly realism** about ourselves and others, while excessive anger tends to crowd this attitude out of our lives. As we become more reasonable and understanding, we are calmer and less stressed by longings for revenge. We are more able to make allowances for others' behavior and at the same time better able to stand up for ourselves.

2. APATHY AS THE VICE OF DEFICIENT ANGER

Aristotle observed that

> The deficiency, whether it is a sort of apathy or whatever it is, is blamed. For those who are not angry at the things they should be angry at are thought to be fools, and so are those who are not angry in the right way at the right time, or with the right persons; for such a man is thought not to feel things nor to be pained by them, and, since he does not get angry, he is thought unlikely to defend himself; and to endure being insulted and put up with insult to one's friends is slavish. (1126a 3-8)

COMMENTARY. Apathetic people seem "not to feel things nor to be pained by them" (F) which implies that their **wishes** (M) are so weak that their being slighted (A) does not trigger an upright sense of anger. As Aristotle says, an apathetic person is "unlikely to defend himself" and the things he believes in (T). His wishes are so weak he is unlikely to persist in them in the face of opposition. It requires courage to want something that others do not encourage or allow, and even more to be angry enough to stand up for oneself.

An apathetic person certainly cannot be **high-minded** (NE IV, 3) about his or her own wishes. Apathy arises rather from the **small-minded** wish simply to get by. As Aristotle says, "to endure being insulted and put up with insult to one's friends is slavish," and insofar as people see themselves as merely the instruments of others, they exist without proper wishes, deliberations and choices of their own. Apathetic people cannot give very deeply of themselves because they do not believe in themselves or know very confidently what they feel and think. As a vice, apathy is thus part of a larger syndrome of attitudes affecting our self-respect, responsibility and creativity as human beings.

A virtuous person should be angry at insulting treatment to his family and friends as well as himself and will never allow himself to act as though they and their welfare were unimportant to him. When we have the vice of apathy, however, we cannot stand up for anybody who needs our help, whether they are close to us or more distant, and let everybody down. But why, though, would someone/ become apathetic? We have discovered two major sources for such apathy, first in examining **hopelessness** (Rh II, 5) in CHAPTER ONE, and then in examining **depression** (NE III, 11) in CHAPTER TWO.

APATHY ROOTED IN HOPELESSNESS AND IDENTIFICATION WITH THE AGGRESSOR. Anger requires us to hold on to the wishes which are being treated as unimportant. If we do not care about our own wishes and our right to them, we will not be very angry when others join us in not taking them seriously. If we do care, however, we need **courage** to handle the fear of realizing people with influence in our lives do not want us to pursue these wishes. Cowardice means we tend to minimize our resources while maximizing those of the people who threaten us. When our confidence that we can act on our wishes falls to zero, we tend to give up the wishes others are threatening as a way to escape the painful uncertainty of being afraid we will make a mess of our lives.

It is a most natural thing in such a state of mind to identify with the wishes of the aggressor and come to act, feel and think according to our anticipation of his expectations. This kind of apathy is closely associated with **obsequiousness** (NE IV, 6) and often with **extravagance** (NE IV, 1). When adopting this general orientation, we lose both our fear and our anger at being treated as though our own wishes were unimportant. We gain a certain calmness and placidity as a result, but only at the cost of losing our integrity and moral and emotional independence.

Women have traditionally been tempted to adopt this attitude out of a lack of confidence in the responsible and encouraging character of the men in their lives and in their own ability to support themselves and their children if they refuse to submit to unjust demands and male indifference to their development and happiness. Submission was exchanged for support, with all its attendant losses in creativity, sincerity and responsibility. There should be no surprise then that so many women have changed from apathy to excessive anger toward men who failed to supply the support and protection owed in return for that submission.

The spread of large organizations and the decline of self-employment and union solidarity has contributed greatly to this problem as more and more men felt in the workplace the same kind of self-betraying dependency that many women felt at home. While the modern workplace has broadened the horizons of many women, it has compromised the sources of confidence and independence for many men by making them feel their security depends on being liked and accepted rather than on performance criteria more under their own control. They then adopt a strategy toward the organization employing them which embodies the same vices and weaknesses we find so wrong when husbands encourage it in their wives and the wives buy into it.

But when such institutional unmanning occurs, they not only feel too weak to stand up for themselves when slighted, they are afraid to accept any deep responsibility for their families' development and well-being. They are inclined to feel everything associated with them is unimportant. Since men do not tend so naturally as women to identify their own state with that of their families, they must be encouraged to develop the moral strength and self-respect derived from providing for their families.

A vicious circle is developed between the sexes as women's loss of confidence in such men drives them to a desperate need to support themselves and their children without the help of men. Denying their disappointment, they no longer expect their men to act like men in being strong and supportive with their families, wishing, deliberating and choosing on their behalf. But with this loss of a moral vision of man's responsible place in securing and developing the human family, men feel irrelevant with no central function around which to organize their identities. They no longer have an honorable, manly place in the transition from one generation of human life to another. This loss of vision and noble expectation can only contribute to the sense of worthlessness fed at work.

All workplace practices which deny the employee's or client's rights to stand up for himself and his fellows against legitimately unjustifiable slights will contribute to people's buying into this apathetic and irresponsible attitude. The denial of the spirit of law and justice thus has grave consequences for both organizational productivity and social policy. There is thus a great deal at stake both individually and for the family and society at large in whether we permit institutions to encourage this syndrome of apathy in either men or women.

APATHY ROOTED IN DEPRESSION. If we can lose our power to be angry by giving up the wishes threatened by authorities, we can also lose it by simply being too afraid to act on our wishes--without giving them up so radically as we described above. This is what we saw with depression's fear to act on its extreme, self-indulgent wishes. The depressed person behaves in a most apathetic and indifferent way, but only on the surface. He appears **small-minded** and not worth worrying with, **obsequious** and desiring to please and cause no trouble. Yet, underneath, he feels great rage. With his overwhelmingly self-indulgent wishes, he has a greatly exaggerated and **vain** sense of what he deserves from others and is enraged when they do not give him all that he secretly desires. But he cannot show his anger, both because he is **ashamed** of his dependency and because he is **afraid** they will no longer help him if they ever see how little he wishes to help himself.

In both these cases, the apathetic person lacks confidence in himself and his resources for taking care of himself and his responsibilities.

And in both, the person wishes more to be taken care of by others than to grow strong himself. The difference between them is that the first wishes to identify with the wishes of powerful figures and act on their deliberations and choices. They are thus more able to act than the depressed person, although certainly not in their own voices. While they can act, they are hollow inside. The depressed person, on the other hand, cannot act and is filled up with desire and anger. Neither can show anger openly and appropriately.

3. TYPES OF EXCESSIVE ANGER

Aristotle identifies several different kinds of excessive anger.

The excess can be manifested in all the points that have been named (for one can be angry with the wrong persons, at the wrong times, more than is right, too quickly, or too long); yet **all** are not found in the same person. Indeed they could not; for evil destroys even itself, and if it is complete becomes unbearable. (1126a 8-12)

First, there are **hot** or **quick-tempered** people.

Now hot-tempered people get angry quickly and with the wrong persons and at the wrong things and more than is right, but their anger ceases quickly--which is the best point about them. This happens to them because they do not restrain their anger but retaliate openly owing to their quickness of temper, and then their anger ceases. By reason of excess choleric people are quick-tempered and ready to be angry with everything and on every occasion; whence their name. (1126a 13-9)

Second, there are **sullen** or **sulky** people.

Sulky people are hard to appease, and retain their anger longer; for they repress their passion, but it ceases when they retaliate; for revenge relieves them of their anger, producing in them pleasure instead of pain. If this does not happen they retain their burden; for owing to its not being obvious no one even reasons with them, and to digest one's anger in oneself takes time. Such people are most troublesome to themselves and to their dearest friends. (1126a 19-27)

Third, and finally, there are **harsh** or **bad-tempered** people.

We call bad-tempered those who are angry at the wrong things, more than is right, and longer, and cannot be appeased until they inflict vengeance or punishment. (1126a 27-8)

COMMENTARY. In dealing with excessively angry people, it is helpful to make these distinctions in the particular quality of their character. We have already seen enough to understand why excessive anger undermines **proper wish, deliberation** and **choice,** but the particular nature of the effect will differ depending on the kind of character.

When we are **hot-tempered**, we are quick to get angry but also quick to get over it. We are open and spontaneous with our feelings. Aristotle suggests a constitutional basis for this quickness with his reference to such people having a choleric temperament. This is the easiest kind of excessive anger to deal with. If we are **sullen** or **sulky**, on the other hand, we are not quick at getting over our anger. We repress our feelings rather than expressing and dealing with them. Since our friends might not even know we are angry, we must simply swallow it and can find no release or relief through talking it out. This attitude is often associated with the **hoarding** orientation (**NE** IV, 1). Finally, if we are **bad-tempered** and **harsh**, we want revenge against others so much that no explanation can satisfy us short of exacting it. We are most likely to be **spiteful** (**Rh** II, 2 & 10) when we feel this way and to drive away the friends who might try to talk us out of our hatred.

4. EXCESSIVE ANGER IS MORE VICIOUS THAN APATHY

Aristotle concluded that

> To good temper we oppose the excess rather than the defect; for not only is it commoner (since revenge is the more human), but bad-tempered people are worse to live with. (1126a 29-31)

COMMENTARY. Aristotle's judgment that anger is a greater vice than apathy might well be culturally determined. The **ILLIAD**, for example, the great fountain of Greek culture, is preoccupied with the consequences of Achilles' excessive anger. In a similar way, Plato's **REPUBLIC** is a study of why spirited intellectuals must discipline their angry, tyrannical natures in order to become philosopher kings. But the role and importance of anger changed over the years between them. The power of great anger and spirit had secured one a ruling position in the age of the Homeric heroes when one's standing depended on military prowess. 800 years later in Aristotle's time, when the modes and relations of production had changed, the Athenians had to be more restrained. The disciplining of their anger was a primary task if they were to adapt to the new political-economic realities and possibilities of the city-state.

One can argue, though, in contrast to this emphasis on excessive anger, that for oppressed people at least, **apathy** has always been the worst vice because it keeps them from standing up and growing stronger. Their problem is to cultivate the proper degree of anger between the vices of apathy and excess which will allow them to overcome the **small-mindedness** built into their subordinated status. The trick is to develop a productive degree of anger while not going over the line into spiteful destructiveness, or into suicidal actions that demoralize people rather than inspiring them to find their strength. Ethical leaders of subordinate groups must arouse their followers' anger, but also counsel them against allowing it to become excessive and turn into **hatred** and **enmity**. When this happens, people become so consumed with **envy** and **spite** (**Rh** II, 10) and their hearts are so hardened, that they lose whatever possibilities for happiness were otherwise available to them.

It would seem then that whether excessive anger or apathy is the worst vice will depend on the particular group of people one is talking about, although it is probably true to say that it is the excessive anger of some that encourages the apathy of others.

5. FINDING THE LINE BETWEEN GENTLENESS AND THE VICES

Aristotle recognized that

> it is not easy to define how, with whom, at what, and how long one should be angry, and at what point right action ceases and wrong begins. For the man who strays a little from the path, either towards the more or towards the less, is not blamed; since sometimes we praise those who exhibit the deficiency, and call them good-tempered, and sometimes we call angry people manly, as being capable of ruling. How far, therefore, and how a man must stray before he becomes blameworthy, it is not easy to state in words; for the decision depends on the particular facts and on perception. But so much is at least plain, that the middle state is praiseworthy--that in virtue of which we are angry with the right people, at the right things, in the right way, and so on, while the excesses and defects are blameworthy--slightly so if they are present in a low degree, more if in a higher degree, and very much if in a high degree. Evidently, then, we must cling to the middle state. (1126a 32-b 9)

COMMENTARY. Aristotle gives us the dimensions along which we must judge the appropriateness of a person's anger: 1) how we responded, 2) with whom we were angry, 3) at what we were angry, 4) how long we were angry, But how do we determine what is appropriate along each of these dimensions?

We can ask then about 1) the appropriateness of **how** we responded. Was it in keeping with our wishes and deliberations about how we should act, or did we go against how we would have chosen to act if we had been more in control of ourselves? Was it a successful defense of our wishes against an unjustified slight or did it leave us more vulnerable? 2) Were we angry at inappropriate persons or were we too forgiving of people we should have been angry at? 3) Were we angry at something that was not a slight or indifferent to things that were? 4) Were we so angry we sulked for a long time about something we should have gotten over? All of these questions require careful examination in individual cases before they can be answered.

A last point should be noted. In a situation of continual slights, we might be justified in being continually angry. But anger is painful and consumes so much of one's energy and attention that it tends to marshall all one's other powers in its service. As such, apathy toward **some** slights can be a prerequisite for freeing one's moral and emotional energy for the nurturing of a family, pursuing an education or being creative in one's work. Such deliberately chosen **apathy in the service of higher wishes** should be counted as a virtue because it allows for the development of our humanity and lays the foundation for a more successful response to the slighting injustice. It reveals the wisdom of the athlete's adage: "Don't get mad, get even"--by playing better and scoring more.

CHAPTER SIX

Handling the Giving of Pleasure and Pain to Others

INVENTORY

A. THE POWER TO BE KIND (Rh II, 7)

1. KINDNESS DEFINED

2. OUR STATES OF MIND WHEN KIND

   a. Generous and friendly rather than greedy,
      self-indulgent or excessively ambitious
   b. Conscious of what we are doing
   c. Not contractually obligated to perform the act
   d. Acting for the sake of the person helped
   e. Realistic about the actual help someone needs

B. THE POWER TO BE FRIENDLY AND TO SHOW ENMITY (Rh II, 4)

1. FRIENDLINESS AND ENMITY DEFINED

2. PEOPLE AROUSING FRIENDLINESS IN OTHERS

   a. Those caring about the same people as we do
   b. Those who have treated us and ours well
      for our own sakes
   c. Those we believe wish to treat us well
   d. Those our friends like or who like them
   e. Those who are the enemies of our enemies
   f. Those who are generous, courageous and just
   g. Those we wish to emulate and who wish to be our friends
   h. Those who are gentle, friendly and witty
   i. Those who praise and support our good qualities
   j. Those who are clean
   k. Those who neither criticize us nor remind us
      of their kindness
   l. Those who do not nurse grudges
   m. Those who are high-minded and do not speak badly
      of others
   n. Those who do not thwart us when we are serious
      or angry
   o. Those who take us seriously, especially
      about qualities we wish to develop in ourselves
   p. Those like ourselves in character and occupation
   q. Those who desire the same things we do
   r. Those whom we respect who do not make us feel ashamed
      for violating a social convention when no real wrong
      was done
   s. Those of our rivals by whom we wish to be respected
   t. Those whom we have helped
   u. Those who are as true to their friends when they
      are absent as when they are present

v. Those who are really fond of us and do not desert us
in trouble

w. Those who are open with us about their own weaknesses

x. Those who make us neither frightened
not uncomfortable

3. BEHAVIOR AROUSING FRIENDLINESS

C. **FRIENDLINESS, OBSEQUIOUSNESS, FLATTERY AND CONTENTIOUSNESS AS THE VIRTUE AND VICES OF THIS POWER (NE IV, 6)**

1. THE VIRTUE AND VICES DIFFERENTIATED

2. FRIENDLINESS AS THE VIRTUE

3. THE VICES DIFFERENTIATED AMONG THEMSELVES

D. **TRUTHFULNESS, BOASTFULNESS, AND MOCK-MODESTY (NE IV, 7) AS THE VIRTUE AND VICES OF THIS POWER**

1. THE VIRTUE AND VICES DIFFERENTIATED

2. TRUTHFULNESS AS THE VIRTUE

3. BOASTFULNESS AS THE VICE OF EXCESS

4. MOCK-MODESTY AS THE VICE OF DEFICIENCY

E. **WIT AND TACT, BOORISHNESS AND BUFFOONERY (NE IV, 8) AS THE VIRTUE AND VICES OF THIS POWER**

1. THE VIRTUE AND VICES DIFFERENTIATED

2. READY-WIT AND TACT AS THE VIRTUE

3. BUFFOONERY AND BOORISHNESS AS THE VICES
OF EXCESS AND DEFICIENCY

4. FRIENDLINESS, TRUTHFULNESS AND READY-WIT COMPARED

A. THE POWER TO BE KIND (Rh II, 7)

1. KINDNESS DEFINED

Aristotle says

> Kindness--under the influence of which a man is said to "be kind"--may be defined as helpfulness towards someone in need, not in return for anything, nor for the advantage of the helper himself, but for that of the person helped. (1385a 17-20)

Kindness can be shown in different degrees.

> Kindness is great if shown to one who is in great need, or who needs what is important and hard to get, or who needs it at an important and difficult crisis; or if the helper is the only, the first, or the chief person to give the help. (1385a 22-3)

But it always meets real needs.

> Natural cravings constitute such needs; and in particular cravings, accompanied by pain, for what is not being attained. The appetites are cravings of this kind: sexual desire, for instance, and those which arise during bodily injuries and in dangers; for appetite is active both in danger and in pain. Those who stand by us in poverty or in banishment, even if they do not help us much, are yet really kind to us, because our need is great and the occasion pressing... The helpfulness must meet, preferably, just this kind of need; and failing just this kind, some other kind as great or greater. (1385a 23-30)

COMMENTARY. Some people seem to have a natural gift for kindness; they take to being kind quickly and easily. Since not everyone is so fortunate, however, there is a special responsibility to teach and promote kindness. In explaining the nature of kindness, Aristotle treats the character trait as a material cause (M), while an act of kindness is a person's form of response (F) when touched or moved by "someone in need" (A). A kind person responds in a helpful way for the sake of the person in need (T) and not for the sake of initiating an exchange of goods or services on an equal or advantageous basis. Kindness can function to establish a relation that is beneficial to the kind person, but this outcome cannot be his intent. The proof of this intent is found in the person's reaction to being given no reward or pay-off for his kindness. Disappointment at the lack of reward reveals the expectation of some payment on a quid pro quo basis. (See, however, Rh II, 2 for a discussion of how the refusal to return a kindness when one is able to can nonetheless stimulate **anger.**)

There is only an apparent paradox, what Piaget calls a "pseudo-contradiction," in the fact that while genuine kindness has no expectation of reciprocity, it nonetheless promotes kindness in return. This dynamic of kindness spreading kindness is particularly important in creating political communities and cooperative work situations. The ability to see the difference between acting from a sense of kindness instead of from a sense of reciprocal compensation is a good mark of one's sensitivity to the importance of attitude and motivation in human behavior.

The degree of kindness shown is measured with reference both to the person needing help (M) and the person helping him (A). Roughly, the greater the need (M) and the fewer the people able or willing to help (A), the more kindness appears to be shown.

Aristotle's list of the needs arousing acts of kindness includes both biological needs such as sex, physical care and security, and political-economic ones arising from banishment and poverty. The basic point, though, is that the person has a painful craving that he or she is not attaining and that it is in the context of this frustrated wish that a person's help appears kind. We might be kind for example to someone whose **ambition** (NE IV, 4) for promotion or for a high grade did not materialize. Interestingly, too, the state of a person's mind which might lead us to be kind to him, might dispose him to be **angry** (Rh II, 2) and touchy toward those seeming to spite him in his distress.

2. OUR STATES OF MIND WHEN KIND

Aristotle recommends various ways in which orators can represent a person's state of mind when he is not acting from genuine kindness. By reversing this description, we can formulate the states of mind when we are kind. Aristotle addressed this problem because it is sometimes necessary to show that someone falsely claims to act out of kindness as a way to promote an interest that would not otherwise appear acceptable. Aristotle notes that "We can... see how to eliminate the idea of kindness and make our opponents appear unkind: we may maintain... "

a. that they are being or have been helpful simply to promote their own interest... (1385b 1)

b. that their action was accidental, or was forced upon them... (1385b 2)

c. that they were not doing a favor, but merely returning one, whether they know this or not--in either case the action **is** a mere return, and is therefore not a kindness... (1385b 3-4)

d. that a smaller service had been refused to the man in need; or that the same service, or an equal or greater one, has been given to his enemies; these facts show that the service in question was not done for the sake of the person helped. (1385b 8-9)

e. that the thing desired was worthless and that the helper knew it: no one will admit that he is in need of what is worthless. (1385b 10-11)

COMMENTARY. All five of these listings concern the person's purpose· (T) in performing what was only an apparently kind act. By identifying the contrary of these purposes we will have the states of mind in which we are actually being kind. They help us see more clearly what it means to be kind.

a. **GENEROUS AND FRIENDLY RATHER THAN GREEDY, SELF-INDULGENT OR EXCESSIVELY AMBITIOUS.** Kindness cannot have an ulterior motive such as **greed** (NE IV, 1), **self-indulgence** (NE III, 10-2) or **ambition** (NE IV, 4), but must be rooted in **generosity** (NE IV, 1) and **friendliness** (Rh II, 4 and NE IV, 6). But where generosity concerns the proper use of money (A), kindness responds to a far greater range of needs (A), such as for one's time, physical attention, etc. Friendliness, on the other hand, is not specifically focused on responding to painful needs the way kindness is. One can be friendly simply through taking pleasure in another's happiness.

Kindness thus seems a hybrid disposition drawing on both generosity and friendliness and responding to an area of peoples' needs that overlaps certain of the forms of agency found in both. It illustrates how the virtues can be blended together to explain other emotional states and forms of action in something like the way the primary colors can be combined to produce fucia, mauve, apricot, and the other colors.

b. **CONSCIOUS OF WHAT WE ARE DOING.** The kind act must be voluntary, and cannot be either accidental or coerced (NE III, 1). In these latter cases, we can speak of a kind **act** that was, nonetheless, not an act **of** kindness because it did not come from an **intention** to be kind. Aristotle makes a similar point about justice at NE V, 8. "Thus it will be possible for a deed to be unjust without yet being an 'unjust act' if the element of voluntariness is absent." (1135a 22-3)

c. **NOT CONTRACTUALLY OBLIGATED TO PERFORM THE ACT.** Seeing an actor's intent to do us a kindness is not enough to make us feel he was actually kind. He must be doing something independently of any obligation he might have to us. Less productive, **hoarding** people (NE IV, 1), for example, tend to picture personal relations in terms of a carefully balanced sense of reciprocity, tit for tat. A person so disposed will tend to construe everything he does as a balancing of accounts. Excessively **receptive** and **exploitative** people are likewise ungenerous and use every opportunity to create the impression they no longer have any obligations to others. There is a striking greediness here as they later pass off as a repayment, what they at the time were happy to praise as a kindness. Whether we focus on the way in which someone is just paying us back, or is genuinely being kind, will depend on whether we are feeling pinched and worried about keeping track of everything owed us, or are feeling confident, expansive and friendly.

   d. **ACTING FOR THE SAKE OF THE PERSON HELPED.** Aristotle gives two arguments to show that a person did not act "for the sake of the person helped." The first is that if the person was committed to our well-being, he would have helped us in a smaller matter also. Since he did not do so, we must assume he did not help us from genuine kindness in the other matter either. In the second case. if he has given "an equal or greater" service to our **enemies**, he certainly cannot be called kind to us.

   e. **REALISTIC ABOUT THE ACTUAL HELP SOMEONE NEEDS.** If we know the help we are offering is worthless in meeting somebody's needs, our offering it seems designed more to make us look kind than really to be so. The more patently useless our offer is, the more insulting it is to the needy person. In the midst of his need, we are manipulating and diverting him from his problem so that he might flatter our vanity about how good we are. Our persistence in reminding him of the worthless offer, combined with our indifference to learning its true value to him, gives us away as not being motivated by genuine kindness. When we sincerely wish to be kind, we want to learn how we can be the most helpful and do not presume we already know what they need.

B. THE POWER TO BE FRIENDLY AND TO SHOW ENMITY (Rh II, 4)

1. FRIENDLINESS AND ENMITY DEFINED

Aristotle says

We may describe **friendly feeling** towards anyone as wishing for him what you believe to be good things, not for your own sake but for his, and being inclined, so far as you can, to bring these things about. A friend is one who feels thus and excites these feelings in return; those who think they feel thus towards each other think themselves friends. (1381a 1-3)

Aristotle seems to treat enmity as the contrary of friendliness. While often confused with simply being angry, enmity involves a different form of response (F) and purpose (T), arises from a different moral source (M), and is triggered by different agents (A).

Enmity may be rooted in either **anger** or **spite**. Now whereas anger arises from offenses against oneself, enmity may arise even without that; we may hate people merely because of what we take to be their character. Anger is always concerned with individuals... whereas hatred is directed also against classes: we hate any thief and any informer. Moreover, anger can be cured by time; but hatred cannot. The one aims at giving pain to its object, the other at doing him harm; the angry man wants his victims to feel; the hater does not mind whether they feel or not. All painful things are felt; but the greatest evils, injustice and folly, are the least felt, since their presence causes no pain. And anger is accompanied by pain, hatred is not; the angry man feels pain, but the hater does not. Much may happen to make the angry man pity those who offend him, but the hater under no circumstances wishes to pity a man whom he has once hated: for the one would have the offenders suffer for what they have done; the other would have them cease to exist. (1382a 2-16)

Enmity finds its source in **spite** and **hate** (**Rh** II, 10).

COMMENTARY. The Greek **philia** has a broad range of reference-- from the love and affection between husband and wife to the kind of friendship that occurs between people in business together. Later in his presentation, Aristotle makes the important observation that "Friendship has various forms--comradeship, intimacy, kinship, and so on." It ranges from true love to simply liking someone and wishing them well in the circumscribed setting of a professional relationship.

The key to the definition is wishing for the other what we believe to be good things for his or her own sake and not our own (T). Cicero grasped this idea nicely when he spoke of Aristotle's idea of a friend as an **alter ego**, rather than simply an extension of our own. The quality of any given friendship can be determined by the particular good things the people wish for each other. Aristotle believes these good things fall under three headings; wishing to be **useful** to each other, to give **pleasure**, or to help each other become **noble** and good.

The wish to promote each other's development as human beings will also include wishing for **utility** and **pleasure**. But without this primary commitment to the promotion of human development and virtue, friends can thoughtlessly urge the excessive (or deficient) pursuit of things which might give pleasure or prove useful in some ways while nonetheless corrupting us in more important ways. Their sense of friendship might have nothing to do with contributing to each other's mature development and happiness. It is not the heart of what they wish, the spirit that animates their deliberations, nor the criteria upon which they base their choices. Friends concerned simply with each other's usefulness, or with pursuing pleasure together, might wish what they think is good for each other. They just do not have the highest goals for the relationship, and probably not for their own lives either.

Erik Erikson says somewhere in his book on Ghandi that "Character solutions sometimes require friendship dissolutions." This is especially true when someone is trying to develop a higher sense of purpose but finds himself or herself in relations which do not support or permit this development. It is simply not true, however, that we should only have the highest kinds of friendship. Such relations are rare, and it is important to develop the power to be friendly at whatever level is natural with others.

This important text on enmity contains Aristotle's most detailed comparison between anger and spite. We saw in the Chapter on anger that this distinction is particularly important in examining the three agents arousing anger--contempt-disdain, insolence-sadism, and spite (**R h** II, 2). Enmity is not, however, normally listed as the direct contrary of friendliness, in the sense of its being the vice of excessive or deficient friendliness. **Flattery** and **obsequiousness** are the excesses of friendliness, and **contentiousness** is the deficiency (**NE** IV, 6), as we will see later in this chapter. The change from friendliness to enmity represents the deficient exercise of friendliness and the suppression of its development through the coming to dominance of spite.

Friendliness, anger and spite are different moral and emotional powers (M) and have different aims or functions (T). Friendliness wishes good for the other's sake; anger wishes to retaliate for, and cure, an unjust slight by causing pain, but not necessarily real harm; while spite actually wishes to harm, or even destroy, the people whose good fortune causes the hater to feel painfully responsible for his own unhappiness and failure.

The three also differ in the agents (A) arousing them. Friendliness is triggered by kindness. Anger is touched off by a particular individual's intentional, unjustified slight. Spite, however, does not require any individual slight by the person subjected to it. He can simply be a member of a hated group or class. The three can also be formally (F) distinguished with reference to the pleasure and pain associated with each. Where friendliness can be pleasurable or painful, depending on what is going on with your friend, being made angry is always painful; and hate is marked by cold satisfaction, if not pleasure.

Erich Fromm has analyzed spite and hate at great length starting with his discussion of **destructiveness** in ESCAPE FROM FREEDOM. Like Aristotle, Fromm distinguishes this attitude from **sadism**. He later expanded his understanding of this trait to include the concept of **necrophilia,** or the love of death as contrasted to **biophilia,** the love of life. Fromm explores these concepts in both THE HEART OF MAN and THE ANATOMY OF HUMAN DESTRUCTIVENESS.

2. PEOPLE AROUSING FRIENDLINESS IN OTHERS

Aristotle gives a long list of the people arousing friendliness in others, but first he notes that

> your friend is the sort of man who shares your pleasure in what is good and your pain in what is unpleasant, for your sake and for no other reason. This pleasure and pain of his will be the token of his good wishes for you, since we all feel glad at getting what we wish for, and pained at getting what we do not. (1381a 4-9)

His pleasure or pain at our welfare is the best sign of his real intentions toward us.

Aristotle characterized the people who can and should arouse other people's feelings of friendliness in the following ways.

> a. Those... are friends to whom the **same things** are good and evil; and those who are, moreover, friendly or unfriendly to the same people; for in that case they must have the same wishes, and thus by wishing for each other what they wish for themselves, they show themselves each other's friends. (1381a 8-12)

> b. We feel friendly to those who **have treated us well,** either ourselves or those we care for, whether on a large scale, or readily, or at some particular crisis; provided it was for our own sake. (1381a 12-3)

> c. And also to those who we think **wish** to treat us well. (1381a 13-4)

> d. And also to our **friends' friends,** and to those who like, or are liked by, those whom we like ourselves. (1381a 14-5)

> e. And also to those who are **e n e m i e s** to those whose enemies we are, or are disliked by those whom we dislike. For all such persons think the things good which we think good, so that they wish what is good for us... (1381a 15-9)

> f. Those who are willing to treat us well where money or our personal safety is concerned: and therefore we value those who are **generous, brave,** or **just.** The just we consider to be those who

do not live on others; which means those who work for their living, especially farmers and those who work with their own hands. We also like self-controlled men, because they are not unjust to others; and, for the same reason, those who mind their own business. (1381a 20-6)

g. Those whose friends we **wish to be**, if it is plain that they wish to be our friends: such are the morally good, and those well thought of by everyone, by the best men, or by those whom we admire or who admire us. (1381a 26-9)

h. Those with whom it is **pleasant** to live and spend our days: such are the good-tempered, and those who are not too ready to show us our mistakes, and those who are not cantankerous or quarrelsome--such people are always wanting to fight us, and those who fight us we feel wish for the opposite of what we wish for ourselves--and those who have the tact to make and take a joke; here both parties have the same object in view, when they can stand being made fun of as well as do it prettily themselves. (1381a 30-5)

i. Those who **praise** such good qualities as we possess, and especially if they praise the good qualities that we are not sure we **do** possess. (1381a 36-b 1)

j. Those who are **cleanly** in their person, their dress, and all their way of life. (1381b 1-2)

k. Those who do not **reproach** us with what we have done amiss to them or they have done to help us, since both actions show a tendency to criticize us. (1381b 2-3)

l. Those who do not **nurse grudges** or store up grievances, but are always ready to make friends again; for we take it that they will behave to us just as we find them behaving to everyone else. (1381b 4-7)

m. Those who are not **evil speakers** and who are aware of neither their neighbors' bad points nor our own, but of our good ones only; as a good man always will be. (1381b 7-8)

n. Those who do not try to **thwart us** when we are angry or in earnest, which would mean being ready to fight us. (1381b 9-10)

o. Those who have some **serious feeling** toward us, such as admiration for us, or belief in our goodness, or pleasure in our company; especially if they feel like this about qualities for which we especially wish to be admired, esteemed, or liked. (1381b 11-4)

p. Those who are **like ourselves** in character and occupation, provided they do not get in our way or gain their living from the same source as we do... (1381b 15-17)

q. Those who **desire the same things** as we desire, if it is possible for us both to share them together; otherwise the same trouble arises here too. (1381b 18-9)

r. Those with whom we are on such terms that, while we respect their opinions, we need not blush before them for doing what is conventionally wrong: as well as toward those before whom we should be ashamed to do anything really wrong. (1381b 19-22)

s. Our **rivals**, and those whom we should like to envy us--though without ill-feeling--either we like these people or at least we wish them to like us. (1381b 22-3)

t. Those whom we **help** to secure good for themselves, pro-vided we are not likely to suffer heavily by it ourselves. (1381b 24-5)

u. Those who feel as friendly to us when we are **not with them** as when we are--which is why all men feel friendly towards those who are faithful to their dead friends. (1381b 25-6)

v. Speaking generally... those who are **really fond** of their friends and do not desert them in trouble; of all good men, we feel most friendly to those who show their goodness as friends. (1381b 27-9)

w. Those who are **honest** with us, including those who will tell us of their own weak points: it has just been said that with our friends we are not ashamed of what is conventionally wrong, and if we do have this feeling, we do not love them; if therefore we do not have it, it looks as though we **did** love them. (1381b 29-32)

x. Those with whom we do not feel **frightened** or uncomfor-table--nobody can like a man of whom he feels frightened. (1381b 33)

COMMENTARY. As we noted earlier, Aristotle explains in **NE** VII that friendship can be based on people being either **useful, pleasurable** or **morally** good for one another. This insight has great practical value in helping us understand where we stand with the important people in our lives. The fact of our being pleased and pained by the same things as another person is the best token of our wishing for and fearing the same things and suggests the quality of the friendships we might have with them. We can be either pleased or pained for example by how useful we are to each other, how much pleasure we give each other, or how we seem to bring out each other's moral goodness. Yet since what we are pleased and pained by also provides a token of our **character**, character provides the real basis of friendship.

It is perhaps obvious that we need confidence in our power to be friendly if we are actually to be so to others. But if the lack of courage undermines friendliness, it is also true that the lack of friendliness can keep us from developing courage, self-control, generosity, gentleness and other virtues as well. Without the faith that we can make friends by being a friend, we are prone to vices such as **self-indulgence** and **depression**, **extravagance**, **small-mindedness** and compensatory **vanity**. Many of the other vices also signal the failure to develop encouraging and self-respecting relations with others and can only be overcome by doing so.

In commenting on Aristotle's list of the people who tend to arouse our friendly feelings, we will note the virtues involved both in their attitude (A) and our state of mind (M) when we respond in a friendly way (F). At the practical level, the list helps us see more clearly when others are being friendly as well as the many things we can do to be friendlier to them. Developing the power of friendliness is crucial for the concept of the proper wish to promote human development in ourselves and others.

Our examination of Aristotle's list will be expedited by noting the **commutative** principle that when two people are friends (or enemies) to a third, they tend to feel friendly toward one another in the same respect. (The principle is found in items a., b., d., e., and g. below.) This friendliness can be overridden, of course, to the extent that the other's success is at our expense, but it is found in a broad range of social phenomena. We see it in the affection nurtured between parents by the love they share for their children, in the solidarity between people with a common sense of social class or nationality, and even between nations participating in international celebrations like the Olympics.

a. **THOSE CARING ABOUT THE SAME PEOPLE AS WE DO.** When two of us wish the same good for a mutual friend, we are sharing the same sense of what is good and evil and are to that extent disposed to feel friendly toward one another. This explains why Ibn Khaldun was right to say that affection (or **philia**) comes from working for the same thing. Fathers and mothers are inclined to such affection when they feel deeply for their children, but this natural affection can obviously be choked off off by their greediness, excessive anger or other vices. Coworkers, too, rather naturally feel friendly to all who share their wish for the good of a project or firm, unless this too is disrupted by management practices setting people against one another in a zero-sum context.

The basic principle in friendliness is sharing the same sense of what things are good and evil and doing so in the win/win context of a **non-zero sum game**. The latter means simply that one person's getting what he wants is not at the expense of others getting what they want. In a zero-sum game, one person's plus comes from another's minus so that the two together always add up to zero.

b. **THOSE WHO HAVE TREATED US AND OURS WELL FOR OUR OWN SAKES.** We are naturally inclined to feel friendly toward those who have been **kind** (**Rh** II, 7) either to us or to our friends. Kindness is a most powerful stimulant to friendly feelings, as we saw earlier in this chapter.

c. **THOSE WE BELIEVE WISH TO TREAT US WELL.** We feel friendly toward those who wish to treat us well either from **kindness** (**Rh** II, 7) or from a sense of **justice** (**Rh** II, 8-9 and **NE** V)--even when circumstances might not permit them to do so. Obviously, however, their wish must be sincere and real. We must know they would, if they could.

d. **THOSE OUR FRIENDS LIKE OR WHO LIKE THEM.** We are inclined to feel friendly to the true friends of our friends--to the people they like and who like them. This inclination holds, however, provided that there is nothing over-ridingly negative about them which off-sets it. We might be more sensitive about some issue than our mutual friend and then be at odds with this third party.

e. **THOSE WHO ARE THE ENEMIES OF OUR ENEMIES.** We feel a certain kind of friendliness toward those whose **enmity** to our enemies makes them wish and work for something that we also wish for. Such friendliness is tightly circumscribed by the area of our common wish, and disappears to the degree conflicting wishes come to the fore. Strategic alliances are impossible (as is all strategic thinking based on them) when people cannot recognize circumscribed areas of common opposition to shared enemies. Groups incapable of such circumscribed friendliness are seriously crippled in taking care of themselves.

f. **THOSE WHO ARE GENEROUS, COURAGEOUS AND JUST.** We feel friendly toward the **generous** (NE II, 1), the **courageous** (NE III, 6-9) and the **just** (N E V and R h II, 8-9) because we can trust them in financial matters and when our personal safety might be at stake. Being around courageous people at a time of danger prompts friendly feelings toward those whose presence reassures us. We feel the same in money matters with generous people. They are not greedy and do not take from others unjustly, nor are they dependent, feeling they have the right to receive more than their share.

So we feel friendly toward the generous not only because they give, but because they support themselves and act justly. We see this with Aristotle's observation that people such as "farmers and those who work with their own hands" stimulate our friendly feelings because they "do not live on others" and "work for a living." This is one of many signs of the favor in which productive hoarding people were held in Athens--both those among the artisan classes, and among the leisured.

Aristotle also mentions that **self-controlled** people (NE III, 10-2) arouse friendly feelings because, unlike the **self-indulgent**, they are not inclined to treat people unjustly. When we control our desires in a life-enhancing way, we are free to commit ourselves to other people and to fine things. We simply cannot do so when indulgent desires forever turn our heads from maintaining any constancy of purpose. We cannot really be trusted when we are self-indulgent--not with people's money nor their personal safety and well-being, and not with their hearts either. Genuine self-control, on the other hand, attracts us, because the person can enjoy himself fully without becoming untrustworthy.

g.**THOSE WE WISH TO EMULATE AND WHO WISH TO BE OUR FRIENDS.** We feel friendly toward those we wish to **emulate** (Rh II, 11), especially when we sense they wish to be our friends. Such a person is someone whose accomplishments and sense of goodness we aspire to for ourselves. For him or her to wish to be friends would be a great honor and a real stimulant to our friendly feelings in return. Here is a clear case of friendliness based on the desire to promote a shared sense of **moral** development rather than simply usefulness or pleasure.

h. **THOSE WHO ARE GENTLE, FRIENDLY AND WITTY.** We feel friendly toward those who give us pleasure in social relations even if we might not be able to establish a deeper relation with them. People "who are not too ready to show us our mistakes" are **gentle** (NE IV, 5) rather than being **irascible, insolent-sadistic** or **spiteful** (Rh II, 2). We certainly cannot feel friendly toward people who are always disagreeing with or making fun of us since they show they do not wish us well. The same is true for "the cantankerous or quarrelsome" who show the vice of **conten-tiousness** (NE IV, 6). On the other hand, "those who have the tact to make and take a joke" show the virtue of **wittiness** (NE IV, 8) and tend to arouse our friendliness by their ability to tease and be teased in return.

i. **THOSE WHO PRAISE AND SUPPORT OUR GOOD QUALITIES.** People arouse friendly feelings when they praise our good qualities, especially those we lack confidence in. They literally en-**courage** us. Their respect helps us build up both our confidence and our high-minded self-respect. If they do so appropriately, they are **friendly** toward us and arouse friendliness in return. If on the other hand they are excessive in their praise, they are either **flatterers** or **obsequious** (NE IV, 6), neither one of which is a proper stimulant to friendliness.

j. **THOSE WHO ARE CLEAN.** Unless taken to extremes, those who keep themselves, their clothes, workplaces and homes clean and tidy tend to arouse friendly feelings, perhaps because of the relaxed sense of security and self-confidence they convey. Aristotle's reference to cleanliness reveals again the productive **hoarding** strain in Athenian culture (NE IV, 1).

k. **THOSE WHO NEITHER CRITICIZE US NOR REMIND US OF THEIR KINDNESS.** People disposed to reproach us for neglect or bad conduct while reminding us how much we owe them for their help do not stimulate very friendly feelings toward them. People less likely to criticize us in these ways are more likely to arouse our friendly feelings. In item h. above, Aristotle mentioned those who do not always show us our mistakes. Here he is talking about people who are genuinely **kind** (Rh II, 7), **generous** (NE IV, 1), or **friendly**, because they are the ones who will not continually remind us of the help they have given.

l. **THOSE WHO DO NOT NURSE GRUDGES.** To nurse grudges and be **sullen** is one of the vices of excessive **anger** (NE IV, 5). For someone to bear a grudge and then treat us less well than others will cause us to be either **angry** (Rh II, 2) at them or **small-minded** (NE IV, 3) and **ashamed** (Rh II, 6) about ourselves. We tend to avoid sullen people and are much more likely to be friendly toward those who are always ready to forgive and do not treat anybody this way.

m. **THOSE WHO ARE HIGH-MINDED AND DO NOT SPEAK BADLY OF OTHERS.** High-minded people tend not to speak ill of others and focus more on people's good points than their bad ones (NE IV, 3). They search for ways to stimulate and challenge people's development and to promote solidarity around life enhancing values. We feel confident and secure around such people and are inclined to be friendly toward them. **Envious** and **spiteful** (Rh II, 10) people, on the other hand, enjoy speaking ill of others and have a generally demoralizing influence. They do not make very attractive friends unless one is envious and spiteful oneself.

n. **THOSE WHO DO NOT THWART US WHEN WE ARE SERIOUS OR ANGRY.** People who respect, rather than show disdain for, our seriousness or anger make us feel friendly toward them. This shows their respect and concern for what we feel is a slight to our just interests or is a matter of some other serious interest to us.Our friendliness is a sign of appreciation for their not belittling or interfering with us when under great pressure. This often happens even with the very person we are angry with. If he takes our anger seriously, we are inclined to calm down and have a much improved chance to get in touch with whatever friendliness we might otherwise feel for him.

o. **THOSE WHO TAKE US SERIOUSLY, ESPECIALLY ABOUT QUALITIES WE WISH TO DEVELOP IN OURSELVES.** Aristotle now universalizes the theme of our feeling friendly toward people who take us **seriously**, whether through admiring any of our powers, believing in them or simply enjoying them. Our friendliness is intensified still further if we lack confidence in the power or gift they take seriously. This explains, for example, our natural friendliness toward encouraging teachers and friends who inspire us to live up to high standards.

This explains too why sadists frequently feel friendly toward the very people they abuse, since masochists take sadists very seriously and often idolize them. We can see why sadists become enraged when people show disdain for their powers and why police often show exaggerated civility toward potentially sadistic drunks to make them more amiable and minimize the chance of setting them off.

p. **THOSE LIKE OURSELVES IN CHARACTER AND OCCUPATION.** There is a natural inclination to feel friendly toward people like ourselves who wish for the same things, provided of course that we like ourselves. A zero-sum game situation tends, however, to override this inclination as people become obstacles to one another, for example, in competing for the same source of income. Times of economic scarcity tend to undermine friendliness especially when people are already inclined to greed and excessive ambition. Those who strongly believe in friendliness, however, always search for possible areas of cooperation in win/win situations.

This need to find complementary interests is why **justice** is so important a factor in friendliness, just as friendliness is decisive in justice. By insisting on distributions in keeping with the ratio of people's contributions and legitimate needs, the just person seeks ways in which one man's gain will not be--in the larger perspective--at another man's expense.

q. **THOSE WHO DESIRE THE SAME THINGS WE DO.** Here Aristotle universalizes the point made in item p. from its focus on sharing the character traits associated with our vocations, to the full range of desires we might share with others. We tend to feel friendly and identify with people who want the same kind of things we want, provided of course that they do not block us from attaining them.

r. **THOSE WHOM WE RESPECT WHO DO NOT MAKE US FEEL ASHAMED FOR VIOLATING A SOCIAL CONVENTION WHEN NO REAL WRONG WAS DONE.** We feel friendly toward people who know the difference between things which are morally wrong, because rooted in vice, and those which are wrong merely by convention. (The Roman jurists labelled these **mala in se** and **mala prohibita**.) To wrongly make us **ashamed** (Rh II, 6 and NE IV, 9) is a powerful way to undermine our self-esteem and promote **small-mindedness** (NE IV, 3). We are not likely to feel friendly toward people who make us feel less worthy as human beings because we violated a social convention.

Clearly, however, there are times when the violation of convention itself expresses a vice. Wearing a business suit, for example, is not by itself a virtue, but in a given circumstance the refusal to wear one can be an act of **insolent** rebelliousness. It can show a **reckless** lack of **courage** to do what must be done to promote a **just** cause and a **self-indulgent** desire to do what one pleases regardless of the circumstances. A person should not treat others **disdainfully** when he genuinely wishes to win them to the justice of his cause.

s. THOSE OF OUR RIVALS BY WHOM WE WISH TO BE RESPECTED.

We can feel friendly even toward our rivals when we see the contest in a broader perspective than a zero-sum game. We can feel friendly toward them when we are both striving for the perfection of the activity itself, and when participation and the virtue of giving our best have become goals in themselves. Everybody in the contest can attain these goals just by virtue of giving the best of themselves. Since there is no limit to what each can gain in this perspective, and one person's success can encourage another's, there is no zero-sum game involved and thus nothing to block the natural impulse toward friendliness.

Envy and **spite** (Rh II, 4 and 10), on the other hand, arise when one is alienated from finding joy in the activity itself. The envious and spiteful person focuses instead simply on financial rewards or success in a limited status hierarchy where one person's success must always be gained at another's expense. Often times, though, we speak of being "envious" of someone in the positive sense of wishing to **emulate** them which is quite the reverse of feeling spiteful toward them. The Greeks seem to have used "envy" in this non-malignant sense, just as we do. We are naturally inclined to feel a certain friendliness toward any rival who wishes to be like us.

t. THOSE WHOM WE HAVE HELPED.

While we help those toward whom we feel friendly, it is also true that we feel friendly toward those we help. We see an important example of this elsewhere when Aristotle observes that parents tend to feel greater friendliness toward their children than children normally feel toward their parents (NE VII). This is attributable at least in part to the process of loving those we help.

u. THOSE WHO ARE AS TRUE TO THEIR FRIENDS WHEN THEY ARE ABSENT AS WHEN THEY ARE PRESENT.

Loyalty to absent or departed friends is often deeply touching, and arouses the desire for similar faithfulness toward ourselves. Those who are "faithful to their dead friends" show this kind of sincerity in a high degree. If they were "two-faced" and assumed "out of sight/out of mind", we would think them inconstant and untrustworthy in their affection, which must inevitably undermine our friendliness toward them.

v. THOSE WHO ARE REALLY FOND OF US AND DO NOT DESERT US IN TROUBLE. It sometimes takes special **courage** (NE III, 6-9), **generosity** (NE IV, 1) and **kindness** (**Rh** II, 7) not to desert us when we are in trouble, so we understandably feel particularly friendly to those who stand by us in such times. Aristotle considers this the single greatest stimulant to feel friendly toward someone.

w. THOSE WHO ARE OPEN WITH US ABOUT THEIR OWN WEAKNESSES. As we have seen friends do not make us feel **ashamed** for violating conventions, as long as no true vice is involved. So when someone is open with us about his own violations, we tend to think he is being friendly toward us, and we feel the same in return.

x. THOSE WHO MAKE US NEITHER FRIGHTENED NOR UNCOMFORTABLE. Unless we have confidence in both ourselves and others, we will be too afraid ever to become close or vulnerable to anyone. If we lack courage, we will not see the friendliness of his telling us a painful truth about ourselves, even though we love learning other, less threatening truths. For us to feel friendly toward someone, he must not act in ways that are more threatening than our **courage** can stand. He can challenge us to face scary things about ourselves, or about social injustice or anything else, but only to the point where we feel we must protect ourselves from what he is doing.

We can become afraid that someone's cowardice or self-indulgence will lead him repeatedly to betray himself or us whenever he is threatened or tempted, that a spouse's extravagance will cost our family its economic security, or that a friend's irrational anger will spoil all of our social activities with him. These and other still stronger fears all tend to undermine our friendly feelings toward the people who cause them.

We might summarize this long list by saying that people with the virtues, including the virtue of friendliness itself, tend to generate friendliness. This holds, however, only when others appreciate virtue as well. People with truly hardened, envious hearts are the least disposed to friendly responses, while flatterers try to appear friendly when it promotes their schemes but lack any genuine interest in others.

Whether a person has the potential for friendliness is an experimental question. The more vices we develop in ourselves, the less will we be able to recognize and respond in kind to the friendliness and goodness of others. It takes some virtue just to see goodness, and considerably more to act on it. There is no guarantee that every individual or group has the capacity for friendliness (M), especially toward groups or categories of people (A) who might have abused him so terribly as to have hardened his heart toward them. But attitudes like those listed above will reveal whatever friendliness he is still capable of.

3. BEHAVIOR AROUSING FRIENDLINESS

Aristotle listed above the types of people and attitudes which tend to arouse friendly feelings in us. Now he mentions the kind of behavior that does so.

Things that cause friendship are: doing kindnesses; doing them unasked; and not proclaiming the fact when they are done, which shows that they were done for their own sake and not for some other reason. (1381b 35-7)

COMMENTARY. Kind acts by themselves are enough to stimulate friendly feelings, although the extent of our friendly feeling will be very much affected by whether the person performing the act falls under any of the headings that tend to limit friendliness. Doing them **unasked** will tend to make us feel friendlier, while bragging about them will make us doubt the person's motives.

C. FRIENDLINESS, OBSEQUIOUSNESS, FLATTERY AND CONTENTIOUSNESS (NE IV, 6) AS THE VIRTUE AND THE VICES OF THIS POWER

1. THE VIRTUE AND VICES DIFFERENTIATED

In keeping with his theory of virtue as the mean between extremes, Aristotle describes three different orientations (M) we can have toward the pleasure and pain of others (A). He begins with **obsequiousness** as a vice of **excessive** desire to please.

> In gatherings of men, in social life and the interchange of words and deeds, some men are thought to be **obsequious**, viz. those who to give pleasure praise everything and never op-pose, but think it their duty "to give no pain to the people they meet." (1126b 12-5)

Second, he speaks of **contentiousness** as the vice of **deficient** con-cern to please others.

> While those who, on the contrary, oppose everything and care not a whit about giving pain are called churlish and **contentious**. (1126b 15-6)

Finally, Aristotle speaks of **friendliness** as the **virtue** and contrasts it with both love and friendship proper.

> That the states we have named are culpable is plain enough, and that the middle state is laudable--that in virtue of which a man will put up with, and will resent, the right things and in the right way; but no name has been assigned to it, though it most resembles **friendship**. For the man who corresponds to this middle state is very much what, with affection added, we call a good friend. But the state in question differs from friendship in that it implies no passion or affection for one's associates; since it is not by reason of loving or hating that such a man takes every-thing in the right way, but by being a man of a certain kind. For he will behave so alike towards those he knows and those he does not know, towards intimates and those who are not so, ex-cept that in each of these cases he will behave as is befitting; for it is not proper to have the same care for intimates and for strangers, nor again is it the same conditions that make it right to give pain to them. (1126b 17-27)

266

COMMENTARY. Aristotle devoted more space to friendship than to any other subject in the **NICOMACHEAN ETHICS**--all of Books VIII and IX, in addition to the present chapter. He thought friendship and love are even more important than **justice** because it is through them that we are able to discover what is just. In the present section he is not talking about the intimate dimensions of friendship and love but about a more impersonal attitude of good feeling toward others. Space does not permit us to follow Aristotle through his rich analysis in these other texts, but we can at least clarify its outline.

Aristotle focuses on how the moral power of friendliness (M) governs those of our responses (F) to others (A) which function (Tfa) as stimulants (A) to their (M) pleasure (F) or pain (F). The vices of this power are classified along the dimensions of both pleasure and pain. **Obsequiousness** shows an excessive disposition to give pleasure and a deficient disposition to give pain. **Contentiousness,** at the other extreme, shows a deficient disposition to please and an excessive one to cause pain. **Friendliness,** as the virtue of this power, disposes us to give both the pleasure and the pain required to promote moral purposes and development in the circumstances.

We must take care to distinguish friendliness from **gentleness,** the virtue of the power of anger (**Rh** II, 2-3 and **NE** IV, 5). **Friendliness** seems to resemble **gentleness** when Aristotle speaks of friendliness as "that in virtue of which a man will put up with, and will resent, the right things and in the right way." This is reminiscent of the way the gentle person deals with situations which might otherwise arouse anger. Friendliness and gentleness differ, however, in that the class of agents (A) arousing **friendliness** is much broader than the class of slighting attitudes and behavior triggering **anger.** Opportunities for friendly responses cover the whole range of occasions in which we might give pleasure or cause pain to others. But they also differ in their forms of response (F) and functions (T).

Gentleness (M), on the other hand, disposes us to understand the motives (F) of those who interfere with our endeavors (A) and to be angry (F) only at those who intentionally slight the importance of what we are doing (A). It is motivated primarily by a high-minded insistence on the respect that should be accorded our legitimate efforts. This means that the gentle response will be a just and considerate one, but not necessarily what we would consider a friendly one. A person might be altogether gentle and understanding when it comes to the appropriateness of his anger while not being particularly friendly. A friendly response is fuller than a gentle one.

Finally, unlike gentleness, friendliness includes an essential aim or purpose (T) of actively wishing for and promoting the other person's well-being.

We must also distinguish **friendliness** from actually being someone's **friend.** Basically, the more intimate relationship is a more developed form of the general attitude of friendliness. A friendly person is disposed to be friendly to everyone and not just to his friends, and does not reserve his friendliness only to those for whom he feels particular affection. He does not even have to know the person to respond to him in a friendly way. This does not mean, however, that he treats everyone the same, only that he wishes all people well (T). He will respond to them in the way (F) they deserve. But other things being equal, friends deserve more than strangers.

2. FRIENDLINESS AS THE VIRTUE

Aristotle explains how virtue functions as a virtue by clarifying the basic wish (T) underlying friendliness (M) and how this aim governs the virtuous person's giving of pleasure and pain. He also clarifies the way in which the genuinely friendly person (M) does not respond in the same form (F) to all people (A), but rather responds in the way that is appropriate to each person and his relation to that person.

> Now we have said generally that he will associate with people in the right way; but it is by reference to what is **noble** and **beneficial** that he will aim at not giving pain or at contributing pleasure. For he seems to be concerned with the pleasures and pains of social life; and wherever it is not noble, or is harmful, for him to contribute pleasure, he will refuse, and will choose rather to give pain; also if his acquiescence in another's action would bring disgrace, and that in a high degree, or injury, **on that other**, while his opposition brings a little pain, he will not acquiesce but will decline. He will associate differently with people in high station and with ordinary people, with closer and more distant acquaintances, and so too with regard to all other differences, rendering to each class what is befitting, and while for its own sake he chooses to contribute pleasure, and avoids the giving of pain, he will be guided by the consequences, if these are greater, i.e. nobility and benefit. For the sake of a great future pleasure, too, he will inflict small pains. (1126b 27– 1127a 7)

COMMENTARY. Friendliness is the virtue disposing us to do what is **noble** and **beneficial** in giving **pain** or **pleasure** to others. An action (F) can be either noble or ignoble for us (M) to take and either beneficial or harmful (Tfa) for the person (M) we are responding to, and either pleasant or painful (F) to him. While a good person is disposed to give pleasure rather than pain, the ethical significance of the pain or pleasure depends on the nobility and beneficence of the act in promoting human development and the institutions which support and encourage it. While friendliness may properly cause either pleasure or pain, it can never lead to ignoble or purposefully harmful acts.

Friendliness calls for us to give pain when doing so might help the person avoid an even greater pain in the future or acquire a greater pleasure. This is why we should be critical and even **disdainful (Rh II, 11)** when people are doing shameful things. In this way we can help them recognize that continuing their behavior will cut them off from us and other honorable people and whatever possibilities for nobility and happiness they might have.

This explains too why friendliness requires **courage**, since we must face the possibility of anger resulting from our taking friendliness seriously in this way. **Self-indulgent, vain,** and excessively **angry** people, for example, tend to get upset even at observations and counsel offered in a spirit of friendly realism. Anger at such friendliness is rather like the captain of a ship being furious at lighthousekeepers trying to warn him off the rocks upon which he is about to crash his ship.

We have already noted that the friendly person's (M) response (F) will be appropriate to the different people (A) he is friendly to. He will not treat a close friend the same as an acquaintance but will adopt the form of behavior which befits the people he is with.

3. THE VICES DIFFERENTIATED AMONG THEMSELVES

Aristotle recognized a significant difference between an **excessive** desire to please others that is based in an exploitative purpose (T) and one that is not. People with the latter attitude are **obsequious**; those with the former are **flatterers**. The contrary vice of **deficiency** is **contentious-ness**.

> Of those who contribute pleasure, the man who aims at being pleasant with **no ulterior object** is obsequious, but the man who does so in order that he may get some **advantage** in the direction of money or the things that money buys is a flatterer; while the man who quarrels with everything is, as has been said, churlish and contentious. And the extremes seem to be contradictory to each other because the mean is without a name. (1127a 7-14)

COMMENTARY. **Obsequiousness** and **flattery** are both vices of excess. They each dispose us to give more pleasure and less pain than is noble for themselves or beneficial from an ethical point of view for the other person and tend to promote the other person's **vanity** (NE IV, 3) by giving him an unjustified sense of his own worth. They differ, however, in that the flatterer has an **exploitative** (NE IV, 1) and possibly **ambitious** (NE IV, 4) aim to take money and other advantages from the person he flatters. We could add **self-indulgence** to the flatterer's aims when he is attempting sexual seduction.

Obsequiousness, on the other hand, tends to be motivated by a **receptive** (NE IV, 1) and dependent person's strategy of survival through identification with the aggressor's wishes. It is an uncourageous response to threatening agents who appear vindictive to those who are dependent on them and do not obey and please them. It is pursued at the obvious expense of the person's own more noble wishes, deliberations and choices. This syndrome of **receptive obsequiousness** combined with **apathy** occurs throughout human history whenever groups of people are terrified and exploited.

Contentiousness is the contrary vice of deficient desire to please others and a correspondingly excessive willingness to cause them pain. Such a person tends to be quarrelsome and oppositional, and does not acknowledge the truth of what others say. You say yes; he says no. His indifference to the pain he causes is overdetermined by the satisfaction he finds in indulging the anger he is normally reluctant to express openly. The attitude is most naturally rooted in a somewhat **depressed** and **hoarding** orientation.

In explaining how these different attitudes come into being, we must start from the fact of the child's dependency which places a premium on his pleasing his parents (M) as a way to stimulate (A) their nurturing behavior (F). While children are natural-born charmers because of its survival value, it is only after several years of development that they are confident, generous and allo-centric enough to wish their parents (or anybody else) well for the other's own good instead of for their own. And as we argued in Chapter Three, the particular way they develop the power of friendliness reflects their strategy of economic survival as well. Together, the two powers of generosity and friendliness give shape to what Marx might call a person's individual **modes** and **relations of production**.

A child's efforts at developing his powers of friendliness and relatedness to others are central in situating him in the world of men and women. Along with whether he is receptive, hoarding, etc., how he handles himself in relating to others (obsequious, flattering, contentious or friendly and self-respecting) will affect what opportunities other people will feel like providing for his or her further development. These efforts can nonetheless be slighted by parents and other authorities who react angrily and make the child frightened to say what he believes about things which might cause them pain. Or they can simply be indifferent to his efforts to please them and promote a deep sense of impotence, envy and spite.

In such a situation, a child can become afraid to be intimate and truthful with others, and of being profoundly disappointed if he risks caring about and wanting to please them. He will understandably feel **small-minded** and incapable of being actively **friendly**, potent to stimulate love and friendship in return. He will also tend to be **angry** at having been slighted in his desire to befriend his parents and at having been made to deny his own thoughts. The development of his power of **truthfulness** will likewise be distorted. His way of handling the situation can be obsequious, flattering or contentious depending on both constitutional and environmental factors.

There will often be an excessive desire to befriend others underlying the vice of deficiency as the contentious person tries to protect himself from the recurrent pain of having cared too much about pleasing **unfriendly** people who did not respond in kind. A child such as the one described would have been better off caring less about pleasing unloving parents and searching for other adults more responsive to his or her growing power of friendliness. Doing so requires both the good fortune of having such people available and the moral and emotional strength required to look for them.

D. TRUTHFULNESS, BOASTFULNESS, AND MOCK-MODESTY (NE IV, 7) AS THE VIRTUE AND THE VICES OF THIS POWER

1. THE VIRTUE AND VICES DIFFERENTIATED

The power (M) Aristotle describes next is closely related to both **friendliness** and **wittiness**. Roughly speaking it has to do with how we respond (F) to opportunities to talk about ourselves (A). We will call this the power of **truthfulness**. Speaking with reference to friendliness, Aristotle says that

> The mean opposed to **boastfulness** is found in almost the same sphere; and this also is without a name. It will be no bad plan to describe these states as well; for we will both know the facts about character better if we go through them in detail, and we shall be convinced that the virtues are means if we see this to be so in all cases. (1127a 13-8)

Since friendliness, truthfulness and wittiness all deal with the pleasures and pains of **social** life, we must pay special attention to the agents (A) and forms of response (F) which allow us to differentiate them. Aristotle says,

> In the field of social life those who make the giving of pleasure or pain their object in associating with others have been described; let us now describe those who pursue truth or falsehood alike in words and deeds and in the claims they put forward. (1127a 18-20)

We must be alert to what he means by this reference to **truth** or **falsehood** in both words and deeds.

Aristotle identifies the virtue and vices of this power as follows, starting with **boastfulness** as the vice of **excess**.

> The **boastful** man... is thought to be apt to claim the things that bring glory, when he has not got them, or to claim more of them than he has... (1127a 21-2)

Second, in speaking of **mock-modesty** as the vice of **deficiency**, he says

> the **mock modest** man on the other hand [tends] to disclaim what he has or belittle it... (1127a 23)

And finally, in speaking of **truthfulness** as the **virtue**, he says

> the man who observes the mean is one who calls a thing by its

own name, being **truthful** both in life and in word, owing to what he has, and neither more nor less. (1127a 23-4)

Since many of the other virtues and vices also involve someone's making true or false claims about himself, it is necessary to pare away the other moral and emotional dimensions to acquire a precise sense of the virtue and vices at issue here. Aristotle does this by identifying a situation in which a person has no ulterior motive in the things he is saying. This effectively excludes the interference of other vices and allows him to focus on the virtue and vices found in this one power.

Speaking with regard to boasting, telling the truth and being mock-modest, he says

Now each of these courses may be adopted either with or without an object. But each man speaks and acts and lives in accordance with his character, if he is not acting for some ulterior object. And falsehood is **in itself** mean and culpable, and truth worthy of praise. Thus the truthful man is another case of a man who, being in the mean, is worthy of praise, and both forms of untruthful man are culpable, and particularly the boastful man. (1127a 26-32)

COMMENTARY. Aristotle tells us he is treating truthfulness as a virtue of social life and thus as it is related to friendliness and wittiness-tact. The three must be seen together to round out his picture of the virtues of sociability. The troubling task here is to understand the difference Aristotle saw between **boastfulness, mock-modesty** and **truthfulness**, on the one hand, and **vanity, small-mindedness**, and **high-mindedness** (NE IV, 3), on the other. Both moral powers have to do with "the claims they put forward," so it is not immediately obvious how they differ.

The difference lies in the fact that **high-mindedness** necessarily entails the presence of the other virtues as part of its material causality, while **truthfulness** as an isolated virtue does not. A robber, for example, could have the virtue of truthfulness but not of high-mindedness (given the absence of exceptional circumstances in which robbery was somehow justifiable).

As we saw earlier, high-mindedness has to do with truthfulness about the high moral expectations one has for himself based on the virtues he has built up over the years. One can even be high-minded about his truthfulness, as something he is proud of. Such a person would be rightly indignant at being treated as a liar by someone who should know his character.

When we say someone is **high-minded** about his truthfulness, we are saying more than that he is being truthful about his truthfulness. The reference to high-mindedness means that the person values truth as an ethical standard which he aspires to and expects himself to adhere to. He expects others to respect him for speaking truthfully and expects that anyone else who speaks the truth should be respected too.

A **small-minded** person, on the other hand, might be small-minded about his truthfulness. He could underestimate the extent of his own truthfulness, and could be small-minded about the noble responsibilities incumbent upon anyone with the power to speak the truth and about the respect he deserves and should expect from others if he is to promote a love of truth among them. If high-mindedness and truthfulness were the same, a vice of the first could not be found this way combined with the virtue of the second.

When we examine the boaster, the mock-modest, and the truthful man, therefore, we must remember that these terms apply simply to the **truth** of their claims, i.e. whether they are exaggerated, deficient or truthful, and not to the larger sense of what the person feels he is worth. Aristotle's observation that the two vices may be "pursued either with or without an ulterior motive" does not mean that either of them can arise without the motivation of other vices. Even though speaking falsely becomes characteristic of a person in the service of **other** vices, it might nonetheless recur when serving no ulterior goal. This is to be expected, after all, when an excessive form of response becomes **characteristic** of someone. The person is disposed to act that way even when it is not appropriate to the agent triggering it.

But it should be remembered that just on their own as characteristic practices, boasting and mock-modesty or self-depreciation are blameworthy even without reference to the other vices that motivate them. We examine these "ulterior motives" further below and expand on Aristotle's observations.

2. TRUTHFULNESS AS THE VIRTUE

Aristotle distinguishes the virtue of truthfulness from other virtues when he explains that

> We are not speaking of the man who keeps faith in his agreements, i.e. in the things that pertain to **justice** or **injustice** (for this would belong to another virtue), but the man who in the matters in which nothing of this sort is at stake is true both in word and in life because his character is such. But such a man would seem to be as a matter of fact **equitable**. For the man who loves truth, and is truthful where nothing is at stake, will still more be truthful where something is at stake; he will avoid falsehood as something base, seeing that he avoided it even for its own sake; and such a man is worthy of praise. He inclines rather to understate the truth; for this seems in better taste because **exaggerations** are wearisome. (1127a 33-b 8)

COMMENTARY. Just as we distinguished the power of **truthfulness** from that of **high-mindedness** to gain a better sense of what truthfulness is in itself, Aristotle here distinguishes truthfulness from being **honest**, **equitable** or **just** (NE V). His point is that while the unjust man will no doubt be a liar when pursuing his unjust gains, and the truthful man will be fair and just, truthfulness and justice are not the same things. Justice entails truthfulness, but truthfulness does not necessarily entail justice. Justice cannot exist without truthfulness, but ironically truthfulness is not always found with justice. One thinks, for example, of cynical people who can speak truthfully about many things, including their own unjust practices.

Aristotle is most concerned with the virtue that makes a truthful life possible, as he says, "both in word and in life." we might speak of the "sincerity" of such a person. A characteristic disposition to truthfulness shows up in the quality of one's sense of realism about the things he talks about and describes. Truthful people are not inclined to exaggerate constantly in evaluating things. We know where we stand with a truthful person who shows his sincerity not only through what he says but in his daily life. This gives us confidence in dealing with him in matters involving justice and injustice.

If anything, the truthful man is given more to understatement than to exaggeration and boasting. So one expects that the things he talks about will be as good or better than he says they are. It is indeed wearisome to listen to people who make little effort to discipline their comments by focusing on the evidence supporting what they are saying.

3. BOASTFULNESS AS THE VICE OF EXCESS

Aristotle distinguishes between different forms of boastfulness depending on whether it shows a simple disregard for truth and delight in falsehood or whether there is an **ulterior motive** leading the person to boast.

> He who claims more than he has with no ulterior object is a contemptible sort of fellow (otherwise he would not have delighted in a falsehood), but seems futile or inept rather than bad; but if he does it for an object, he who does it for the sake of reputation or honor is (for a boaster) not very much to be blamed, but he who does it for money, or the things that lead to money, is an uglier character (it is not the capacity that makes the boaster, but the purpose; for it is in virtue of his state of character and by being a man of a certain kind that he is a boaster); as one man is a liar because he enjoys the lie itself, and another because he desires reputation or gain. (1127b 9-16)

The purest form of this vice occurs when the person is just inept and prefers making things up to paying attention to what he is talking about. But people can also lie out of ulterior motives such as excessive **ambition** (NE IV, 4) and **exploitativeness** (NE IV, 1) which introduce further vices into the picture.

Some things lend themselves more readily to getting away with boasting than others when one's aim is winning either **honor** or **money**.

> Now those who boast for the sake of **reputation** claim such qualities as win praise or congratulation, but those whose object is **gain** claim qualities which are of value to one's neighbors and one's lack of which is not easily detected, e.g. the powers of a seer, a sage, or a physician. For this reason it is such things as these that most people claim and boast about; for in them the above-mentioned qualities are found. (1127b 16-22)

COMMENTARY. When Aristotle says the "inept" person "enjoys the lie itself," he seems to refer to someone who is hopelessly unreliable in his exaggerations and whose judgment is not to be counted on. Such a person tends not to carry through on the things he claims. Someone, on the other hand, who boasts for the sake of reputation or honor is either **vain** (NE IV, 3) or excessively **ambitious** (NE IV, 4) while the one who does so for the sake of money is **unjust** (NE V) and **exploitative** (NE IV, 1). Reputation, honor and money can trigger vices in our other moral and emotional powers and bring our power of truthfulness in their train. The man, on the other hand, who exaggerates simply for the enjoyment of "the lie itself" shows the vice of excess in this moral power unmixed with other vices.

The different motives for lying--honor or money--are revealed in the different claims they lead people to make. The claims differ because they have different purposes and functions to perform. The claims of a **vain** or **ambitious** person (M) are in a form (F) that he believes will stimulate (Tfa) other people (M) to honor him (F) with praise and congratulation.

An **exploitative** person, on the other hand, claims to have abilities (Tfa) that should cause other people (M) to give him their money (F). Aristotle mentions fortune-tellers, sophists, and physicians or quacks as examples of people who make such claims. These arts and powers, and others like them, would be well-worth paying for if the person actually had them. They are particularly tempting claims for exploiters to employ because they combine high market value in terms of what people will pay, with considerable ease at escaping detection.

The love of lying would seem to occur in the context of failing to develop virtues in our other powers. In an important sense we all start out incapable of being truthful because as infants and young children we cannot initially distinguish between reality and illusion. (Imaginative creations often penetrate to important realities so we are not talking about illusions in this sense.) As we saw earlier with adult **self-indulgence** and **vanity**, what requires explanation is not how we might develop the vice of exaggeration and boastfulness but how we can grow out of such attitudes.

This focuses one on understanding how social environments can encourage people not to become truthful. A little girl with a harsh, threatening mother who punishes her excessively for minor wrongs, for example, might begin to lie to protect herself from a mother unresponsive to truth. But she might also have an older girl friend who is a **flatterer** (NE IV, 6), **self-indulgent** (NE III, 10-2) and an accomplished liar. She comes to **emulate** (Rh II, 11) this child and begins to lie even when there is nothing to be gained beyond the pleasure she takes in her skill at crafting falsehoods and manipulating people's credibility. (We even speak of such people as "crafty.") In the process, she fails to develop a virtuous attitude toward others which would bring with it a corresponding love of truth and sincerity of character.

4. MOCK-MODESTY AS THE VICE OF DEFICIENCY

Aristotle observed the interesting fact that extreme forms of **modesty**, the vice of **deficiency**, can actually be a disguised form of **boasting**, the vice of **excess**. He thought too that within certain limits modesty is more attractive than boasting.

> Mock-modest people, who understate things, seem more attractive in character; for they are thought to speak not for gain but to avoid parade; and here too it is qualities which bring reputation that they disclaim, as Socrates used to do. Those who disclaim trifling and obvious qualities are called humbugs and are more contemptible; and sometimes this seems to be boastfulness, like the Spartan dress; for both excess and great deficiency are boastful. But those who use understatement with moderation and understate about matters that do not very much force themselves on our notice seem attractive. And it is the boaster that seems to be opposed to the truthful man; for he is the worse character. (1127b 23-33)

COMMENTARY. Where **boastfulness** deals with what people **claim**, **mock-modesty** deals with what people **disclaim**. There the problem was exaggeration, here it is understatement and irony. The mock-modest person disclaims things that would win him honor and reputation. Aristotle is talking about what, in its minor form, appears to be shyness and the desire "to avoid parade," or to be in the spotlight.

While there is a connection, **mock-modesty** is not the same as **small-mindedness**. The latter undermines our capacity to act nobly and reflects our expectation that we will not be thought worthy of others' respect. A **high-minded** and noble person might none the less be shy about people making a fuss over him. And surely the desire "to avoid parade" is not the same as feeling unworthy to do fine things and be respected.

Mock-modesty is not limited, however, to shyness or an attractive form of understatement. The more extreme it becomes, the more offensive and unpleasant it is. Aristotle thought that instead of sincere simplicity, Spartan clothing was a boastful affectation. As Shakespeare has Julius Ceasar say, "Me thinks he doth protest too much."

In this relation between **mock-modesty** and **boastfulness**, we see again the way a tendency toward **deficiency** masks an even stronger tendency toward **excess**. This is the same kind of fibrillation we saw earlier in the way depression, as a **deficiency** in finding **pleasure**, can actually result from **excessively self-indulgent desires** (NE III, 11), and the way in which someone can vacillate back and forth between the **deficiency** that is **small-mindedness** and the **excess** that is **vanity** (NE IV, 3).

276

E. WIT AND TACT, BOORISHNESS AND BUFFOONERY (NE IV, 8) AS THE VIRTUE AND THE VICES OF THIS POWER

1. THE VIRTUE AND VICES DIFFERENTIATED

We also have the power (M) to respond (F) to opportunities for **social amusment** (A).

> Since life includes rest as well as activity, and in this is included leisure and amusement, there seems here also to be a kind of intercourse which is **tasteful**; there is such a thing as saying--and again listening to--what one should and as one should. The kind of people one is speaking or listening to will also make a difference. (1127b 34-1128a 3)

There is a virtue and vices of excess and deficiency which govern not only what we say ourselves (F) but also what we will put up with from others (A).

Aristotle first describes the vice of **excess**, found in the **buffoon**.

> Those who carry humor to excess are thought to be vulgar buffoons, striving after humor at all cost, and aiming rather at raising a laugh than at saying what is becoming and at avoiding pain to the object of their fun... (1128a 5-7)

Second, he describes the vice of **deficiency**, found in the **boorish** person.

> Those who can neither make a joke themselves or put up with those who do are thought to be boorish and unpolished. (1128a 7-8)

Finally, he describes the **virtue**, found in the **witty** person.

> But those who joke in a tasteful way are called ready-witted, which implies a sort of readiness to turn this way and that; for such sallies are thought to be movements of the character, and as bodies are discriminated by their movements, so too are characters. The ridiculous side of things is not far to seek, however, and most people delight more than they should in amusement and jesting, and so even buffoons are called ready-witted because they are found attractive; but that they differ from the ready-witted man, and to no small extent, is clear from what has been said. (1128a 9-18)

COMMENTARY. This power (M) has to do with the things (A) that cause us to laugh (F) and be amused (F). Aristotle's analysis reveals two different levels of response, one when we make a joke (F) about someone (A), the other when we laugh at a joke (F) someone else (M) has made about a third person (A). In both cases we can go wrong in the number of things (A) we laugh at and in the form of our response (F).

The virtue can be called a kind of **tactful wittiness.** As always, the aim or purpose is the governing dimension or cause of causes. It is ignoble to make a fool of oneself, or to cause needless pain and offense to others, and respect for this governs the virtuous person's humor. He subordinates his power to make jokes to a **high-minded** sense of what is becoming and seemly. And with his **friendly** spirit, he avoids doing things that are unnecessarily painful to the people he teases or tells jokes about, while nonetheless believing in laughter and amusement.

Aristotle also points to a certain lability of character in the witty person, i.e. "a sort of readiness to turn this way and that." He even speaks of humorous behavior as "movements of the character." This implies that when we tease or make fun of **someone else**, we put ourselves in their place and act out some aspect of their character in an exaggerated way. We can do this only to the extent that our own character is not so rigid and set as to preclude our identifying with somebody else and approach the world, at least momentarily, the way he does. If we cannot put ourselves in his place, we cannot tease him in a friendly and knowing spirit.

We must have the same kind of emotional and moral lability to laugh at **ourselves.** Our wishes and traits cannot be so dominant as to preclude our seeing ourselves from a different perspective. To laugh at our stinginess in small things or at our insecurities is to look at ourselves from a more **generous** and **confident** point of view. To laugh at our **vanity** and **anger** is to be more **gentle** and realistic about ourselves. In all such cases, emotional-moral perspective is like spatial perspective in vision. It is a matter of looking at the same point from more than one point of view. Visually, that is a matter of a physical change of place; in humor, it is a matter of altering the moral trait dominating our behavior.

The **buffoon,** on the other hand, is characterized by his allowing the desire to make people laugh become a goal in itself (T), and to override any concern for what is becoming to himself, or for his desire to act nobly. **Boorish** people seem to lack the wish to be happy (T) and to find amusement and enjoyment in life. Their unwillingness "to put up with those who do" find humor and amusement even suggests a **spiteful** and **destructive** wish (T) (**Rh** II, 10). They have an unethical influence on others; they slight and demoralize people by deadening their enjoyment. Where **boorishness** seems related to **spite, buffoonery** seems related either to **disdain** or **insolence-sadism.** Both buffoonery and boorishness are **slighting** forms of behavior treating other people's interests and happiness as unimportant, and both make people angry. (See **Anger, Rh** II, 2).

2. READY WIT AND TACT AS THE VIRTUE

Aristotle thought that

To the middle state belongs also tact; it is the mark of a tactful man to say and listen to such things as befit a good and well-bred man; for there are some things that it befits such a man to say and to hear by way of jest, and the well-bred man's jesting differs from that of a vulgar man, and the joking of an educated man from that of an uneducated one. One may see this even from the old and the new comedies; to the authors of the former indecency of language was amusing, to those of the latter innuendo is more so; and these differ in no small degree in respect of propriety. Now should we define the man who jokes well by his saying what is not unbecoming to a well-bred man, or by his not giving pain, or even giving delight, to the hearer? Or is the latter definition, at any rate, itself indefinite, since different things are hateful or pleasant to different people? The kind of jokes he will listen to will be the same; for the kind he will put up with are also the kind he seems to make. There are, then, jokes he will not make; for the jest is a sort of abuse, and there are things that lawgivers forbid us to abuse; and they should, perhaps, have forbidden us even to make a jest of such. The refined and well-bred man, therefore, will be as we have described, being as it were a law to himself. (1128a 18-33)

COMMENTARY. The tactfully or tastefully witty person is concerned with both what is becoming for himself and for the pain and pleasure he or she gives others. The latter aim (T) is **indefinite**, however, in that it depends on what pains or pleases a given person or group. We would hardly call someone a virtuously humorous person who pleased, and did not pain, a group of **macho males** with demeaning jokes about women, or pleased a group of **Ku Klux Klansmen** with jokes about Black people. The judgment of such audiences is perverse and provides no standard for who is a good man.

Aristotle's analysis points to the way the virtuous man or woman must look ultimately to his own judgment of what is noble and ignoble, fitting and unbecoming. While he is tactful and sensitive to other's feelings, he does not rely on their judgment of what is right and wrong to determine his feelings and actions. Just because some group enjoys making fun of certain things does not mean he will feel comfortable participating in their doing so. At the same time, he will not readily listen to jokes he would not tell. And while he will be a man of humor and wit, there are things he will hold sacred and not joke about.

3. BUFFOONERY AND BOORISHNESS
AS THE VICES OF EXCESS AND DEFICIENCY

Aristotle considered **buffoonery** the vice of **excess** and believed it has damaging consequences on the character of both the person with the vice as well as the people he affects.

> Such, then, is the man who observes the mean, whether he be called tactful or ready-witted. The buffoon, on the other hand, is the slave of his sense of humor, and spares neither himself nor others if he can raise a laugh, and says things none of which a man of refinement would say, and to some of which he would not even listen. (1128a 33-b 1)

Boorishness, the vice of **deficiency**, also has destructive consequences.

> The boor, again, is useless for such social intercourse; for he contributes nothing and finds fault with everything. But relaxation and amusement are thought to be a necessary element in life. (1128b 1-3)

COMMENTARY. When humor becomes a goal in itself, the **buffoon** becomes "the slave of his sense of humor." This means its dominance overrides his **wishes, deliberations** and **choices** for more noble behavior. As a slave to the wish to make jokes, he loses his freedom in the same way as someone does to self-indulgent desires, greediness for money or excessive ambition.

We glimpse possible motives (T) for the buffoon's behavior when Aristotle says he "spares neither himself nor others if he can raise a laugh." Not sparing himself is a sign of **small-mindedness** (NE IV, 3) while not sparing others shows excessive **anger, disdain**, or **insolence-sadism** (Rh II, 2). The buffoon seems to aim at satisfying **vanity** and **ambition** (NE IV, 3) by claiming the right to be recognized and respected for his wit even though his acts are ignoble. Abusing oneself or others in public is hardly a **high-minded** approach to humor.

Aristotle underlines the importance and value of laughter, relaxation and amusement when he says they are "thought to be a necessary element in life." The **boorish, contentious** person is thus missing something essential to the fullness of life. Norman Cousins has recently argued that laughter is important even to physical health. He claims it has a salutary effect on the immunological system. Boorishness and contentiousness have a close affinity to **spite**.

4. FRIENDLINESS, TRUTHFULNESS AND READY-WIT COMPARED

Aristotle concludes with a summary of the relation between **friendliness, truthfulness,** and **ready-wit** or **tact.**

The means in life that have been described, then, are three in number, and all are concerned with an interchange of words and deeds of some kind. They differ, however, in that one is concerned with truth, and the other two with pleasantness. Of those concerned with pleasure, one is displayed in jests, the other in the general social intercourse of life. (1128b 4-8)

COMMENTARY. Here Aristotle summarizes the agents (A) and forms of response (F) of the virtues of friendliness, truthfulness and tactful wittiness. They are all concerned with social interchange but are judged according to different criteria. **Friendliness** and **wittiness** are judged according to the quality of the **pleasure** they give, while **truthfulness** is judged by itself, i.e. the truth.

These three aim less at **justice** than at saying what is true and making people happy. Generosity and anger are also concerned with our relations to others, but they are governed by the sense of what others **deserve** and what is just. We should not be as generous to undeserving flatterers, for example, than to self-respecting people trying to make something of themselves, nor angry toward slights seen as justified.

We are not, however, friendly, truthful, and humorous because people **deserve** it or because we would be unjust to them if we were not. These do not necessarily involve questions of justice at all. We are friendly, truthful and humorous because these things are good in their own right and because they further other good things.

CHAPTER SEVEN

Handling the Disgrace of Having Acted Badly

INVENTORY

A. THE POWER TO BE ASHAMED (Rh II, 6)

1. SHAME DEFINED

2. ACTIONS AROUSING SHAME

a. Cowardice or apathy in a fight
b. Failing to live up to our debts
c. Self-indulgence in sexual and other matters
d. Making money through exploitation or hoarding
e. Begging from others while being ungenerous ourselves
f. Flattery
g. Cowardice in enduring hardship
h. Ingratitude and disloyalty
i. Boastfulness and vanity
j. Any of the other vices
k. Deficient ambition
l. Passivity in being sexually abused

3. PEOPLE BEFORE WHOM WE FEEL ASHAMED

a. People we admire or love
b. Our rivals
c. Those who are sensible, older or well-educated
d. The general public as well as those we live
   and work among
e. Those who cannot be criticized for the same thing
   we did
f. Those who are indignant at people who do wrong
g. The angry and spiteful
h. The sadistic and disdainful
i. Those admiring us, wishing to be friends
   or asking for help
j. Not before infants and animals
k. More before intimates than strangers

4. OUR STATES OF MIND WHEN ASHAMED

a. Haviong people we admire or who admire us
b. Having personal, family or group accomplishments
   to live up to
c. Having people whose own bad actions
   would make us ashamed
d. Having a position exposing us to public scrutiny

B. SHAME, SHAMELESSNESS AND BEING ABASHED (NE IV, 9) AS THE VIRTUE AND VICES OF THIS POWER

1. SHAME IS NOT A VIRTUE
2. THE GOOD ASPECT OF SHAME

A. THE POWER TO BE ASHAMED (Rh II, 6)

1. SHAME DEFINED

Once again we are fortunate to have treatments of the same moral and emotional power from the **RHETORIC** and the **ETHICS**. Beginning as always with the former, we see that Aristotle thought

> Shame may be defined as pain or disturbance at the appearance of disgraceful things, whether present, past or future, which seem likely to involve us in discredit; and shamelessness as contempt or indifference in regard to these same bad things. (1383b 15-8)

COMMENTARY. We will see as this chapter unfolds that shame is an essential part of mankind's cybernetic, self-correcting feed-back mechanism and plays a major role in the development of proper wish, deliberation and choice. When properly developed, shame allows us to deliberate about our actions, recognize our mistakes, and choose to do only those which are in keeping with our highest wishes for ourselves and the people we care about.

Shame is a painful disturbance in our actions when we see we have done something disgraceful and unseemly in violation of our wish to do noble and fine things. The time frame can extend from disgraceful things remembered from our past to those we might be planning for the future.

We have seen throughout this work how the way we picture things (A) determines our choices, actions and emotions (F). But we have also seen that it is the state of our moral virtues and vices (M) which disposes us to see things either appropriately or in excess or defect (F) of the way they are. (See the **INTRODUCTION**.) With regard to shame, this means that a deficient number of things will appear shameful to a **shameless** person. He or she will just not see the disgrace in the bad things he has done. At the other extreme, an **excessively ashamed** person will see more things as shameful than actually are so and will be crippled by a small-minded sense of unworthiness.

That shame is "a kind of fear of dishonor" tells us that it is related both to **courage** (NE IV, 6-9) and to **high-mindedness** (NE IV, 3) and **ambition** (NE IV, 4), both of which concern honor. Since shame is painful we must have courage to face it virtuously, turn from it and act rightly. People having high values but lacking courage, self-control, and the other virtues, live with lots of pain and are continually ashamed. They are sorely tempted to give up their values to the extent they do not see how much happier they would be by becoming more virtuous.

Shame always implies our relation to some person or group in whose eyes we will be discredited if we do bad things. We must distinguish, however, between the case in which we wish to **emulate** (Rh II, 11) this person's values and the case in which we are simply afraid their behavior toward us will change as a result of our action. American usage tends to reserve "shame" for the first case and "embarrassment" for the second, although this is by no means always the case.

Shame occurs in those situations in which our actions and character threaten a high-minded evaluation of our own worth. Embarrassment, on the other hand, occurs when our actions threaten the satisfaction of our ambition. While the two states are distinct, they can be related in several ways. For example, a high-minded person in a dishonorable occupation can be ashamed of an action that promotes his ambitions even though it was by no means a source of embarrassment among his or her corrupted colleagues. On the other hand, one could feel no shame but considerable embarrassment when he must give a business presentation right after a co-worker spills coffee on the front of his white shirt. Shame and embarrassment can be difficult to distinguish in a society of virtuous people. For example, a good person will be embarrassed by his or her shameful actions when virtuous people who care about such things have a say in determining his success.

One suspects that excessively ambitious, career-oriented people are embarrassed only when they act badly in front of people who can affect their advancement but tend to be indifferent when subordinates, neighbors, even their families, see the same behavior. It is as though their careers rather than they themselves suffered the embarrassment. A person who aspires to greater nobility will be ashamed for anyone to see him act badly--although he will be more ashamed the more he respects the other person's virtue.

Appropriate shame is tied to the wish to emulate good people. The examination of shamelessness shows the importance of emulating noble people instead of showing disdain for them. A shameless person is contemptuous of what a good person thinks about acting in a bad way and has no desire to emulate his rejection of bad things. The development of proper emulation and disdain in turn arises through just and encouraging social interactions between adults and children and authorities and subordinates in general. A society whose authorities fail to be worthy of such emulation will be characterized by the shamelessness of its people.

While emulation of good people is decisive in strengthening our virtues, we must not assume they are the only persons before whom we feel ashamed. We will see that we can feel ashamed before people we do not wish to emulate because they might tell others who we genuinely admire of our misdeeds.

2. ACTIONS AROUSING SHAME

Aristotle distinguishes three different kinds of agent which can arouse feelings of shame. They are

- "evils due to moral badness,"

- "lacking a share in the honorable things shared by everyone else," and

- "having done to us, having had done, or being about to have done to us acts that involve us in dishonor and reproach."

They are all either things we have done or failed at or which others have done to us. But at a deeper level, they are shameful only to the extent they are caused by the moral badness of our own vices.

Aristotle gives the following list of agents arousing shame.

a. Throwing away one's shield or taking to flight: for these... are due to **cowardice**. (1383b 21-2)

b. Withholding a deposit or otherwise **wronging people about money**; for these acts are due to **injustice**. (1383b 22-3)

c. Having carnal intercourse with forbidden persons, at wrong times, or in wrong places; for these things are due to **self-indulgence**. (1383b 23-4)

d. Making profit in petty or disgraceful ways, or out of helpless persons, e.g. the poor, or the dead... for all this is due to low **greed** and **meanness**. (1383b 24-6)

e. Also in money matters, giving less help than you might, or none at all, or accepting help from those worse off than yourself, so also borrowing when it will seem like begging; begging when it will seem like asking the return of a favor; asking such a return when it will seem like begging; praising a man **in order that** it may seem like begging; and going on begging in spite of failure; all such actions are tokens of **meannness**. (1383b 27-32)

f. Praising people to their face, and praising extravagantly a man's good points and glossing over his weaknesses, and showing extravagant sympathy with his grief when you are in his presence, and all that sort of thing: all this shows the disposition of a **flatterer**. (1383b 32-5)

g. Refusing to endure hardships that are endured by people who are older, more delicately brought up, of higher rank, or generally less capable of endurance than ourselves; for all this shows **effeminacy**. (1384a 1-2)

h. Accepting benefits, especially accepting them often, from another man, and then abusing him for conferring them: all this shows a mean, ignoble disposition. (1384a 2-4)

i. Talking incessantly about yourself, making loud professions and appropriating the merits of others; for this is due to **boastfulness**. (1384a 4-5)

j. The same is true of the actions due to any of the other forms of badness of moral character, of the tokens of such badness, etc.: they are all disgraceful and shameless. (1384a 6-8)

k. Lacking a share in the honorable things shared by everyone else, or by all or nearly all who are like ourselves. By "those like ourselves" I mean those of our own race or country or age or family, and generally those who are on our own level. Once we are on a level with others, it is a disgrace to be, say, less well educated than they are; and so with other advantages: all the more so, in each case, if it is seen to be our own fault; wherever we are to blame for our present, past or future circumstances, it follows at once that this is to a greater extent due to our own moral badness. (1384a 10-7)

l. Having done to us, having had done, or being about to have done to us acts that involve us in dishonor and reproach, such as prostituting one's person or performing disgraceful actions, including unnatural lust. And the acts of yielding to the lusts of others are shameful whether willing or unwilling (yielding to force being an instance of unwillingness), since unresisting submission to them is due to unmanliness or cowardice. (1384a 18-21)

COMMENTARY. Each of these bad actions is felt to be shameful only to the extent we wish for the corresponding virtue. Shame is a sign we are not disdainful of what is right and good, although, as we will see, because it entails our having done wrong in the first place, its moral status is equivocal. The following explains the virtues violated and the vices committed in each of Aristotle's examples. The list is by no means exhaustive.

a. COWARDICE OR APATHY IN A FIGHT. Throwing away one's shield and running away from one's comrades in a fight is an act of **cowardice** (NE III, 6-9). We could expand this cause for shame to include all those instances of **apathy** when we fail to stand up to injustice against ourselves and others. While it requires a certain amount of courage to be genuinely ashamed of standing our ground, none is required simply to be embarrassed and afraid of what others might think of us as a result.

b. FAILING TO LIVE UP TO OUR DEBTS. Injustice (NE V), and more particularly, **exploitativeness, excessive receptiveness** or **hoarding** (NE IV, 1) are involved in withholding a deposit, wronging people about money and in general refusing to pay our debts. These things are shameful, no matter the specific vice from which they spring.

c. SELF-INDULGENCE IN SEXUAL AND OTHER MATTERS. There is nothing innately shameful about sexuality or other physical pleasures and to believe that there is is a life-crippling vice of excessive shame. **Self-indulgence** is expressed, however, by intercourse that is improper in its object, time or place (NE III, 10-12). As indicated in the Chapter on self-indulgence, we should add indulgences in eating, drinking and drugs as well.

d. MAKING MONEY THROUGH EXPLOITATION OR HOARDING. Again, **exploitativeness** or **hoarding** motivates making profit in disgraceful ways from poor or helpless people (NE IV, 1). Such practices are shameful.

e. **BEGGING FROM OTHERS WHILE BEING UNGENEROUS OURSELVES.**
Again we are talking about the power of **generosity**, but this time about
failing to be helpful rather than outright taking from others. The vice of
excessive receptiveness (**NE** IV, 1) leads us to accept help from people
worse off than ourselves. There is nothing wrong with borrowing as such
so long as one does not become so dependent on others as to ignobly beg
for their help. It seems to be the self-abasement and **small-mindedness**
(**NE** IV, 3) involved in begging that Aristotle criticizes.

On the other hand, to pretend that one is requesting the return of a
favor when he is actually begging is **exploitative** (**NE** IV, 3). Rather than
appealing to the person's **generosity**, one is trying to take money by
manipulating his sense of honesty and propriety. Aristotle suggests that a
high-minded person (**NE** IV, 3) would not ask for the return even of a
legitimate favor in conditions that would make him appear to be begging.
Finally, an **obsequious** person (**NE** IV, 6) will praise someone in the hope
he will be supported and cared for by the person he abases himself
before.

It is bad enough to beg in the first place; it is even worse when
we persist in the face of failure. One should be ashamed of all these
practices.

f. **FLATTERY.** Praising people too much and to their face, protecting them from the slightest criticism, and in general being excessively
concerned with their pleasures and pains, all done with an ulterior, exploitative motive, are the marks of a **flatterer** (**NE** IV, 6).

g. **COWARDICE IN ENDURING HARDSHIP.** Refusing to endure the
hardships that older, more protected, higher ranking or less able people
are willing to endure shows one's **cowardice** (**NE** III, 6-9). Men used to
call this effeminacy. We need a non-sexist term like "softness" for this
shameful weakness of character.

h. **INGRATITUDE AND DISLOYALTY.** What kind of person would accept
benefits from another and then abuse him for having conferred them? Certainly an ungrateful one. Such **kindness** (**Rh** II, 7) should have aroused
friendliness (**NE** IV, 6 and **Rh** II, 4) instead of abuse and **anger** (**Rh** II,
2 and **NE** IV, 5). Excessively **receptive** people, however, especially when
they are also **insolent-sadistic**, are inclined to accept many benefits and
then feel slighted when even more are not forthcoming or when they find a
more promising means of support. They often abuse the very people from
whom they have accepted benefits in the past as a way to mask the fact
of their ingratitude and disloyalty. This is a shameful thing.

i. **BOASTFULNESS AND VANITY.** Talking constantly about oneself and
making exaggerated claims is indicative of both **boastfulness** (**NE** IV, 7)
and **vanity** (**NE** IV, 3). It is not something to be proud of.

j. **ANY OF THE OTHER VICES.** Aristotle's Greek assumes that the
vices are not only something to feel ashamed of but that they also lead
to **small-mindedness** (**NE** IV, 3). We would want to add to his list of actions arousing shame examples of other vices such as **recklessness, excessive anger, buffoonery** and **boorishness.**

k. **DEFICIENT AMBITION.** Aristotle seems to be talking about a lack of **ambition** (NE IV, 4) when he speaks of the shame of not having a share in the honorable things had by other people like ourselves. **Emulation** (**Rh** II, 11) is the productive response to this painful shame, **envy** and **spite** (**Rh** II, 10) the vicious response. This does not mean emulation must be grounded in shame, however, since we can wish to emulate people older or more experienced than ourselves to whom we are not yet equal in these regards. Since our not already having what they have is not "due to our own moral badness," it is not a source of shame.

If we are ashamed of not having what "those like ourselves" have yet lack the courage required to live with it while emulating their accomplishments, we are likely either to become envious and spiteful or give up thinking of ourselves as equal to them. Either way, excessive shame cuts us off from our internal resources and isolates us from others.

l. **PASSIVITY IN BEING SEXUALLY ABUSED.** Aristotle focuses here on the passive suffering of such outrages rather than on how **self-indulgence** (NE III, 10) might lead us to find pleasure in actively pursuing them. One should find the **courage** to fight back and resist such advances and should be ashamed at not doing so. This is quite a comment on homosexuality in Athenian society lending immediacy to some of Plato's dialogues in which older men try to force themselves on younger ones.

3. PEOPLE BEFORE WHOM WE FEEL ASHAMED

Aristotle next considers who the people are before whom we feel ashamed. He begins with something which distinguishes the concept of shame from embarrassment.

> Now since shame is a mental picture of disgrace, in which we shrink from the disgrace itself and not from its consequences, and we only care what opinion is held of us because of the people who form that opinion, it follows that the people before whom we feel shame are those whose opinion of us matters to us. (1384a 24-8)

Shame is activated by seeing the disgrace of our actions themselves while embarrassment focuses on their consequences in jeopardizing something we want. Where with shame we care about the opinions of people we genuinely respect, with embarrassment we care about the opinions of anyone who might influence our interests.

In general, the people before whom we feel ashamed are those

- "who admire us,"

- "those whom we admire,"

- "those by whom we wish to be admired,"

- "those with whom we are competing, and"

- "those whose opinion of us we respect." (1384a 28-9)

The following can be said more specifically about these people.

a. We admire those, and wish those to admire us, who possess any good thing that is highly esteemed; or from whom we are very anxious to get something that they are able to give us--as a lover feels. (1384a 29-31)

b. We compete with our equals. (1384a 31)

c. We respect, as true, the views of sensible people, such as our elders and those who have been well educated. (1384a 32-3)

d. We feel more shame about a thing if it is done openly, before all men's eyes... For this reason we feel most shame before those who will always be with us and those who notice what we do, since in both cases eyes are upon us. (1384a 33-5)

e. We also feel it before those not open to the same imputation as ourselves: for it is plain that their opinions about it are the opposite of ours. (1384b 1-2)

f. Also before those who are hard on any one whose conduct they think wrong; for what a man does himself, he is said not to resent when his neighbors do it: so that of course he does resent their doing what he does not do himself. (1384b 3-5)

g. And before those who are likely to tell everybody about you; not telling others is as good as not believing you wrong. People are likely to tell others about you if you have wronged them, since they are on the look out to harm you; or if they speak evil of everybody, for those who attack the innocent will be still more ready to attack the guilty. (1384b 5-9)

h. And before those whose main occupation is with their neighbor's failings--people like satirists and writers of comedy; these are really a kind of evil-speakers and tell-tales. (1384b 9-11)

i. And before those who have never yet known us to come to grief, since their attitude to us has amounted to admiration so far: that is why we feel ashamed to refuse those a favor who ask one for the first time--we have not as yet lost credit with them. Such are those who are just beginning to wish to be our friends... and such also are those among our old acquaintances who know nothing to our discredit. (1384b 12-8)

j. And, generally, we feel no shame before those upon whose opinions we quite look down as untrustworthy (no one feels shame before small children or animals). (1384b 18-9)

k. Nor are we ashamed of the same things before intimates as before strangers, but before the former of what seem genuine faults, before the latter what seem conventional ones. (1384b 25-7)

COMMENTARY. Although there is a real difference between shame and embarrassment, Aristotle's list shows it is not always easy to draw the line between them. The key seems to be whether we share the agent's judgment that the value we have violated is in fact virtuous. The fact that they know of our disgrace makes it that much more painful for us. Not only is it harder to hide our moral failing, we are also diminished in their eyes with respect to the value we share.

With shame we are concerned about what good people think of us because we value and share their judgment about what is good. We feel with them that what we did was not fine or noble. Regardless of its practical consequences, we do not want to be like that. With embarrassment, on the other hand, we are preoccupied with the effects our action might have on people who can affect our careers regardless of the moral quality of the act itself. We are only incidentally concerned about what good people think of us. The first is a matter of principle, the second a matter of expediency.

a. **PEOPLE WE ADMIRE OR LOVE.** We feel ashamed if we do something bad in front of someone we admire, whether that person is broadly respected for his excellence and goodness or is simply someone we love. We wish the people we admire to admire us and are pained when we do something to lower their estimation of us. In the case of a lover, we are afraid we might lose his or her love. If our fear is simply that we will lose sexual favors, gifts, etc., we are not so much ashamed as embarrassed.

b. **OUR RIVALS.** We wish to be respected and admired by the people we compete with, who we consider our equals and are not **disdainful** of (**R h** II, 11). Sharing the same values, we care what they think of us. We want to be at our best in front of them and certainly do not wish to give them cause to think less of us.

c. **THOSE WHO ARE SENSIBLE, OLDER OR WELL-EDUCATED.** If a person has good judgment, broad experience or is well-educated, we are inclined to respect his opinion and to be ashamed if we betray before his or her eyes the values we share.

d. **THE GENERAL PUBLIC AS WELL AS THOSE WE LIVE AND WORK AMONG.** Our shame is intensified the more public it is and the more other people's eyes are turned upon it. This is revealed, for example, in the characteristic gesture of trying to cover one's face seen on television when accused persons are taken in or out of court. (This is no doubt embarrassment in many cases.) The exposure of our vice can either be broad in terms of the number of people who know of our action, or intensive in the sense of a few people "who will always be with us and... notice what we do."

e. **THOSE WHO CANNOT BE CRITICIZED FOR THE SAME THING WE DID.** We feel ashamed before people who we know do not share our temptation to the bad thing we have done. We know they do not share the opinion we held when we surrendered to the temptation. Wishing to be like them in this judgment, we are ashamed at having acted in a contrary way.

f. THOSE WHO ARE INDIGNANT AT PEOPLE WHO DO WRONG. Aristotle gives here the kind of case psychoanalysts make a great deal of. We feel shame before those who are very hard on people they think have done wrong. This suggests **righteous indignation** (**Rh** II, 9), but people often confuse this virtue with the vices of **envy** and **spite** (**Rh** II, 10).

Many acts of indignation at sexual behavior, for example, are actually envious and spiteful, committed by **depressed** people whose **self-indulgent** impulses are so excessive, and whose cultural backgrounds so repressive, that they are afraid to act on natural desires in a virtuous manner. Nietzsche is the great student of this resentful attitude. Such a person does "resent" others "doing what he does not do himself," but he does so because he must fight so hard against his own temptation to similar action. The freer from temptation he becomes, the less harsh and frightened he will be.

g. THE ANGRY AND SPITEFUL. We feel shame before those who are likely to tell others of our vice. Aristotle mentions two classes of such people. The first are those who are **angry** (**Rh** II, 2 and **NE** IV, 5) because they feel we have wronged them and they want revenge. The second are the **spiteful** (**Rh** II, 10) who cut down everyone. The latter attack with special relish because other people's shameful acts seem to legitimate their negative views about life as a whole. We make their vicious attitude seem realistic and are ashamed both to contribute to it as well as to think of their exposing our disgrace to people we respect.

h. THE SADISTIC AND DISDAINFUL. Satirists and comedy writers preoccupied with "their neighbor's failings" should be contrasted with both tragedians who approach people's failings with the wish to promote nobility (see the discussion of "a catharsis of pity and fear" in the **POETICS**) and those satirists and comic writers whose **wit** (**NE** IV, 8) is kind and promotes realism and perspective. Aristotle is thus talking here about humor motivated by **insolence-sadism** or **contempt-disdain** (**Rh** II, 2). We are ashamed to give them the opportunity to make fun of our disgrace.

i. THOSE ADMIRING US, WISHING TO BE FRIENDS OR ASKING FOR HELP. We feel shame before people who have never known us to do anything bad, especially those who admire us or who wish to be or to become our friends (**Rh** II, 4 & **NE** IV, 4). We are pained by having acted in a way harming their admiration. Our wish for them to think us good also explains our being ashamed to deny them a first favor. Their desiring to be our friend and asking for our help shows they think us good, and we wish to preserve this view.

j. NOT BEFORE INFANTS AND ANIMALS. Obviously, we will feel ashamed before an infant only to the extent we care about what the child will think when he or she is older. It is only through imagining the child (or even an animal) as having the power of moral judgment that we feel shame before him or her. The child's own moral development at a given

time determines the actions about which he can make a trustworthy judgment. He or she can judge blatant cruelty and lying long before he can
complicated questions of justice requiring broad experience of the factors
involved in determining what is fair.

In general, we are not so ashamed in front of people for whom we
feel disdain. This explains why morally upright servants   feel their
employers are committing a most offensive slight when they act shamelessly in front of them. This shows the employer's complete **disdain** for
their moral judgment (**Rh** II, 2).

k. **MORE BEFORE INTIMATES THAN STRANGERS.** Aristotle combines
here the distinction between what is appropriate in relating to intimates
versus strangers, and that between genuine and merely conventional faults.
Before intimates we are ashamed only of things which are genuinely
wrong, while before strangers we are ashamed to do things which merely
appear wrong.

4. OUR STATES OF MIND WHEN ASHAMED

The states of mind in which we feel shame always involve "having
people before whom, as has been said, we feel shame." Aristotle says

a. These are... persons whom we admire, or who admire us, or by
whom we wish to be admired, or from whom we desire some service that we shall not obtain if we forfeit their good opinion.
These persons may be actually looking on... or again they may be
near at hand, or may be likely to find out about what we do. This
is why in misfortune we do not wish to be seen by those who
once wished themselves like us; for such a feeling implies admiration. (1384b 28-34)

b. And men feel shame when they have acts or exploits to their
credit on which they are bringing dishonor, whether these are
their own, or those of their ancestors, or those of some other
persons with whom they have some close connection. (1385a 1-3)

c. Generally, we feel shame before those for whose own miscon-
ducts we should also feel it--those already mentioned; those who
take us as their models; those whose teachers and advisers we
have been; or other people, it may be, like ourselves, whose
rivals we are. For there are many things that shame before such
people makes us do or leave undone. (1385a 3-7)

d. And we feel more shame when we are likely to be continually
seen by, and go about under the eyes of, those who know of our
disgrace. Hence, when Antiphon the poet was to be cudgeled to
death by order of Dionysius, and saw those who were to perish
with him covering their faces as they went through the gates, he
said, "Why do you cover your faces? Is it lest some of the spec-
tators should see you **tomorrow**?" (1385a 7-13)

COMMENTARY. Shame requires us to have the virtue we are a-shamed of having violated, although we cannot have it strongly enough always to act on it. We must also have people whom we wish to **emulate** in having this virtue, or who admire us or who we wish would do so. They are people who already have the virtue, who aspire to it, or who support our belief that we have it. The belief that we have the virtue helps us expect, and give, the best of ourselves. To lose this person's belief in us is to lose a potent agent supporting our development and high performance.

There is a developmental dynamic, or virtuous circle, at work here. Success brings the pleasing respect and admiration of others. This in turn encourages greater success and makes us more afraid to surrender to corrupting temptations. When, on the other hand, people are "down on our case," and neither respect nor have faith in us, we find it that much easier to become vicious. When we have no social function through which to gain others' respect, we are actively disposed to shamelessness. With no respect to gain or lose in anyone's eyes, we feel little pain in doing shameless things.

This dynamic explains why "peer pressure" can be so powerful among teenagers, in military combat units, and work groups. Our peers are the people "we are likely to be continually seen by and go about under the eyes of" when we are involved in these groups. If one becomes emotionally tied to the group, its judgment on his behavior is likely to be decisive in determining what he will be ashamed of either doing or not doing.

a. **HAVING PEOPLE WE ADMIRE OR WHO ADMIRE US.** The basic possibility condition for feeling ashamed is that we have "persons whom we admire, or who admire us, or by whom we wish to be admired." We cannot feel ashamed without having such people in our lives. Whether we actually have such people, however, is a matter not just of our own virtue (which others after all help us develop), but of our good fortune in being exposed to people who will play such a role for us.

Aristotle observes that for them to make us feel ashamed, they may be either looking at our disgraceful behavior, or merely be close at hand and likely to learn of it. This implies having living persons before our mind's eye, but people can also be ashamed before the memory of a dead parent or teacher and perhaps of historical and even fictional characters who come to play living roles in their psychic lives.

Aristotle's comments on being ashamed at the loss of another's admiration explain why proud people try to hide their misfortunes and weakness from others. His remarks show too how highly he valued the good opinion of others when their judgment is grounded in virtue. (See **High-mindedness**, NE IV, 3.)

b. **HAVING PERSONAL, FAMILY OR GROUP ACCOMPLISHMENTS TO LIVE UP TO.** People are disposed to be ashamed, if they or their ancestors or close associates have been honored for achievements they can bring discredit on. If no one thinks well of us in the first place (see item a. above) and we have no role models to emulate, we are that much less likely to be ashamed of our disgraceful behavior.

    c. **HAVING PEOPLE WHOSE OWN BAD ACTIONS WOULD MAKE US ASHAMED.** We are disposed to be ashamed at our own bad conduct, if we have other people we care enough about to be ashamed when they do bad things. We are inclined to be ashamed of people's bad actions when they model themselves on us, when we have taught or advised them, or when they are like us and are our rivals in common endeavors. We try to maintain high standards before such people. We do and refuse to do many things to keep their respect, promote their development and bring credit to our common endeavors.

    d. **HAVING A POSITION EXPOSING US TO PUBLIC SCRUTINY.** We are disposed to feel ashamed when our social position exposes us to continual scrutiny by people who know of our indiscretion. A corollary of this is that people are disposed to be **shameless** when they are socially isolated and no one around them knows how they actually live. This fact helps explain why urbanization causes the "loosening" of moral norms. (See Durkheim's **THE DIVISION OF LABOR IN SOCIETY** and **SUICIDE** for information on the way changes in a person's social function in an increasingly complex division of labor tend to sever his ties with groups before whom he might otherwise feel ashamed.)

B. SHAME, SHAMELESSNESS AND BEING ABASHED (NE IV, 9) AS THE VIRTUE AND VICES OF THIS POWER

1. SHAME IS NOT A VIRTUE

Aristotle thought that

Shame should not be described as a virtue; for it is more like a feeling than a state of character. It is defined, at any rate, as a kind of fear of dishonor, and produces an effect similar to that produced by fear of danger; for people who feel disgraced blush, and those who fear death turn pale. Both, therefore, seem to be in a sense bodily conditions, which is thought to be characteristic of feeling rather than of a state of character. (1128b 9-14)

Aristotle also thought that while shame has an essential role in moral development, it has a different significance in adulthood and in youth.

The feeling is not becoming to every age, but only to youth. For we think young people should be prone to the feeling of shame because they live by feeling and therefore commit many errors, but are restrained by shame; and we praise young people who are prone to this feeling, but an older person no one praises for being prone to the sense of disgrace, since we think he should not do anything that need cause this sense. For the sense of disgrace is not even characteristic of a good man, since it is consequent on bad actions (for such actions should not be done; and if some actions are disgraceful in very truth and others only according to common opinion, this makes no difference; for neither class of actions should be done, so that no disgrace should be felt); and it is a mark of a bad man even to be such as to do any disgraceful action. To be so constituted as to feel disgraced if one does such an action, and for this reason to think oneself good, is absurd; for it is for voluntary actions that shame is felt, and the good man will never voluntarily do bad actions. (1128b 14-30)

COMMENTARY. Aristotle builds his case for why shame is not a virtue from the fact that virtue belongs to the genus of character traits instead of feelings or emotions. In Aristotle's view, moral and emotional phenomena can be classed as 1) capacities or gifts, 2) the characteristic traits or dispositions developed in those capacities, or 3) the actualizations of these capacities and character traits in our choices and actions which always have determinant feelings and emotions accompanying them. (See the discussion of the causal diagram in the INTRODUCTION.)

Aristotle insists that "shame" refers to the feeling people have when they are ashamed rather than to the characteristic disposition of having that feeling. He uses fear as an analogy. Fear refers to a state of feeling, while cowardice refers to one's excessive disposition to having that feeling. People can be afraid without being cowards. To be cowardly is to be characteristically afraid when it is inappropriate to be so. Both fear and shame are thus forms of response (F) rather than material dispositions (M) the way courage and cowardice are. And as emotional responses, they have physical correlates, turning pale in the first case, blushing in the second.

Even if we considered shame a character trait, however, it is still not a virtue in the truest sense. Virtues constitute the perfected condition of an organ or organism which allows it to function properly. Shame, on the other hand, tends only to promote the perfecting of a person in the face of his imperfections, and disappears as the person becomes more virtuous. There is no need to actualize the power of feeling ashamed except insofar as one has done wrong.

The case is different with the true virtues. They are themselves perfections of our powers which we can never outgrow and which we need whenever confronted by their respective agents. As perfections, we can be proud of them without having to admit that they come into play (as shame does) only when we are at fault for voluntarily wishing to do something wrong.

Shame is decisively important in the transition to maturity when we are developing the other virtues, particularly when as teenagers and young adults we are struggling to identify and discipline powerful emotions in order to meet the expectations of the social groups we want to join and the social functions we want to perform. A proper sense of shame is much to be praised during this transition, but it is not to be honored as a perfection of some kind.

2. THE GOOD ASPECT OF SHAME

Aristotle noted, nonetheless, that

shame may be said to be conditionally a good thing; if a good man does such actions, he will feel disgraced; but the virtues are not subject to such a qualification. And if shamelessness--not to be ashamed of doing base actions--is bad, that does not make it good to be ashamed of doing such actions. Moral strength or "continence" too is not virtue, but a mixed sort of state. (1128b 30-5)

COMMENTARY. The basic point again is that shame is not unconditionally good because it depends on our doing something bad. But Aristotle makes a new point when he relates shame to "moral strength." This refers to the technical concept of the **morally-strong** person as opposed to the **self-controlled, morally-weak** or **evil** person. The shame involved in moral strength is good because it is part of an effective cybernetic mechanism of self-correction. We can see this quite clearly by comparing the four concepts.

The evil person wishes evil things shamelessly, without moral conflict. Of the four types of person, his disposition to virtue is the weakest.

The morally-weak person wishes virtue enough to know what is right for him to do, but not strongly enough to do it even when he sees it. The morally-strong person sometimes surrenders to vicious impulses, but is ashamed and works to right the wrong as soon as he recognizes what he has done. His shame at the act and turning to correct it shows he did not do it in a fully voluntary way, and marks his moral strength. The truly self-controlled person is not tempted to act in conflict with his wish to live rightly and thus does not need shame to right himself.

CHAPTER EIGHT

Handling the Good and Bad Fortune of Others and the Challenge to be Just

INVENTORY

A. THE POWER TO FEEL PITY (Rh II, 8)

1. PITY DEFINED

2. OUR STATES OF MIND WHEN WE FEEL PITY

   a. Those who have courage and hope
   b. Those who are not insolent and sadistic
   c. Those such as the elderly who have experienced
      bad fortune themselves
   d. Those who are cowardly
   e. Those who are educated with a long view
      of our vulnerability as human beings
   f. Those whose parents, children and spouses are living
   g. Those between the extremes of excessive
      and deficient anger, confidence and fear
   h. Those who have a friendly belief in the goodness
      of some people rather than being envious and spiteful

3. THE BAD FORTUNE AROUSING PITY

   a. Being cut off from one's family and friends
   b. Being deformed, weak or mutilated
   c. Being hurt by people who should be good to us
   d. Good things happening when they will no no good
   e. Having repeated bad fortune in one's life

4. PEOPLE AROUSING OUR PITY

5. HOW TO MAKE PEOPLE FEEL PITY

B. THE POWER TO FEEL INDIGNATION (Rh II, 9)

1. INDIGNATION DEFINED AND
   DIFFERENTIATED FROM ENVY AND SPITE

2. THE GOOD FORTUNE AROUSING OUR INDIGNATION

   a. Goods which cannot be unjustly distributed
   b. Goods that can be unjustly distributed

3. THE PEOPLE AROUSING OUR INDIGNATION

   a. The nouveau riche more than those
      with long-established privileges
   b. Those who have fine things beyond what
      they deserve

4. OUR STATES OF MIND WHEN INDIGNANT

    a. Being a good person and truly accomplished
       at something
    b. Being a good and honest person, though
       less accomplished
    c. Being ambitious to attain rewards others
       are receiving unfairly
    d. Being no longer obsequious, small-minded
       and unambitious

C. THE POWER TO FEEL ENVY AND SPITE (Rh II, 10)

1. ENVY AND SPITE DEFINED

2. OUR STATES OF MIND WHEN ENVIOUS

    a. Feeling equal to others in fact
       or by ignoring significant differences
    b. Feeling we should have it all
       because of our privileged status
    c. Being distinguished at something or ambitious to be so
    d. Feeling so small-minded that whatever other people have
       seems better than what we have

3. THE GOOD FORTUNE AROUSING OUR ENVY

4. THE PEOPLE AROUSING OUR ENVY

    a. Those like outselves with whom we compete
    b. Those who are after the same things we are
       regardless of whether we are alike in other ways
    c. Those whose good fortune seems to put us down
    d. Those who have what we want and once had
    e. Those who get the things we want more easily
       than we do

D. THE POWER TO FEEL EMULATION AND CONTEMPT (Rh II, 11)

1. EMULATION AND CONTEMPT DEFINED

2. OUR STATES OF MIND WHEN EMULOUS

    a. Young and high-minded
    b. Having wealth, many friends or public responsibilities,
       or at least being thought to deserve them

3. THE GOOD FORTUNE AROUSING EMULATION

   a. Things for which our ancestors, relatives, friends,
      race or country are especially honored
   b. Moral virtue
   c. Skills that are useful and of service to others
   d. Things by which we can give pleasure to others

4. THE PEOPLE AROUSING EMULATION

   a. Those with moral and intellectual virtue
   b. Those with power and influence who are helpful
      to others
   c. Well-known people whom others wish to be like
   d. People for whom we do not feel contempt

A. THE POWER TO FEEL PITY (Rh II, 8)

1. PITY DEFINED

Aristotle says that

> Pity may be defined as a feeling of pain caused by the sight of some evil, destructive or painful, which befalls one who does not deserve it, and which we might expect to befall ourselves or some friend of ours, and moreover to befall us soon. (1385b 13-6)

COMMENTARY. Pity has acquired an undeservedly bad reputation in recent years, perhaps because of its association with disdainful or insolent-sadistic people who have raised money for charity by depicting disabled people or famine victims as so hopelessly dependent as to be qualitatively different from the rest of humanity. Pity appeals have come to be associated with sentimentality, condescension, moralistic self-promotion and the exploitation of people's sense of guilt. There is however a finer dimension to pity which has to do with being in solidarity with others in the face of their unjustifiable bad fortune. This finer sense of pity is a crucial component of human civilization in that it expands our care and concern to include those beyond our own families and friends. The cultivation of this finer sense of pity is thus a prime concern for anyone working for social justice and human solidarity.

Because of its association with pain, pity entails the way we have developed our power to feel fear and confidence (**R h** II, 5 and **NE** III, 6-9). Pity, however, requires a more complex judgment about the threat than **courage** does. We will see that it stands in the same relation to fear as **indignation** stands to **anger**. Where the agents arousing fear and anger victimize us either directly or through those we think of as our own, those arousing pity (and we will soon see, **indignation**) victimize other people who we think of as being like us. Pity and indignation are thus higher-order powers than fear and anger because they include the additional power of concern for the welfare of people beyond our circle of intimates and a more complex set of judgments.

The proximate agent of pity is picturing someone as suffering a serious evil which he does not deserve, and which might soon befall us or one of our friends or loved ones. This complex picture entails judgments of 1) the severity, and 2) the justice of the evil befalling the person, as well as 3) the threat it poses to us and ours. This latter determination is made by judging the agent's power and disposition to harm us in relation to our own power to resist him. There is also the additional judgment about 4) the emotional distance between ourselves and the victim which is discussed further below. We must feel friendly, but not be so identified with him that we feel as though what has happened has happened to us or one of ours, in which case we would feel fear rather than pity.

Pity (M) and fear (M) function in immediate response to the person (M) who is unjustly injured (Tfa). Indignation (M) and anger (M), on the other hand, function (T) in response to the agent (A) causing this suffering. At times it is appropriate to comfort and calm people (M) when they are afraid or hurt. But pity can be inappropriate when circumstances call for us to be indignant or angry at the agents (A) causing the unjust suffering so that no further abuse is committed.

2. OUR STATES OF MIND WHEN WE FEEL PITY

The basic point is that

In order to feel pity, we must obviously be capable of supposing that some evil may happen to us or some friend of ours. (1385b 16)

Unless we can feel afraid for ourselves or our friends, we cannot feel pity for others.

We cannot, however, feel vulnerable to evil when we feel ourselves in extreme states of either good or bad fortune. Aristotle's list of the states of mind affecting our power to feel pity begins with two which make us incapable of feeling it. They include

a. Those completely ruined, who suppose that no further evil can befall them. (1385b 19-20)

b. Those who imagine themselves immensely fortunate . . . [who feel] presumptuous insolence... [and include in their imagined good fortune] the impossibility of evil befalling them. (1385b 21-4)

He adds to this list further states of mind and types of people who are capable of feeling afraid and having pity for others.

c. Those who have already had it befall them and have safely escaped... [and] elderly men owing to their good sense and their experience (1385b 25-6)

d. Weak men, especially men inclined to cowardice (1385b 27)

e. Educated people, since they can take long views (1385b 28)

f. Those who have parents living, or children or wives; for these are our own, and the evils mentioned above may easily befall them (1385b 28-9)

g. Those who are neither moved by any courageous emotions such as anger or confidence (these emotions take no account of the future), nor by a disposition to presumptuous insolence (insolent men, too, take no account of the possibility that something evil will befall them)--nor yet by great fear (panic-stricken people do not feel pity, because they are taken up with what is happening to themselves); only those feel pity who are between these two extremes (1385b 30-4)

h. We must also believe in the goodness of at least some people; if you think nobody good, you will believe everybody deserves evil fortune (1385b 35-1386a 1)

Aristotle sums up what can be said about a pity-prone state of mind with the observation that

we feel pity whenever we are in the condition of remembering that similar misfortunes have happened to us or ours, or expecting them to happen in the future. (1386a 2-3)

COMMENTARY. Anyone who has tried to educate people about issues of social justice soon learns that people differ very greatly in their ability to feel for others and care about what happens to them. Aristotle lists here states of mind affecting our ability to feel solidarity with others and shows the central role of courage and friendliness in shaping our power to feel pity. Applying this analysis should help those trying to identify the most promising groups to work with in promoting a broader concern for others and in devising strategies for doing so.

a. **THOSE WHO HAVE COURAGE AND HOPE.** It follows from the fact that people who are "completely ruined, who suppose no further evil can befall them" cannot feel fear for themselves (**R h** II, 5), that they will be that much less likely to feel pity for others. Having lost all they cared about and wished for, they have nothing left that anyone could threaten, nothing of importance whose fate is uncertain. Such a radical state of loss and resignation precludes caring about the fate of other people. If we still cared about them, we would not feel completely ruined by our own personal misfortune. We would still wish for and rejoice in their well-being and happiness, even when things are not going so well for us personally. The importance of courage and hope for the possibility of pity explains the hard-heartedness and lack of compassion found among truly defeated people.

b. **THOSE WHO ARE NOT INSOLENT AND SADISTIC.** "Those who imagine themselves immensely fortunate" and act with "presumptuous insolence" are **sadistic** (**Rh** II, 2). Sadistic people are marked by their lack of pity for the people they belittle and abuse. In this state of mind, we are often **reckless** and feel excessively **confident** (Rh II, 5). Where in item a. our fearlessness came from a deficiency of confidence, here it comes from an excess. In either case, we must be able to feel fear, if we are to be able to feel pity.

c. **THOSE SUCH AS THE ELDERLY WHO HAVE EXPERIENCED BAD FORTUNE THEMSELVES.** The general "experience" of the "elderly" as well as the particular experience "of those who have already had [evil] befall them and have safely escaped" give one a healthy respect for how threatening things can be, and make one more capable of pity for others undergoing similar suffering. The same kind of experince can increase our confidence in mankind's ability to endure as well as to feel pity (**Rh** II, 5).

   d. **THOSE WHO ARE COWARDLY.** As cowards (**NE** III, 7) we are excessively threatened even by things that might cause only mild pain. This state inclines us to be equally excessive in judging others as pitiable. We judge their pain and distress as more serious than would a more courageous person, and we judge the agent causing it as more of a threat to us than we should.

   When we approach people as though their suffering is more pitiful than it is, we tend to magnify their picture of the pain (F) and the agent (A) they (M) must endure and cope with. In the process, instead of encouraging them (M) to feel stronger and more courageous (F), we support their view of themselves (M) as small and of the task they must struggle with (A) as all but overwhelming. Is it any wonder then that people trying to find their courage are angry at those whose pity is excessive? Or that "bleeding hearts" have given pity an undeservedly bad name?

   e. **THOSE WHO ARE EDUCATED WITH A LONG VIEW OF OUR VULNERABILITY AS HUMAN BEINGS.** "Educated people" who "can take the long view" are capable of pity because they see how the working out of what a harmful agent is doing to somebody else might affect them or the people they consider their own. Part of what it means to take the long view is precisely to imagine ourselves in other circumstances, to think about how and why things develop the way they do, and to speculate about how we would feel and respond in circumstances different from our present ones.

   It is essential to pity that we put ourselves in the other fellow's shoes and see the potential consequences for ourselves of their seemingly unrelated sufferings. Since appropriate pity must transcend the way things appear from a parochial and private point of view, there is a high correlation between being truly educated and having a just sense of pity.

   f. **THOSE WHOSE PARENTS, CHILDREN AND SPOUSES ARE LIVING.** Why should our having "parents living, or children or wives" make us more capable of pity? We should not be misled into thinking that Aristotle's point is that we pity our own parents, children or wives when they suffer unjustly. We would only pity them if we were alienated from them and did not feel them to be "our own." When we feel them to be our own and something bad happens, we are afraid for them; we do not pity them. Aristotle's real point here is that by caring for our families and intimate friends, we strengthen our capacity for **friendship** and **love** (**Rh** II, 4 and **NE** IV) and that puts us in a state of mind where we are more capable of feeling pity.

   The explanation for this is found in the fact that the source of the person's suffering must be at least potentially a threat to us and ours. Loving someone (M) as our own makes us very sensitive to their pleasures (F) and pains (F) and thus to the agents (A) which might cause them pleasure and pain. The range of our own material sensitivity (M) expands to include the agents (A) affecting their well-being and interests as well as our own. This means in practice that we become sensitive to a whole range of agents (A) that might never have concerned **us** (M) before, or which might not have seemed real to us even though we had been exposed to them time and time again.

Having a son approaching draft age, for example, makes one more sensitive to world affairs and threats to peace, and makes one feel for those mothers and fathers in other lands who might be sending their sons off to senseless wars. Having an intimate black, or handicapped, friend makes one more attuned to questions of discrimination. Ambitious men with daughters become more sensitive to sexism in employment. Close friendships with foreign students make one more aware of international practices which people from other countries consider unjust.

In sum, close friendships and family relations--especially with people who are not the same as us sexually, emotionally, physically, culturally, economically--broaden our basic material sensitivity (M). This enlarges the number of both the agents (A) we will judge as potential threats to us, and the people (M) we can recognize as suffering unjustly at the hands of those agents. By identifying with more people, we become more concerned to determine the justice of how they are treated.

g. **THOSE BETWEEN THE EXTREMES OF EXCESSIVE AND DEFICIENT ANGER, CONFIDENCE AND FEAR.** We have already seen reasons why **insolent sadism** and both excessive and deficient fear and confidence undermine the power to feel pity. Aristotle adds several new observations here, however. The first is that when we are courageously or angrily facing some threat we are caught up in the present struggle and are not in any position to be thinking about how the source of somebody else's suffering might affect us or ours in the future. In the same way when we are terrified, we are so worried about ourselves we cannot feel pity for anyone else.

While these comments add to our understanding of the dispositions that keep us from feeling pity, Aristotle introduces them to clarify what allows us to feel pity. He notes that "only those feel pity who are between these two extremes" of being so confident or angry that we do not feel threatened, or so deficiently confident we are terrified. We must feel vulnerable, but not too vulnerable. Only when our power is between the extreme states of fear and confidence can we feel pity.

h. **THOSE WHO HAVE A FRIENDLY BELIEF IN THE GOODNESS OF SOME PEOPLE RATHER THAN BEING ENVIOUS AND SPITEFUL.** Believing "in the goodness of at least some people" requires **friendliness** (**Rh** II, 4 & NE IV, 6) and the wish that they fare well. By disposing us to believe in the goodness of people and the justice of their expectations, friendliness disposes us to feel the badness and injustice of the harm that befalls them, thus making pity possible. When, on the other hand, we feel great **e n v y** and **spite** we "believe everybody deserves evil fortune" and pity no one.

3. THE BAD FORTUNE AROUSING PITY

Aristotle examines here the form (F) of people's (M) suffering which we pity and, to a certain extent, the nature of the actions (A) by which it comes about. In the next section, he examines our relation to the people (M) we pity. The basic point is that

> All unpleasant and painful things excite pity if they tend to destroy and annihilate; and all such evils as are due to chance, if they are serious. (1385a 4-6)

The "evils due to chance" are

a. Friendlessness, scarcity of friends (it is a pitiful thing to be torn away from friends and companions) (1386a 10-1)

b. Deformity, weakness, mutilation (1386a 11)

c. Evil coming from a source from which good ought to have come; and the frequent repetition of such misfortunes. (1386a 12-3)

d. The coming of good when the worst has happened: e.g. the arrival of the Great King's gifts for Diopeithes after his death. (1386a 14-5)

f. That either no good should have befallen a man at all, or that he should not be able to enjoy it when it has. (1386a 15-7)

COMMENTARY. Aristotle's list of the bad fortune arousing pity is by no means exhaustive, but it does give us headings under which to try to grasp the forms of unjustifiable bad fortune with which people can most readily identify. He makes a distinction between two kinds of bad fortune which, according to the definition of pity, must "befall one who does not deserve it." The first group of "unpleasant and painful things" arouse pity simply because they destroy and annihilate someone, while the second do not have to destroy someone so long as "they are serious" and occur by chance or unnecessarily. He thus distinguishes two criteria, a thing's seriousness and its being a matter of chance rather than being seen as a natural outcome of some kind.

This latter point is particularly important because it means that we cannot simultaneously feel that a person's suffering was an inevitable consequence of his own action and pity him for bringing it down on his own head. This means that for us to see someone's suffering as pitiful, we must not see it as his or her own fault or as a natural part of life. Death in old age is not by itself pitiful in this sense. And it means in practice that depicting unjustifiable bad fortune as being the inevitable outcome of a given social system can actually dimenish people's solidarity with the system's victims in so far as people take the system to be simply a fact of life and believe the victim should have known better.

The strategic point would seem to be that people cannot pity the victims of an unjust system that they see as either inevitable or incapable of transformation into a more virtuous form of operation. This formulation is actually just another way of saying that people must feel that the suffering was neither necessary nor justifiable by the requirements of the only way they know how to do business. They have to feel that somebody could have done his job better and this suffering would not have had to happen. If they don't feel anybody could have resisted causing such suffering and that the system requires it, they will not pity the victim but resign themselves to his suffering and perhaps even feel superior to him by being more realistic about what you should not even try to do.

Here then are Aristotle's basic headings for the kinds of unjustifiable bad fortune which most arouses the sense of pity, although it should always be remembered that we must be in a state of mind which allows us to feel pity in the first place.

a. **BEING CUT OFF FROM ONE'S FAMILY AND FRIENDS.** It is a pitiable thing for people who are capable of friendship and who have families and dear friends to be separated from them or otherwise isolated from people. Because of their feelings for others and the way they have developed their character, it is not natural for them to be so alone. Perhaps Aristotle was thinking of people who were banished from Athens where all their relatives and friends lived. (To befriend and stand by a person at such a time is cited as an important act of kindness at **R h** II, 7, item b.) We could add to this the thousands of political exiles in modern America, and if we were not so hardened to the reality we would probably add the millions of American families repeatedly uprooted when the bread-winner moves them from city to city.

Though we might feel compassion for his suffering, the friendlessness of a misanthropic character is not a cause for pity, however, because the misfortune of his isolation is not accidental. He has not had bad luck and ended up with no friends. Rather, his envy, contentiousness or whatever has driven people away.

b. **BEING DEFORMED, WEAK OR MUTILATED.** "Deformity" (or ugliness), "weakness" and "mutilation" are pitiable because of the way they limit what one can do physically, but also because of their tendency to isolate us. While we might always feel compassion for people with such problems, we are not so disposed to pity them insofar as they bring their troubles on themselves through excessive drinking, drug abuse or other forms of self-indulgence. As Aristotle says at **NE** III, 5:

> Let us assume the case of a man who becomes ill voluntarily through living a dissolute life and disobeying doctors' orders. In the beginning, before he let his health slip away, he could have avoided becoming ill: but once you have thrown a stone and let it go, you can no longer recall it, even though the power to throw it was yours, for the initiative was within you. (1114a 15-9)

Such people seem to be reaping what they have sown. Suffering which follows sadly enough as the consequence of the life one has indulged is less pitiable than the deformity, weakness, or mutilation resulting from accidental causes or from torture that one does not see as a necessary part of maintaining an irreplaceable regime.

c. **BEING HURT BY PEOPLE WHO SHOULD BE GOOD TO US.** In the POETICS, Aristotle explains that the most powerful agent for arousing pity is unknowingly harming someone one loves through making a chance mistake. This seems an instance of "evil coming from a source from which good ought to have come." But other examples come to mind as well. The abuse of cruel parents, mean-spirited teachers, and authoritarian officials all elicit pity for the people they should be befriending. But again one must feel that such goodness is both psychologically and politically possible before he can feel the suffering was not inevitable and as such was unjustifiable.

d. **GOOD THINGS HAPPENING WHEN THEY WILL DO NO GOOD.** The bad timing of good fortune arriving when it is too late to do any good is pitiful and seems unfair when the person deserved better. Aristotle's example is of a gift coming after someone's death, but it is perhaps equally pitiful when something good occcurs such as the birth of a child or signing a contract right before someone's death.

e. **HAVING REPEATED BAD FORTUNE IN ONE'S LIFE.** People are thought to have particularly pitiful lives when they have had repeated bad luck and misfortune on occasions when "good should have befallen" them. That they are not able to enjoy it when it does come seems to be the same case as item d. above.

4. PEOPLE AROUSING OUR PITY

Here Aristotle examines our relation to the people (M) whose suffering (Tfa) arouses our pity. He first establishes the need for distance between ourselves and the victim.

> The people we pity are: those we know, if only they are not very closely related to us--in that case we feel about them as if we were in danger ourselves. For this reason Amasis did not weep, they say, at the sight of his son being led to death, but did weep when he saw his friend begging: the latter sight was pitiful, the former terrible, and the terrible is different from the pitiful; it tends to cast out pity, and often helps to produce the opposite of pity. (1386a 18-23)

There must, however, be some relation between us and the victim since

> we feel pity when the danger is near ourselves. Also we pity those who are like us in age, character, disposition, social standing, or birth; for in all these cases it appears more likely that the same misfortune may befall us also. (1386a 23-7)

The need for closeness in age, character, gifts, etc. follows the general principle that "what we fear for ourselves excites our pity when it happens to others." (1386a 28)

COMMENTARY. For us to pity someone, we must identify with the goodness of his or her efforts in order to feel the undeservedness of his suffering. This is made possible by our being alike in age, character, ability, etc. But this identification cannot be with him as an individual person, because we would then feel ourselves hurt and experience **fear**, or **anger**, rather than **pity** or **indignation**. There must be a distance between us that our friendliness is able to leap across without eliminating.

The people we pity thus reflect the way we have developed the powers we identify with in others, and particularly the power of friendliness. This allows us to explain the often noted class and character based nature of many people's sense of justice and injustice. We pity those who suffer from the things which scare us. Who are they? They are the people who are doing, or trying to do, the same kinds of things we are. Our common aims and efforts make us vulnerable to the same kinds of things.

A major function of political ideologies is to establish the priority of the moral traits that have seemed virtuous in a given group's practice of life--even though they might be so situation-specific, and rigidified, as not to be morally applicable in other circumstances. Such ideologically-supported traits as tight self-control, a hoarding desire to amass property, high ambition, etc. are then used as the criteria for determining whose side one is on in distributing the hardships and rewards of social life. People who lack the dominant traits of the time will be thought to deserve that portion allotted the unfit. In this way, we are encouraged to feel no pity for people whose character type does not thrive under the given conditions.

We think what we are doing is good--otherwise we would try not to do it. So we naturally think that other people's similar efforts deserve better than the mistreatment befalling them, especially when the misfortune seems threatening to us too. This is the psychological mechanism behind the class-based sense of justice, pity, and indignation.

Such limitations on one's sense of justice can be transcended only as people engage in life practices that cultivate a broader concern for the lives and development of human beings. Anything which promotes a noble sense of pity must at the same time create a more mature sense of justice.

5. HOW TO MAKE PEOPLE FEEL PITY

Aristotle offers the following advice to orators.

Since it is when the sufferings of others are close to us that they excite our pity (we cannot remember what disasters happened a hundred centuries ago, nor look forward to what will happen a hundred centuries hereafter, and therefore feel little pity, if any, for such things): it follows that those who heighten the effect of their words with suitable gestures, tones, dress, and dramatic action generally, are especially successful in exciting pity: they thus put the disasters before our eyes, and make them seem close to us, just coming or just past. Anything that has just happened, or is going to happen soon, is particularly piteous: so too therefore are the tokens and the actions of the sufferers--the garments and the like of those who have already suffered; the words and the like of those actually suffering—of those, for instance, who are on the point of death. Most piteous of all is it when, in such times of trial, the vic-tims are persons of noble character: when-ever they are so, our pity is especially excited, because their in-nocence, as well as the setting of their misfortunes before our eyes, makes their misfortunes seem close to ourselves. (1386a 31–b 8)

COMMENTARY. These remarks were intended to show how orators can heighten people's feelings of pity. Aristotle's advice turns on the impor-tance of bringing "the sufferings of others... close to us," when we would otherwise think of them as distant, and suggests doing so temporally, spa-tially, and morally. Temporal closeness means referring to suffering that has either just happened or is about to happen since that in the distant past or future is not so piteous. One can make the suffering spatially close by acting it out, or putting "the disasters before our eyes" through tokens like the victim's garments. The spatial and temporal dimensions reinforce one another. But the main point would seem to be the moral closeness between the sufferer and the audience.

Aristotle thought that the "Most piteous of all... victims are persons of noble character." Was this because the Greek audience was itself noble, or at least aspired to moral nobility even when they did not achieve it? Some such answer seems required to explain the sympathy they appear to have felt for noble victims. Their strong response to the suffer-ing of the noble cannot be explained simply by saying that the person's moral nobility made his or her suffering that much less deserved and therefore more piteous. While this is certainly true, we must not overlook the fact that only those who love and honor nobility themselves will per-ceive this.

A significant contrast to the Athenian case is found, for example, in Willie Loman the central character of Arthur Miller's "DEATH OF A SALES-MAN." Loman is not a noble character, yet he has elicited as much, or more, pity from American audiences than any figure in our theater. The dif-ference, no doubt, is in the moral basis of identification between audience and victim. Americans saw something of themselves in this man who sold his right to a personality of his own in order to advance a shoddy career. This suggests that, while the suffering of the finest people might arouse the greatest pity, pity operates wherever moral identification occurs between an audience and someone that is seen as suffering naturally enough from his own choices but in a way that is ultimately unnecessary and without justification.

B. THE POWER TO FEEL INDIGNATION (Rh II, 9)

1. INDIGNATION DEFINED
AND DIFFERENTIATED FROM ENVY AND SPITE

Aristotle thought indignation and pity are the two forms of response (F) made by a virtuous moral character (M) to the unmerited good and bad fortune of others (A).

Most directly opposed to pity is the feeling called indignation. Pain at unmerited good fortune is, in one sense, opposite to pain at unmerited bad fortune, and is due to the same moral qualities. Both feelings are associated with good moral character; it is our duty both to feel sympathy and pity for unmerited distress, and to feel indignant at unmerited prosperity; for whatever is undeserved is unjust, and that is why we ascribe indignation even to the gods. (1386b 9-16)

Where pity is a matter of feeling pain at **unmerited bad** fortune, indignation is a matter of pain at **unmerited good** fortune.

Aristotle sought immediately, however, to distinguish indignation from envy.

It might indeed be thought that envy is similarly opposed to pity, on the ground that envy is closely akin to indignation, or even the same thing. It is true that it also is a disturbing pain excited by the prosperity of others. But it is excited not by the prosperity of the undeserving but by that of people who are like us or equal with us. The two feelings have this in common, that they must be due not to some untoward thing being likely to befall ourselves, but only to what is happening to our neighbor. The feeling ceases to be envy in the one case and indignation in the other, and becomes fear, if the pain and disturbance are due to the prospect of something bad for ourselves as the result of the other man's good fortune. (1386b 16-24)

Where envy is excited by good fortune whether or not others deserve it, indignation concerns only undeserved good fortune.

It is important to understand that in their true form pity and indignation are moral responses made by good men.

The feelings of pity and indignation will obviously be attended by the converse feelings of satisfaction. If you are pained by the unmerited distress of others, you will be pleased, or at least not pained, by their merited distress. Thus no good man can be pained by the punishment of parricides or murderers. These are

things we are bound to rejoice at, as we must at the prosperity
of the deserving; both these things are just, and both give
pleasure to any honest man, since he cannot help expecting that
what has happened to a man like him will happen to him too. All
these things are associated with the same type moral character.
And their contraries are associated with the contrary type; the
man who is delighted by others' misfortunes is identical with the
man who envies others' prosperity. For anyone who is pained by
the occurrence or existence of a given thing must be pleased by
that thing's non-existence or destruction. (1386b 25-1387a 3)

A good person will be pained by undeserved bad fortune, but he will also
be pleased by deserved bad fortune. And of course he will be pleased and
rejoice at deserved good fortune. The envious person, on the other hand,
is pained by anybody's good fortune whether it is deserved or not. He is
also inclined to be spiteful and to find pleasure in their bad fortune,
again, whether or not it is deserved.

Spite, envy and indignation can each block feelings of pity.

We can now see that all these feelings tend to prevent pity
(though they differ among themselves, for the reasons given), so
that all are equally useful for neutralizing an appeal to pity.
(1387a 3-5)

When we are feeling any one of these three, we cannot be feeling pity for
others.

Aristotle defined indignation this way.

Indignation is pain caused by the sight of undeserved good fortune. (1387a 8-9)

COMMENTARY. Mastering proper indignation is one of the greatest
challenges in being just because, while it is an essential attitude for
those wishing to maintain high standards of justice, one can slip so
easily into being envious and spiteful. It is thus understandable that Aristotle first clarifies the relations between indignation and pity, envy, and
spite. Pity and indignation are actually the different forms of response (F)
which a single virtue (M) makes when exposed to different agents (A).

Pity is this virtue's response to those who have not deserved to
suffer bad fortune, while indignation is its response to those who have
not deserved to enjoy some particular good fortune. Pity is aroused by
picturing people as receiving less of the good things and more of the bad
than they deserve. Indignation, on the other hand, is aroused by picturing
them as receiving less of the bad and more of the good than they
deserve. It is a general principle, of course, that the same moral character (M) responds in different forms (F) when exposed to different agents
(A).

The same moral power (M) which responds in these ways to undeserved good and bad fortune (A) also responds to that which is deserved
(A) which will be explained further below. Envy and indignation are both
pained by the good fortune of others, but envy makes us indifferent to
whether people deserve their good fortune. Indignation, on the other hand,
is aroused by good fortune only when it is unjust for a given person to

have that particular reward (**Rh** II, 10). For now though, it should be clear that we mean by indignation, pity and emulation the responses a just person makes to the good and bad fortune of others.

This is especially important with regard to indignation which is often confused with the vice of envy and spite. Alasdair MacIntyre for example, in his early **A SHORT HISTORY OF ETHICS,** expressed what has become a common misconception about the moral status of indignation.

> The righteously indignant man is one who is upset by the undeserved good fortune of others (this example is perhaps the first indication that Aristotle was not a nice or a good man: the words "supercilious prig" spring to mind very often in reading the **ETHICS.**) (Macmillan Publishing Co., Inc., 1966, p. 66)

MacIntyre's comment shows surprisingly little reflection on the essential function (T) of truly righteous (i.e. non-spiteful) indignation in maintaining a just form of social life.

One need only think, for example, of the indignation felt by civil rights supporters at President Nixon's desire to appoint men with established segregationist records and poor judicial craftsmanship to the Supreme Court. These men did not deserve such high honor, and very nearly everyone committed to the integrity of the judicial system was indignant at their nomination.

More generally, though, how could any system of social expectations and rewards function if people were not indignant at their being violated? As always, forms of response must be appropriate to the agents that stimulate them. But surely, an appropriately indignant response that is neither envious nor spiteful shows one's belief in the rules of the game and his faith in their ability to provide for the sense of justice social life requires. When one loses his belief in the system's justice, the heart goes out of his desire to hold other people (and himself) accountable to those standards.

Without the high-minded ambition to succeed within and maintain the standards of a just system, people become fatalistic about corruption. A servile acceptance of whatever people with power wish to do, or allow others to get away with, and the accompanying loss of faith in the system's values and standards, makes people incapable of indignation. Indignation is an angry, courageous response to the violation of the system of responsibilities and rewards people expect to follow from virtuous or vicious behavior.

All movements for social reform and against injustice must promote people's power to be indignant at the undeserved good fortune which corrupts the society's leaders. But it is equally important to recognize that corrupt systems tend to corrupt the poor and the weak as well as the rich and the powerful. So, too, the envious leaders of revolutionary classes can be exploitative and spiteful in dispossessing unjust rulers and then replace them as the beneficiaries of similar injustices. Truly righteous indignation, however, rejects not just a particular system of unjust advantage, but all social arrangements which violate the fundamental wish to protect and promote virtuous human development.

2. THE GOOD FORTUNE AROUSING OUR INDIGNATION

Aristotle begins his discussion of the things arousing indignation by eliminating those which we might envy or wish to emulate but about which we cannot be truly indignant.

> Thus a man may be just or brave, or acquire moral goodness: but we shall not be indignant with him for that reason, any more than we shall pity him for the contrary reason. (1387a 11-3)

On the other hand

> Indignation is roused by the sight of wealth, power, and the like--by all those things, roughly speaking, which are deserved by good men and by those who possess the goods of nature-- noble birth, beauty and so on. (1387a 13-6)

COMMENTARY. We have seen that indignation responds to undeserved good and deserved bad fortune. The difference between the good fortune about which we can feel indignant, and that about which we cannot, turns on the difference between the good fortune which can be undeserved and that which cannot. It is only those goods which can be unjustly distributed which arouse indignation.

a. **GOODS WHICH CANNOT BE UNJUSTLY DISTRIBUTED.** It is certainly one's good fortune to possess a virtuous character such as being "just or brave," but such moral goodness can never be undeserved since it is always the result of purposely responding in a virtuous form (F) to the proper agents (A). One deserves the character he or she has developed, in the same way as it is said that people deserve the faces they have acquired after age forty. By then our faces reflect our lives and character more than the natural endowment we start with.

We might wonder, though, why Aristotle would say vice is not a cause for pity. We can imagine, for example, feeling that a given person did not deserve being born into a situation which tempted and pressured him or her into doing corrupting and harmful things. Some people have terribly hard lives and it is often a pity to see how little they are expected to make of themselves. But for their own sakes, we must make a careful distinction here between compassion for the unjust conditions a person must deal with and realism about what he or she comes to wish and work for.

For their own sakes as well as ours, we must be indignant when the subjects of injustice practice injustice against others. Vicious characters should arouse indignation whenever they seek undeserved good fortune at the expense of others whether or not they have been victimized themselves. But for our indignation to be virtuous and in the service of the wish to promote human development, it must always be grounded in friendly realism about the conditions a person has had to face in developing him or herself.

It is here that a legitimate sense of pity comes in. While there remains no place for pity insofar as people contribute to their own undoing, there is an important place for pitying people who are struggling against unjustly taking out their own suffering on others. Rather than pitying their vice (which we should be indignant at), we pity their being placed in a situation requiring so much moral strength to keep from becoming vicious.

b. **GOODS THAT CAN BE UNJUSTLY DISTRIBUTED.** The goods about which people can be indignant are those that can be unjustly distributed. In describing the causal structure of such cases, we can treat the goods of fortune as material (M) which the person has unjust control over as an agent (A). The person has excessive agency (A) in controlling either the direct enjoyment and use of wealth (M), or in the exercise of power and influence over people (M). To be honored unjustly, for example, is to be given a status (A) that commands greater deference (F) from others (M) than one's own achievements merit.

Just as we saw in examining **vanity** (**NE** IV, 3), having excessive expectations and exercising agency over others beyond what one's virtue warrants leads to a distorted and even ideological consciousness that inflates one's sense of his own worth so as to appear to deserve what are actually unjustifiable rewards. Our power to be indignant at such injustice is dependent on the development of the other virtues involved in assessing the justice of given distributions of burden and reward.

3. THE PEOPLE AROUSNG OUR INDIGNATION

Aristotle first considers a temporal factor about people arousing our indignation.

> Again, what is long established seems akin to what exists by nature; and therefore we feel more indignation at those possessing a given good if they have as a matter of fact only just got it and the prosperity it brings with it. The newly rich give more offence than those whose wealth is of long standing and inherited. The same is true of those who have office or power, plenty of friends, a fine family, etc. We feel the same when these advantages of theirs secure them others. For here again, the newly rich give us more offence by obtaining office through their riches than do those whose wealth is of long standing; and so in all other cases. The reason is that what the latter have is felt to be really their own, but what the others have is not: what appears to have been always what it is is regarded as real, and so the possessions of the newly rich do not seem to be really their own. (1387a 16–27)

And then he examines the proper fit between people and the agency they should be allowed to exercise over various materials.

> Further, it is not any and every man that deserves any given kind of good; there is a certain correspondence and appropriateness in such things; thus it is appropriate for brave men, not for just men, to have fine weapons, and for men of family, not for parvenus, to make distinguished marriages. Indignation may therefore properly be felt when anyone gets what is not appropriate for him, though he may be a good man enough. It may also be felt when

any one sets himself up against his superior, especially against his superior in some particular respect... but also... when the inferior in any sense contends with his superior; a musician, for instance, with a`just man, for justice is a finer thing than music. (1387a 27-b 2)

COMMENTARY. We can identify two distinct factors concerning the people arousing our indignation.

a. **THE NOUVEAU RICHE MORE THAN THOSE WITH LONG-ESTABLISHED PRIVILEGES.** While Aristotle's judgment on long-held privilege reflects aristocratic influences, we nonetheless still feel greater indignation at unjust exercises of power coming from the **nouveau riche** than from people of old wealth or established position who have long indulged in such excesses. A tradition of abuse blunts its edge--at least for those who have become adjusted to it. The abuse of new economic or political opportunities, even by traditional wealth, is a different matter exciting greater indignation.

The explanation of this phenomenon is found in the dynamics of character formation at both the moral and emotional and the cognitive levels. At the moral and emotional level, we can develop vices such as cowardice, depression, small-mindedness, apathy and obsequiousness in response to traditional injustice which keeps us from being able to feel indignant about it. These moral vices in turn distort our cognitive powers as well.

As Aristotle observes, "what appears to have been always what it is is regarded as real." People irrationally come to think that just because someone has successfully gotten away with his unjustifiable claims of superior rights, he really has the superior powers he bases his claims on. This affect of longevity makes the rights of the **nouveau riche** appear less real and thus more of a cause for indignation than people who have had power and privilege longer.

b. **THOSE WHO HAVE FINE THINGS BEYOND WHAT THEY DESERVE.** The ruling concept in indignation--and justice generally--is the appraisal of what people are due. Virtue is required, however, if one is to make such a determination properly. We have often commented, for example, on how vices such as **insolent sadism** and **vanity** can lead us to assume ourselves superior and thus to have a deficient sense of what others are due. They dispose us to be indignant whenever anyone we look down on challenges someone we identify with--even when they have justice on their side.

We are talking here, however, about more legitimate instances of indignation when a person is not really due the fine thing he has or claims a right to. Aristotle's examples are the appropriateness of a man with less courage having a finer weapon than one with more courage, of an ignoble man presuming that his wealth makes him worthy of marriage into a family with real accomplishments, of arrogantly insulting someone superior in a particular area or, finally, acting as though superiority in a less important area made one superior to someone who is better in a more important area.

Clearly, inferiority in some respects does not spell inferiority in all. Physical bravery is inferior to (because more limited in its range than) an excellent sense of justice. But when it comes to defending us in a fight, it is the brave man who deserves the best weapon. If the weapon is to function most effectively, the brave man will wield it in the most appropriate form.

4. OUR STATES OF MIND WHEN INDIGNANT

Aristotle lists the following kinds of people as being disposed to feeling indignant or as being incapable of it.

a. We feel it if we do ourselves deserve the greatest possible goods and moreover have them, for it is an injustice that those who are not our equals should have been held to deserve as much as we have. (1387b 5-8)

b. We feel it if we are really good and honest people; our judgment is then sound, and we loathe any kind of injustice. (1387b 8-9)

c. If we are ambitious and eager to gain particular ends, especially if we are ambitious for what others are getting without deserving to get it. (1387b 9-11)

d. And, generally, if we think that we ourselves deserve a thing and that others do not, we are disposed to be indignant with those others so far as that thing is concerned. Hence servile, worthless, unambitious persons are not inclined to indignation, since there is nothing they can believe themselves to deserve. (1387b 13-4)

COMMENTARY. The power to judge something to be unjust, and thus to be indignant about it, stands or falls with the development of our other powers which constitute our state of mind when indignant. If one has the virtue of **friendship** (NE IV, 6), for example, he will be indignant at the betrayal of a friend and at organizational policies that set friends against each other.

The four items in Aristotle's list describe other factors affecting our power to be indignant and provide helpful insight in explaining why someone should care about a particular instance of unmerited good fortune. They are presented in a descending order of people's ability to respond appropriately to instances of unmerited good fortune.

a. **BEING A GOOD PERSON AND TRULY ACCOMPLISHED AT SOMETHING.** The person of real accomplishment who not only deserves much but has attained it is capable of truly righteous and appropriate indignation when someone in his area is rewarded or claims rewards beyond his merits. The broader the area of one's accomplishments, including of course the whole range of the virtues, the better one's judgment will be. Because he deserves much in the area himself, he knows how to apply high standards correctly. Because he has been well rewarded himself, his judgment is less likely to be distorted by envy and he can more appropriately say when others receive more than they deserve.

b. **BEING A GOOD AND HONEST PERSON, THOUGH LESS AC-COMPLISHED.** The person who loves justice and is honest but who has not himself attained great things will be a good judge of what people are due insofar as his general moral attitude is concerned, but will have less of a personal incentive to maintain high standards in his field and may well lack a cognitive character that is as sharply developed. For example, a very just person without acknowledged accomplishments in ice-skating will be less indignant about (because less sensitive to) undeserved awards in that sport than a skating champion who knows what he sees. He will have the added incentive of wanting to maintain not only the high standards he attained within the field, but the value of the honors he rightfully earned.

c. **BEING AMBITIOUS TO ATTAIN REWARDS OTHERS ARE RECEIVING UNFAIRLY.** The ambition to meet certain expectations and gain appropriate rewards will clearly enhance one's sensitivity to injustice in the field of his or her chosen endeavors. The difference between such a person and the accomplished champion is that not only is his judgment less proved, but he is more inclined to envy a rival who already has what he has not yet attained. He will be more tempted to disguise spite as indignation and falsely accuse the person of receiving unmerited rewards.

d. **BEING NO LONGER OBSEQUIOUS, SMALL-MINDED AND UNAMBITIOUS.** The basis of all indignation is feeling that we and the people like us have rights and deserve a certain level of response from others. Without this feeling there can be no indignation and obviously no standing up for shared rights. When we are "servile" and **obsequious** (NE IV, 6), when we feel "worthless" and are **small-minded** (NE IV, 3), or when we are simply **"unambitious"** (NE IV, 4) we do not feel indignant at the abuse of people like ourselves because we do not feel any of us deserve better. Real friendliness, high-mindedness and an appropriate degree of ambition, as the contraries of these vices, are required for us to feel indignant.

C. THE POWER TO FEEL ENVY AND SPITE (Rh II, 10)

1. ENVY AND SPITE DEFINED

Aristotle says that

Envy is pain at the sight of such good fortune as consists of the good things already mentioned; we feel it toward our equals; not with the idea of getting something for ourselves, but because the other people have it. (1387b 21-4)

The same moral character (M) which responds to the good fortune of equals in an envious form (F), responds to their bad fortune (A) in a spiteful way (F).

We can also see what things and what persons give pleasure to envious people, and in what states of mind they feel it: the states of mind in which they feel pain are those under which they will feel pleasure in the contrary things. (1388a 23-6)

Envy is pain at good fortune; spite is pleasure at bad.

A noteworthy function (T) of envy is to destroy one's concern for justice and one's pity for the undeserved suffering of equals and rivals.

If therefore we ourselves with whom the decision rests are put in an envious state of mind, and those for whom our pity, or the award of something desirable, is claimed are such as have been described, it is obvious that they will win no pity from us. (1388a 26-9)

COMMENTARY. In contemporary English we tend to use "envy" and "jealousy" interchangeably. For our purposes here, when we are talking about wanting to be like someone we admire without wishing him or her any harm, we will speak of "emulation" and will reserve the term "envy" for the vice described in this section.

Aristotle does not examine spite separately here because he sees it as the obverse of envy and has examined it in detail elsewhere (**Rh**, II, 2 & 4). It is important to see how unproductive and even destructive envy and spite are. Its telos or purpose is not to acquire for oneself the kind of thing another has. **Emulation** (**Rh** II, 11) strives to do that through just means, while exploitation (**NE** IV, 1) does so unjustly. But where emulation promotes a genuine development of oneself and one's resources, envy and spite lead to the tearing down of others.

Envy is pained simply because another person has something that seems to make him happy. The envious person tries to find satisfaction through undermining the happiness of others as a way to escape his pain at their being happy when he is not. Envy thus takes a perverse satisfaction in spiteful acts that establish one's power at least to destroy.

The harder we are on ourselves, and the less respect we have for the natural processes and limitations involved in accomplishing fine things, the greater will be our envy. (This is why inculcating an exaggerated sense of duty and guilt is immoral and irresponsible.) The success of others can then all the more easily trigger our anger at ourselves for not having their success, and lead us to picture their success as the cause of the pain we actually bring on ourselves. Spiteful action against them is then a tempting way to keep from blaming ourselves for how unhappy our lives have become. Most envious and spiteful people would probably be horrified to realize they actually take pleasure in other people's misfortunes.

Envy and spite are the core of evil because in their destructiveness they are actively opposed to the proper wish of promoting development in oneself and others. Spiteful people might be coldly calculating and decisive in their destruction, but they should never be thought rational or free because they do not act in the service of life. The other vices are not necessarily evil in that they do not embody this wish to destroy and do away with signs of the fullness of life or simply that others might be more fortunate. Unjust social conditions which undermine people's confidence in their own powers while promoting envious and spiteful strategies of life are tainted by the evil they produce.

2. OUR STATES OF MIND WHEN ENVIOUS

We are disposed to feeling envious--and by implication, spiteful--when we are in the following states of mind.

a. If we have, or think we have, equals; and by "equals" I mean equals in birth, relationship, age, disposition, distinction, or wealth. (1387b 25-6)

b. If we fall but a little short of having everything; which is why people in high place and prosperity feel it--they think everyone else is taking what belongs to themselves. (1387b 27-8)

c. If we are exceptionally distinguished for some particular thing, and especially if that thing is wisdom or good fortune. Ambitious men are more envious than those who are not. So also those who profess wisdom; they are ambitious--to be thought wise. Indeed, generally, those who aim at a reputation for anything are envious on this particular point. (1387b 28-33)

d. Small-minded men are envious, for everything seems great to them. (1387b 34)

COMMENTARY. Aristotle's analysis of states of mind in which we feel envious shows how much this destructive attitude depends upon developing vices in the powers of **high-mindedness** and **ambition**. And we see here the various areas in which we can work to keep from instilling envy in others or overcoming it in ourselves. We see too the different kinds of social environment which promote it.

a. **FEELING EQUAL TO OTHERS IN FACT OR BY IGNORING SIGNIFI-CANT DIFFERENCES.** The importance of picturing ourselves as equal to the object of our envy explains why we often feel bitterly envious about the relatively minor advantages of someone like ourselves, yet are indifferent to the much greater advantages of Arab sheiks, rock and roll stars, or economic entrepreneurs. Feeling that there might be a significant difference in our talents, personalities or culture which explains and justifies their good fortune keeps us from envying such people as much as one might expect.

The equality aspect explains too a certain levelling process that is always involved in the way envy leads us to ignore the issue of whether other people deserve their good fortune. One can envy people in this bitter sense only by ignoring significant differences which might legitimately account for their good fortune. So lazy people, for example, ignore the talent, hard work and risks taken by the people they envy. **Vanity** (NE IV, 3) and **excessive ambition** (NE IV, 4) are states of mind which dispose people to this sort of disrespectful levelling.

Aristotle thought democracies are inclined to celebrate the real equality which exists between people but in a way that ignores significant differences which should also be respected. This leveling tendency helps explain why envy is so broadly cultivated in modern societies. He thought we needed the additional term "polity" for more virtuously developed democracies which hold out high standards while aiming for human development for all its people. Without such high moral standards, democracies tend to be governed by those who pander to either the self-indulgence or the envy of their people.

The leaders of a polity, on the other hand, are like good coaches and teachers in holding fast to the realities of differences in how well people have developed themselves, and of the strenuous requirements involved in attaining excellence. Their recognition of the natural processes of human development and character formation allows them to believe in the equal right of all people to develop themselves without this implying that, at any given time, all people are equal in what they deserve.

b. **FEELING WE SHOULD HAVE IT ALL BECAUSE OF OUR PRIVILEGED STATUS.** People living prosperous, privileged lives are ironically inclined to envy people less well-off than themselves. The vanity which is often stimulated by having so much already makes them excessive in what they think they deserve. It is then natural to feel envious at the painful sight of someone else being the center of attention or the recipient of some element of good fortune which has escaped them. Having grown accustomed to good things naturally coming to them, they are all the more easily pained by even the merited good that goes to others.

This might seem inexplicable to less-privileged people who do not understand how corrupting it can be to have just about anything one wants. Considerable ethical education and training is required if the children of the rich and powerful are not to suffer all their lives from envious hearts. It is important that they be taught to **emulate** the noble lives of the men and women who have contributed to mankind's development and appreciation of our place in nature. Their own happiness and that of the people they will affect depends on it.

c. BEING DISTINGUISHED AT SOMETHING OR AMBITIOUS TO BE SO. We are prone to feeling envy within the given context of our particular ambitions. If we are vying with others for reputation or standing, it is understandable that we might be pained by their having something thought good. Aristotle singles out as an example those aspiring to a reputation for wisdom as being prone to envy. Academic put-downs apparently have an ancient history of their own.

But one of the most striking things is that we can also envy things even when we do not particularly want them ourselves. Envy is not emulation and does not truly desire to attain its object. Envy simply registers our outrage at feeling inferior at the sight of others' good fortune, while spite promotes pleasure at their misfortunes. Being hurt this way by lacking things we do not really want has a damaging effect on our ability to commit ourselves to anything we really could distinguish ourselves at.

d. FEELING SO SMALL-MINDED THAT WHATEVER OTHER PEOPLE HAVE SEEMS BETTER THAN WHAT WE HAVE. Small-mindedness can incline us to believe that whatever somebody else has is greater than what we have because we feel that whatever is associated with us is less valuable on that account. But while small-mindedness can incline us to picture others as more fortunate than we are, it would seem that we must have a strong latent vanity to feel we deserve better than this and to be pained by that fact. If **small-mindedness** promotes envy, it does so only through such concealed **vanity**.

Small-mindedness does, however, occur without this envious edge to it, as in the case of excessively humble people who harbor no resentment against others' good fortune.

3. THE GOOD FORTUNE AROUSING OUR ENVY

Aristotle identified the things which arouse envy this way.

The good things which excite envy have already been mentioned. The deeds or possessions which arouse the love of reputation and honor or the desire for fame, and the various gifts of fortune, are almost all subject to envy; and particularly if we desire the thing ourselves, or think we are entitled to it, or if having it puts us a little above others, or not having it puts us a little below them. (1387b 35-1388a 4)

COMMENTARY. As we have seen, almost anything which others value or which will increase our reputation can be an object of envy. The range of envy-promoting things is thus far broader than the things about which people can feel indignation and pity. People can even envy others' virtue, or at least the honor shown them for it. Aristotle's analysis points, however, to the essentially hierarchical nature of envy and spite which we have not commented on so directly before. Envy leads one to raise the issue of superiority-inferiority in all of his relations with others. Feeling put down by the happiness and good fortune of others, one then tries to promote the feeling of superiority through putting them down.

This feature of envy explains a most remarkable fact about any culture which promotes excessive ambition and conspicuous consumption. If advertisers can lead people to think that having their product "puts us a little above others, or not having it puts us a little below them," ambitious people will feel like buying that product. To the extent people's relation to the use value of commodities changes, they will no longer approach things in terms of their quality and usefulness so much as in terms of how much pain they are led to feel at not having them.

One's sense of self-worth and social standing will tend no longer to be measured according to one's own individual wishes, interests and judgments but will shift instead to whatever is the object of passing fashion. One's **choices** will be the group's choices, and the felt need to identify one's own proper **wishes** and to **deliberate** for oneself will be eclipsed. But beyond this loss of the sense of self is the fact that we come to see one another's good fortune and happiness as a source of pain and spiteful impulses rather than of rejoicing and emulation.

4. THE PEOPLE AROUSING OUR ENVY

Aristotle lists the following as people arousing our envy.

a. We envy those who are near us in time, place, age, or reputation... Also our fellow-competitors, who are indeed the people just mentioned—we do not compete with men who lived a hundred centuries ago, or those not yet born, or the dead, or those who dwell near the Pillars of Hercules, or those who, in our opinion or that of others, we take to be far below or far above us. (1388a 6-11)

b. We compete with those who follow the same ends as ourselves: we compete with our rivals in sport or in love, and generally with those who are after the same things; and it is therefore these whom we are bound to envy beyond all others. (1388a 11-5)

c. We also envy those whose possession of success in a thing is a reproach to us: these are our neighbors and equals; for it is clear that it is our own fault we have missed the good thing in question; this annoys us, and excites envy in us. (1388a 17-20)

d. We also envy those who have what we ought to have, or have got what we did have once. Hence old men envy younger men, and those who have spent much envy those who have spent little on the same thing. (1388a 20-3)

e. And men who have not got a thing, or not got it yet, envy those who have got it quickly. (1388a 23-4)

COMMENTARY. Aristotle's five headings are useful in alerting us to the kinds of people and situations that are likely to create problems with envy and thus to where we should work to minimize the threat.

a. **THOSE LIKE OURSELVES WITH WHOM WE COMPETE.** The focus here is on the appearance of material equality between the agent (A) and the person (M) whose envy he arouses as expressed by their nearness in "time, place, age, or reputation." The requirement of seeing him or her as our equal explains why we are not envious of those "we take to be far below or far above us."

Whenever we are envious of another, we assume our equality with them. We assume they have no greater need nor right to the thing we covet. But this fact is more revealing than one might expect. When a well-positioned person, for example, is envious of someone in a much poorer life situation, he or she is revealing a **small-minded** (NE IV, 3) self-assessment that makes them feel as bad off as the people they envy. In such cases, envy displays the hollowness of all success that is not grounded in **high-minded** self-respect.

b. **THOSE WHO ARE AFTER THE SAME THINGS WE ARE REGARDLESS OF WHETHER WE ARE ALIKE IN OTHER WAYS.** The agents (A) who are capable of triggering our envy (M) can simply be competitors within a given form of life (F) that we are either in or aspire to. Going after the same goal (T) when that life is taken to be a zero-sum game disposes us very strongly to envy. Envy knows no win/win situation.

We have seen though that our **rivals** can also arouse **friendliness** (R h II, 4) in us when we share common values and can see the competition in the larger context of the proper wish to promote human development in ourselves and others.

c. **THOSE WHOSE GOOD FORTUNE SEEMS TO PUT US DOWN.** Even if we are not so clearly competing with someone like a neighbor or some other equal, we envy their success when it seems like "a reproach to us" and a sign "that it is our own fault we have missed the good thing in question." The central point again is the assumption of equal material capacity that makes one attribute his lack of the desired good to his own moral-emotional failing. It is this angry, self-accusing, small-mindedness that the other's success triggers in the envious person.

d. **THOSE WHO HAVE WHAT WE WANT AND ONCE HAD.** Old people are inclined to envy young ones, just as those who paid high for an item are disposed to envy those who paid low. The equality between the parties is that the old were once equally young and the shopper who paid high feels equal to the one who paid low. This dynamic of envy between generations is particularly important when the society's values promote envy already. Generational conflict is inevitable when young people still living at home demand the right to adult pleasures and rewards which were traditionally dependent on a person's attaining higher stages of development and assuming responsibility for his own support. How could today's adults not become at least somewhat envious and even spiteful when they must carry the responsibilities for young people who they might have spoiled but whose self-indulgence as teenagers has finally come to interfere with their parent's own pleasure? Such envy is accentuated by parental fears about growing older and serves to undermine the legitimacy of parental authority which can only be rooted in wishing the child well.

     e. **THOSE WHO GET THE THINGS WE WANT MORE EASILY THAN WE DO.** People who have gotten things quickly and easily are envied by those who are having a hard time getting them. Such people will be particularly arousing to someone lacking faith in his own ability to **generate** (NE IV, 3) what he wants and needs.

D. THE POWER TO FEEL EMULATION AND CONTEMPT (Rh II, 11)

1. EMULATION AND CONTEMPT DEFINED

Aristotle says that

> Emulation is pain caused by seeing the presence, in persons whose nature is like our own, of good things that are highly valued and are possible for ourselves to acquire; but it is felt not because others have these goods, but because we have not got them ourselves... Emulation makes us take steps to secure the good things in question, envy makes us take steps to stop our neighbor having them. (1388a 31-8)

And with regard to contempt or disdain he says that

> Those who are such as to emulate or be emulated by others are inevitably disposed to be contemptuous or disdainful of all such persons as are subject to those bad things which are contrary to the good things that are the objects of emulation: despising them for just that reason (1388b 23-7)

Because emulation and contempt-disdain promote human development, each of them is "a good feeling felt by good persons, whereas envy is a bad feeling felt by bad persons." (1388a 34-5)

    COMMENTARY. Unlike envy which focuses on the fact of other people appearing to be happier and more accomplished than ourselves, emulation's focus on others' accomplishments makes us feel a painful sense of urgency to make more of ourselves so that we do not waste our lives pursuing contemptible goals. Rather than promoting spiteful put-downs of their contributions, emulation's pain causes us to develop, or justly acquire, the things we admire and to look for role models who will help us bring out what is best in ourselves and live up to our highest wishes.

    Since emulation is a painful emotion, it requires courage and faith to try to master the skills of someone more accomplished than ourselves. During the prolonged process required to develop anything that is really fine, we must withstand the paiful realization that the people we wish to emulate are better than we are at the things we aspire to, and perhaps better than we will ever be. This shows too how emulation requires **high-mindedness** rather than **vanity** (**NE** IV, 3), the wish genuinely to live according to high standards rather than simply appearing to do so. We must believe in ourselves through all of the developmental stages we must endure.

    Whether we approach the noble accomplishments of other men and women in a spirit of emulation or of envy and spite will have a profound effect on our **wish** to develop ourselves. As we have seen, an envious and spiteful attitude betrays hopelessness about the prospects about our own development and sets us on an isolated and destructive path. Emulation, on the other hand, draws us to a respectful appreciation of the accomplishments of others which allows us to apprentice ourselves so that we might learn the lessons of their lives. In so doing we develop our powers of **deliberation** and **choice** as we follow the history of their own decision-making. We learn to recognize how much is at stake in even the small things we do, and begin to develop some narrative sense of our own place in the traditions we are part of and the larger scheme of things.

So far we have spoken of the productive pain we can feel at someone like ourselves doing or having a good thing which it would be possible for us to acquire too. We should remember here Aristotle's earlier remark that the same person who feels pity for unjustified bad fortune and indignation for unjustified good fortune will **delight** in people's justified good fortune. Such sympathetic joy is an essential part of **friendliness** (**R h** II, 4). Joy differs from emulation insofar as it is a pleasurable response to another's good fortune and because it can be aroused by people's accomplishments even when we do not want them for ourselves. A husband, for example, can rejoice at, but not emulate, his wife's easy labor and delivery.

Finally, as harsh as it might sound, just as we must emulate the admirable if we are to draw on the accomplishments of the past and grow to our own full stature, so too we must learn to see as contemptible those attitudes and practices which abuse, belittle and demoralize people. But one will see the rightness of advocating disdain for despicable actions and conditions that should not be emulated only so long as he recognizes the difference between spiteful and arrogant vanity, on the one hand, and standing up for life-affirming principles, on the other. (See the discussion of this idea in **high-mindedness** at **NE** IV, 3 and the reference to unjustified disdain as an agent arousing **anger** at **Rh** II, 2.)

2. OUR STATES OF MIND WHEN EMULOUS

The general principle is that

Emulation must... tend to be felt by persons who believe themselves to deserve certain good things that they have not got, it being understood that no one aspires to things which appear impossible. (1388a 38–b 2)

And the type of people who are inclined to feel this way are

a. The young... and high-minded people. (1388b 3)

b. Those who possess such good things as are deserved by men held in honor--these are wealth, abundance of friends, public office, and the like; believing that they ought to be good men because such things ought to belong to men whose state of mind is good, they are emulous to preserve them. And those are emulous whom others think worthy of them. (1388b 4–8)

COMMENTARY. Unlike envy, emulation is not tied to a zero-sum game conception of superiority-inferiority. Here, somebody else's accomplishments actually heighten our expectations of ourselves and what we deserve if we will only work for it. We also see the productive effect of emulation in promoting deliberation and choice about how to attain our wishes.

a. YOUNG AND HIGH-MINDED. The young are inclined to emulation because they are naturally hopeful and searching for goals toward which to aim their energy and development. If, however, they are allowed to become so **self-indulgent** (NE III, 10-2) that they lack the power to concentrate their energy and so **cowardly** (NE III, 7) that they feel hopeless about testing their resources against the challenges of maturity, they will be too cynical to emulate anyone. Conversely, finding fine figures to emulate will greatly promote their acquisition of both self-control and courage. We saw elsewhere how important having such a person to emulate is if a young person is to develop a proper sense of **shame** (Rh II, 6 & NE IV, 9).

Older persons of lofty disposition also aspire to high things and follow those who have set high standards. Contrary to a common misperception, the **high-minded** and truly independent person (NE IV, 3) finds no servility or self-betrayal in following principles which others have shown to be the path to a noble and generous individuality.

b. HAVING WEALTH, MANY FRIENDS OR PUBLIC RESPONSIBILITIES, OR AT LEAST BEING THOUGHT TO DESERVE THEM. The wealthy, the influential and the powerful emulate good men and women not necessarily because they aspire to goodness themselves, but because doing so is thought part of the role expected of anyone in their position. Acts of philanthropy are part of their strategy for retaining their powerful positions and possessions. Imitating noble actions tends to minimize both the indignation honorable people might show toward the wealthy person's self-centered and indulgent life, and the envy and spite the general public might express toward their having so much good fortune.

But there are more benign reasons as well. Imitating noble actions tends to satisfy a good person's sense of there being special responsibilities that come with having so much more money, friends, influence or power than others. How is he to live up to having so much more than others unless he emulates those whose character and accomplishments meant they were thought to deserve their good fortune?

When, however, a critical mass of a society's people become excessively ambitious and envious, the privileged will no longer feel any legitimate moral authority in demands that they emulate the magnificent practices of the finest people of the past. So if it is obviously true that leaders can corrupt the rest of us, it is equally true that we can contribute to their corruption by not expecting them to emulate those who have used their influence well to promote human development and well-being.

3. THE GOOD FORTUNE AROUSING EMULATION

Aristotle lists these things as arousing emulation.

a. Anything for which our ancestors, relatives, personal friends, race, or country are specially honored, looking upon that thing as really our own, and therefore feeling that we deserve to have it. (1388b 8-10)

b. Since all good things that are highly honored are objects of emulation, moral goodness in its various forms must be such an object (1388b 10-2)

c. All those good things that are useful and serviceable to others; for men honor... those who do them service. (1388b 12-4)

d. Those good things our possession of which can give enjoyment to our neighbors--wealth and beauty rather than health. (1388b 14-5)

COMMENTARY. After an opening comment about how we are affected in our choice of things to emulate by the people we identify with, Aristotle then addresses the three possible aims of friendship: usefulness, pleasure, and nobility (**NE** VIII, 3).

a. **THINGS FOR WHICH OUR ANCESTORS, RELATIVES, FRIENDS, RACE OR COUNTRY ARE ESPECIALLY HONORED.** People do not want just to be good; they want to be a good one of their kind. But saying this underscores the fact that we must always learn who a given person identifies with and feels he or she is like. It might well be something less obvious than the family or group he was born into and point to a more spiritual kinship based on sharing an otherwise unrecognized talent with someone who made something notable of theirs.

At any rate, we see here once again the great power of shared cultural goals in focusing and refining what we wish to make of ourselves. It is another reason why people are so lost--and inclined to become spitefully destructive--when they have no person, or group, with whom they identify and who holds out the expectation that they will make something fine of themselves. Lacking positive ideals to emulate, their life expression is likely to become aimless and capable of leaving nothing better than a destructive mark.

b. **MORAL VIRTUE.** Moral goodness or virtue falls under the general heading described in item a. above. Aristotle's adding it here calls attention to the fact that item a. includes all kinds of abilities in addition to moral virtue such as cooking, athletics, military prowess, etc. People aspiring to excellence in these different groups and cultures are inclined to emulate whatever is honored there regardless of its real moral worth.

c. **SKILLS THAT ARE USEFUL AND OF SERVICE TO OTHERS.** Things that are "useful and serviceable to others" are emulated because many people wish to help others and because they are likely to be honored for doing so. Learning CPR, how to cook or repair simple machines are easy examples of useful skills lots of people want to emulate.

d. **THINGS BY WHICH WE CAN GIVE PLEASURE TO OTHERS.** People also emulate things like the possession of expensive and beautiful things like cooking equipment, boats or stereos which allow them to "give enjoyment to... neighbors."

4. THE PEOPLE AROUSING EMULATION

The following kinds of people tend to arouse feelings of either emulation or contempt.

a. Those who have the sorts of good things already mentioned such as courage and wisdom... (1388b 16-17)

b. Holders of public office--generals, orators, and all who possess such powers--who do many people a good turn. (1388b 17-8)

c. Those whom many people wish to be like; those who have many acquaintances or friends; those whom many admire, or whom we ourselves admire; and those who have been praised and eulogized by poets or prose-writers. (1388b 18-21)

d. Persons of the contrary sort are objects of contempt. (1388b 21-2)

COMMENTARY. Aristotle's list gives us some headings under which to think about the kinds of people who are emulated for either good or ill.

a. **THOSE WITH MORAL AND INTELLECTUAL VIRTUE.** Moral virtues such as courage and intellectual virtues such as practical wisdom are often very attractive to people and inspire emulous feelings in those who have not given up hope for their own higher development. But it is quite common today, for example, for many youth to be conflicted about whether they can integrate their moral aspirations with their desires for social influence. It is hard for them to find adults to emulate who have integrated moral excellence with worldly success.

b. **THOSE WITH POWER AND INFLUENCE WHO ARE HELPFUL TO OTHERS.** People with power and influence who use them to promote human development are especially emulated by those ambitious people who are unwilling to give up their self-respect for success. It is refreshing to see Aristotle note that people in his time emulated the powerful and influential out of a desire to be virtuous and helpful to others.

c. **WELL-KNOWN PEOPLE WHOM OTHERS WISH TO BE LIKE.** In general, anyone with a large reputation will be emulated such as athletes and rock stars. Popularity and broad admiration are signs that many people wish to be like such a person, and the wish-to-be-like is the heart of emulation. We see again the way people take their lead in what they should go after in their lives from following what others respect, praise and seek in theirs. Obviously, on these grounds less noble people will be just as readily emulated as the very finest people.

     d. **PEOPLE FOR WHOM WE DO NOT FEEL CONTEMPT.** People held in contempt are the contrary of those we emulate. This includes people who have many vices or whose thinking is irrational and impractical. It includes also those with power and influence whose fearfulness and selfishness keeps them from using their advantages to promote the development of others. Finally, we should not emulate people just because they are famous or popular without regard to their moral character and real contributions.

GLOSSARY AND REFERENCE GUIDE

GLOSSARY & REFERENCE GUIDE

The reader will find here insights & reviews of material that sometimes go beyond that contained in the body of the text. The list identifies the various virtues & vices & locates their principal, but not their only occurrence in the text. The list also includes commonly used moral & emotional adjectives & identifies the classical virtues & vices to which they refer. OMC aims throughout to clarify concepts concerning the fundamental states of moral character & their interaction rather than to prescribe a definitive set of terms for those concepts. Given this goal, consistency of terminology has been striven for within the work. In practical affairs, on the other hand, one must often search for other terms to convey the same concept in a more palatable & emotionally nuanced way--even at the risk of betraying one's precise meaning. The reader should note, however, in tracking down the classical referents of contemporary terms how often modern usage is ambiguous & glosses over the moral significance & true motive of the emotional attitude referred to.

Chapter references are identified by number & frequently by a section designation such as -A, -B or -C. The reader should supplement the readings in these sections by following up on the cross-references contained therein & in the INVENTORIES at the beginning of each Chapter. "Appl" stands for "applicable" throughout & "syn" for "synonym." "He" should always be interpreted as applying to both women & men.

ABASHED - vice of excess shame, Ch 7-B
ADAPTATION - the changing of one's character, or simply his behavior or perception & thinking, to fit environmental circumstances; can be either virtuous or vicious depending on whether it is in keeping with proper wish, deliberation & choice; an adaptation's success can be judged in terms of whether it promotes the person's moral well-being & development or simply his attaining rewards within a given social system without regard to their personal cost
ADJUSTMENT - see adaptation
AGGRESSIVE - appl to self-indulgence, Ch 2, exploitativeness, Ch 3-A. or ambition, Ch 4-B
AMBITIOUS - Ch 4-B, appl to virtue or vice of excess; see also fanatic
AMBIVALENCE - coexistence of seemingly contradictory attitudes in different moral-emotional powers, e.g. self-indulgent desire combined with contempt toward the same person, or love & anger; sometimes a mark of lack of integrity, other times an appropriate response as when being angry at someone one loves who has been thoughtless
ANAL - Freud's term for the hoarding character & developmental stage preoccupied with retention & deficient giving, CH 3-A
ANGRY - appl to virtue or vice of excess, Ch 5
ANXIETY - generalized lack of courage, Ch 1-B
APATHETIC - here vice of deficient anger, Ch 5; also appl to depression, Ch 2, the vices of deficient ambition, Ch 4-B, & indignation, Ch 8-B
APPROPRIATE - here a virtuous response in keeping with proper wish, deliberation & choice & the environmental agents to which one must respond
ARCHON - a leader whose character is committed to promoting the virtues

& proper wish, deliberation & choice & to creating institutions which support human development; generically a leader whose character maintains the spirit & culture of an institution or community for either good or evil, e.g. a person whose bad attitude sets a demoralized tone for a whole group, office or team

ASHAMED – appl to virtue or vice of excess, Ch 7

ASOCIAL – appl to depressed, Ch 2-B, the vice of deficient ambition, Ch 4-B, contentiousness as the vice of deficient friendliness, Ch 6-C, & envy-spite, Ch 8-C

ASSERTIVENESS – appl to virtue or vice of excess anger in standing up for one's rights, Ch 5; see also aggressiveness

BAD-TEMPERED – vice of excess anger, Ch 5-C

BASHFUL – here vice of excess shame, Ch 7-B; associated with small-mindedness, Ch 4-A

BEAUTIFUL – here appl to noble acts & people of noble character

BLEEDING-HEART – appl to vice of excess giving, extravagance, Ch 3-A, & vice of excess friendliness, obsequiousness, Ch 6-C

BOASTFUL – appl to vice of excess talk about oneself, Ch 6-D, & the macho-boaster vice associated with cowardice, Ch 1-B

BOORISH – vice of deficient wittiness, Ch 6-E

BRAGGART – see boastful, Ch 6-D, & macho-boaster, Ch 1-B

BRAVE – see courageous, Ch 1-B

BUFFOONISH – vice of excess wittiness, Ch 6-E

BULLY – see macho-boaster, Ch 1-B, & insolent-sadist, Ch 5-A

CALCULATING – here deliberation inspired more by vice than virtue; contrast with rational

CALM – here contrary of angry, Ch 5-B; also appl to developing courage, Ch 1-B, self-control, Ch 2-B, proper ambition, Ch 4-B, & overcoming obsequiousness, Ch 6-C

CAPACITY – here someone's constitutional gifts, talents or potential as opposed to how they have developed their character or skill in using those talents; in secondary sense one's character determines the range in which he can actualize his capacities unless forced to stretch & go beyond himself by exceptional circumstances; such stretching shows one has a greater capacity than one had normally revealed

CHARACTER – here the particular form of development of a person's moral & emotional powers which dispose him to excessive, deficient or appropriate responses; developed through the interaction between one's constitutional capacities or gifts & environmental opportunities & pressures; while relatively fixed & marked as an adaptation & strategy toward life, one's character can become either more or less virtuous

CHARITABLE – see generosity, Ch 3-A, magnificence, Ch 3-B, & pity, Ch 8-A

CHOICE – the activating desire to do what our deliberation shows is within our power to accomplish in pursuing what we properly wish in developing ourselves & promoting the development of others; not an opinion about the action we should select but the act of pursuing the opinion we come to at the conclusion of our deliberation; a person who has developed the power of choice desires to do what his deliberations show to be required by his proper wishes; virtue gives a person the power of choice, vice takes away this power; the choices we make build up either virtuous or vicious character traits

CLEVER – appl to either virtuous practical reason or vicious calculation

COMPANYMAN - see receptive character, Ch 3-A

COMPASSIONATE - see friendly, Ch 6-B, & pity, Ch 8-A

COMPULSIVE - appl to hoarding & exploitative characters, Ch 3-A, but also self-indulgence, Ch 2, the vice of excess ambition, Ch 4-B, some forms of excess anger, Ch 5-C, & hatred, Ch 6-B

CONCEITED - see vanity, Ch 4-A

CONCENTRATION - governed by one's wish & the development of virtuous interests in the world; destroyed most fully by cowardice, Ch 1, & self-indulgence or depression, Ch 2; developed in a distorted way by vices associated with being compulsive

CONFIDENCE - root element in courage, Ch 1-B

CONNIVING - see calculating

CONSCIENCE - rooted in the power of high-mindedness, Ch 4-A, can be developed in excessive, deficient or appropriate forms; registered through the power of shame, Ch 7; can activate anger, Ch 5, or friendliness, Ch 6, toward oneself in the process of deliberation & self-correction

CONTEMPTUOUS - see contempt-disdain, Ch 8-D, & anger, Ch 5-A

CONTENTIOUS - here vice of deficient friendliness, Ch 6-C, often associated with hoarding, Ch 3-A

COURAGEOUS - virtue of fear & confidence, Ch 1-B

COWARDLY - vice of excess fear & deficient confidence, Ch 1-B

CRAFTSMAN - virtuous development of hoarding character, Ch 3-A

CYBERNETIC - here the power of deliberation is considered a cybernetic function involving communication between a person & the environment of external agents he must deal with in the light of his highest wishes & potentially competing desires & fears, & the control of his behavior through analyzing feed-back to determine the particular forms of response he should choose in pursuing his wish. By leading us to develop false pictures of the world, the vices undermine this cybernetic function through distorting our communication with the external environment. They distort communication further by leading us to ignore our larger interest as human beings when pursuing a vice at the expense of everything else & in inhibiting our ability to choose the self-correcting course of behavior even when we know what it is. Cybernetic deliberation, animated by the proper synergistic wish for integrated human development, allows us to maintain our equilibrium by optimalizing our responses to environmental agents which might otherwise lead us to lose our balance & sense of purpose.

CYNICAL - appl to envy & spite, Ch 8-C, the contentious, Ch, 6-C, & the depressed, Ch 2-B

DEATH WISH - appl to envy & spite, Ch 8-C

DEFENDER - virtuous development of exploitative character, Ch 3-A

DEFENSIVE - fearful, Ch 1; the internal issue in defensiveness is always the wish felt to be threatened

DELIBERATION - the investigation into the means by which we can attain our wishes & those of the people we care about; culminates in an opinion about the action we should choose; ends are wished for, not deliberated about or chosen--although deliberation can reveal that pursuing one wish will result in consequences damaging to more important wishes; deliberating on these conflicts & making choices based on it contributes to strengthening some wishes & character traits while weakening others

DEPRESSED - here vice of deficient pleasure, Ch 2-B

DESPAIRING - the loss of hope & courage, Ch 1

DESTRUCTIVE - see spite, Ch 8-C, also enmity, Ch 6-B, & disdain,

Ch 5-A

DIGNIFIED – see high-minded, Ch 4-A

DISDAINFUL – see Ch 8-D, but also anger, Ch 5-A

DISGRACE – see shame, Ch 7

DISTINGUISHED – appl to high-minded, Ch 4-A

DUTY – here appl to excess ambition, Ch 4-B, to please authorities, excess shame, Ch 7, & anger turned inward, Ch 5, with resulting small-mindedness, Ch 4-A; an improper wish & attitude toward ethics associated with feeling guilty; here the contrary of responsibility, see also conscience

DYSERGISM – here conflicting desires & diminished energy resulting from moral & emotional vices; a quality of moral weakness; the contrary of synergism

EGOTISTICAL – appl to vanity, Ch 4-A, boastfulness, Ch 6-D, & macho-boaster, Ch 1-B

EMPATHY – rooted in the virtue of friendliness, Ch 6, appl to pity, Ch 8-A

EMULATION – a virtue, Ch 8-D

ENCOURAGE – to inspire someone to find his or her courage, 1-B

ENMITY – see Ch 6-B

ENTREPRENEURIAL – see the exploitative character, Ch 3-A

ENVIOUS – see Ch 8-C

EQUILIBRIUM – maintained by virtue, undermined by vice

EVIL – contrary of proper wish, deliberation & choice to promote human development; the wish to destroy that which is alive & joyous; rooted most fully in envy & spite, Ch 8-C; most vices are not evil because they do not display a destructive hatred of life even though they do undermine proper wish, deliberation & choice to a more or less great degree

EXPLOITATIVE – as a vice, excess taking, as virtuously developed, an entrepreneur, builder & defender of common interests against a jungle mentality, Ch 3-A

EXTRAVAGANT – vice of excess giving, here seen as rooted in the overly receptive character, Ch 3-A

FAITHFUL – the firmness of one's convictions & commitments, the root of confidence & courage, Ch 1-B

FANATIC – here the vice of recklessness or deficient fear, Ch 1-B; appl to not only religious & political zealots but those who sacrifice everything to career ambitions

FEAR – see Ch 1

FINE – here a syn of noble & beautiful actions & the people who perform them

FLATTERING – along with obsequiousness one of two forms of the vice of excess friendliness, Ch 6-C; normally motivated by exploitativeness, Ch 3-A

FORTITUDE – see faithful, & confidence-courage, Ch 1

FRIENDLINESS – a virtue, see Ch 6-B&C

FUNNY – appl to virtue of wittiness & vice of buffoonery, Ch 6-E

GENEROUS – a virtue, see Ch 3-A

GENITAL – Freud's term for the generous character & developmental stage at which one begins to be able to work & be thoughtful & giving to others, Ch 3-A

GENTLE – a virtue, see Ch 5-C

GOAL-ORIENTED – can be rooted in either virtue or vice; see aggressive

GRACEFUL – a quality of the high-minded & noble character, Ch 4-A

GREEDY – appl to the vices of self-indulgence, Ch 2-B, receptiveness, exploitativeness & hoarding, Ch 3-A, & excess ambition, Ch 4-B

GROUCHY – appl to some forms of the vice of excess anger, Ch 5-C

GUILTY – here a form of self-correction associated more with embarrassment than shame, Ch 7; shows a high component of fear for the consequences of failing to please authority rather than displeasure at having failed to live up to one's own higher wishes; anger, Ch 5, turned inward with resulting small-mindedness, Ch 4-A, & tendency toward depression, Ch 2-B, & masochism, Ch 4-B; see duty

HAPPY – here, state of functioning according to proper wish, deliberation & choice

HATEFUL – see enmity, Ch 6-B, & envy-spite, Ch 8-C, & evil

HELPER – virtuous form of development of the companyman, receptive character, Ch 3-A

HEROIC – see courage, Ch 1-B

HIGH-MINDED – a virtue, see Ch 4-A

HOARDING – here vice of deficient giving, Ch 3-A; when virtuously developed the craftsman character trait

HONORABLE – properly speaking, virtuous action & character; in corrupted societies, people honor things giving one advantage or having status in others' eyes, regardless of whether they are virtuous or vicious

HOPEFUL – a root of confidence, characteristic of the courageous, falsely claimed by the macho-boaster, Ch 1

HOSTILE – vice of excess anger, Ch 5-C, or spite, Ch 8-C

HUMAN DEVELOPMENT – see INTRODUCTION on Erikson & Gilligan

HUMAN NATURE – in normative sense, perfected through development of the moral-emotional & cognitive virtues & expressed through functioning according to proper wish, deliberation & choice; while people can develop in the direction of either goodness or evil, goodness alone makes the fullness of human life possible; in generic sense, the whole range of possible development of the virtues & vices, & the system of their possible interdependencies; determined in individual cases by the interaction between a person's constitutional gifts & environmental factors

HUMILITY – as a virtue, high-mindedness in responding to those less powerful & influential, as a vice, small-mindedness, Ch 4-A

HUMOROUS – appl to the witty & to buffoons, Ch 6-E

IMMODERATE – appl to vices of both excess & deficiency

IMPULSE – a disposition that is not necessarily characteristic of a person, as when someone acts on impulse in contrast to his normal behavior (although see impulsive), found frequently when one's character is changing; in another sense, one's character governs one's impulses, as when the impulse of a hoarding person is to save

IMPULSIVE – appl to indulgent people lacking self-control, Ch 2, but also the reckless, Ch 1-B, & excessively angry, Ch 5-C

INDIGNATION – a virtue, Ch 8-B; often confused with the vices of envy & spite, Ch 8-C

INFANTILE – appl particularly to self-indulgence, Ch 2-B, extreme receptiveness, Ch 3-A, vanity, Ch 4-A, & excess anger, Ch 5-C

INSOLENT-SADISTIC – here an attitude of excess ambition, Ch 4-B, & vanity, Ch 4-A, which deals with feeling small-minded, Ch 4-A, by hurting & belittling others to make oneself appear powerful in their eyes; an attitude stimulating anger, Ch 5-A; see masochistic

INSTINCT – sometimes a constitutionally given, highly formatted capacity such as the infant's sucking instinct in contrast to a socially acquired & purposive character trait; other times syn for character-rooted impulses, as when the instinct of the hoarding character is to save

INSULT – a slight stimulating anger, Ch 5-A

INTEGRITY – appl to high-mindedness, Ch 4-A, & truthfulness, Ch 6-D, & justice, Ch 8; a quality of synergism & proper wish

INTEMPERATE – appl to either self-indulgence, Ch 2, or the vice of excess anger, Ch 5-C

INTENTION – one's wish & motive, whether pursued consciously or unconsciously

INTERNALIZED – appl to the qualities one makes his own from a person he emulates, Ch 8-D, which he expects of himself in a high-minded, small-minded or vain way, Ch 4-A, & which serve as the standard for his sense of shame, Ch 7; also appl to the wishes of an aggressor one identifies with when he loses the confidence & hope he can escape from the aggressor & be himself, Ch 1-A

INVOLUNTARY – an action done either under external compulsion or in ignorance of its consequences & shown to be involuntary by the remorse the actor feels for what he has done; the vices lead us to do things which are voluntary at the time but which are involuntary when seen in the light of their violating our higher wishes—unless we are evil or continue to do lesser vices voluntarily & wholeheartedly

IRASCIBLE – vice of excess anger, Ch 5-C

IRRATIONAL – vices of both excess & deficiency lead one to perceive & act in irrational ways that run counter to one's deliberations & choices when his wishes are virtuous & proper, as when an excessively angry person is disposed to see others as unjustifiably slighting him & abuses even those whom he otherwise wishes to befriend

JEALOUS – virtuously, natural fear of losing a loved one to a rival or the desire to emulate another's accomplishments, Ch 8-D, viciously, envy-spite, Ch 8-C

JUDGMENT – people can have either good or bad judgment in assessing the character & motives of others; people wrongly identify exercising judgment with being judgmental; see disdain, insolent sadism & spite, Ch 5-A, for judgmental attitudes arousing anger; moral vice undermines good judgment, virtue promotes it

JUNGLE-FIGHTER – see the exploitative character, Ch 3-A

KIND – Ch 6-A

LIBERALITY – syn for generosity, Ch 3-A

LOVING – see friendship & love, Ch 6-B&C

LUST – see self-indulgence & self-control, Ch 2; people wrongly think of sensuous pleasure as indulgent & bad; see duty, guilt, over-controlled & depressed

MAGNIFICENT – here the virtue of grand expenditure, Ch 3-B

MALICIOUS – see evil & insolent-sadism

MASOCHISTIC – see small-mindedness, Ch 4-A, anger turned inward, Ch 5

MEANNESS – Aristotle speaks of two forms of it, here hoarding & exploitative, Ch 3-A

MEMORY – moral character provides a principle of selection according to which we remember some things & forget others; the theory of moral character provides a framework for sorting & retrieving what we learn about others both directly & through cultural media, when we try to understand them in a spirit of friendly realism

MISERLY - syn for hoarding character, Ch 3-A

MOCK-MODESTY - a vice in talking about oneself, Ch 6-D

MODERATE - here the quality virtue has of disposing one to situationally appropriate responses animated by proper wish, deliberation & choice

MODESTY - quality of the high-minded when dealing with those less strong, Ch 4-A, also of the truthful, Ch 6-D; but see mock-modesty, Ch 6-D, & small-mindedness, Ch 4-A

MOTIVATE - to activate the particular character traits of a person or group; normally implies activating traits thought to be positive, but clearly cowardly people are motivated by fear, self-indulgent people by pleasing seductions, excessively ambitious people by status, angry people by slights, etc.

MOTIVE - from the root word "motion" & designating the internal principle or source governing how we respond to stimuli; our motives are rooted in our character unless we are acting on an uncharacteristic impulse; they are inferred directly from our behavior & from our response to recognizing what we have done & can be either conscious or unconscious to us; "Know thyself" means learning to know our motives, supporting those in keeping with a proper wish for our development & allowing those conflicting with our higher wishes to atrophy; rationalists assume our only motives are those we are conscious of & that we can change them at will, positivists have often assumed our motives are unknowable & irrelevant since they believe we are environmentally determined

MUTUALITY - a property of friendships whether based on being useful or giving pleasure to one another or on furthering one another's development as human beings, Ch 6-B&C

NARCISSISTIC - an extreme form of vanity, Ch 4-A, in which one becomes so fixated on an image of himself & the importance of the things pertaining to him as to distort realistic perception of the motives & feelings of others & resulting in a serious distortion of one's own emotional & practical responses; a fearful defense against seeing the reality of one's true situation; can be a source of strength for leaders & innovators who persist against all odds & inspire others by their confidence; see archon

NEUROTIC - a dysergistic, function-crippling condition resulting from the development of vices of excess or deficiency beyond the range of the psychopathology of normalcy; implies a conflict between virtuous & vicious impulses neither set of which is dominant, as opposed simply to surrendering to self-indulgence or spite without shame, fear or struggle; the truly evil are not neurotic & can function with great concentration & calculation

NOBILITY - the capacity to function according to proper wish, deliberation & choice in defending human rights & promoting human development while functioning on a high plane of excellence & beauty; made possible internally by the development of both moral & intellectual virtue, & externally by institutions & social relations stimulating & expecting what is best in us

NON-VOLUNTARY - an action done in ignorance of its consequences but about which one feels no remorse; see involuntary

OBSEQUIOUS - along with flattery one of the two forms of excess concerned with the pleasure of others, Ch 6-C, normally motivated by excess receptiveness, Ch 3-A

OPTIMALIZE - virtue disposes us to respond to environmental agents to obtain the optimal result we can in the light of our highest wishes & resources, for ourselves & the others involved; vices of excess dispose us to obtain maximal results without regard for anyone's higher wishes & well-being & tend always toward a runaway situation in which a given moral & emotional power takes over the whole of our lives; vices of deficiency dispose us to under utilize our resources & thus to fail to attain an optimal result

ORAL-AGGRESSIVE - Freud's term for the exploitative character & developmental stage preoccupied with excess taking, CH 3-A

ORAL-RECEPTIVE - Freud's term for the receptive character & developmental stage preoccupied with excess receiving, CH 3-A

OSTENTATIOUS - here syn for vanity, Ch 4-A, or vulgar display of wealth, Ch 3-B

OVER-CONTROLLED - characteristic of hoarding character, Ch 3-A, with tendency toward self-denial & depression, Ch 2-B, small-mindedness, Ch 4-A, anger turned inward, Ch 5, & excess shame, Ch 7; see duty & guilt

PAMPER - obsequious people, Ch 6-C, pamper others by feeding their self-indulgence, Ch 2, & trying to protect them from all pain, Ch 1, in ways encouraging cowardice

PIRATICAL - Aristotle's term for the exploitative character, Ch 3-A

PITY - a virtue, Ch 8-A; today often thought of as condescending & disdainful & replaced with syn like empathy or compassion

PRACTICAL REASON - the cognitive power by which we deliberate, animated by our moral & emotional powers; perfected when energized by moral virtue, distorted by moral vice; see calculating

PRACTICAL SCIENCE - an applied science whose sense of what is good is a good action seen in the light of our best deliberation about what is good & bad for ourselves & other people; if practical reason is thought of as hardware, practical science is the soft-ware to run on it; **OMC** is a work of practical science; it is out of our practical lives & the theories we develop in pursuing those lives that both technological & theoretical science emerge & find their sense of direction & purpose, but not their content

PRAGMATIC - in good sense--realistic, experimental & exploratory; in bad sense--positivistic, opportunistic, unprincipled

PRINCIPLED - a self-controlled, Ch 2-B, person who holds himself accountable for living up to certain values & corrects his behavior when it is pointed out that he has violated his values; the high-minded, Ch 4-A, have the highest principles, but many others have high principles with regard to money or truthfulness without necessarily holding themselves to the highest standards for their lives as a whole

PRODIGAL - syn for extravagant, Ch 3-A

PROUD - in virtuous sense, high-minded, in vicious sense, vain, Ch 4-A

PSYCHOPATHOLOGY OF NORMALCY - the characteristic disposition to inappropriate responses within the range of excess or deficiency which, while undermining proper wish, deliberation & choice, does not become either neurotic or psychotic

PSYCHOTIC - a dysergistic extreme in which one's moral & emotional powers are approaching their asymptotic limits & are so conflicted as to distort realistic perception, deliberation & action; but see evil

RASH - syn for reckless, Ch 1-B

RATIONAL – thought & action animated by the wish to respect the nature & promote the development of living things & the ecosystems within which they can thrive

READY WIT – the virtue in handling humor, Ch 6-E

RECEPTIVE – the vice of excess dependency, Ch 3-A

RECKLESS – the vice of deficient fear, Ch 1-B

RESENTFUL – a quality of envy & spite, Ch 8-C, often confused with anger, Ch 5, or indignation, Ch 8-B

RESILIENCE – a quality of the courageous in responding to set-backs, Ch 1-B

RESPONSIBLE – a basic attitude in which one's virtues allow him to respond to the life around him in a caring & rational way; in contrast see duty

RESTLESS – appl to the fearful, Ch 1, the self-indulgent, Ch 2, the exploitative, Ch 3-A, the excessively ambitious, Ch 4-B, angry, Ch 5, obsequious, Ch 6-C, or guilty & shameful, Ch 7; see also calm

RIGHTEOUS INDIGNATION – a virtue, Ch 8-B, often confused with envy & spite, Ch 8-C

ROLE MODEL – see emulation, Ch 8-D

RUDE – appl to the insolent-sadistic, Ch 5-A, the contentious, Ch 6-C, & to buffoons, Ch 6-E

SAD – see courage, Ch 1-B, & depression, Ch 2-B

SADISTIC – see insolent

SARCASTIC – see insolent, CH 5-A, & buffoon, Ch 6-E

SELF-ACTUALIZATION – most properly, functioning according to proper wish, deliberation & choice, & made possible by the development of the virtues; more broadly, since vice is as much a part of man's potential as virtue, one must stipulate the moral principles governing the particular form of one's self-actualization

SELF-CONTROLLED – the virtue of enjoying sensual pleasures properly, Ch 2

SELF-HATRED – anger, Ch 5, or spite, Ch 8-C, turned inward, involving depression, Ch 2-B, small-mindedness, Ch 4-A, & excess shame, Ch 7

SELFISH – appl to self-indulgence, Ch 2, receptiveness, exploitativeness or hoarding, Ch 3-A, vanity, Ch 4-A, or excess ambition, Ch 4-B, boastfulness, Ch 6-D, or buffoonery, Ch 6-E

SERVILE – appl to obsequiousness, Ch 6-C, & apathy, Ch 5-C

SEX – see self-control & indulgence, Ch 2

SHAMELESS – the vice of excess, Ch 7

SINCERE – see high-mindedness, Ch 4-A, & truthfulness, Ch 6-D

SLIGHTING – the behavior of people making others angry, Ch 5

SMALL-MINDED – the vice of deficient self-respect, Ch 4-A

SPITEFUL – see Ch 8-C, Ch 5-A, & Ch 6-B; also evil

SPOILED – appl to self-indulgence, Ch 2, excess receptiveness, Ch 3-A, vanity, 4-B, & excess anger, Ch 5; disposed to cowardice, Ch 1-B, depression, Ch 2-B, & envy, Ch 8-C

SPOILING – promoting the vices found among the spoiled; a profoundly unfriendly thing to do; see obsequiousness, Ch 6-C

STIMULI – here identified with regard to the moral & emotional powers they activate; each of **OMC**'s chapters is organized around a different class of agents such as painful things, money & the things it will buy, etc.

STINGY – see hoarding, Ch 3-A

STRAIGHT-FORWARD - appl to both the high-minded, Ch 4-A, & the shameless, Ch 7

STRESSOR - a subset of stimuli

SUBSERVIENT - obsequious, Ch 6-C, apathetic, Ch 5-C; see servile

SULLEN - a form of excess anger, Ch 5-C

SYMPATHY - friendliness, Ch 6-B&C, or pity, Ch 8-A; with today's emotional inflation, commonly treated as a condescending form of pity & replaced with empathy

SYNERGISM - here the way in which our moral-emotional & intellectual powers can be developed to work together in a life-enhancing way rather than conflicting with one another & leading us to work at cross purposes; each of our desires & fears is pursued according to the wish to fulfill ourselves & others as a whole instead of each part of ourselves in isolation; an energy generating, efficient attitude rather than energy wasting & diffusing

TECHNOLOGICAL SCIENCE - an applied science whose sense of what is good is a good product technically considered without regard to its effect on man & the ecosystem; always exists within a larger context of the realms of both practical & theoretical science which it challenges with new powers & to which it looks in defining its function & possibilities

TEMPERATE - syn for self-control, Ch 2-B, or gentleness, Ch 5-C

THEORETICAL SCIENCE - an applied science whose sense of what is good is a good theory; properly developed it strives to understand the nature of things & what causes them to be what they are & in the case of living things how their nature instructs us about what is good for them; as such theoretical science arises from an ethical attitude of respect & reverence for what is real & to that extent arises from a practical science commitment to finding the truth as a basis for policy rather than finding data that will support a policy generated without regard for the truth; theoretical science has profited greatly from technological science & contributed to its development as well; only by working with theoretical science can practical science hope to develop a properly focused & disciplined technological science

TIGHT-WAD - syn for niggardly, Ch 3-B

TIMID - syn for fearful, lacking courage, Ch 1-B; see aggressive

TRUTHFUL - a virtue, Ch 6-D

UNEASINESS - all vices generate an internal sense of uneasiness; more particularly, see restless & calm

UNFEELING - appl to meanness, Ch 3-A, contentiousness, Ch 6-C, & spite, Ch 8-C

UNREASONABLE - see rational & irrational

UNSELFISH - appl to courage, Ch 1-B, generosity, Ch 3-A, high-mindedness, Ch 4-A, kindness, Ch 6-A, & friendliness, Ch 6-B&C

VAIN - vice of excess self-regard, Ch 4-A

VICE - a character trait undermining our ability to function according to proper wish, deliberation & choice & disposing us to make either excessive or deficient responses to a given class of stimuli; the contrary of virtue

VIRTUE - a character trait generating our ability to function according to proper wish, deliberation & choice & disposing us to make appropriate responses to a given class of stimuli; the contrary of vice

VOLUNTARY - an action in which the person knows what he is doing & desires to do it in the circumstances; both virtuous & vicious actions are done voluntarily in that they are desired, but as one comes to wish more for his development & well-being vicious actions that were voluntarily performed previously come to seem involuntary & ignorant because of their harmful nature

VULGAR – here the vice of excess display in making large public expenditures, Ch 3-B

WILL – here a syn for wish used in the rationalist tradition to refer to a dutiful character structure; see duty & over-controlled

WILLFUL – the demanding, impulsive quality of the self-indulgent, Ch 2, or the imperious & disdainful, Ch 8-D & Ch 5-A, quality of the vain, Ch 4-A

WISH – the desire which is the starting point of our deliberations & choices, as well as our dispositions to perceive, think & act from a given perspective; most properly, the wish to develop ourselves & function in an integrated, synergistic way while contributing to the well-being & development of others; more broadly, the ultimate internal principle governing a person's motivation & thus the most important thing to be known about him

WITTY – the virtue of being humorous, Ch 6 E

WORTHLESS – the feeling of the extremely small-minded, Ch 4-A, also the depressed, Ch 2-B, the apathetic, Ch 5-C, the obsequious, Ch 6-C, the excessively ashamed, Ch 7-B, & the envious & spiteful, Ch 8-C

Photo by Karl Poyry

Jody Palmour

Dr. Palmour has recently founded the ARCHON INSTITUTE FOR LEADER-
SHIP DEVELOPMENT to promote research in moral character and the training
of practitioners in this area. His next major works include a similar study
on Aristotle's **POLITICS**, tentatively titled **ON MORAL LEADERSHIP**, and a
historical sketch of the **THREE PHILOSOPHICAL OPERATING SYSTEMS**. He
hopes to work with others in creating a monograph series designed to
high-light the moral character dimension in the most commonly taught
texts in high school and college teaching, and to create a seminar series
to introduce a larger audience to this perspective. He has a private practice in moral counseling and in the assessment of moral character in
Washington, D.C.

Dr. Palmour earned the Ph.D. with distinction in moral philosophy
from Georgetown in 1984. Prior to that time, he worked for five years on
the Harvard Project on Technology, Work and Character. He has taught in
an Adjunct capacity at American University and then Georgetown University
since 1973.

MAIL ORDERS

Will you help us get this book in the hands of others who might find it useful?

- teachers, youth workers and students
- professionals involved in leadership development or staff training
- counselors
- priests and ministers
- columnists and speech writers
- newsletter editors and subscribers
- libraries

To order **ON MORAL CHARACTER**, please indicate

_____ copy(ies) @ $13.95 for paperback

_____ copy(ies) @ $24.95 for hardback

plus $2 postage and handling for first book, 50 cents for each additional book.

Total $ _____

Your name _____

   address _____

_____

Person(s) to whom you would like copy(ies) sent

Their name _____

   address _____

_____

Send check or purchase order to

ARCHON INSTITUTE FOR LEADERSHIP DEVELOPMENT
3700 Massachusetts Ave. NW, Suite 121
Washington, DC 20016